The Hastings Center Series in Ethics

ETHICS TEACHING IN HIGHER EDUCATION
Edited by Daniel Callahan and Sissela Bok

MENTAL RETARDATION AND STERILIZATION
A Problem of Competency and Paternalism
Edited by Ruth Macklin and Willard Gaylin

THE ROOTS OF ETHICS: Science, Religion, and Values
Edited by Daniel Callahan and H. Tristram Engelhardt, Jr.

ETHICS IN HARD TIMES
Edited by Arthur L. Caplan and Daniel Callahan

VIOLENCE AND THE POLITICS OF RESEARCH
Edited by Willard Gaylin, Ruth Macklin, and Tabitha M. Powledge

WHO SPEAKS FOR THE CHILD: The Problems of Proxy Consent
Edited by Willard Gaylin and Ruth Macklin

ETHICS, THE SOCIAL SCIENCES, AND POLICY ANALYSIS
Edited by Daniel Callahan and Bruce Jennings

IN SEARCH OF EQUITY: Health Needs and the Health Care System
Edited by Ronald Bayer, Arthur L. Caplan, and Norman Daniels

DARWIN, MARX, AND FREUD: Their Influence on Moral Theory
Edited by Arthur L. Caplan and Bruce Jennings

ABORTION: Understanding Differences
Edited by Sidney Callahan and Daniel Callahan

REPRESENTATION AND RESPONSIBILITY: Exploring Legislative Ethics
Edited by Bruce Jennings and Daniel Callahan

APPLYING THE HUMANITIES
Edited by Daniel Callahan, Arthur L. Caplan, and Bruce Jennings

REPRESENTATION AND RESPONSIBILITY

Exploring Legislative Ethics

Edited by
Bruce Jennings
and
Daniel Callahan

The Hastings Center
Institute of Society, Ethics and the Life Sciences
Hastings-on-Hudson, New York

PLENUM PRESS • NEW YORK AND LONDON

Library of Congress Cataloging in Publication Data

Main entry under title:

Representation and responsibility.

(Hastings Center series in ethics)
Bibliography: p.
Includes index.
1. United States. Congresses — Ethics — Addresses, essays, lectures. 2. Legislative bodies — United
States — States — Ethics — Addresses, essays, lectures. I. Jennings, Bruce, 1949–   . II. Callahan,
Daniel, 1930–   . III. Series.
JK1051.R46   1985   328.73'0766   85-17008
ISBN 0-306-41994-7

© 1985 The Hastings Center
Institute of Society, Ethics and the Life Sciences
360 Broadway
Hastings-on-Hudson, New York 10706

Plenum Press is a division of
Plenum Publishing Corporation
233 Spring Street, New York, N.Y. 10013

Printed in the United States of America

Contributors

Richard Allan Baker is Director of the United States Senate Historical Office and previously served as a specialist in American history with the Congressional Research Service. He is the author of *Senator Clinton P. Anderson and the Politics of Conservation* and numerous articles on congressional history.

Daniel Callahan, a philosopher by training, is Director of The Hastings Center and an elected member of the Institute of Medicine, National Academy of Sciences. His many books include: *The Tyranny of Survival, Ethics in Hard Times,* and *Abortion: Understanding Differences.*

Roger H. Davidson is Senior Specialist in American National Government and Public Administration at the Congressional Research Service. He has taught at Dartmouth College, the University of California, Santa Barbara, and the University of Maryland. His books include: *The Role of the Congressman, Congress Against Itself, A More Perfect Union,* and *Congress and Its Members.*

Jean Ford is presently a public affairs consultant and a member of the Nevada Tourism Commission. She has served as a Nevada State Assemblyman (1972–76) and a Nevada State Senator (1978–82).

Amy Gutmann is Associate Professor of Politics at Princeton University. She is author of *Liberal Equality* and *Ethics and Politics* and is currently writing a book on political theory and democratic education.

Jay H. Hedlund is Senior Lobbyist on the staff of Common Cause, specializing in ethics legislation and nuclear arms control. As Executive Director of Common Cause/Massachusetts from 1976 to 1980, he was involved in the creation of the Massachusetts State Ethics Commission.

Thomas Kingsley Houston is currently Deputy Mayor of the City of Los Angeles. From 1979 to 1983 he was the Chairman of the California Fair Political Practices Commission.

Gary C. Jacobson is Professor of Political Science at the University of California, San Diego. His books include: *Money in Congressional Elec-*

tions, The Politics of Congressional Elections, and *Strategy and Choice in Congressional Elections.*

Bruce Jennings, a political theorist by training, is Associate for Policy Studies at The Hastings Center. His publications include: *Ethics, the Social Sciences, and Policy Analysis, The Ethics of Legislative Life,* and *Congress and the Media: The Ethical Connection.*

James C. Kirby is Professor of Law at the University of Tennessee. He has served as a United States Senate staff member and directed a study of congressional ethics conducted by the Association of the Bar of the City of New York. His publications include: *Congress and the Public Trust, The Rights of Americans,* and *The Rewards of Public Service.*

Vanessa Merton is Associate Professor of Law at City University of New York Law School at Queens College. She has taught at New York University and Columbia University and is the author of numerous articles on legal education, biomedical ethics, and professional ethics.

James A. Morone is Assistant Professor of Politics at Brown University. His publications include *The Politics of Innovation* and numerous articles on political representation and health policy. He is currently at work on a book on citizen representation in America.

Richardson Preyer served in the United States House of Representatives from 1968 to 1980. He is currently Adjunct Professor at the University of North Carolina, Chapel Hill, and President of the Private Adjudication Center at the Duke University School of Law.

David E. Price is Professor of Political Science and Policy Sciences at Duke University. His publications include: *Who Makes the Laws?, Policymaking in Congressional Committees,* and *Bringing Back the Parties.* He has worked as a legislative aide in the United States Senate and in 1983–84 served as Chairman of the Democratic Party of North Carolina.

John D. Saxon is currently Director of Corporate Issues, RCA Corporation. He has served as Counsel on the staff of the United States Senate Select Committee on Ethics and as a White House Fellow. He has lectured widely on legislative ethics and congressional disciplinary proceedings.

Robert M. Stern is currently General Counsel for the California Commission on Campaign Financing, a nonprofit organization studying California campaign finance laws. From 1974–1983 he served as General Counsel on the staff of the California Fair Political Practices Commission.

John M. Swanner is Staff Director of the Committee on Standards of Official Conduct of the United States House of Representatives.

Dennis Thompson is Professor of Politics at Princeton University. He is author of *The Democratic Citizen: Social Science and Democratic Theory in the 20th Century* and *John Stuart Mill and Representative Government*.

Contents

Introduction   xi
    BRUCE JENNINGS AND DANIEL CALLAHAN

     PART I.   **Evolving Ethical Standards for Legislators:**
                A Historical Overview

CHAPTER 1.   **The History of Congressional Ethics**   3
           RICHARD ALLAN BAKER

CHAPTER 2.   **The Role of the Electorate in Congressional**
           Ethics   29
           JAMES C. KIRBY

       PART II.   **Ethics and Legislative Life**

CHAPTER 3.   **Political Action Committees, Electoral Politics, and**
           Congressional Ethics   41
           GARY C. JACOBSON

CHAPTER 4.   **Ethics in Political Campaigns**   67
           THOMAS KINGSLEY HOUSTON

CHAPTER 5.   **Lobbying and Legislative Ethics**   89
           JAY H. HEDLUND

CHAPTER 6.   **Socialization and Ethics in Congress**   109
           ROGER H. DAVIDSON

CHAPTER 7.   **Legislative Ethics in the New Congress**   129
           DAVID E. PRICE

      PART III.   **Toward a New Framework for Legislative Ethics:**
                Theory and Practice

CHAPTER 8.   **Legislative Ethics and Moral Minimalism**   149
           BRUCE JENNINGS

CHAPTER   9.   The Theory of Legislative Ethics   167
                    AMY GUTMANN AND DENNIS THOMPSON

CHAPTER 10.   The Scope of Legislative Ethics   197
                    JOHN D. SAXON

CHAPTER 11.   Legislative Codes of Ethics   221
                    DANIEL CALLAHAN

CHAPTER 12.   Enforceable Standards and Unenforceable
                    Ethics   235
                    JOHN M. SWANNER

              PART IV.   Legislative Ethics in the States

CHAPTER 13.   Ethics in the States: The Laboratories of
                    Reform   243
                    ROBERT M. STERN

CHAPTER 14.   An Insider's View of State Legislative Ethics   263
                    JEAN FORD

CHAPTER 15.   Legislative Ethics at the State and Federal Levels:
                    A Comparison   273
                    RICHARDSON PREYER

              PART V.   Representation in Nonlegislative Settings

CHAPTER 16.   Representation without Elections: The American
                    Bureaucracy and Its Publics   283
                    JAMES A. MORONE

CHAPTER 17.   Legislative Ethics and Professional
                    Responsibility   303
                    VANESSA MERTON

Index   325

Introduction

The practice of representation permeates our society and is essential to its routine functioning. Much of this representation is informal and goes unnoticed. Every day individuals stand in or up for someone else, acting for them, on their behalf, in their stead, in their name. And just as each of us informally "represents" our friends, colleagues, or families, so too are we represented by them in turn. In contemporary America—or indeed in any but the most rudimentary society—social institutions and practices of all kinds rest on a thick web of representations.

When we do think explicitly about representation, however, we normally think of a more formal arrangement in which some sort of voluntary agreement is entered into by the representing and the represented parties. This agreement is based on a transfer of authority, a (limited) surrender of autonomy, and a set of shared expectations about the rights of the represented and the duties of the representative. The relationships between professionals and their clients have this character—perhaps most clearly and self-consciously in the practice of law, but in other professions as well. So, too, do situations involving surrogate decision making in cases involving incompetent persons. Other examples abound. Whenever individuals lack the time, the knowledge and expertise, or the competence to act for themselves on behalf of their own legitimate interests, they must rely on prevailing structures of representation. In our complex corporate and technological society, individuals increasingly find themselves in that position and their dependency on representation grows. It is little wonder, then, that the ethical responsibilities or obligations of representatives have become a topic of increasing preoccupation and concern.

Nor is it surprising that this concern about the ethics of representation has focused not only on professional representatives in the private sector but also on public officials who act as political representatives. For political representation is the paradigmatic, quintessential form of formal representation in our society, and governmental institutions most of all have been built around representation as their organizing and legitimating principle. From the White House to local community boards and councils the exercise of political authority and power is considered acceptable and legitimate on democratic grounds because it is tempered by the legal, procedural, and ethical norms that have been built into the concept of representation. That is to say, public officials are not free to exercise their authority however they will; their intentions and purposes in the exercise of their authority must be representative of the collective will of their constituents.

This re-presentation of the will of others in the will of an individual office holder is an exceedingly complex phenomenon—conceptually and legally as well as psychologically and socially. Philosophers have distinguished several different senses of representation, and political theorists have argued for competing normative accounts of representation, such as "delegate theories" on one hand and "trustee theories" on the other. Social scientists studying the process of representation in legislatures or other governmental settings have found that the relationships between representatives and constituents are varied and that the roles representatives play are far more multifaceted than the familiar delegate/trustee dichotomy allows.

Representation in legislatures, particularly the United States Congress, has been the focal point for much of this research. And yet, despite the more refined theoretical and descriptive accounts of legislative representation developed in the last twenty years, the ethical implications of these findings have not been systematically developed or adequately explored. We have a tolerably clear sense of how political representation fits into the normative scheme of a democratic political system, and we know a good deal about the factors influencing the actions of legislators and the structure and functioning of legislatures, but we have not yet fully elaborated the distinctive ethical obligations that should be attached to the role of the legislator.

At the practical level, discussions of legislative ethics are rather more frequent these days, but for the most part they have tended to focus narrowly on the area of conflict of interest and the misuse of office for personal gain. In recent years, interest in legislative ethics has grown in response to successive scandals and the awareness that certain traditional practices—such as the outside practice of law, the assignment of legislative staff members to campaign activities, the maintenance of "unofficial office accounts" (slush funds), and the undisclosed receipt of substantial gifts from lobbyists—invited serious abuse.

In the late 1960s the United States Senate and House of Representatives adopted their first official codes of ethics in response to problems revealed in scandals involving Bobby Baker, Representative Adam Clayton Powell, and Senator Thomas Dodd. In the 1970s other scandals—and the tremendous public concern with ethics in government generally created by the Watergate investigations—led to the strengthening of these codes, to the establishment of permanent ethics committees to enforce them, and to the passage of the landmark Ethics in Government Act of

1978. During the same period, approximately thirty states adopted new ethics laws and codes and established ethics committees or commissions.

By the end of the decade these reforms, and related measures such as new campaign finance laws and open-meeting rules or "sunshine" acts, had clarified some traditional ethical expectations concerning the obligation of legislators to remain accountable and to keep a distance from influences and pressures that would improperly bias their judgment and decision making. But because these reforms were largely reactions to scandals and the perceived decline in public confidence and because they were designed to correct or deter specific ethical abuses, they did not provide a full account of the ethical duties of legislators. In their wake, some problems have been mitigated and a new moral circumspection has emerged in legislative life. But no consensus has emerged concerning the broader ethical expectations that legislators should have about themselves and that citizens should have about those who represent them. When we try to push the conversation about legislative ethics beyond the issue of corruption, we begin to stutter and lapse into silence with a shrug or a shake of the head. In a democracy that silence is debilitating and dangerous.

Today there is both an intellectual and a practical need for a systematic and comprehensive study of legislative ethics and the ethics of representation. The ethical implications of various theories of representation must be explored. Traditional understandings of the special moral responsibilities of legislators as democratic public servants must be recovered, critically examined, and, where appropriate, revitalized. Recent changes in the electoral system, the role of political parties, campaign practices, and the institutional distribution of power within legislatures must be analyzed in ways that will help us understand the dilemmas and pressures that contemporary legislators face in attempting to fulfill their ethical obligations. The basic rationales behind recent ethics reforms in Congress and the state legislatures must be clarified so that these reforms can be made more secure or improved upon in the future. These are the issues, we believe, that should be on the agenda for the future study and discussion of legislative ethics.

This book has been designed to address that agenda. Its aim is to explore the broad range of ethical responsibilities that arise in legislative life and in the practice of political representation and to place those responsibilities in the context of recent changes in the electoral system and the legislative environment on both the federal and the state level.

Part I provides a historical background to current discussions of legislative ethics. Richard Baker traces the evolution of ethical norms pertaining to legislative service and indicates how those norms, which until quite recently have been largely unwritten and informal, have changed in response to shifts in the political power and influence of Congress. James Kirby examines how the "reelection imperative" has served—and failed to serve—as a check on unethical legislative behavior and shows why the constitutional mechanism of periodic elections alone is not a sufficient safeguard in the absence of other formal ethics enforcement procedures.

Part II shifts to the current electoral and legislative environment as a context within which moral dilemmas arise for conscientious legislators. Gary Jacobson focuses on the organizational and financial pressures legislators face in the electoral environment and cautions against any hasty conclusion that relatively new forces there, such as political action committees (PACs), are necessarily going to produce unprecedented or unmanageable ethical conflicts. Thomas Houston discusses a disturbing trend toward deceptive and abusive practices in some recent legislative campaigns and sketches the beginnings of a new code of ethics for legislative candidates.

Chapters by Jay Hedlund, Roger Davidson, and David Price concentrate on the ways the internal legislative environment affects ethical decision making. Generally less sanguine about the effects of PACs than is Jacobson, Hedlund discusses some new problems raised by the ways in which lobbyists are now becoming involved in the systems of campaign fund raising upon which legislators increasingly depend. More generally, he discusses the ethical dimensions of the entire legislator–lobbyist relationship. Davidson and Price examine the informal ethical norms and the system of folkways that exist in Congress. Davidson calls attention to the positive ways in which learning the "rules of the game" of legislative service provides a form of ethics socialization. Price observes that declining party discipline and a decentralization of power in Congress has made legislators more independent and entrepreneurial. He argues that legislators have a positive ethical obligation to take more responsibility for the effective functioning of the legislature as an institution.

Part III focuses on the theory and scope of legislative ethics. Bruce Jennings examines the relationship between the political and the ethical considerations that influence legislative conduct and argues that the political purposes of representation in a democracy are compatible with— and indeed require—a broadening of the ethical responsibilities that citizens demand of their legislators and that legislators demand of themselves. Amy Gutmann and Dennis Thompson indicate what a suitably broad account of the ethical obligations of legislators contains, by analyzing the fundamental duties of autonomy, accountability, and responsibility. The duties of autonomy and accountability capture the creative tension that exists between political leadership and responsiveness in a democracy. The duty of responsibility addresses the moral relationship between the individual legislator and the legislature as an institution—the problem underscored earlier by Price. John Saxon critically responds to the call to broaden the scope of legislative ethics by discussing how legislators might practically respond to a more inclusive definition of the moral dimensions of their role.

The discussion then turns to the range of ethical considerations that might be incorporated in a formal code of legislative ethics. Daniel Callahan examines the present codes in the Senate and House and finds them overly narrow and legalistic. Arguing that a legislative code can be an important public affirmation of the ethical expectations legislatures have for their members, he recommends that existing codes should be restructured to contain both aspirational ideals and specific disciplinary standards. In his commentary on Callahan's chapter, John Swanner outlines a way of classifying and ordering the various levels and types of ethics rules that codes and other regulations might encompass.

Part IV is devoted to a specific examination of legislative ethics at the state level. Robert Stern provides an overview of recent ethics reforms in states across the country and identifies the lessons that have been learned from the various approaches taken in different states. Jean Ford discusses the particular ethical dilemmas state legislators face. Richardson Preyer concludes this section with some reflections on the similarities and the differences between ethical issues arising in Congress and the state legislatures.

Finally, Part V examines the ways in which the issues of legislative ethics might be illuminated by comparison with ethical issues of representation in nonlegislative contexts. James Morone discusses the ethics and politics of representation in the federal bureaucracy. Vanessa Merton discusses the analogies between professional ethics and legislative ethics.

The papers collected in this volume grew out of a two-and-one-half year research project on Legislative and Representative Ethics conducted by The Hastings Center, supported by a grant from the Ford Foundation. The findings and conclusions of that project are contained in *The Ethics of Legislative Life: A Report by The Hastings Center* (Hastings-on-Hudson, NY: The Hastings Center, 1985).

In six extended conferences from 1982 through 1983, the authors of these commissioned papers and other members of The Hastings Center project discussed the issues raised here and critically responded to earlier drafts of these papers. Our discussions were lively and often heated, for in our explorations of legislative ethics we were moving into largely uncharted and often controversial territory. Over time, we gradually moved toward a general agreement about the main problems of legislative ethics today, if not their resolution. As a result of that process, each of the papers included here went through several drafts and was carefully and substantially revised. We would like to thank our authors and the other project participants for their cooperation and their willingness to take part in this long, but fruitful, process.

In addition, we would like to thank the Ford Foundation for the support and encouragement which made our project and this book possible.

Finally, special thanks are due to Eric Feldman, who provided research assistance, and to Mary Gualandi and Eva Mannheimer for their skillful and good humored support in typing and retyping the manuscript of this book.

BRUCE JENNINGS
DANIEL CALLAHAN

I

EVOLVING ETHICAL STANDARDS FOR LEGISLATORS
A HISTORICAL OVERVIEW

I

The History of Congressional Ethics

RICHARD ALLAN BAKER

Throughout most of its history, the American Congress has been reluctant to establish formal, institutionally based rules of conduct for its members. Rather, it has chosen to deal, on a case-by-case basis, only with the most obvious acts of wrongdoing, those clearly "inconsistent with the trust and duty of a member." In a large measure, this attitude reflects the inherent difficulty of enforcing ethical standards in an institution whose members are selected from outside its precincts. Whenever possible, congressional leaders have chosen to administer the lesser of available remedies, leaving the ultimate judgment of a senator's or representative's fitness to the electorate. Reinforcing this attitude has been the notion that ethical behavior of those in Congress is generally neither better nor worse than that of society as a whole. As long as the government of the United States remained small, with only limited impact on the daily lives of its citizens, isolated cases of congressional corruption caused little general concern. Following the Civil War, this began to change and Congress began to pass legislation restricting members' freedom to conduct private law practices and to accept corporate campaign contributions without public accountability. During the three decades that followed World War II, as Congress significantly expanded its staff resources and policy review capabilities, members were forced to reassess past practices and to examine the necessity and scope of formal codes of ethical behavior.[1]

[1] Congressional Quarterly, *Congressional Ethics*, (2nd ed.; Washington: Congressional Quarterly, Inc., 1980), pp. 147–68. This provides a useful summary of the historical record with valuable lists of exclusion, expulsion, and censure cases. Its narrative coverage for the pre-1945 period is uneven.

RICHARD ALLAN BAKER ● Director, Historical Office, United States Senate, Washington, D.C. 20510.

For nearly two centuries, a simple and informal code of behavior existed. Prevailing norms of general decency served as the chief determinants of proper legislative conduct. Public officials who obtained private profit at the expense of the general welfare were widely considered to be corrupt. However, those who reaped financial profit as a concomitant of their public roles generally escaped censure.[2]

Senator Joseph Weldon Bailey gave a classic expression to this attitude early in the twentieth century. Defending his commercial dealings, the forthright Texas Democrat said,

> I despise those public men who think they must remain poor in order to be considered honest. I am not one of them. If my constituents want a man who is willing to go to the poorhouse in his old age in order to stay in the Senate during his middle age, they will have to find another senator. I intend to make every dollar that I can honestly make, without neglecting or interfering with my public duty.[3]

Several decades later former Senator and Navy Secretary Claude Swanson attributed his successful political career to an "unfailing adherence to three maxims of political conduct." First, he advised, "be bold as a lion on a rising tide. Second, when the water reaches the upper deck, follow the rats. And third, and most important, when in doubt, do right."[4]

The framers of the Constitution set only minimum standards of fitness for congressional service. They provided that "each house shall be the judge of the elections, returns, and qualifications of its own members" and they allowed punishment of "members for disorderly behavior," with the ultimate penalty being expulsion upon concurrence of two-thirds of the body's membership.[5] These powers were deemed essential for preserving the independence of the legislative branch. They took on particular importance in the context of the Constitution's "speech and debate" clause that provided members with immunity from being "questioned" elsewhere about their legislative conduct on the floor of their respective houses. If Congress lacked the power to discipline its members, they would in effect be allowed to operate outside the law, a concept for which the framers obviously had no sympathy. Also, the framers believed that Congress had the duty to protect the nation from the dangerous actions of its individual members. Whether or not a member's constituency chose to

[2] This point is developed in Estes Kefauver, "Past and Present Standards of Public Ethics in America: Are We Improving?," *Annals of the American Academy of Political and Social Science* 280 (March 1952), 1–8.

[3] *Congressional Record* (hereafter cited as *CR*), June 27, 1906, pp. 9375–76.

[4] Quoted in Joseph S. Clark, "Some Ethical Problems of Congress," *Annals of the American Academy of Political and Social Science* 363 (January 1966), 16.

[5] U.S. Constitution, Art. I, sec. 5, cl. 2.

deal with errant behavior, each house of Congress would retain the right of exclusion by a simple majority vote at the start of the member's next term, or censure by a similar majority, or expulsion by two-thirds at any time. The power of exclusion sprang from Congress's right to determine the qualifications of its own members, whereas expulsion had a more directly disciplinary purpose. Members need not be in violation of a statute to be subject to expulsion. Over the years, the fundamental governing consideration has been whether the individual has displayed conduct "inconsistent with the trust and duty of a member."[6]

Despite its constitutional and statutory tests of fitness for service, Congress, throughout the nation's history, has displayed great reluctance to discipline members.[7] In the majority of early incidents up to the Civil War, Congress seemed content to extract an apology from those involved, allowing the attendant publicity to serve as sufficient punishment. There were, however, notable exceptions. Examination of these exceptions provides an outline of emerging, if unstated, ethical norms in Congress during the Republic's early years.

The Senate, in 1797, for the first time, exercised its powers of expulsion for a member's unacceptable behavior. President John Adams initiated the process, sending the Senate evidence that Tennessee Senator William Blount had been involved in a conspiracy to wrest Florida and Louisiana from Spanish control on behalf of Great Britain. Adams' attorney general believed such behavior deserved swift punishment. While the Senate considered a resolution of expulsion, the House quickly voted to impeach Blount. As the Senate pondered the request of Blount's counsel for additional time in which to prepare his defense, the House committee arrived in the Senate chamber to present its bill of impeachment. The Senate overwhelmingly adopted the expulsion resolution, affirming that the Tennessee senator had been "guilty of a high misdemeanor, entirely inconsistent with his public trust and duty as a senator." He was then ordered to appear three days later to answer the impeachment articles. Blount ignored his pledge to attend and on the appointed date was spurring his horse in the direction of Tennessee.[8]

---

[6] An excellent study of the constitutional and statutory bases for Congress to determine the qualifications of its membership is P. A. Dionisopoulos, *Rebellion, Racism, and Representation: The Adam Clayton Powell Case and Its Antecedents* (Dekalb, Ill.: Northern Illinois University Press, 1970), pp. 19–33.

[7] Allan J. Katz, "The Politics of Congressional Ethics," in *The House at Work* ed. by Joseph Cooper and G. Calvin Mackenzie (Austin: University of Texas Press, 1981), pp. 97–98.

[8] William Masterson, *William Blount* (Baton Rouge: Louisiana State University Press, 1954), pp. 320–23; U.S. Senate, *Senate Election, Expulsion and Censure Cases from 1793 to 1972*, S. Doc. 92–7 (Washington, D.C.: Government Printing Office, 1972) p. 3.

Seventeen months later, failing in its efforts to return Blount to the capital, the Senate convened an impeachment trial and proceded to consider whether a member was, indeed, an impeachable officer. Subsequently, the Senate concluded that it lacked jurisdiction and dismissed the impeachment, failing to make clear whether its action stemmed from its belief that no senator was liable for impeachment or the assumption that someone who had ceased to hold a "civil office" was no longer impeachable.[9]

Within a decade, the Senate faced its second expulsion case when Ohio Senator John Smith was indicted as a coconspirator with Aaron Burr in a plot to lead western territories out of the Union. Although the indictments were subsequently dropped on a legal technicality, the Senate decided to initiate its own probe to determine Smith's eligibility for continued membership. The debate focused on the Senate's jurisdiction over the conduct of its members and established that the Senate could entertain a motion of expulsion whether or not a criminal statute had been violated and independent of moves toward legal prosecution. The upper house concluded that its constitutional authority to expel a member did not fall under the same rubric that courts had established for criminal prosecution. The Senate's prerogative in this instance represented a political power to be exercised when necessary for preserving the purity of the legislative branch.

In the Smith case, arguments centered on the definition of Senate "purity." Although Smith's attorneys, Francis Scott Key and Robert Goodloe Harper, contended that the Senate had no jurisdiction to inquire into an offense covered by a code of civil law, the chamber's majority disagreed, concluding that a person who accepts a cloak of legislative membership becomes to some extent responsible to that body for his conduct. Although the Senate failed by a single vote to expel Smith, the Ohio legislator recognized that the publicity had destroyed his political future and he resigned shortly thereafter. His case led the Senate to affirm its exclusive constitutional power to determine the suitability of its members' qualifications without limiting its jurisdiction to indictable offenses commited in its immediate environs.[10]

Two years later, in 1810, the Senate again asserted jurisdiction over the conduct of a member. Massachusetts Federalist Timothy Pickering, an uncompromising and abrasive partisan, sought to embarrass former President Thomas Jefferson by reading on the Senate floor an 1804 letter

[9] *Annals of Cong.*, 5th Congress, 2nd and 3rd sess., Vol. 2, (1798–99), pp. 2245–2416.

[10] *Dictionary of American Biography* 17, p. 296; *Annals of Congress*, 10th Cong., 1st sess., pp. 184–331; *Senate Election, Expulsion, and Censure Cases*, pp. 4–5.

from French minister Tallyrand that disputed certain Louisiana territorial claims. Senator Henry Clay submitted a resolution charging that Pickering's reading of a secret document violated Senate rules and jeopardized the Senate's advice and consent role. For the first time in its brief history, the Senate moved to censure a member, condemning Pickering's action by an impressive 20–7 margin. Later that year, the Massachusetts legislature defeated Pickering's reelection bid. The Pickering case established the Senate's determination to move quickly against members who commited offenses in clear violation of that body's rules.[11]

The House of Representatives, during those early years, followed a course similar to the Senate's, preferring to leave the ultimate determination of a member's suitability to the voters, but stepping in on those occasions on which the offense brought such discredit to the legislature that it could not be prudently ignored. One of the most blatant acts of congressional misconduct, within the immediate jurisdiction of the House, occurred in 1798 when Republican Congressman Matthew Lyon spat in the face of Federalist Roger Griswold after the latter had taunted Lyon about his military record. The body's Federalist majority narrowly failed to achieve the two-thirds vote necessary to expel Lyon, in part because he argued that he believed the House was not technically in session at the time of the offense, as the Speaker had briefly left the chair. Griswold subsequently took matters into his own hands by attacking Lyon with his cane, prompting Lyon to retaliate with a convenient pair of fire tongs. After other members separated the combatants, the House took little notice of the altercation, choosing instead of expulsion or censure a resolution admonishing them against further acts of violence.[12]

There was little basis for consistency in the enforcement of ethical standards in the pre–Civil War era. In neither house of Congress did there exist party organizations of sufficient coherence and strength to establish clear disciplinary guidelines for members. Senators and representatives set their own political and ethical agendas, relatively free from interference other than the dictates of their local and regional support bases. The relative lack of institutional continuity, pursuant to high rates of membership turnover, led to an inconsistent application of discipline. For example, in 1832, the House rose up in wrath to censure Ohio Democrat William Stanbery for saying, in objection to a ruling by the chair, "The eyes of the Speaker are too frequently turned from the chair you occupy

---

[11] *National Cyclopedia of American Biography*, 14, p. 565; *Annals of Congress,* 11th Cong., 3rd sess., pp. 66–83.

[12] Dionisopoulos, pp. 49–50; *Debates and Proceedings of the U.S. Congress*, 4th Cong. 1st sess., pp. 786–98, 1007, 1043.

to the White House.''[13] A year later, however, Congress reacted with indifference to the revelation of Senator Daniel Webster's financial ties to the Bank of the United States. In December, 1833, he wrote to bank president Nicholas Biddle to report that he was coming under increasing pressure to join those who opposed the bank's recharter. Webster assured Biddle that he would resist such pressures, but he boldly reminded the banker, "I believe my retainer has not been renewed or refreshed as usual. If it be wished that my relation to the bank be continued, it may be well to send me the usual retainers."[14]

Webster was hardly alone among those public officials who profited from the bank's largess. As many as one quarter of the members of Congress benefitted from largely unsecured loans totalling over $1.6 million during the five-year recharter campaign in the early 1830s. Consequently Congress turned aside calls for an investigation in 1835 when Congressman John Quincy Adams reminded his colleagues that a similar effort in 1832 had failed because it had become clear that members of all political factions were involved.[15]

Only Webster's most resolute congressional foes chose to condemn his conduct. Few of his colleagues, however, were so brazen as to imitate his example of parading a contingent of homestate bankers onto the Senate floor to witness his ministrations on their behalf. Yet, in the absence of clear contrary standards, little fuss was made. Less objectionable, under the norms of the day, was Webster's practice of shuttling between the chambers of the Senate and the Supreme Court, one floor apart, to argue cases in which he had a substantial legislative or personal interest. Webster made no effort to keep his business ties secret, and few could doubt the nature of his connection to the Bank of the United States after he successfully argued forty-one cases on its behalf before the high court.[16]

A few years later, in the House of Representatives, John Quincy Adams refused to follow Webster's example of serving as legislator and lawyer. In 1845 he turned down an offer of $5,000 to argue a separation of powers case before the Supreme Court. In doing so, Adams said that as a representative he would give his constituent his opinion on the question

---

[13] Dionisopoulos, p. 50; *Register of Debates in Congress*, 22nd Cong., 1st sess., pp. 3876–3887, 3907–08.

[14] Charles McGrane, ed., *The Correspondence of Nicholas Biddle* (Boston: Houghton Mifflin, 1919), p. 218; Richard N. Current, *Daniel Webster and the Rise of National Conservatism* (Boston: Little Brown, 1955), pp. 80–81.

[15] Robert Luce, *Legislative Assemblies* (New York: Da Capo Press, 1974, Reprint of 1924 edition), pp. 411–12.

[16] Irving H. Bartlett, *Daniel Webster* (New York: W. W. Norton, 1978), pp. 142–43, 198–200, 205–206.

free of charge. He then noted the conflict of interest in the prospective transaction:

> It occurs to me that this double capacity of a counsellor in courts of law and a member of a legislative body affords opportunity and temptation for contingent fees of a very questionable moral purity. It is a sad contemplation of human nature to observe how the action of members of legislative bodies may be bought and sold, and how some of the brightest stars in that firmament may pass in occultation without losing their lustre.[17]

Webster and Adams represented two poles on a spectrum of attitudes regarding dealings with parties having a personal financial interest in the activities of the federal government. From the nation's earliest years, congressmen had appeared in cases before federal courts, as well as before commissioners appointed to settle claims growing out of wars with Great Britain and Mexico. Following the War of 1812, several members of Congress and Vice President George Dallas received fees for prosecuting cases before federal departments. Before establishment of the federal Court of Claims in 1855, such matters were handled informally within the agencies involved or through private bills introduced in Congress.

A major scandal involving Ohio Senator Thomas Corwin brought that procedure to an end. In the years following the Mexican War, he represented a "Dr. Gardiner" before the Mexican Claims Commission in a suit for damages arising from the wartime destruction of a silver mine. Corwin won a $500,000 settlement for his client, but in 1852 it became known that Gardiner was a fraud and the silver mine had never existed. By that time, Corwin had become Secretary of the Treasury and the resulting uproar brought about swift reform of federal claims settlement procedures. Tennessee Congressman Andrew Johnson, in 1853, expressed the emerging attitude of revulsion within Congress for such activities, noting, "The Government and the functionaries of Government are beginning to stink in the very nostrils of the nation; it is now dead and rotten in many of its parts. Its putrid stench is sent forth upon every wind and is arresting the attention of the voracious vultures throughout the land."[18] Shortly thereafter, Congress enacted legislation forbidding members to accept fees for prosecuting claims before federal agencies.[19]

By 1856 sectional discord over the issue of slavery in the territories had greatly intensified and had led to an act of congressional violence that tested both chambers' willingness to discipline miscreants. On May 20,

---

[17] Quoted in Luce, p. 455.

[18] Association of the Bar of the City of New York, *Congress and the Public Trust* (New York: Atheneum, 1971), pp. 80, 116; *Congressional Globe*, 32nd Cong., 2nd sess., A1853.

[19] Association of the Bar of the City of New York, *Conflict of Interest and Federal Service* (Cambridge, Mass.: Harvard University Press, 1960), pp. 36–37, 40.

1856, Massachusetts Senator Charles Sumner made a scathing verbal attack on his South Carolina colleague, Andrew Butler. Two days later, Butler's kinsman, Congressman Preston Brooks, went to the Senate chamber, waited for that body to adjourn for the day, and then assaulted the unsuspecting Sumner. Badly wounded, Sumner fell to the floor, bleeding and unconscious. Although he recovered from his wounds, Sumner was unable to muster the emotional strength to return to the Senate for three years. In responding to the attack, the Senate decided that the offense could only be punished by the House. The House agreed, but its vote to expel Brooks failed to achieve the necessary two-thirds majority. Brooks then made a boastful speech and resigned his House seat. Shortly thereafter, his South Carolina constituents returned him to the House. That body successfully censured Congressman Lawrence Keitt for having prior knowledge of Brooks' intentions and for failing to prevent the beating.[20]

Two years later the House refused to pursue its case against Congressmen William Gilbert and Orsamus Matteson, both New York Whigs. They had resigned in the final days of the previous Congress to escape expulsion for alleged bribery in connection with an Iowa land grant. Matteson, who had been reelected before the charges surfaced, was also subject to House action for declaring that many members had agreed not to vote for any measure providing money or lands unless they were paid to do so. The House investigating committee decided, however, that that chamber had no jurisdiction over events of an earlier Congress.[21]

Senator Stephen A. Douglas (Democrat, Illinois), willing to set aside his strong moral objections to slavery to secure political compromise and national stability, drew the line at outright bribery. As he was recovering from surgery, resting on a couch with his crutches in easy reach, Douglas was visited by a man who proposed that the senator give him a specific document rather than sending it to the Illinois secretary of state. "Do this," the man allegedly said, "and I will give you in exchange, the deed of a tract of land containing two and a half million acres, and worth twenty millions of dollars." Douglas reportedly grabbed his crutches and struck the man as he fled from the room.[22] Looking back to that era, Horace Greeley, who had served in the House during the winter of 1848–49,

---

[20] David Donald, *Charles Sumner and the Coming of the Civil War* (New York: Alfred A. Knopf, 1960), pp. 278–311.

[21] A. R. Spofford, "Lobby," *Lalor's Cyclopedia of Political Science*, Vol. 2, p. 781.

[22] James Parton, "The 'Strikers' of the Washington Lobby," *Atlantic Monthly* 24 (August 1869), 231.

concluded, "There were ten or twelve members—not more than twelve, I am confident—who were generally presumed to be 'on the make', as the phrase is; and they were a class by themselves, as clearly as if they were so many black sheep in a large flock of white ones."[23]

The Civil War brought in its wake a massive political, social, and economic revolution. The departure of Southern states from the halls of Congress cleared the way for legislation authorizing construction of a transcontinental railroad and broad distribution of the public domain. The war and its aftermath promoted an environment of growth and profiteering that raised new and vastly more difficult ethical questions for those who served in Congress. As Ohio Congressman James A. Garfield later commented, the Civil War "awakened a reckless spirit of adventure and speculation, and greatly multiplied the opportunities and increased the temptations to evil."[24]

A major issue of public propriety during the war centered on whether members of Congress could freely represent clients before military courts-martial. Some members agreed with Connecticut Senator Lafayette Foster's argument that military judges could hardly be expected to be impartial when their promotions and careers were subject to congressional approval. Foster observed, "Taking human nature as it is, it is utterly inconceivable that members of these military courts should not have this fact in mind when they are trying cases brought before them." He related an account of a senator dissatisfied with a court's preliminary judgment who told a member of the court, "You expect soon to be promoted and I give you to understand that your confirmation will not get through the Senate without some difficulty."[25]

With the war barely a year old, the Senate moved to expel Rhode Island Senator James F. Simmons for corruption. On July 2, 1862, a resolution was submitted charging that he had blatantly misused his official influence to secure a war contract for two Rhode Island rifle manufacturers. In exchange for his lobbying efforts, Simmons allegedly received promissory notes amounting to $20,000 as initial payment on a $50,000 share of the manufacturers' profits.

Simmons did not contest the validity of the charges against him. Instead he professed astonishment that anyone should question efforts to help constituents seeking a contract and the federal government seeking weapons in a time of national emergency. The unabashed senator made no move to deny that he still held the promissory notes or that he

---

[23] Quoted in Luce, p. 415.
[24] James A. Garfield, "A Century of Congress," *Atlantic Monthly* 40 (July 1877), 63.
[25] *Congressional Globe*, 38th Cong., 1st sess., p. 557.

expected them to be paid in full. The Senate investigating committee set forth Simmons' case in most deferential terms citing his advanced age and honorable public record, but ultimately finding his behavior inexcusable. Consequently, the committee reported the expulsion resolution back to the full Senate with the recommendation that the Senate take whatever action it deemed appropriate. The Senate adjourned three days later without further considering this matter. Rather than face certain expulsion in the session scheduled to begin in December, 1862, Simmons resigned in August. In the aftermath of the Simmons case, Congress expanded the provisions of its 1853 statute in 1864 in a law that provided maximum penalties of a $10,000 fine and two years in prison for any senator or representative found guilty of illegally receiving compensation for services before a federal agency. The statute also provided that members convicted thereunder "shall be rendered forever thereafter incapable of holding an office under the government of the United States."[26]

Eight years after the Simmons case, the House of Representatives confronted a more explicit case of corruption by its members as three of them were charged with attempting to sell appointments to the military academies. On February 21, 1870, the House Military Affairs Committee recommended the expulsion of South Carolina Congressman B. F. Whittemore for having "been influenced by improper pecuniary considerations" in making academy appointments. In Whittemore's defense, several members argued that the sale of cadetships was so widespread that it had become sanctioned by custom. Before the House had the opportunity to act on the expulsion resolution, however, Whittemore resigned. Consequently, the House passed a censure resolution by a margin of 187–0. That body responded in similar fashion to identical charges against Congressmen John Deweese of North Carolina and Roderick Butler of Tennessee. Although both men received unanimous votes of censure, the cases were apparently of so little concern to leading members of the era that they failed to mention them in the discussion of the era's scandals included in their memoirs.[27]

Whittemore immediately stood for reelection and his constituents returned him to the House. His arrival in the House chamber with fresh credentials reopened the issue of his earlier conduct. Opponents urged that he be excluded in light of the 1853 statute that permanently barred from public office any person convicted of bribery. Although Whittemore

---

[26] *Senate Election, Expulsion, and Censure Cases*, p. 34; *Congress and the Public Trust*, p. 31.
[27] Dionisopoulos, pp. 101–105.

had not been convicted under that law, Illinois Congressman John A. Logan argued that the House had a constitutional right to rule that a prospective member "shall not be a man of infamous character." He contended that without such power Congress could be seriously damaged by a congressional district that sent a representative willing to sell his vote. In response to charges that this would undermine the fundamentals of representative government, Logan countered that the people do not have the right to "destroy their own liberties by filling Congress with men who, from their conduct, show themselves capable of the destruction of the Government." The House agreed with Logan's reasoning and voted, 130–24, to exclude Whittemore, consistent with the previous action of both houses in excluding ex-Confederates and rebel sympathizers, despite their presentation of valid election certificates.[28]

The Whittemore case gave the House a strong precedent to employ two years later when faced with one of the most notorious scandals of its history. During the 1872 election campaign the nation was confronted with charges of widespread corruption by leading Republican officeholders in connection with construction of the recently completed Union Pacific Railroad. To divert profits to themselves, promoters of the railroad had organized a construction company known as the Credit Mobilier of America. The railroad's directors then awarded highly profitable contracts to the company with the result that as the railroad approached bankruptcy, the Credit Mobilier shareholders reaped dividends of 348 percent in a single year.

On December 2, 1872, at the beginning of the final session of the Forty-second Congress, a House committee launched an investigation in response to charges that Massachusetts Congressman Oakes Ames had bribed other members "to perform certain legislative acts for the benefit of the Union Pacific Railway Company by presents of stock in the Credit Mobilier of America, or by presents of a valuable character derived therefrom." In its subsequent report, the panel charged that Ames had sold shares to members at par value, although the actual value had more than doubled. When members so favored had asked Ames whether this would prove ethically embarrassing, he responded that it would not, for "the Union Pacific has received from Congress all the grants and legislation it wants and shall ask for nothing more."[29]

The House committee, however, concluded that Ames was looking for "friends in Congress who would resist any encroachment upon or interference with the rights and privileges already secured, and to that end

---

[28] Ibid.; *Congressional Globe* 41st Cong., 2nd sess., pp. 4670–73.
[29] *Congressional Globe*, 42nd Cong., 3rd sess., p. 11.

wishes to create in them an interest identical with his own."[30] As examples of such "encroachment" the panel pointed to pending legislation to regulate the Union Pacific's rates. Among those identified as stockholders in the profitable company were fifteen House members, including chairmen of almost every major committee, six senators, and Vice President Schuyler Colfax. Of this number, the House charged only Ames and New York Congressman James Brooks with misconduct in violation of antibribery legislation. The committee recommended that both members be expelled, arguing that the commission of the offenses during a previous Congress did not erase the current Congress's responsibility.

Acting several days before the end of the congressional term, the House concluded that it did not have authority to judge members' behavior prior to the existing term of Congress. This came despite arguments that the offenses were of a continuing nature. As long as Congress considered railroad rate legislation, Credit Mobilier shareholders would be subject to a conflict of interest. Consequently, the House rejected expulsion resolutions but curiously agreed, by decisive margins, to censure both men. One observer noted the inconsistency of the House's action in this case:

> Since the power to censure and the power to expel claim the same constitutional basis, and since the power to punish, whether by censure or expulsion, is applicable only to its members, the House could not logically doubt or deny that it had one power but not the other. This act of censure, therefore, was an expedient device for protecting two esteemed colleagues while making a concession to the public trust.[31]

For its part, the Senate created a special committee in the final month of its term to examine charges referred by the House committee. Among those members who came under the panel's scrutiny was John A. Logan. Logan explained that while a House member he had refused Ames's offer of stock but that a few months later he did accept a dividend check for $329 from him. Reluctantly, he took the check, but after two days he returned the money with $2 interest. The Senate committee accepted Logan's explanation as well as that of Massachusetts Senator Henry Wilson. Wilson claimed that his wife had purchased Credit Mobilier stock on his recommendation but that he had in no way benefitted from her transaction. Despite an earlier denial of knowledge about the company's existence, Wilson survived the scandal and later became vice president in place of Schuyler Colfax, whose association with the scandal destroyed

---

[30] Ibid., pp. 1462–66.
[31] Dionisopoulos, p. 109.

his political career. The Senate committee looked with disdain on New Hampshire Senator James Patterson's conflicting testimony and recommended on February 27, 1873, that he be expelled. The full Senate chose not to act on the case during the few days that remained in the congressional session. As Patterson's term expired with the end of that Congress, the Senate waited until the start of the new session before passing a resolution stating that its inaction should not be interpreted as expressing either approval or disapproval of his conduct.[32]

While embroiled in the Credit Mobilier scandal, the Senate was also concluding an investigation of charges that Kansas Senators Samuel Pomeroy and Alexander Caldwell had secured their respective seats through bribery. The Pomeroy case brought melodramatic tales of a midnight rendezvous in Pomeroy's hotel suite with a state legislator who received a $2,000 downpayment against a $5,000 fee for his vote to reelect Pomeroy. Pomeroy claimed he had given the money to a friend who wanted to establish a bank in Kansas. He was spared from Senate disciplinary action only by the poor credibility of the witnesses against him and by the action of the Kansas legislature early in 1873 of refusing to reelect him. Alexander Caldwell, Pomeroy's Kansas colleague, faired less well amidst allegations that he had volunteered to pay as much as $250,000 in 1871 for a Senate seat. After he won that contest, Caldwell reportedly told friends that it had cost him $60,000. He unwisely displayed an arrogant attitude to the Senate investigating committee, demanding to know under what authority it presumed to examine him. He argued that bribery of state legislators was not a federal offense and that the Senate could not discipline a member for conduct prior to his election. As the case against him gained momentum, he recognized that further resistance was futile and resigned rather than face resolutions designed to expel him or invalidate his election.[33]

In deliberations on these and related cases throughout the remainder of the nineteenth century, both houses of Congress left little doubt that they possessed the standing to judge such matters as bribery and corruption among their members, both before and during their terms of office. The application of these precedents, however, proved to be uneven and dictated by strongly partisan considerations. Whenever possible, unless the offense appeared to be a direct assault on the dignity and

[32] J. B. Crawford, *The Credit Mobilier of America* (Boston: C. W. Calkins and Co., 1880), chapters 8–10; Willard H. Smith, *Schuyler Colfax* (Indianapolis: Indiana Historical Bureau, 1952), pp. 350–51.

[33] *CR*, 43rd Cong., 1st sess., pp. 195–97; *Senate Election, Expulsion, and Censure Cases*, pp. 52–53; Dionisopoulos, pp. 119–20.

prerogatives of the House or Senate, those bodies chose to allow the electorate to take the ultimate disciplinary actions. This course was particularly evident in cases that came before both houses after the member in question had already been defeated for reelection. Affirming their constitutional rights to judge the qualifications of their members, the two houses simply allowed a member's term to expire, thereby avoiding a protracted and ultimately futile diversion from more pressing matters.[34]

Despite the aura of corruption surrounding Congress in the three decades following the Civil War, close contemporary observers found that scandal was specific rather than endemic to the House and Senate. Writing in 1869, journalist and biographer James Parton noted that although "Congress has its weak members and its weak moments," it contained "a laborious, able, and respectable body of men, intent on doing the best they could for the country." Members of Congress, he continued, "are not all the immaculate, disinterested, and devoted men whom we could wish to see sitting in those cane-bottomed chairs. If they were, they would not represent *us*." Parton concluded,

> The average ability is much higher than the people in general, and the standard of morals not lower. Congress can do wrong one hundred times from carelessness, indolence, ignorance, timidity, caprice, or good-nature, to once that it does wrong from a motive that so much as savors of corruption.[35]

Two decades later, the astute British observer of American political life, James Bryce, echoed Parton's analysis. He noted the "opportunities for corruption and blackmailing, of which unscrupulous men are well known to take advantage." Recognizing that "such men are fortunately few," Bryce provided a classic assessment of how these few were allowed to continue unchecked except in the most blatant behavior:

> The contagion of political vice is nowhere so swiftly potent as in legislative bodies, because you cannot taboo a man who has got a vote. You may loathe him personally, but he is the people's choice. He has a right to share in the government of the country, . . . you are grateful to him when he saves you on a critical division; you discover that "he is not such a bad fellow when one knows him"; people remark that he gives good dinners, or has an agreeable wife; and so it goes on till falsehood and knavery are covered under the cloak of party loyalty.[36]

In an era when railroads, seeking federal subsidies for preferred routes and rates, were considered the chief agents of corruption, the

---

[34] Dionisopoulos, chap. 5.

[35] Parton, pp. 219, 228, 230.

[36] James Bryce, *The American Commonwealth* (London: Macmillan & Co., 1888), I, pp. 160–61.

testimony of Southern Pacific President Collis Huntington was revealing. During a battle in 1876 with the Texas and Pacific Railroad, he confided that he might have won over certain congressmen "had they not been offered large sums" to vote against him. He added, "You know our rule is never to buy a vote." He recognized that a few politicians could be influenced by money, but there was little advantage in dealing with them. As historian David Rothman has concluded,

> The dangers of discovery and scandal were great, and buying two or three officials drove away ten honest men. A vote purchased by one bidder could easily be won over by another; then too, the strategy was too expensive to adopt as a habitual practice. Occasionally a supporter could be picked up with a generous gift—short weight men we always have with us—but economic interests did not influence the political process through bribery.[37]

Rather, they turned to well-placed loans, but also with little predictable success. When Georgia Senator John Gordon approached a Texas and Pacific Railroad lobbyist for a loan, his request was granted. Later, when a bill important to that company was before the Senate, Gordon told the lobbyist, "I cannot vote for it. There is nothing as you know which I could do consistently, at which I would hesitate to oblige you; but not only my convictions but my constituents are against it." He added, "I know you would not have me guilty of a shadow of turning from my convictions on any matter of legislation."[38]

During the first decade and a half of the twentieth century, Progressive reformers demanded an expanded role for government in offering protection to the citizenry from the economic, social, and political chaos that had engaged the energies of the post–Civil War generation. As one historian has observed, reformers at the start of the new century were faced with "the ethical confusion which resulted from attempting to apply the moral code of an individualistic, agrarian society to a highly industrialized and integrated social order."[39]

The alliance, both apparent and real, between members of Congress and captains of industry became a major item on the Progressives' reform agenda. To loosen these bonds, they advocated an end to the election of United States senators by state legislatures. That procedure had worked without serious difficulty until after the Civil War. As political parties grew stronger and better organized, state legislatures became battle-

---

[37] David J. Rothman, *Politics and Power: The United States Senate, 1869–1901* (Cambridge, Mass.: Harvard University Press, 1966), pp. 198–99.

[38] Ibid., pp. 199–200.

[39] Samuel Eliot Morison, Henry Steele Commager, William E. Leuchtenburg, *A Concise History of the American Republic* (New York: Oxford University Press, 1977), p. 499.

grounds for contending factions and seedbeds for bribery and other corruption. Under federal law, senatorial elections were the first order of legislative business in the state bodies. This often produced stalemate and deadlock, frustrating efforts to move ahead with matters of local concern and fueling charges that business interests were trying to purchase Senate seats. One contemporary magazine editor asserted that a rich man who wanted to buy a public office looked "first to the Senate for whereas a whole state may not be purchasable, a legislature may."[40]

In March, 1906, *Cosmopolitan Magazine* began a series of nine monthly articles by the muckraking journalist David Graham Phillips entitled "Treason of the Senate." Phillips's series purported to document the venality of twenty-one of that body's most senior members. As historian George Mowry has observed, Phillips's writing set forth a plea for "a return to the old moral standards, for the hard-headed integrity of the frontier farmer, for the revival of democratic methods of selecting public officials in place of the boss-ridden, money dominated political practices of his day."[41] In the months prior to the appearance of the series, the Senate had come into particular public disrepute as a result of the actions of two members who had recently been convicted under the 1864 statute on charges of fraud and corruption. One of them, Oregon's John Hipple Mitchell, was found guilty of receiving fees for expediting land claims before the United States Land Claims Commission. He died as the Senate was preparing to take disciplinary action against him.

The other, Joseph Burton of Kansas, was awaiting the results of an appeal of his conviction for taking fees for interceding with postal authorities in a mail fraud case against a St. Louis grain company. Burton expressed his innocence and also the prevailing sentiment of some of his colleagues in saying, "Other senators and representatives had built up large private practices during their terms of office and I, in a small way, desired to emulate them." Other senators told Burton that they would not move to expel him until all his appeals had been exhausted and provided that he remained away from the Senate floor. In May, 1906, amidst the publicity fanned by the Phillips series, the Supreme Court upheld Burton's conviction rejecting arguments that the 1864 statute, in prohibiting further federal service for convicted members, violated the Senate's constitutional right to decide on expulsion of its members. Justice John M. Harlan wrote that the "final judgment of conviction did not operate,

---

[40] Quoted in Robert and Leona Rienow, *Of Snuff, Sin and the Senate* (Chicago: Follett Publishing Co., 1965), p. 110.
[41] David Graham Phillips, *The Treason of the Senate*, ed. by George E. Mowry and Judson A. Grenier (Chicago: Quadrangle Books, 1964), p. 17.

ipso facto, to vacate the seat of the convicted senator nor compel the Senate to expel him or to regard him as expelled by force alone of the judgment." On the following day, the Senate referred the matter to its Committee on Privileges and Elections. Before it could take further action, Burton resigned to begin serving a six-month prison sentence.[42]

The "Treason of the Senate" series, combined with vast popular dissatisfaction with the indirect method of electing senators, led in 1913 to ratification of the Seventeenth Amendment to the Constitution. The direct election amendment became one of the hallmarks of successful Progressive era reform. These reforms extended beyond direct election to include a ban on financial contributions by corporations to congressional candidates. Early in 1907, Congress passed the Tillman Act, which made it unlawful for a corporation or national bank "to make a money contribution in connection with any election" to federal office. In 1910 and 1911, Congress extended this statute to provide for public reporting of receipts and expenditures as well as a maximum spending limit of $10,000 for Senate candidates and $5,000 for House aspirants.[43]

Investigations into four disputed senatorial elections shaped subsequent campaign spending legislation during the first quarter of the twentieth century. In 1911, the Senate received charges from a member of the Illinois state legislature that he and three colleagues had been bribed in 1909 to throw the Senate election to William Lorimer. A Senate investigating committee concluded that this action had no bearing on Lorimer's election, for he had won by a fourteen-vote margin, rendering the four purchased votes of no effect. The Senate decided not to expel Lorimer, noting that none of the legislators who had been charged with vote fraud had been convicted and all had been reelected. In May, 1911, however, the Illinois state legislature declared that Lorimer had obtained his election through corrupt means. More than a year passed before the Senate reversed its earlier stand, voting to invalidate Lorimer's election and thereby making him the last senator deprived of office for corrupting a state legislature.[44]

Six years later, in 1918, Michigan industrialist Truman H. Newberry defeated automobile magnate Henry Ford in a Republican senatorial primary. Newberry admitted spending nearly $200,000 in that bitterly contested campaign. Although he went on to win the general election

---

[42] "John Hipple Mitchell," *Dictionary of American Biography,* 13 pp. 53–54; *Senate Election, Expulsion, and Censure Cases,* p. 100.

[43] Elizabeth Drew, *Politics and Money: The New Road to Corruption* (New York: Macmillan, 1983), pp. 7–10; *Congressional Ethics,* p. 194.

[44] George H. Haynes, *The Senate of the United States* (Boston: Houghton Mifflin, 1938) I, pp. 131–33.

against Ford, who had also entered and won the Democratic primary, he was subsequently convicted of violating the 1910 campaign spending statute. In 1921, the United States Supreme Court set aside Newberry's conviction, ruling that the right of Congress to regulate elections did not extend to primaries. Although the Senate had seated the Michigan Republican in 1919, it undertook a thorough investigation of his campaign conduct. While concluding that he had been duly elected, the Senate expressed strong distaste for his ethical conduct. "The expenditure of such excessive sums in behalf of a candidate, either with or without his knowledge or consent," the committee report explained, "being contrary to sound public policy, harmful to the honor and dignity of the Senate, and dangerous to the perpetuity of a free government, such expenditures are hereby severely condemned and disapproved."[45] Facing the likelihood of expulsion, Newberry resigned his seat late in 1922.

As a result of the Newberry case and other government scandals during the presidency of Warren Harding, Congress moved to tighten campaign spending restrictions, passing the Federal Corrupt Practices Act in 1925. That measure set specific reporting requirements, prohibited solicitation of contributions from federal employees, and extended the ban on corporations' contributions to include "a gift, subscription, loan, advance, or deposit of money, or anything of value."[46]

Shortly after this act received President Calvin Coolidge's signature, the Senate again became embroiled in two protracted and sensational election cases. They involved Senators-elect William S. Vare of Pennsylvania and Frank L. Smith of Illinois. They began, as did Newberry's, with reports of excessive primary campaign spending. Smith reportedly received $125,000 from public utilities tycoon Samuel Insull, while retaining his seat on the powerful Illinois Commerce Commission. The Senate received a letter from Pennsylvania Governor Gifford Pinchot declaring, "The stealing of votes for Mr. Vare and the amount and sources of money spent in his behalf make it clear to me that the election returns do not in fact represent the will of the sovereign voters of Pennsylvania." After an extended inquiry, the Senate voted in January, 1928 to exclude Smith. Vare's illness delayed a similar finding until December 1929.[47]

As it was disposing of the Vare case, the Senate took another

---

[45] "Truman Handy Newberry," *Dictionary of American Biography*, Supplement 3, p. 549; *Congressional Ethics*, pp. 148–49; *Senate Election, Expulsion and Censure Cases*, pp. 111–13.

[46] *Congressional Ethics*, p. 194.

[47] *Senate Election, Expulsion and Censure Cases*, pp. 119–24; Reuben Momsen, "The Right of the Senate to Exclude a Senator-Elect," *The Notre Dame Lawyer* 4 (September–October 1928), 1–20.

significant step in defining ethical standards for its members by ruling on charges that Connecticut Senator Hiram Bingham had placed a lobbyist on his official Senate payroll. Following a seven-month investigation, the Senate voted to censure Bingham observing that his actions, "while not the result of corrupt motives," were "contrary to good morals and senatorial ethics and tend to bring the Senate into disfavor and disrepute."[48]

Early in 1933, Senate Sergeant-at-Arms David Barry, in a published article, assessed the contemporary state of congressional morality. In a statement that resulted in his being hauled before the bar of the Senate to explain himself, Barry observed, "there are not many Senators or Representatives who sell their votes for money, and it is pretty well known who those few are." Unimpressed with Barry's assertion that he intended his remark as a defense of a majority of members, the Senate found his behavior inappropriate and removed him from office.[49] This incident underscored Congress's desire to maintain the appearance of ethical propriety and its ability to deal swiftly with those who called it into question.

Preoccupied during the 1930s with New Deal era efforts to revive the nation's economy and during the 1940s with the conduct and aftermath of World War II, Congress found little time to focus on matters related to misconduct of members. The House of Representatives took no action in matters involving exclusion, expulsion, and censure in either decade. The end of the war, however, brought major changes to Capitol Hill. Long frustrated over its inability to counter executive branch domination, Congress passed the Legislative Reorganization Act of 1946, providing expanded staff resources and improved machinery for fomulating legislative policy. The combination of increased legislative independence in policy determination and the expansion of those policies through a wider sector of American life raised new concerns about the need for formal standards of legislative behavior.

These concerns led to establishment in 1951 of a Senate Subcommittee on Ethical Standards, under the chairmanship of Illinois Senator Paul Douglas. Although the panel's mandate extended throughout the entire federal government, it gave special consideration to the intensifying pressures facing members of Congress. Among its strongest recommendations, the committee urged both houses to develop voluntary codes of conduct to clarify new or complex situations where the application of

---

[48] *Senate Election, Expulsion and Censure Cases*, pp. 126–28.
[49] David Barry, "Over the Hill to Demagoguery," *The New Outlook* 161 (February 1933), 40–42; *CR* February 3, 1933, pp. 3269–82; Ibid., February 7, 1933, p. 3511.

basic moral principles was far from obvious and to keep well-intentioned members from blundering into error.[50] The committee placed on members of Congress special responsibility for maintaining high moral standards in the conduct of public affairs. It noted that "each is a public figure who is watched by thousands, sometimes by millions of people. His example influences the standards of conduct in the lives of people he never meets and does not know by name."[51] The Douglas Committee issued one of the earliest calls for mandatory disclosure by public officials, including congressmen, of income, assets, and financial transactions. It observed that such reporting would serve as "an antibiotic" to cure "ethical sicknesses in the field of public affairs."[52]

Although the Douglas Committee did not immediately achieve its objectives, it stimulated thoughtful and systematic study of the proper boundaries of legislative behavior. At the same time, in the House of Representatives, Charles Bennett introduced a resolution calling for a somewhat tamer code of conduct exhorting federal officials to "give a full day's labor for a day's pay," to "expose corruption wherever discovered," and to exhibit in their behavior consistent "devotion to God and country." Bennett and his supporters hoped that an ethical code would deter officials from wrongdoing and provide voters with a standard for measuring a candidate's behavior.[53] No action resulted from Bennett's proposal, but as with the Senate's deliberations, it paved the way for future initiatives.

As dust began to gather on the Douglas and Bennett reports, two members of the Senate became targets of investigations concerning management of outside sources of income. During the 1952 presidential campaign the Republican Vice Presidential candidate, Senator Richard Nixon, was reported to have received $16,000 from wealthy California businessmen to help pay office expenses for phone calls, trips, stamps, and Christmas cards. Although Nixon successfully defended his practice of receiving more money from private than from public sources, the furor

[50] For the work of the Douglas Subcommittee and a view of congressional ethics in the early 1950s see U.S. Senate, Committee on Labor and Public Welfare, *Establishment of a Commission on Ethics in Government, Hearings*, June–July, 1951; Paul Douglas, *Ethics in Government* (Cambridge, Mass.: Harvard University Press, 1952); H. H. Wilson, *Congress: Corruption and Compromise* (New York: Rinehart and Co., 1951). A more recent brief survey of Senate ethical codes with historical background is Jim Sasser, "Learning From the Past: The Senate Code of Conduct in Historical Perspective," *Cumberland Law Review* 8 (Fall 1977), 357–84.

[51] U.S. Senate, Committee on Labor and Public Welfare, *Ethical Standards in Government*, Committee Print, 82nd Cong., 1st sess., (1951), pp. 63–64.

[52] Ibid., pp. 37–39.

[53] *CR*, June 26, 1951.

that ensued alerted many congressmen to the need for care in establishing such funds.

Between 1950 and 1954 Senator Joseph R. McCarthy rocked the nation and the Senate with his campaign to expose alleged communist infiltration in the United States government. During the 1950 election season he sowed the seeds of his eventual undoing by defaming the character of Senate colleague Millard Tydings. Shortly after Tydings went down to defeat at the hands of a McCarthy protégé, Senator William Benton offered a resolution calling for a special investigation of McCarthy's actions. McCarthy refused to cooperate in the resulting probe by the Senate Rules Committee's Subcommittee on Privileges and Elections. Instead, he lodged charges questioning the propriety of Benton's conduct as a public official. By mid-1954, McCarthy had become an embarassment to his party, which in 1953 had taken control of both the Congress and the White House. The Senate devoted the latter half of 1954 to an investigation of charges against McCarthy and in December formally voted to "condemn" him for conduct "contrary to Senatorial traditions." The Wisconsin senator's downfall came as a result of his noncooperation with and abuse of the 1952 subcommittee investigation and his contempt for the select committee appointed to consider his censure.[54]

The absence of a clearly stated code of conduct for federal officials became a decided political liability for members of Congress by 1958. In that year the Eisenhower administration found itself ensnared as a consequence of influence-peddling charges involving presidential assistant Sherman Adams and Boston industrialist Bernard Goldfine. A House committee investigation uncovered plentiful evidence that Adams, a vocal apostle of morality in public life, had accepted favors from Goldfine while intervening on his behalf with the Federal Trade Commission. During his own testimony before the House committee, Goldfine revealed himself, in the words of an observer, to be "a sleazy, amoral, double-shuffle con man."[55] Shortly after the House committee concluded its investigation with a call for Adams' ouster, Maine's Republican Senator Frederick Payne suffered a surprising defeat at the hands of Democrat Edmund Muskie in that state's September general election. Republican congressional candidates feared that a similar fate awaited them in the upcoming November contests. Their concern triggered Adams' resigna-

---

[54] *Senate Election, Expulsion and Censure Cases*, pp. 152–53; Robert Griffith, *The Politics of Fear: Joseph R. McCarthy and the Senate* (Lexington: University Press of Kentucky, 1970).

[55] William Manchester, *The Glory and the Dream: A Narrative History of America, 1932–1972* (Boston: Little, Brown, 1974), p. 840.

tion and led to establishment of the first formal government-wide code of ethics. That code was identical to the version Representative Charles Bennett had prepared in 1951. Aspirational in tone and without legal force, it paved the way for the congressional codes of the 1960s.[56]

By the beginning of 1963, influential members of Congress called for creation of a joint congressional ethics committee to identify standards of behavior appropriate to legislative life on Capitol Hill. Noting the inadequacy of the 1958 Code of Conduct for senators and representatives, Senator Jacob Javits declared that it was "completely incongruous for Senate committees to question executive appointees vigorously on their financial affairs when those of us in Congress and our staffs are not subject to similar standards and requirements." He concluded, "We cannot continue to function on this double standard of ethics—a complete set for the executive branch but none for the legislative branch."[57]

Within days of Javits's statement, the Senate was faced with charges of corruption and influence peddling against one of its top staff aides, Majority Secretary Robert G. ("Bobby") Baker. A protégé of former Senate barons Lyndon Johnson and Robert Kerr, Baker resigned his post before the Senate Rules Committee began a broad investigation of the financial activities of Senate employees. That probe focused on the conditions that permitted Baker to amass a large personal fortune, and it resulted in a call for limited disclosure by Senate officers and senior employees of their assets and income. In the midst of the Rules Committee's inquiry, the Senate decided, on July 24, 1964, to establish a strictly bipartisan Select Committee on Standards and Conduct.[58]

Less than two years after its creation, the Select Committee launched its first full-scale investigation in response to newspaper charges that Senator Thomas Dodd had improperly exchanged favors with a public relations representative of West German interests, that he had used campaign funds to meet personal expenses, and that he had double-billed the government for travel expenses. On April 27, 1967, the committee recommended that the Senate formally censure Dodd on the last two charges. Two months later, the Senate voted by an unprecedented margin of 92–5 to censure Dodd for using campaign contributions for personal purposes, noting that his conduct, "which is contrary to accepted morals, derogates from the public trust expected of a Senator, and tends to bring the Senate into dishonor and disrepute."[59]

---

[56] House Concurrent Resolution 175, 85th Cong., 2nd sess.; *CR*, July 11, 1958, p. 13557.

[57] *CR*, January 16, 1963, p. 405.

[58] *CR*, July 24, 1964, p. 16929.

[59] *Senate Election, Expulsion and Censure Cases*, pp. 155–57.

While the Senate acted on the Dodd case, the House of Representatives deliberated the fate of the flamboyant Adam Clayton Powell. Throughout his two decades in Congress, the Harlem representative had been subject to numerous legal difficulties including charges of tax evasion. In 1966, his long absences from Congress and cavalier disregard for his legislative responsibilities led the Education and Labor Committee's members to remove him as that panel's chairman. Further revelations of Powell's pleasure trips at government expense and his practice of keeping his wife on the House payroll while she lived in Puerto Rico resulted in a challenge to his right to a seat in the House at the start of the 1967 congressional term. On March 1, 1967, after an investigating committee recommended that Powell be fined and censured, the House decided on sterner action and voted 307–116 to deny him his seat. Powell was quickly reelected, sworn in, fined $25,000, and deprived of his seniority. He decided, however, not to appear in the House until the courts had disposed of his challenge to the House's act of exclusion.[60]

The Dodd and Baker cases in the Senate and the Powell case in the House led each chamber in 1968 to adopt their first formal codes of ethical conduct. The Senate code contained four rules but provided no specific punishment for their violation other than the implied threat of censure or expulsion. They prescribed limits on outside employment for members and their staffs, required disclosure of campaign contributions and set restrictions on their use, prohibited all except designated Senate employees from receiving, soliciting, or distributing campaign funds, and required members and senior staff to file annual financial disclosure statements. In drafting these rules, the Senate Select Committee on Standards and Conduct followed several basic guidelines. The panel's first chairman, John Stennis, articulated the fundamental themes running through the history of Congress's concern with ethical behavior in explaining his committee's priorities:

> First, we resolved to deal with practical and actual situations, not with theoretical or imagined ones, and to provide workable procedures to head off trouble. Second, we did not want to interfere with a Senator's constitutional and legal duties, nor did we want to displace the electorate in judging his performance. It seemed unwise to treat senators like adolescents by imposing long lists of do's and don'ts.

The respected Mississippi senator concluded, "Finally, we thought it

[60] Congressional Quarterly, *Guide to Congress* (3rd ed.; Washington, D.C.: Congressional Quarterly, 1982) pp. 824–26.

would be prudent to measure what we thought the Senate would accept."[61]

In the wake of the Powell case, the House of Representatives established a twelve-member bipartisan standing Committee on Standards of Official Conduct. In 1968 that panel recommended and the House adopted a code of conduct that declared that a member may "accept no gift of substantial value, directly or indirectly, from any person, organization or corporation having a direct interest in legislation before Congress" or accept an honorarium for a speech or article "in excess of the usual and customary value for such services." House members were also required to disclose publicly financial interests of more than $5,000 and income of more than $1,000 from companies having business with the government.[62]

In the decade that followed the 1968 adoption of the Senate and House codes, one president, two senators, and fifteen members of the House of Representatives were subject to congressional or judicial investigation for ethical misconduct. Under threat of impeachment, President Richard Nixon resigned in August, 1974. Senators Daniel Brewster and Edward Gurney were indicted, in 1969 and 1974 respectively, for bribery. Thirteen of the fifteen House members were convicted of a series of crimes including bribery, conflict of interest, perjury, extortion, conspiracy to hide kickbacks, and income tax evasion.[63] During 1976 alone, seven members of the House were involved in criminal proceedings. Hostile public reaction to the apparent tendency within Congress to ignore these cases of wrongdoing led the Senate and House early in 1977 to toughen their codes of conduct.

Senate and House floor leaders tied consideration of a long overdue congressional salary increase to passage of stronger ethics codes. They reasoned that a pay increase would make less objectionable strict limits on outside earned income. Without such a limitation, it would be impossible to devise a meaningful code. On February 7, 1977, the bipartisan House Commission on Administrative Review released a proposed code and the House adopted it within a month. Early in April, the Senate agreed to a similar code. The codes limited outside earned income to 15 percent of a member's congressional salary, although the Senate subsequently voted to delay the effective date of that provision.

[61] U.S. Senate, Special Committee on Official Conduct, *Senate Code of Conduct, Hearings*, 95th Cong., 1st sess., p. 58.

[62] U.S. House, Committee on Standards of Official Conduct, *Proposals for Standards, Hearings*, 90th Cong., 1st sess., (August–September 1967).

[63] For a summary of these cases see Congressional Quarterly, *Congressional Ethics*, 2d ed., pp. 173–74.

The revised codes also abolished office accounts, a favorite device for masking the source and uses of outside contributions, and they placed new limits on the use of the franking privilege for sending congressional mail. Members and their spouses were also required to make public detailed financial data. The Senate code went further than that of the House by prohibiting its members from affiliating with law firms for compensation and restricting them from lobbying in the Senate for one year after leaving office.[64]

With the passage of the 1977 codes, both the House and Senate strengthened the powers of their respective ethics committees. The combination of tighter codes and more effective enforcement mechanisms brought to a close nearly two centuries of congressional reluctance to sit in judgment on individual colleagues. Through the years most members had agreed with the spirit of the nineteenth-century observation that although "Congress has its weak members and its weak moments" it contained a "laborious, able and respectable body of men intent on doing the best they could for the country." As the Senate completed work on its 1977 code, Mississippi's John Stennis expressed satisfaction with that body's handiwork in the face of pressing political realities. He summarized two hundred years of congressional ambivalence over the regulation of members' conduct when he observed, "It has been our experience that senators want to do the right thing when they are confronted with an ethical dilemma, but they find that making a judgment is not only difficult but risky." Referring to the Senate Committee on Official Conduct, Stennis concluded:

> This is where our committee has done some of its best work, for it can not only deal with a Senator or his representative on an individual basis, but it can address the particular facts that gave rise to his trouble and distinguish those facts from others. The alternative to advice and counsel from a committee of Senators assisted by an able staff is a list of precepts and admonitions that will begin to resemble the Internal Revenue Code in length and complexity.[65]

---

[64] Ibid., pp. 48–56.
[65] *Senate Code of Conduct Hearings*, p. 57.

2

The Role of the Electorate in Congressional Ethics

JAMES C. KIRBY

No convicted felon is now a member of either house of Congress. Furthermore, in twenty-seven years only one incumbent has been re-elected after conviction on felony charges.

No senator has gained reelection after formal disciplinary action by the full Senate. Only one incumbent representative has survived in office despite having been subjected to formal discipline by the House.

The basis for these narrow findings will be developed later. The response of the electorate to congressional misconduct which does not produce criminal prosecution or disciplinary proceedings is more difficult to assess.

A valuable beginning point is a study by John G. Peters and Susan Welch of the University of Nebraska. It was published in the September, 1980, issue of the *American Political Science Review* under the title "The Effects of Corruption on Voting Behavior in Congressional Elections."[1] They examined all known instances, eighty-one in number, wherein charges of political corruption or unethical behavior were campaign issues in elections for the House of Representatives from 1968 to 1978, relying largely on *Congressional Quarterly* to identify such contests.

The first noteworthy fact is that only eighty-one instances were found in six pairs of primary and general elections for 435 House seats. Sixteen of these were elections in which the accused candidate was not an incumbent. Thus, in only sixty-five instances were incumbent represen-

---

[1] John G. Peters and Susan Welch, "The Effects of Corruption on Voting Behavior in Congressional Elections," *American Political Science Review* 74, 3 (September 1980), pp. 697–708.

JAMES C. KIRBY ● University of Tennessee College of Law, Knoxville, Tennessee 37916.

tatives even accused of unethical conduct in several thousand primary and general elections. It is surprising that there were so few elections in which the voters were called on to "throw the rascal out" on ethical grounds. A more encouraging fact is that the number has steadily increased from four in 1968 to twenty-eight in 1978.

Peters and Welch analyzed elections for "electoral retribution," meaning loss in a candidate's vote total, not necessarily electoral defeat. In this sense, all types of candidates were found to suffer some degree of retribution at the polls, with significant numbers being defeated or resigning before risking defeat.

Electoral retribution varied widely according to the severity of the charges. Campaign violations and conflict of interest engendered the lowest levels of retribution, bribery and morals charges the highest.

Peters and Welch broke down accused incumbents into five categories: those who resigned during their terms, those who chose not to seek reelection, those defeated in primaries, those defeated in general elections and those who won reelection. Only sixty-two percent survived the entire process. Considering the possibility that many of the charges may have been minor or unfounded, this attrition speaks well for the process.

Within the incumbent group, Peters and Welch found significant electoral retribution against all incumbents, but senior incumbents were better able to survive their vote slides, resulting in their enjoying a high degree of electoral security. The "average" Democrat accused of corruption had served six terms in Congress and had polled over sixty-seven percent of the votes in his last election. The average Republican had served three terms and polled fifty-eight percent of the vote.

The high degree of security of senior incumbents is troubling. It was interpreted as showing that many voters treat an ethical charge as a single issue to be considered with others. It may be outweighed by the senior representative's voting record, important committee chairmanships, and casework for individual constituents. The relative severity of the charges may also aid in assessing voter reaction. There was no breakdown connecting accused senior incumbents with particular categories of misconduct.

The section below on congressional discipline will suggest remedies which might lessen voter tolerance of senior members' misconduct.

EFFECTS OF CRIMINAL PROSECUTIONS

As former congressman Richard Bolling of Missouri warned a dinner meeting of our Hastings Institute conference, criminal prosecution is a dangerous weapon and carries serious implication for congressional independence of the executive branch. Nonetheless, its use has proliferated in recent years.

The "Abscam" defendants are the most notable group.[2] Not one of the seven was able to survive in congressional office. Four won primary elections after indictment but were defeated in the general election: Michael ("Ozzie") Myers of Pennsylvania, John W. Jenrette, Jr., of South Carolina, John W. Murphy of New York, and Frank Thompson, Jr., of New Jersey. Richard Kelly of Florida was defeated in his primary. Raymond F. Lederer was reelected, but this occurred after indictment and before his conviction. He later resigned to avoid expulsion, as did Senator Harrison Williams, of New Jersey, the only Abscam senator.

In the past twenty years ten other representatives have either chosen not to run or have been defeated after criminal prosecutions were initiated.[3] In the majority of cases mere indictment has been fatal in either the primary or the general election. Of those surviving primaries, only three have survived general elections. They are Abscam's Lederer, mentioned above, and Representatives John Dowdy of Texas, in 1971, and Daniel J. Flood of Pennsylvania, in 1979. Dowdy and Flood were reelected after indictment but before conviction. Flood resigned during his term. Dowdy served his term but did not seek further reelection.

Veteran Charles C. Diggs of Michigan stands alone as the only recent member to gain reelection after conviction. He was chairman of the House District of Columbia Committee and the International Relations Subcommittee on Africa. In 1978, after his primary election, he was convicted of salary kickback charges, but he won reelection in November from his heavily black Democratic district in Detroit. He was censured by the House and agreed to give up his chairmanships. He resigned when his appeal failed.

Thus, criminal prosecution has proved to be highly effective in engendering fatal electoral retaliation. The voters are more likely by far to respond to this stimulant than any other.

---

[2] Unless otherwise indicated, all factual references to Congress are based on the appropriate publication of *Congressional Quarterly*.

[3] Thomas F. Johnson of Maryland (1962), Frank W. Boykin of Alabama (1962), John Dowdy of Texas (1970), Martin B. McKneally of New York (1970), Henry Helstoski of New Jersey (1976), James F. Hastings of New York (1976), Daniel J. Flood of Pennsylvania (1978), Joshua Eilberg of Pennsylvania (1978), J. Herbert Burke of Florida (1978), and Robert E. Bauman of Maryland (1980). Prior to 1962, *Congressional Quarterly* could identify only eighteen instances of alleged "corrupt practices," seven of which did not involve criminal proceedings. "Corrupt Practice Cases Involving Congressmen," *1962 CQ Almanac,* p. 389.

One would be slow to advocate increased uses of this remedy, but criminal prosecutions of members of Congress have increased substantially in the past two decades, with a corresponding increase in voter retaliation.

EFFECTS OF CONGRESSIONAL DISCIPLINE

Several of the criminal cases discussed above were accompanied by formal discipline. We turn now to the effects on the electorate of congressional discipline unaccompanied by criminal prosecution and presumably based on noncriminal conduct.

Many view congressional sanctions short of expulsion as innocuous. The censure of Senator Joe McCarthy in 1954, the beginning point of the modern history of congressional discipline, is compelling evidence to the contrary. Ostensibly, McCarthy was not disciplined for "McCarthyism" but for abusing fellow senators, first the members of a committee which was investigating his conduct and later those on the special committee considering his censure. In the floor debates on censure recommendations, he aggravated his misconduct by saying that "the Communist party has now extended its tentacles to the United States Senate." His censure was in part an action taken by the Senate to protect itself institutionally.

The practical effect of censure was the ruin of McCarthy. He was totally discredited and was never again effective in the Senate. He drank himself to death and died of cirrhosis of the liver in 1957. He was never a candidate for reelection but surely would have been defeated.[4]

It was not until 1967 that another member of Congress, Congressman Adam Clayton Powell, was to see peer discipline help to bring ruin to his career. His case is notable as an example of ascending disciplinary sanctions, formal and informal, being applied over a period of time.[5]

Powell entered the House from the Harlem district of Manhattan in 1945. He was regularly reelected thereafter and rose by virtue of seniority to chairmanship of the Education and Labor Committee. By 1963 he had come under widespread public and congressional criticism for an accumulation of misconduct, including indiscretion in his private life, absen-

---

[4] McCarthy's isolation and total decline in national and local influence is well described by Thomas C. Reeves, *The Life and Times of Joe McCarthy* (Briarcliff Manor, N.Y.: Stein and Day, 1982), pp. 639–671.

[5] The facts of Powell's treatment by the House are extracted from Association of the Bar of the City of New York, Special Committee on Congressional Ethics, *Congress and the Public Trust* (New York: Atheneum, 1970), pp 205–210.

teeism, junketing, contempt of New York courts, and misuse of public funds.

Powell's difficulties with fellow members of Congress came into the open on February 5, 1963, when Senator John J. Williams raised several charges against him and challenged his fitness to conduct a proposed House investigation of juvenile delinquency. Powell soon answered charges based upon his wife's being on his office payroll and his personal use of overseas counterpart funds by accusing other unnamed members of doing the same things. He also attributed Senator Williams's charges to the fact that he (Powell) was black.

A unique series of disciplinary steps was then launched in the House against Powell. On March 6, 1963, it cut Powell's committee's funds from a requested two-year grant of $697,000 to a one-year figure of $200,000. In an even more extraordinary move, $150,000 of this sum was made directly available to subcommittees and placed beyond Powell's control.

In 1966 a bipartisan revolt against Powell arose within the Education and Labor Committee. Frustrated by his absenteeism and erratic actions in handling legislation, the committee adopted new rules which stripped him of much of his power. It empowered subcommittee chairmen to take bills directly to the House floor in certain circumstances, thus depriving Powell of the traditional ability of a chairman to delay legislation. New restrictions were placed on Powell's power over funds and staff.

An official investigation was soon begun of Powell's alleged misuse of committee funds and personnel. It was conducted by the House Administration Committee's Special Subcommittee on Contracts. The subcommittee reported on January 3, 1967, and made several findings adverse to Powell. It condemned his misuse of public funds and recommended that Mrs. Powell be discharged from her position. She resided in Puerto Rico and obviously did no work for Congress.

Powell declined the subcommittee's invitation to testify and responded by offering to prove nepotism and junketing by other members. When the newly elected Ninetieth Congress convened on January 10, 1967, there were widespread public and congressional demands for punitive action against Powell. The House Democratic Caucus stripped him of his party seniority and the chairmanship of the Education and Labor Committee. Proponents of this move claimed it was designed to salvage Powell's seat, arguing that otherwise the House would exclude him. Nonetheless, by a 363-to-65 vote the House moved against Powell the next day and required him to stand aside without being seated while a select committee investigated his qualifications.

A select committee, headed by the liberal Emanuel Celler of New York, proceeded to investigate Powell's qualifications. This committee was carefully chosen from representatives who could not be charged with racial bias and included one black representative. Nonetheless, Powell angered his House colleagues by public statements that the movement against him was racially motivated, calling it a "lynching Northern style" and himself a "black Dreyfus." Powell refused to respond to any charges of misconduct or to answer any questions unrelated to his age, citizenship, and inhabitancy, contending that the committee lacked power to consider any grounds for excluding him other than the stated grounds of constitutional eligibility for the House.

The Celler Committee moved slowly and did not report until February 23. The committee agreed with Powell that he possessed the requisite constitutional qualifications and could not be excluded. However, it found punishment to be warranted and recommended that Powell be seated but then censured, denied seniority, and fined $40,000.

The committee stated four specific categories of Powell's misconduct: (1) contumacious conduct toward New York courts; (2) maintaining his wife on the Congressional payroll while she performed no services; (3) expenditure of government funds for private purposes; and (4) refusal to cooperate with the two congressional committees which had investigated his activities. Powell's public statements did not help him. When temporarily denied his seat, he told the House that those "without sin should cast the first stone. There is no one here who does not have a skeleton in his closet. I know, and I know them by name." The House took up Powell's dare and rejected the committee's recommendations as inadequate by voting 222 to 202 against a motion to bring them to a vote. The committee's resolution was then amended to require Powell's exclusion and passed by a final vote of 307 to 116.

Powell was overwhelmingly reelected in the special election which was held to fill the vacancy but did not present himself again to the Ninetieth Congress. Instead, he initiated a suit in federal court challenging the validity of his exclusion.

Before his litigation was finally decided, Powell was elected to the Ninety-first Congress. This time the House seated him and imposed a fine of $25,000 which Powell did not contest. (His later victory in the United States Supreme Court had no legal consequences other than to establish his right to his salary for the Ninetieth Congress.[6])

Powell lost his next bid for reelection to Charles Rangel. Although his constituents were slow to react, the massive congressional discipline undoubtedly played a role in his downfall.

The next senator to feel the sting of peer-discipline after Joe

[6] Powell v. McCormack, 395 U.S. 486 (1969).

McCarthy was Senator Thomas J. Dodd of Connecticut in 1967.[7] Members of Dodd's staff covertly copied records temporarily removed from his office and delivered the material to columnists Drew Pearson and Jack Anderson, who proceeded to expose Dodd on a number of allegations of misconduct and made it impossible for the Senate to ignore Dodd's case. He was censured for deliberately raising campaign surpluses. Dodd's defense was that a sum of $116,000 raised over a four-year period was intended by his constituents to be personal gifts to be spent at his discretion. Ninety-two Senators voted against Dodd in approving a censure resolution which accused him of violating customary standards of Senate conduct.

Dodd sought reelection in 1970. After rejection as the Democratic nominee, he ran in the general election as an independent. He received less than one-fourth of the vote in losing to Lowell Weicker.

In 1979 Herman F. Talmadge of Georgia joined McCarthy and Dodd and became the third modern Senator to be formally disciplined by that body. His former wife testified before the Senate Ethics Committee that he kept large sums of cash in the pocket of a coat hanging in their Washington home. The cash was available to both for their expenses. She turned over $7,700 in one-hundred-dollar bills to the committee and testified that it came from this coat. Talmadge denied this and the committee made no findings on this issue. The committee reported five findings adverse to Talmadge based on irregularities in his handling of office and campaign funds. The Senate "denounced" Talmadge by a vote of eighty-one to fifteen.

Talmadge won the Democratic nomination in his 1980 reelection bid but then suffered a surprising loss to Republican nominee Matt Mattingly, who became Georgia's first Republican Senator since Reconstruction. The Senate's discipline of Talmadge undoubtedly contributed to his defeat.

Since the Powell case there have been four other instances in which the House of Representatives has imposed formal discipline in the absence of criminal proceedings. John McFall and Charles H. Wilson were defeated at the polls after being reprimanded for accepting gifts from Korean lobbyist Tongsun Park. Wilson's case was a particularly aggravated one. In 1978 he was reprimanded for accepting cash from the Korean lobbyist and lying to the Ethics Committee. The next year he was censured for accepting cash from a person with an interest in pending

---

[7] For a full account of Dodd's case, see James Boyd, *Above the Law* (New York: New American Library, 1968), written by Dodd's former legislative assistant who turned against him.

legislation and converting campaign funds to personal use. In 1980 Wilson was overwhelmingly defeated in his primary, receiving only fifteen percent of the vote.

Veteran Congressman Robert L. F. Sikes of Florida survived reprimand briefly. In 1976 he was exposed by *The New York Times* on a number of egregious conflict-of-interest charges. His worst offense was failing to report his ownership interest in the First Navy Bank, Pensacola Naval Air Station, while he was attempting to assist the bank in obtaining a national charter and FDIC coverage. Sikes was reprimanded but was unopposed and won reelection. The House Democrats then removed him from his chairmanship of the Military Construction Appropriation Subcommittee. He did not seek reelection in 1978.

Edward Roybal of California is the only incumbent to have survived reprimand and to have continued in the House for more than one term. His discipline arose out of the 1978 "Koreagate" scandal and involved receipt of cash from Tongsun Park. Roybal was a former chairman of the Hispanic Caucus and charged his accusers of racism. Key votes in the House on Roybal were closer than usual in such cases and the Koreagate scandal lacked the customary stimulants of adverse public opinion found in such cases.

The Sikes case is one of several in which internal sanctions, short of formal action by the full House, have been used to discipline errant members. In the Powell case, the full array of such measures was employed. The Diggs and Dowdy cases included similar organizational sanctions. Before his resignation, Wayne Hays was forced by the Democratic leadership to give up his committee chairmanship because of the Elizabeth Ray scandal.

The potential of using organizational sanctions for ethical violations deserves study. It indicates peer disapproval, which aids Congress institutionally in the public's eye. It removes a member of questionable fitness from a position of power. It may cause voter retaliation and help to unseat the member in the preferred way.

CONCLUSION

Criminal convictions are virtually certain to be followed by electoral rejection of a member of Congress.

Criminal indictments carry a high likelihood of causing electoral rejection when a member must stand for election before trial.[8]

[8] Peters and Welch, p. 706.

Formal discipline of a member has a high likelihood of causing electoral defeat. Increased use of formal disciplinary proceedings would undoubtedly result in a corresponding increase in electoral defeats.

A more likely prospect is that Congress might make greater use of its organizational disciplinary powers. Such sanctions as denying committee chairmanships would be a partial solution to the problem of the high degree of electoral security enjoyed by senior incumbents.

As examples of secure incumbents who had figured in prominent scandals of recent years, Peters and Welch cited Powell, Hays, Diggs, Roybal, Flood, McFall, and Wilbur Mills. Of these seven, only Roybal is still in Congress. However, of the six who have departed, only Powell and McFall were defeated at the polls. The other four voluntarily gave up their seats after undergoing some form of organizational discipline. (Mills was stripped of the chairmanship of the Ways and Means Committee.) Thus, this disciplinary process and the electoral process working together have an impressive track record of promoting electoral defeat or voluntary departure among senior incumbents. Even a modest increase in the use of organizational discipline might well help to reduce the instances for which it is appropriate.

II

ETHICS AND LEGISLATIVE LIFE

3

Political Action Committees, Electoral Politics, and Congressional Ethics

GARY C. JACOBSON

Ethical dilemmas are intrinsic to the American system of electoral politics, an inevitable consequence of the diverse values elections are supposed to promote. To people pursuing public office they appear as recurrent conflicts between electoral expediency and other values, between doing what will help win election and what otherwise would be "right." They are experienced as personal challenges to individual integrity, and the questions they raise in the minds of most observers concern the honesty and character of politicians as individuals.

There is, it seems, no want of reason to worry on this score; unethical—or at least questionable—behavior appears common enough. But in a larger sense, such concern is misplaced. Ethical quandaries are inherent in the basic structure of electoral politics; they admit of no simple solution. Certainly they cannot be resolved merely by enlisting a better class of candidates, if only because the principled alternative is so rarely obvious. Fundamental problems would remain no matter how virtuous individual politicians were to become. Neither are there easy or obvious structural reforms that are not likely to create equal or greater difficulties, or so I shall argue in this essay.

The difficulty originates in basic democratic theory. Elections make political authority legitimate. They do so by giving ritual expression to the notion that we are governed, however indirectly, by our own consent and to the democratic ideal of political equality: one person, one vote. In this

GARY C. JACOBSON ● Department of Political Science, University of California, San Diego, La Jolla, California 92093.

guise elections imply that people will enjoy some manner of equality in representation; legitimate authority does not play favorites. If not perfect equality, some minimal degree of fairness is expected. At the very least, widely shared interests should enjoy precedence over narrower "special interests." Influence should reside more in numbers than in wealth or position. Beyond that, popular elections are expected to bind elected officials to conscientious service of the public interest.

But conferring legitimacy is by no means the only function of elections; among other things, they are expected to produce political leaders who can govern effectively, making difficult social choices in the face of widespread social disagreement on values and policies and deep uncertainty about what constitutes the public good. Neither is equality the only important democratic value; just as basic are such things as freedom of expression and association. Nor are votes the only important political resource; money, organization, and political skill also matter, and they are distributed very unequally. Inevitably, the ideal of political equality is, in practice, routinely violated. So is the public interest, however conceived, routinely neglected.

Because electoral politics necessarily fails to deliver on the promises of equal representation and dependable devotion to the public good, the integrity of politicians and the legitimacy of political institutions is always open to question. The tension between theory and practice, though finding permanent expression in the caricature of the duplicitous politician common in popular culture, has usually been muted. But from time to time it becomes acute. In recent years, for example, evolving campaign finance practices and the rising cost of political campaigns have brought it to prominence once again. Privately financed elections naturally invite suspicion that the interests of contributors will take precedence over the interests of voters. Suspicion is sharpened when campaign contributions are unmistakably linked to specific private interests, as are those made by most political action committees (PACs). It is no coincidence that campaign contributions by PACs have excited the most concern.

Because the ethical questions raised by PACs have received so much attention, they provide a useful starting point for considering the more general ethical problems posed by electoral politics. I therefore begin with a discussion of PACs and refer to them frequently in the pages that follow. I do so, however, only to argue that the focus on PACs and their distinctive threat to the integrity of legislators is basically misguided. PAC contributions raise no ethical problems for individual legislators that do not appear in many other guises in the struggle to stay in office. The most important ethical problems they raise are systemic; they are not a

Table 1. Political Action Committees Registered with the Federal Election Commission, 1974–1982

			Date		
	12/74	12/76	12/78	12/80	7/82
Type of PAC					
Labor	201	224	217	297	350
Corporate	89	433	784	1204	1415
Other	318	489	652	1050	1484
Total	608	1146	1653	2551	3249

Source: Federal Election Commission.

function of individual lapses in ethics and so will not be solved by more scrupulous behavior on the part of individuals.

Furthermore, the systemic problems created by PACs are not unique, nor are they or the others easily corrected without creating worse problems. Ironically, coping effectively with systemic weaknesses bred by the electoral politics of Congress probably requires that greater, rather than lesser, outside pressure be brought to bear on individual members, augmenting rather than reducing their burden of ethical quandaries. Structural problems require structural solutions which are by no means guaranteed to make individual ethical choices any easier, although they may serve to enhance the integrity of the system as a whole.

It is not difficult to see why people concerned with congressional ethics should inevitably cast a cold eye on political action committees. PACs are organized by corporations, unions, ideologues, trade and professional associations, and many other sorts of groups to provide campaign money to congressional candidates. Since their legal status was clarified by the Federal Election Campaign Act Amendments of 1974, the number of active PACs has increased with every election (Table 1); so, too, has the amount of money they contribute to congressional candidates (Table 2).[1] Campaign contributions from other sources have also increased, but not so fast; therefore PAC contributions account for a growing share of campaign funds (Table 3).

PACs do not, of course, raise and bestow campaign money for the pure joy of it; they mean to influence public policy. A distinction is often

[1] PAC contributions continued to grow in 1982. Final figures are not yet available, but as of June 30, PAC fundraising was 61 percent ahead of 1980. See Brooks Jackson, "Democrats Holding Lead in Donations from Interest Groups," *Wall Street Journal,* 4 October 1982, p. 16.

Table 2. The Growth of PAC Contributions to Congressional Candidates,
1974–1980

	Contributions (in millions)			
	1974	1976	1978	1980
Type of PAC contribution				
Labor	$6.3	$8.2	$10.3	$13.1
	(50)[a]	(36)	(29)	(24)
Corporate	2.5	7.1	9.8	19.2
	(20)	(31)	(28)	(35)
Trade/membership/health	2.3	4.5	11.5	16.1
	(18)	(20)	(33)	(29)
Other	1.4	2.8	3.5	6.9
	(11)	(12)	(10)	(12)
Total PAC contributions	12.5	22.6	35.1	55.3
Adjusted for inflation (1980 = 1.00)	20.9	32.7	44.3	55.3

	Percentage change (adjusted for inflation)			
	1974–76	1976–78	1978–80	1974–80
Type of PAC contribution				
Labor	13	7	0	24
Corporate	146	17	55	359
Trade/membership/health	169	117	11	319
Other	73	6	56	195
Total PAC contributions	57	32	24	189

Source: Federal Election Commission.

[a] Percentage of all PAC contributions; numbers may not sum to 100 because of rounding.

drawn between PACs that define their policy objectives broadly and those
that pursue much narrower special—generally economic—interests. The
former deploy their funds to help elect candidates whose views on policy
are congenial; they often support nonincumbent candidates, and they
concentrate their resources in close races, where they are most likely to
make a difference. The latter give money not so much to affect the
outcome as to curry favor with whoever winds up in a position to serve or
damage their interests. They contribute to safe incumbents who do not
need the money, to members of both parties sitting on committees dealing
with legislation they care about, to newly elected members *after* the
election.[2] Such PACs bear the brunt of suspicion and criticism, but there

---

[2] Gary C. Jacobson, *Money in Congressional Elections* (New Haven: Yale University Press,
1980), pp. 76–88.

Table 3. Sources of Campaign Contributions to Major Party House and Senate General Election Candidates, 1972–1980

	1972[a]	1974	1976	1978	1980
House elections					
Average contribution:	$51,752	$61,084	$79,421	$111,232	$148,268
Percentage from:					
Individuals	60[b]	73	59	61	67[b]
Parties[c]	17	4	8	5	4
PACs	14	17	23	25	29
Candidates[d]	—	6	9	9	—
Unknown	9	—	—	—	—
Senate elections					
Average contribution:	$353,933	$455,515	$624,094	$951,390	$1,079,346
Percentage from:					
Individuals	67[b]	76	69	76	78[b]
Parties	14	6	4	2	2
PACs	12	11	15	14	21
Candidates	0	1	12	8	—
Unknown	8	6	—	—	—

Sources: Compiled by author from data supplied by Common Cause (1972 and 1974) and the Federal Election Commission (1976–1980).

[a] Some contributions before April 7, 1972, may have gone unreported.

[b] Includes candidates' contributions to their own campaigns.

[c] Does not include party expenditures on behalf of candidates.

[d] Includes candidates' loans unrepaid at time of filing.

is no reason to single them out. If a group's contributions give it undue influence over public policy, the substance of its goals is irrelevant. In any case, the democratic ideal is violated and the integrity of individual legislators brought into question.

PACs are not without their defenders, of course. The involvement of organized groups in financing campaigns fits easily into the hallowed tradition of Madisonian pluralism. The ceiling on how much any PAC can give to a candidate is low enough to ensure that no single PAC can make much difference and therefore acquire much influence (and very few give the limit as it is). Three-quarters of the money spent on campaigns comes from sources other then PACs (see Table 3). PACs represent groups that politicians would take into account in any case. Some mechanism for representing the enormous variety of economic and political interests that are not easily encompassed within the framework of single-member districts is clearly essential; why not PACs? At best, PACs provide a new way to involve large numbers of people in electoral politics.[3]

[3] See Michael J. Malbin, "Of Mountains and Molehills: PACs, Campaigns, and Public Policy," *Parties, Interest Groups, and Campaign Finance Laws,* ed. by Michael J. Malbin

Such arguments do little to reassure critics who are persuaded that, apart from any virtues they may have, PACs do in fact exercise illegitimate influence over members of Congress and consequently on policy decisions. Evidence offered for this conviction is largely anecdotal and circumstantial. Typically, Common Cause or an enterprising newspaper reporter finds that congressmen pushing legislation desired by some group—maritime unions, milk producers, beer distributors, defense contractors are recent examples—get campaign money from PACs representing the group. This, for some, closes the case. But it is no proof of influence. Recipients of such contributions invariably argue that the PACs are merely helping out those members who have the good sense to agree with their own quite defensible view of the public interest.

At this level of analysis, ambiguity is inevitable. Recently, for example, the *Wall Street Journal* ran a front-page article headlined "A Liberal Congressman Turns Conservative; Did PAC Gifts Do It?"[4] The article traced the evolution of Thomas A. Luken, a Democrat who represents western Cincinnati, from the liberal reformer first elected in 1974 to the vigorous proponent of actions backed by special economic interests (e.g., to weaken the Clean Air Act, to prevent hospital cost controls, and to exempt medical professionals from FTC consumer-protection and antitrust regulations). In the course of this transformation, Luken has become a major recipient of campaign funds from business-oriented PACs; in 1980, he received $174,778 from PACs, an extraordinarily high fifty-nine percent of his total contributions. His case was presented as an example of "the growing clout of business-oriented political action committees," of how "the sheer gravitational pull of their money . . . draws incumbents away from their old moorings."[5] The clear implications was that he had adapted his politics to finance his campaigns.

Luken naturally denied the charge, and the reporter went on to admit, "There is, in truth, a chicken-and-egg problem here. Which came first, the congressman's conservative views or the promise of business PAC contributions?"[6] This is exactly why such evidence is always inconclusive. In Luken's case, there is the additional circumstance that he represents a conservative district, "a Republican bastion that would be

(Washington, D.C.: American Enterprise Institute for Public Policy Research, 1980), pp. 152–184; Joseph E. Cantor, *Political Action Committees: Their Evolution and Growth and Their Implications for the Political System* (Washington, D.C.: Congressional Research Service, 6 November 1981), pp. 149–184.

[4] Dennis Farney, "A Liberal Congressman Turns Conservative; Did PAC Gifts Do It?" *Wall Street Journal*, 29 July 1982, p. 1.
[5] Ibid.
[6] Ibid.

difficult for any Democrat to hold."[7] Business PAC money was not a necessary condition for his political transformation.

More systematic evidence of PAC influence—or the absense thereof—is generally lacking. A few careful studies have been conducted on the relationship between PAC contributions and roll-call votes which attempt to untangle the causal links.[8] But all suffer from severe technical problems (no criticism of these scholars—the specification problems here are ferocious) and have produced decidedly inconclusive results. PACs do evidently support members whose votes they like; but no one ever doubted this. The evidence that PAC contributions affect individual roll-call votes is much more limited and doubtful. We simply do not yet know how commonly PAC contributions influence behavior, if at all.[9]

Politicians seem equally uncertain as to just how contributions affect what they do. It is a decidedly touchy subject for them. Senator Hugh Scott, then Senate Minority Leader, put the issue this way:

> I think every person in the Senate . . . realizes that every time a contribution is made, some sort of obligation is implied at least by the general public, some sort of obligation is very often felt by the recipient, some sort of obligation may be in the mind of the donor. The obligation may be slight, . . . some minor favor. On the other hand, the donor may expect benefits which he has no right to expect."[10]

The ethical ambiguity involved in fund raising is one reason why so many members of Congress find it, in the late Senator Humphrey's frequently quoted words, "a disgusting, degrading, demeaning experience."[11] People accustomed to deference do not enjoy pleading for money, and the sense that the money never comes without some kind of strings only makes the process more unpleasant. This does not prevent some members from making what one reporter called "shameless campaign solici-

---

[7] Ibid.

[8] See Candice J. Nelson, "Counting the Cash: PAC Contributions to Members of the House of Representatives" (paper delivered at the 1982 Annual Meeting of the American Political Science Association); James B. Kau and Paul H. Rubin, "The Impact of Labor Unions on the Passage of Economic Legislation," (unpublished paper, 1979); Benjamin Ginsburg, *The Consequences of Consent: Elections, Citizen Control, and Popular Acquiescence* (Reading, Mass.: Addison-Wesley, 1982), pp. 220–233.

[9] This is, to my mind, the most important outstanding question in research on campaign finance politics; we can expect some progress as each election adds to the sequence of contributions, votes, contributions, votes.

[10] U.S., Congress, Senate, Committee on Rules and Administration, *Public Financing of Federal Elections, Hearings,* before a Subcommittee on Privileges and Elections, 93rd Congress, 1st session, September 18–21, 1973, p. 34.

[11] David W. Adamany and George E. Agree, *Political Money: A Strategy for Campaign Financing in America* (Baltimore: The Johns Hopkins University Press, 1975). p. 130.

tations," involving "a lot of pandering, hyperbole, and even outright misrepresentation."[12] And few of the rest are willing to forego PAC contributions if the price is an appreciably greater chance of defeat at the polls. But it does leave many members uneasy and unhappy about the campaign finance system and breeds proposals for reform after every election.

The delicacy of the issue of contributors' influence is evident throughout congressional discussions of campaign finance legislation. Members who contend that PAC and other campaign gifts are corrupting necessarily imply that at least some of their colleagues have been corrupted. Their opponents challenge them to provide specifics; certainly their *own* contributors want only to keep fine public servants in office. Since members do not lightly attack one another's integrity (at least in public), the specifics are usually not forthcoming, and the case is left open.

Nonetheless, political contributions are generally believed to be productive investments. Although whether or not politicians or policies can be bought is a matter of vigorous argument, it is widely conceded by lobbyists and politicians alike that contributions buy, at minimum, access to members of Congress. The lobbylist for a group whose PAC sent a check to a member's last campaign will at least get a polite hearing from the member. And this, the most vehement critics of PACs claim, is sufficient to make relations between PACs and politicians illegitimate. "It's not a question of buying [votes]," argues Fred Wertheimer, president of Common Cause. "It's a question of relationships that get built, obligation and dependencies that get established. . . . It puts PACs at the head of the line, as opposed to the great bulk of a congressman's constituents."[13]

By this argument, it is not necessary for campaign contributions to buy favorable decisions directly for PACs to exercise illegitimate influence over policy. Access alone guarantees that members will be inveigled into serving interests contrary to those they are supposed to serve. Any favors beyond an attentive hearing merely make matters worse, but the argument against PACs does not depend on them. The ethical issues raised by PACs are not resolved if legislators owe only a hearing, not a favorable decision, to their contributors. Some interests are given an

---

[12] Albert Hunt, "An Inside Look at Politicians Hustling PACs," *Wall Street Journal,* 1 October 1982, p. 1.
[13] Congressional Quarterly, *Dollar Politics* (3rd ed.; Washington, D.C., 1982), p. 57.

unfair advantage, and this is sufficient to undermine the individual integrity of congressmen and collective integrity of Congress.

Regardless of whether PACs buy influence or merely access, the coincidence of campaign contributions and favorable votes is read by much of the press and public as evidence of corruption. For some critics of PACs, this is sufficient to justify legislation to reduce or eliminate their role in financing campaigns. The *appearance* of corruption undermines public confidence in the political system and its leaders, requiring corrective action no matter what the reality. Variations on this theme have always been popular with congressional advocates of campaign finance reform, for it allows them to argue their case without suggesting that their colleagues can be bought. It enjoys the imprimatur of the Supreme Court, which acknowledged in *Buckley v. Valeo*[14] the government's legitimate interest in "the prevention of corruption *and the appearance of corruption* spawned by the real *or imagined* coercive influence of large financial contributions on candidates positions and on their actions if elected to office" (emphasis added).

The strength of this argument is that its empirical premise—that PAC contributions are widely *perceived* to buy illegitimate influence—is demonstrably true. It is given added force by extensive evidence that the public's faith in political leaders and institutions of all kinds has declined rather drastically over the past twenty years;[15] surely proposals designed to reverse this trend deserve serious consideration. But it is by no means clear that anything done about PACs will make much difference. Dubious campaign finance practices are hardly the primary source of popular dissatisfaction with government; failure to deal adequately with basic social and economic problems has been far more damaging. Special interests will be observed lobbying vigorously—and often successfully— for favorable policies no matter how campaigns are financed. Scandals unconnected with campaign fund-raising (witness Abscam) occur frequently enough to maintain widespread public suspicion of politicians as a class.

Furthermore, the wisdom of basing campaign finance policy on public perceptions is open to serious question. Public understanding of the issue is minimal. Few people realize how much money is required to conduct competitive campaigns, for example.[16] Improving appearances requires material changes in campaign finance regulation that may pro-

---

[14] 424 U.S. 1, 96 S.Ct. 612,46 L.Ed. 2nd 659 (1976).

[15] Gary C. Jacobson, *The Politics of Congressional Elections* (Boston: Little, Brown, 1983), p. 2.

[16] Jacobson, *Money*, pp. 224–226.

duce a variety of undesirable consequences (of which more later) scarcely imagined by the general public. Even granting that appearances *would* improve, the value of a marginal increase in popular trust in government must be balanced against potentially formidable costs, and it is not at all certain that it would be worth incurring them.

All of the foregoing arguments, like most criticism of PACs, focus on the questionable relationship between the legislator and the people who contribute to his campaign. But if PACs are indeed a serious menace, this focus is much too narrow, and is in fact misdirected. The reason has to do with the electoral politics of Congress. It is abundantly clear from research on congressional elections that the electoral fates of incumbents depend largely on the kind of opposition they face.[17] The political assets and skills of the challenger and the money and other resources he assembles for the campaign have a powerful effect on the outcome; more specifically, the more the challenger spends, the better he does on election day. The money raised and spent by the incumbent has comparatively little consequence when the strength of the challenge is taken into account. In fact, the more incumbents spend, the *worse* they do in the election—not because the spending costs them votes, but because they raise and spend money in direct proportion to the vigor of the challenge they face, and a vigorous challenge does cost them votes.[18]

This means that an incumbent's most effective reelection strategy is to avoid strong opposition—something which members of Congress know well.[19] Denying resources to potential opponents is more important than acquiring resources oneself (although raising a lot of money is one way in which members try to discourage opponents). Members thus have a powerful incentive to avoid doing things that incite any group that has resources to mobilize against them. And this can certainly affect their choices quite apart from their own fund-raising needs.

Such considerations clearly broaden the range of influence that might be exercised by PACs. They can succeed not only by supporting friends (or making friends through their donations) but also by implicit or explicit threats to support the opponents of members who displease them sufficiently. They may not expect members to rally to their side simply to avoid opposition, but merely to abjure opposing their interests too vigorously or prominently. Again, the effectiveness of the group does not

---

[17] See Jacobson, *Politics,* pp. 37–48 and 86–119; Thomas E. Mann and Raymond E. Wolfinger, "Candidates and Parties in Congressional Elections," *American Political Science Review* 74 (1980), 617–632.

[18] Jacobson, *Money,* pp. 136–157; 234–238.

[19] Richard F. Fenno, Jr., *Home Style: House Members in Their Districts* (Boston: Little, Brown, 1978), p. 13.

depend on its preferences, be they narrowly economic or broadly ideological. It depends only on its potential for generating electoral headaches for incumbent members. No "access" is even required; no question of "appearances" need even arise.

Environmental Action, a conservation lobby, provided an example of how this can work. At one time Environmental Action compiled and publicized a list of the "Dirty Dozen," twelve congressmen who had (by its standards) exceptionally bad records on environmental issues and who appeared to be vulnerable. Opponents of members who made the list received contributions from environmentalists and environmental groups all over the country. Over five elections, twenty-four of the fifty-two who made the Dirty Dozen list were defeated. A consultant who worked on the campaigns said that the tactic "was very effective at making congressmen think twice about certain votes. There were numerous examples of members or their staffs calling and saying 'Is the congressman close to being on the list?' or 'Is this vote going to be used to determine the list?' "[20]

Influence of this kind need have nothing to do with campaign contributions, of course. Money is by no means the only important electoral resource; any group with a large and mobilizable membership is in a position to have its interests taken into account. Single-issue groups like environmentalists, Right-to-Lifers, and opponents of gun control can be influential without contributing a dime directly to any candidate.

No matter what form PAC influence is understood to take, criticism of PACs rests on the assumption that some values or interests that ought to be served are slighted because of the way campaigns are financed. These interests are never clearly specified, and for good reason: there are too many potentially contradictory options. Presumably, members ought to be attentive to (1) the preferences of a majority of their constituents or of a majority of those who voted for them, (2) the objective interests of their constituents or of a majority of them or of a majority of those who voted for them, (3) objective national interests, or (4) their own personal values.

With the possible exception of the final item, all of these things are often exceedingly difficult to ascertain. This is one reason why experienced politicians rarely find it difficult to argue that virtually any position they take is in the "public interest." Leaving such considerations aside, members knowing what they *should* do by whatever standard they follow who are tempted to vote otherwise for the sake of campaign contributions

[20] "The Trail of the 'Dirty Dozen,' " *Congressional Quarterly Weekly Report* 39 (21 March 1981), 510.

face difficult choice with serious ethical implications. But it is no different from a host of other choices they have to make in pursuit of reelection.

If members extend extra courtesies (or more concrete favors) to representatives of PACs, it is because they believe that PAC contributions are necessary for winning elections and staying in office. But no member believes that the money received from PACs in general, let alone from any individual PAC, is the only thing that matters. Many other things affect electoral fates, and taking account of them inevitably involves choosing between doing what will help win an election and doing what would otherwise be preferred. PACs represent only one example of a far more general problem for legislators, a problem that is inherent in electoral politics and that would remain even if PACs did not exist.

Most members of Congress—and, presumably, of most legislatures—want to stay in office. Indeed, the electoral incentive is so pervasive that David Mayhew could construct an insightful and persuasive account of congressional behavior and organization on the simple assumption that members are "single-minded seekers of reelection."[21] But winning and holding office is not (for all but a few, anyway) an end in itself. It is only valuable as a means to other ends: making what is, by their lights, good public policy and winning influence and respect in Washington.[22] Still, holding office is essential to these ends, and it comes first.

The problem is that what serves reelection does not always serve other important ends; frequently, the contrary is true. Members therefore continually confront choices between doing what helps them stay in office and doing what they hold the office in order to be able to do. There is nothing surprising about this. Weighing choices between conflicting goals, making trade-offs, is an integral part of legislative life. Indeed, it is an integral part of democratic politics. Everyone in political life—voters, activists, candidates, legislators—must decide when to give up something valued in order to achieve something else valued. The problems raised by electoral politics are not unique. Neither are those raised by the need for campaign contributions.

Consider the policy decisions made by members of Congress. Members may indeed feel compelled to weigh the effects of their policy choices on campaign finances—both theirs and their potential opponents'—and thereby face challenges to their integrity. But this is surely not the only way in which electoral politics poses difficult ethical questions. For

[21] David R. Mayhew, *Congress: The Electoral Connection* (New Haven: Yale University Press, 1974), p. 16.
[22] Richard F. Fenno, Jr., *Congressmen in Committees* (Boston: Little, Brown, 1973), p. 1.

example, do I, as a member of Congress, support a policy that I know to be foolish, wasteful, ineffective, or even immoral because I would have trouble with my district if I did not?

Pork-barrel politics raises such questions all the time. Do I vote for a package of projects I know to be wasteful and unnecessary in order to get that dam for my district (which is itself wasteful and unnecessary, though very popular locally)? Do I push a project widely condemned as massively cost-ineffective because my constituents would benefit? (Does Senator Baker push the Clinch River Breeder Reactor?) Similarly, do I support policies that would help local industries at the expense of consumers everywhere? (Does Senator Proxmire, that scourge of government-fostered rip-offs, support beer distributorship monopolies?) Do I set aside ideological principles when the local economy is at stake? (Does Senator Cranston, a dovish liberal Democrat, push weapon systems that will be built in California?) Or, perhaps more profoundly, do I cater to local prejudices I find thoroughly distasteful as the price of staying in office? (Did former Senator William Fulbright ever vote in favor of a civil rights law?)

The ethical answer to such questions is by no means self-evident. A member who sticks to principles against political logic courts defeat by someone less punctilious who follows different principles. A member can only pursue his vision of the public good if he remains in office; refusal to slight some values in order to survive to pursue others may make it less likely that any of them will be served. It would be hard to convince a Fulbright that bowing to local racial mores (assuming he did not share them) was morally questionable when the alternative was losing his seat to someone who *would* conform to local prejudices without serving the national interest (as Fulbright understood it) in other ways. Part of political wisdom is knowing when to settle for less than the whole loaf.

The difficulty lies, of course, in recognizing the line between political wisdom and self-serving rationalization. At what point does electoral necessity demand too much? The question has no objective answer; each member is forced to decide for himself, and it is not surprising to discover wide variation in the extent to which members are willing to adapt principle to necessity. But it is clear that the electoral process will, over time, tend to weed out members who are overly scrupulous.

The issues raised by pork-barrel and similar policy choices are easy to grasp. Electoral necessity can also have more subtle, and ultimately more disturbing, effects on policy making. Mayhew argues that members seek (and get) electoral credit for taking the proper positions, making agreeable speeches, casting correct votes, without these actions having any necessary connection to real policy decisions. They are rewarded, electorally, for adopting the proper *symbolic* stance regardless of its concrete results:

> We can all point point to a good many instances in which congressmen seem to have gotten into trouble by being on the *wrong* side in a roll call vote, but who can think of one where a member got into trouble by being on the *losing* side?[23]

Offering as an example a vote on a bill to stop busing, Mayhew notes that "congressmen had every reason to worry about whether they were voting on the right side but no reason to worry about what passed or was implemented."[24] The temptation, then, is to traffic in symbolism instead of trying to make effective policy. Giving in to it may well have more profoundly negative consequences for congressional peformance than anything done for the sake of campaign funds.

Mayhew, Fenno, and others have also pointed out how electoral pursuits can absorb so much of a member's time, staff, and other resources that little is left over for serious legislative work. The electoral incentives are thoroughly one-sided. The most effective way to retain electoral support is to conduct a permanent campaign. This requires spending a great deal of time in the district, meeting constituents, cultivating ties of friendship and trust, appearing accessible and attentive. It also means concentrating on casework, soliciting and responding to constituents' requests for personal assistance.

Hard legislative work, on the other hand, is rarely noticed or valued back in the district. Other members may recognize it as essential to Congress's institutional performance and reward it accordingly with respect and deference. But that does not help on election day. Indeed, the 1980 House elections, for example, suggested that the more important a member becomes in Washington, the more vulnerable he becomes at home. Eight Democrats with nine or more terms behind them, including the majority Whip and the chairmen of the Ways and Means and the Public Works and Transportation committees, lost. The dilemma this raises for members who want to win reelection but who recognize that holding office is not an end in itself is obvious. It is conceivable that the more one contributes to governing, the more one is likely to be defeated. The dilemma is built into the structure of contemporary electoral politics; a better developed sense of duty will do nothing to resolve it.

The pursuit of reelection raises ethical questions in another way. Members of Congress have given themselves an astonishing array of

[23] Mayhew, p. 117.
[24] Ibid., p. 115.

official services and resources that can be used to cultivate the support of constituents. Official resources have grown spectacularly over the past two decades; salary, staff, travel, office, and communications allowances estimated to be worth more than $1 million over a two-year term are now allotted to every member.[25] Of course members argue that they need all of these perquisites to do a proper job of representing their constituents; but no one denies their value in pursuing reelection. They clearly give incumbent members an enormous head start in their campaigns. Questions of fairness have arisen whenever Congress has increased them. Members naturally argue that they need more resources simply to meet the growing demand by constituents for services and assistance. But Fiorina makes a plausible case that much of the demand is stimulated by members themselves in order to take credit for responding to it. His explanation for the striking electoral success of incumbent members of the House in recent years is their shift in focus of attention from making policy to delivering district services. Larger staff, office, and communications allowances are an integral part of this development.[26]

The advantages of incumbency must especially be kept in mind when considering the politics of campaign finance regulation. The marginal returns on campaign spending are much less for incumbents than for challengers in large part because incumbents have already used their official resources to saturate the electorate with information about their accomplishments and virtues *before* the election campaign. Campaign money is much more important to challengers than to incumbents. But incumbents make the laws regulating campaign finance. It is no coincidence that campaign finance "reforms," whatever else they have accomplished, have done nothing to make it easier for challengers to raise money. Because of the way money works in congressional elections, any restriction on the flow of funds benefits incumbents. Many proposals that have been made for additional changes—including all of those that would, on one ground or another, limit the amount candidates can raise or spend—would clearly make incumbents even safer than they already are.[27]

Indeed, a case can be made to demonstrate that growth of PACs is a good thing because any increase in campaign money tends to help challengers and therefore to generate more competitive elections in which voters have a choice between candidates they actually know something

---

[25] Morris P. Fiorina, *Congress: Keystone of the Washington Establishment* (New Haven: Yale University Press, 1977), p. 61.
[26] Ibid.
[27] See Jacobson, *Money,* pp. 209–220.

about. Although PACs give most of their money to incumbents, the marginal electoral benefit incumbents derive from campaign expenditures is, according to statistical analyses, very small. The additional money available to challengers does make a substantial difference, however. Proposals to put a ceiling on how much a candidate could accept from PACs (Representative Obey has recently suggested a limit of $90,000) are ostensibly aimed at decreasing interest-group influence in campaigns. But such limits are also likely to make it more difficult for challengers to mount campaigns against incumbents. This has not been lost on Republicans, who have opposed ceilings on the belief that they would make it more difficult for Republicans to achieve their dream of taking over the House.[28]

Congressional regulation of campaign finance naturally raises the issue of conflict of interest. Ralph Winter, of Yale Law School, testifying before the Senate Subcommittee on Communications in 1971, argued that "systematic regulation of political campaigns by Congress must inevitably lead to those in power regulating in favor of themselves."[29] It is important to keep in mind that he has yet to be proven wrong.

I have not exhausted all the possibilities here, but enough has been said to make the point: political action committees do force members of Congress to make choices between doing what helps win election and doing what they otherwise think they ought to do. But there is nothing unique about PACs in this regard. Members must make decisions of this sort all the time. Many of these decisions have much more profound consequences for the quality of government. A member is unusual and fortunate indeed if electoral necessity always coincides with doing what he thinks is right. When it does not, the question always arises: what am I willing to compromise in order to remain in office to do the good I can do there?

PACs are by no means a unique threat to the integrity of members of Congress. Furthermore, if PAC money and the many other electoral considerations I have mentioned do pose real problems for the political system, they are not the kinds of problems that will be cured by greater ethical sensitivity on the part of politicians. Such an assertion of course goes against the venerable reform tradition in American politics that works from the implicit assumption that the way to improve politics is to improve politicians.

First of all, arguments about the corrupting influence of contributions

---

[28] Ibid., pp. 238–240.
[29] Ibid., p. 175.

are, in an important sense, moot. Members of Congress need not vote to please financial backers (or to avoid stimulating opposition) in order for organized interests to exercise undue influence over public policy. An analogy drawn from an old controversy among evolutionary biologists is instructive. Lamarck believed that species change through heritable individual adaptions to environmental pressures. But Darwin showed that natural selection could produce the same result: the environment selectively enhances or diminishes the survival and reproductive chances of individuals according to their fixed characteristics, which are thus transmitted differentially to subsequent generations.

By this line of reasoning, campaign contributors might influence policy just as effectively by favoring candidates who already agree with them; no direct venality—a member changing his position for the sake of campaign money—is required. The financial environment affects the congressional species through differential selection of candidates. Of course, this analysis applies to anyone who controls campaign resources, not merely to PACs. Since about three-quarters of the money spent in campaigns does come from sources other than PACs, there is no particular reason to single them out. But the point is that if one is worried about the democratic ideal of political equality, PACs—or anyone else with disproportionate political resources—may undermine it without corrupting anyone.

A kind of natural selection also operates in all the other situations in which a legislator must chose between doing what helps win reelection and doing what he considers right. Members who feel compelled to reject the pork barrel, concentrate on serious legislative work rather than on cultivating constituents, or pursue national rather than local interests are more likely to be defeated. Those more easily guided by electoral necessity are more likely to remain in office. The problem lies in a system that tends to reward behavior that detracts from effective national policy making and punish its opposite.

Second, the greatest systemic problem created by PACs is not that they bring outside pressures to bear on what should be independent, publically interested decisions, but that they bring the wrong pressures to bear on them. It is a mistake to think that elected politicians should be independent spirits, beholden only to the people who elected them—if, indeed, to anyone. The most serious barrier to effective national government in the United States is not unresponsive or subservient legislators but the incapacity of leaders to lead. Presidents and party leaders in Congress have, in recent years, found it increasingly difficult to assemble legislative coalitions behind any policy that might deal coherently with pressing national problems.

There are a number of reasons for this. Organizational changes have fragmented congressional authority down to the subcommittee level; much more of the work of Congress is now done in public; the public itself is badly divided on issues and self-contradictory in its preferences; the list could go on.[30] For our purposes, the point is that PACs—and many other organized and active interest groups—contribute to political fragmentation and therefore immobilism and stalemate. They reinforce divisive impulses and add to the cacaphony of voices making competing demands on government. By offering a remarkable variety of ways to assemble campaign resources, they make it easier for members of Congress to resist the persuasive efforts of presidents and other party leaders. By keeping a close watch on what members are doing, they make it harder for them to resolve conflicts through compromise and horse-trading—that is, to do *politics*.

The problem is not that members are open to outside influences, but that they are subject to influences that weaken rather than strengthen governing coalitions. This is true regardless of whether one thinks of PACs and other politically active organizations as corrupt purchasers of politicians or as healthy manifestations of a vigorous pluralism. The problem is particularly acute at present because the economy has been performing so poorly. Political options increasingly involve distributing costs rather than benefits. Any of the proposed solutions to basic economic (and, for that matter, social) problems require that costs be imposed on some groups; think of the current options for the Social Security system. If we have not actually become what Lester Thurow calls a "zero-sum society," in which a gain by any group necessitates an equal loss by some other group,[31] it is certainly true that *redistribution* of limited resources is a more pressing issue than it used to be. The electoral politics of Congress renders it painfully difficult to impose costs on any politically significant group. Most are too alert and too well organized, the policy process is too transparent, and members of Congress are too sensitive to too many demands. PACs are part of the problem, but it would exist even if they did not.

Electoral politics produces a Congress that combines great individual *responsiveness* with equally great collective *irresponsibility*. Emphasis on constituency services becomes more attractive as policy matters become more divisive. The safest way to cope with a host of conflicting policy demands is to be acutely sensitive to what electorally important groups

---

[30] Jacobson, *Politics*, pp. 157–177.

[31] Lester Thurow, *The Zero-Sum Society: Distribution and the Possibility for Economic Change* (Harmondsworth, England: Penguin Books, 1981).

want in taking positions on issues but to avoid responsibility for the costs they would impose. The pervasive temptation to engage in symbolic position taking rather than working to find real solutions to national problems is harder to resist when every solution is likely to anger one politically important group or another. It does not help that members are rewarded individually (at election time) for taking pleasing positions but are not punished for failing to turn them into national policy or, when they do become policy, for seeing that they work.

The only instrument we have developed for imposing collective responsibility on legislators is the political party. Fiorina has outlined the connections succinctly:

> A strong political party can generate collective responsibility by creating incentives for leaders, followers, and popular supporters to think and act in collective terms. First, by providing party leaders with the capability (e.g., control of institutional patronage, nominations, etc.) to discipline party members, genuine leadership becomes possible. Legislative output is less likely to be a least common denominator—a residue of myriad conflicting proposals—and more likely to consist of a program actually intended to solve a problem or move the nation in a particular direction. Second, the subordination of individual officeholders to the party lessens their ability to separate themselves from party actions. Like it or not their performance becomes identified with the performance of the collectivity to which they belong. Third, with individual candidate variation greatly reduced, voters have less incentive to support individuals and more to support or oppose the party as a whole. And fourth, the circle closes as party line voting in the electorate provides party leaders with the incentive to propose policies which will earn the support of a national majority, and party backbenchers with the personal incentive to cooperate with leaders in the attempt to compile a good record for the party as a whole.[32]

To be sure, American parties have never been particularly well disciplined, and pristine party government has never been characteristic of our politics. But insofar as collective responsibility has been enforced, parties have been the means. Even if, at present, members of Congress can safely ignore the collective consequences of their individual actions, party leaders, presidents in particular, cannot. They have to concern themselves with the practical as well as the symbolic consequences of what the government does, if only because their own interests are clearly at stake. Theirs is the chore of assembling policy coalitions out of disparate congressional fragments. Whatever makes this more difficult weakens their capacity to lead and the ability of the government to govern. It also diminishes the capacity of voters to reward or punish

[32] Morris P. Fiorina, "The Decline of Collective Responsibility in American Politics," *Daedalus* 109 (Summer 1980), 26–27.

members for collective policy outcomes, thereby undermining an important component of democratic control.

If this is true, we are better off with legislators who are less, rather than more, independent, who are not protected from outside influence but rather are subject to the influence of party leaders much more than they are. In this light, the recent blossoming of national Republican party strength is encouraging. National-level Republican campaign committees have developed effective direct-mail fund-raising operations that now provide them with tens of millions of dollars to spend for congressional candidates. They can offer a wide array of electoral services, including polling, advertising production, and training in how to organize an effective campaign. They also coordinate campaign donations from a substantial group of cooperative PACs. For the first time ever, national party organizations have the capacity to intervene extensively in local congressional campaigns.[33]

What this can mean is suggested by the Reagan administration's fights during the Ninety-seventh Congress to cut the budget and alter the tax laws. An official of the Republican National Committee explained how he persuaded a pair of reluctant Republicans to vote for the budget cuts:

> They said, "This'll kill us." I said, "Look—what if I can guarantee we'll max out on you? [*Maxing out* means giving as much help as the party legally can: $30,000 in cash, $36,880 in services.] We'll help you do a quick and dirty newsletter, make a commercial, organize a town meeting."

The members went along with the administration. If they had not? "I would have nailed them to the wall."[34]

The same tactics were used on the tax-increase bill. The administration faced stiff opposition to any election-year tax increase from its own partisans in Congress. They won the fight in part through aggressive use of their access to campaign resources. The fund raiser for one freshman Republican, calling the Republican National Committee to find out when his first campaign check would be arriving, was asked, "How is he on the tax bill?"[35] Others reported similar pressures. Democratic leaders give the Republican campaign operation a great deal of credit for Republican unity in the Ninety-seventh Congress. "The Republicans have been

[33] See Gary C. Jacobson, "Congressional Campaign Finance and the Revival of the Republican Party," *The U.S. Congress: Proceedings of the Thomas P. O'Neill, Jr., Symposium,* ed. by Dennis Hale (Chestnut Hill, Mass.: Boston College, 1982). pp. 313–330.

[34] "How Reaganites Push Reluctant Republicans to Back Tax-Rise Bill," *Wall Street Journal,* 18 September 1982, p. 1.

[35] Ibid., p. 14.

marching in lockstep," claimed James Jones, head of the House Budget Committee, "and the key to that is finance."[36] Tony Coelho, chair of the Democrats' congressional campaign committee, agreed. "The conventional wisdom is that business political-action committees have taken over Congress. The reality is different. The Republicans have transcended PACs. They've become the PAC of PACs."[37]

Party demands may, of course, confront members with ethical dilemmas no different from those generated by PACs: to cooperate with the party for the sake of campaign assistance, or to follow constituency, conscience, or one's own sense of what is good public policy. Perhaps the individual predicament is softened somewhat by the greater legitimacy of parties; after all, parties claim to represent the interests of the entire nation, and they manifestly do represent coalitions much broader than any interest group serves. Bowing to party demands may thus seem less objectionable than other concessions to electoral necessity. Either way, I see no reason to be concerned about greater pressure from parties. Political processes exist to allow social cooperation despite strong disagreements over values. If no one has to give in or compromise or trade off one good against another, nothing gets done and the result is stalemate, a failure of politics and thus of democracy. Politics requires followers as well as leaders, and who should lead if not the party leaders? We have suffered much more, in recent years, from weak party leadership than from an excess of party discipline.[38]

If stronger parties are desirable, what can be done about the present system of electoral politics to strengthen them? Fundamentally, not much, at least not without major structural changes in political institutions and equally dramatic changes in political values. The roots of political individualism and entrepreneurial electoral politics go very deep.[39] But marginal improvements are certainly conceivable. The problem is in coming up with "improvements" that do not actually make things worse.

For example, if PACs act as a counterforce to parties, why not strengthen parties by weakening PACs? This is a favorite argument of people who wish to limit the total amount candidates can receive from all PACs. But this will not necessarily solve the problem and is likely to

[36] Ibid.
[37] Ibid.
[38] See William J. Crotty and Gary C. Jacobson, *American Parties in Decline* (Boston: Little, Brown, 1980), pp. 202–240.
[39] See Jacobson, *Politics, passim,* for the evidence.

create new ones. It will not solve the problem because even if candidates were forbidden to accept any money at all from organized groups, PACs would not necessarily fold their tents and quietly slip away. Having already incurred the costs of organization, many would doubtlessly continue their work through independent expenditures; there is no way to stop them from doing this without suspending the First Amendment. If our recent experience with independent campaigning is any guide, this would scarcely improve the tone of political life. More to the point, it would not relieve individual members of the need to worry about doing things that mobilize groups to work for or against them. It would also take more of the campaign out of the hands of candidates, a development that neither they nor, I think, most objective observers would welcome.

Limiting PAC contributions may also weaken political competition by strengthening incumbents. No candidate can be competitive without reaching voters, and in most circumstances there is no way to do this without spending a lot of money. Congressional incumbents' campaigns are in fact heavily subsidized, and there is no way to eliminate this subsidy without impairing their ability to represent constituents. Challengers normally need a great deal of money to overcome the advantages automatically available to incumbents; any restriction on fund raising works to their disadvantage. It is often argued that because PACs contribute much more to incumbents than to challengers, limits on PACs would favor challengers. But the marginal returns on campaign spending are much greater for challengers than for incumbents; what matters to challengers is the absolute, not the relative amount of money they can put into the campaign. Furthermore, incumbents raise money more readily from all sources, not just PACs; limiting PACs could by no means be guaranteed to reduce their fund-raising advantage. And finally, limits on contributions in any guise add to the advantage enjoyed by wealthy candidates, since the Supreme Court has decided that no restrictions may be placed on how much a candidate may contribute to his own campaign.

The most commonly proposed general solution to campaign finance problems is public financing of congressional campaigns. This would scarcely strengthen parties, of course, unless party leaders controlled the funds and were allowed discretion in deciding how they were to be distributed (an approach not likely to find much support in Congress). But public money could obviate the need for PACs and reduce the advantage conferred by personal wealth. And it would certainly take some fund-raising pressure off members of Congress. However, the real effect of public funding would depend on the scheme chosen. One which placed a ceiling on expenditures—unless that ceiling were much higher than either Congress or the public is likely to tolerate—would only add to the incumbents' advantage.[40] If it did not apply to primary elections, private money would still be necessary. If it did, it might inspire and subsidize frivolous candidacies (a half-million of the taxpayers' dollars went to Lyndon LaRouche for his 1980 campaign for the Democratic presidential nomination).

Most public subsidy schemes include a provision for matching small donations from private individuals. In the mythology of campaign finance reform, the individual who gives a small amount of money to the candidate of choice is the hero. But the most effective way to raise money from individuals is through direct mail solicitation, and appeals are most successful when they can arouse emotions of fear, anger, and hatred. Candidates and groups espousing extreme views do this best and so would benefit from a system that places a premium on small individual donations. A set of electoral incentives that enhances the influence of a Richard Viguerie or the Moral Majority is, to my mind, hardly an improvement over one that offers advantages to beer distributors or used-car dealers.

I do not mean to argue that nothing can be done to alter the campaign finance system to reduce divisive influences on members of Congress. For example, the FECA could be amended to make it easier for parties to raise money (for example, by raising or eliminating entirely limits on what individuals and groups can give to national party organizations) and to allow them to put more of it into campaigns. This will not be easy to do as long as Republican party committees continue to raise seven times as much money as their Democratic counterparts and Democrats control the House. Still, the cause is not hopeless. The chairman of the Democrats' congressional campaign committee said recently that he favored lifting the ceilings on party aid to candidates, albeit in slow increments to give Democrats a chance to catch up with Republican fund raising.[41]

Another practical step would be to raise the limits on the amounts individuals can contribute to campaigns. At present, individuals can give a maximum of $1,000 per candidate per campaign, while the same limit for PACs is $5,000. There is little justification for this disparity; by all accounts individuals tend to expect less in the way of a direct return on their investment than do PACs. Because the limit has not been changed since 1974, in real dollars it is less than half of what it was originally. The

---

[40] See Gary C. Jacobson, "Public Funds for Congressional Campaigns: Who Would Benefit?" *Political Finance,* ed. by Herbert E. Alexander (Beverly Hills, Calif.: Sage Publications, 1979), pp. 99–127.

[41] Brooks Jackson, "The Problem With PACs," *Wall Street Journal,* 17 November 1982, p. 30.

costs of campaigning have risen with inflation (outstripping it, really); therefore candidates have had to solicit a larger number of contributions just to stay even. This no doubt accounts for some of the undignified scrambling after PAC dollars observed in the most recent campaign.[42] Raising the limit would probably not have a dramatic impact on fund raising, since few contributors give the limit even now. Still, it might be a small improvement and would involve little risk of making things worse.

It is clearly possible to make at least marginal improvements in campaign finance regulation. Some changes might even make life a bit less hectic for members of Congress by reducing the number of conflicting demands electoral necessity imposes upon them. But the difficult choices forced on legislators by the contrary requirements of duty and expediency emerge from the basic structure of electoral politics in the United States; they will remain no matter what is done about financing campaigns.

REFERENCES

Alexander, Herbert E., ed. *Political Finance*. Beverly Hills, California: Sage Publications, 1979.

Adamany, David W., and Agree, George E. *Political Money: A Strategy for Campaign Financing in America*. Baltimore: The Johns Hopkins University Press, 1975.

Cantor, Joseph E. *Political Action Committees: Their Evolution and Growth and Their Implications for the Political System*. Washington, D.C.: Congressional Research Service, 6 November 1981.

Congressional Quarterly, *Dollar Politics*. 3rd ed. Washington, D.C., 1982.

Crotty, William J., and Jacobson, Gary C. *American Parties in Decline*. Boston: Little, Brown, 1980.

Farney, Dennis. "A Liberal Congressman Turns Conservative: Did PAC Gifts Do It?" *Wall Street Journal*, 29 July 1982, p. 1.

Fenno, Richard F., Jr. *Congressmen in Committees*. Boston: Little, Brown, 1973.

_____. *Home Style: House Members in Their Districts*. Boston: Little, Brown, 1978.

Fiorina, Morris P. *Congress: Keystone of the Washington Establishment*. New Haven: Yale University Press, 1977.

_____. "The Decline of Collective Responsibility in American Politics," *Daedelus* 109 (Summer 1980), 1–31.

Ginsburg, Benjamin. *The Consequences of Consent: Elections, Citizen Control, and Popular Acquiescence*. Reading, Mass.: Addison-Wesley, 1982.

Hale, Dennis, ed. *The United States Congress: Proceedings of the Thomas P. O'Neill, Jr., Symposium*. Chestnut Hill, Mass.: Boston College, 1982.

"How Reaganites Push Reluctant Republicans to Back Tax-Rise Bill," *Wall Street Journal*, 18 September 1982, p. 1.

Hunt, Albert. "An Inside Look at Politicians Hustling PACs," *Wall Street Journal*, 1 October 1982, p. 1.

---

[42] Hunt, p. 1; "Running with the PACs," *Time*, 25 October 1982, pp. 18–26.

Jackson, Brooks. "Democrats Holding Lead in Donations from Interest Groups," *Wall Street Journal,* 4 October 1982, p. 16.

———. "The Problem With PACs," *Wall Street Journal,* 17 November 1982, p. 30.

Jacobson, Gary C. *Money in Congressional Elections.* New Haven: Yale University Press, 1980.

———. *The Politics of Congressional Elections.* Boston: Little, Brown, 1983.

Kau, James B., and Rubin, Paul H. "The Impact of Labor Unions on the Passage of Economic Legislation." Unpublished paper, 1979.

Malbin, Michael J., ed. *Parties, Interest Groups, and Campaign Finance Laws.* Washington, D.C.: American Enterprise Institute for Public Policy Research, 1980.

Mann, Thomas E., and Wolfinger, Raymond E. "Candidates and Parties in Congressional Elections," *American Political Science Review,* 74 (1980), :617–632.

Mayhew, David R. *Congress: The Electoral Connection.* New Haven: Yale University Press, 1974.

Nelson, Candice J. "Counting the Cash: PAC Contributions to Members of the House of Representatives." Paper delivered at the 1982 annual meeting of the American Political Science Association.

"Running With the PACs," *Time,* 25 October 1982, pp. 18–26.

Thurow, Lester. *The Zero-Sum Society: Distribution and the Possibility for Economic Change.* Harmondsworth, England: Penguin Books, 1981.

"The Trail of the Dirty Dozen," *Congressional Quarterly Weekly Report* 39 (21 March, 1981), 509–512.

United States, Congress. Senate. Committee on Rules and Administration. *Public Financing of Federal Elections. Hearings* before a Subcommittee on Privileges and Elections, 93rd Cong., 1st sess., September 18–21, 1973.

4

Ethics in Political Campaigns

THOMAS KINGSLEY HOUSTON

The use of false and misleading political advertisements, or advertisements which unfairly attack the integrity or character of candidates,
reached new heights during the 1982 elections. California, an innovative
state where new campaign techniques often originate, produced campaigns for federal and state office that deteriorated to an all-time low.
Candidates were falsely accused of tax evasion, criminal conspiracy,
anti-Semitism, and one family man of not being married to his wife. But
California was not alone. A television ad was broadcast in Tennessee
showing a Fidel Castro look-alike gleefully lighting up his cigar with a
$100 bill while thanking "Senor Sasser." The false implication was that
incumbent Senator Jim Sasser, who had done nothing of the sort, had
voted for foreign aid for Cuba. In Maine, a mailing was sent to veterans
throughout the state charging that the incumbent United States Senator
had voted no on ninety-two veteran benefits bills. In truth, most of the
bills had been defeated before the Senator assumed office. Nevada voters
were subjected to a spate of fake public opinion polls actually designed to
convey false charges and innuendo against candidates rather than to
register voter sympathy. And in Alabama a sophisticated whispering

The author served as chairman of the California Fair Political Practices Commission
(FPPC) from 1979 to 1983. The FPPC, which was established by voter initiative in 1974,
regulates contributions and expenditures in political campaigns, the activities of registered
lobbyists, and conflicts of interests among state and local government officials. During 1982,
the FPPC held extensive public hearings on the problem of misleading, last-minute and
negative campaign advertising and developed the model Fair Campaign Practices
Code/Agreement which is discussed in this chapter.

THOMAS KINGSLEY HOUSTON • Deputy Mayor, Los Angeles, California 90012.

campaign was utilized to imply that a candidate for governor was homosexual.

These examples, as well as others from other states, have resulted in mounting concern on the part of the national press, state ethics commissions, and political observers. There is a strong feeling that something must be done, and done now, to eliminate unethical campaign practices and to correct the problems caused by such conduct.

Unfortunately, there has been little written of a scholarly nature on the purposes served by political campaigns in a representative democracy.[1] There is a related dearth of information concerning what type of conduct should be permitted or tolerated during political campaigns. My own thinking as to what constitutes unethical conduct on the part of candidates is based on personal observations made and opinions formed while I served as chairman of California's Fair Political Practices Commission and as a member of the staffs of various political campaigns. Over the years I have also conducted numerous interviews with candidates, campaign managers, political correspondents, and professional pollsters.

I take as a given that conduct by candidates which results in their fraudulently gaining elective office or being elected under false pretenses is unethical. As a society, we provide criminal penalties for those who defraud the election process by bribing voters, stuffing ballot boxes, or preventing certain groups from casting ballots. The damage inflicted upon the electoral process as well as the public's confidence in that process is just as bad, however, when a candidate gains elective office by deceiving the public about his opponent's character or qualifications for office. In either case, a mockery is made of the public's right to exercise a meaningful franchise.

It is obviously difficult to draw precise lines between statements or political ads which are false or misleading and those which simply reflect bad taste or a candidate's aggressive campaigning style. Many recent political ads, however, have so clearly fallen into the deceptive category that there is no question that an unethical label can be placed on their perpetrators. It is this type of conduct and not the preparation or distribution of ads which teeter on the deceptive-nondeceptive line that is the primary focus of this paper. At the same time, however, it appears

[1] For brief discussions of the various purposes served by political campaigns, consult V. O. Key, *Politics, Party and Pressure Groups*, (5th Ed.; New York: Crowell Co., 1964), pp. 482–485; Alexander Heard, *The Cost of Democracy* (Chapel Hill: University of North Carolina Press, 1960) pp. 426–427; and Dan Nimmo, *The Political Persuaders* (Englewood Cliffs, N.J.: Prentice Hall, 1970) pp. 6–8. For a fuller discussion see Stanley Kelley, Jr., *Political Campaigning: Problems in Creating an Informed Electorate* (Washington, D.C.: Brookings Institution, 1960) pp. 8–84.

clearly that candidates who adopt campaign styles or strategies that cause them to hover near the unethical line are more likely to cross over the line as their campaigns become heated. I have a positive view, therefore, of procedures and standards which will cause candidates to operate their campaigns far away from any ethical line.

Distributing falsehoods about oneself or one's opponent is but one form of deceit, albeit the most obvious. A subtler form of unethical conduct occurs when a candidate fails to perform certain affirmative tasks such as appearing at public events where his skills and qualifications can be displayed and judged, personally participating in debates and discussions of issues of importance to the office sought, and repudiating false statements made on his behalf by third parties. Although the exact extent of these duties may not be definable, it is clear that a candidate's failure to provide certain information or to take corrective action in appropriate instances can be as deceitful as the distribution of false information. I therefore tend to favor procedures and standards which encourage or require candidates to assume certain affirmative duties as well as the obligation not to distribute lies or falsehoods.

In the first two sections of the chapter I discuss the various problems posed by unethical campaign conduct and explore some of the underlying reasons for the increase in false and misleading political advertising. In the course of that discussion, I stress the lack of any practical restraints upon unethical campaign conduct given the current state of campaign technology and voter apathy. In the concluding two sections, I develop a conceptual framework for assigning certain ethical responsibilities to candidates and propose a voluntary Fair Campaign Practices Agreement as one way of reducing or eliminating unethical campaign conduct.

PROBLEMS POSED BY UNETHICAL CAMPAIGN ACTIVITIES

Many problems are engendered by false and misleading or the personal-attack type of political advertising. Some are blatantly obvious, others quite subtle. In either case such advertising unfairly destroys or taints the reputations of many candidates and public officials. The fear of being personally impugned along with the hardships inflicted upon candidates and their families, has cost the republic the services of many dedicated and experienced public servants.[2] To many, public office is

[2] There is rising evidence that many otherwise interested and qualified candidates are shying away from running for office because of the threat of being muddied by unfair campaign

simply not worth the risk of putting their reputation on the line. The result is that the pool of available qualified and competitive candidates is being artifically drained.

Of course, when numerous candidates hurl false charges at one another, or even when only a few candidates engage in such destructive conduct, their activities receive wide media coverage. The sorry spectacle thus presented to the voters can only further erode their confidence in the election process and the caliber of elected officials it produces. There is little doubt that public confidence in government institutions and elected officials is fast declining, and irresponsible campaign charges are clearly hastening this decline.

There is also mounting concern that voters who are constantly subjected to false and misleading campaign advertisements are simply voting with their feet—staying away from the polls—rather than attempting to sort out the various charges and countercharges. And those voters who do get to the polls may well feel that they are being asked to choose the lesser of two evils rather than the candidate of their choice. Such a situation is unlikely to inspire increased confidence or faith in either elections or elected officials.

False and misleading advertising also serves to skew election results by confusing the voters and distracting from the more substantive or important issues in a campaign. Most campaign professionals believe that negative and personal-attack advertising, particularly if it is done in the closing weeks of a campaign, can turn an election in favor of a less well known or less experienced candidate. Of course, the more sensational the charges the greater the impact of a last minute "hit piece." The upshot is that false and misleading advertising may be propelling less qualified candidates into public office.

Finally, and perhaps most importantly, it is likely that candidates who engage in unethical conduct on the campaign trail will be more likely to engage in or tolerate unethical conduct once elected to office.[3] Having cast aside ethics during the campaign, they may well find it easier to breach official standards or to look the other way when unethical conduct occurs on the part of their colleagues or staff. This is particularly true of the candidate who owes his election to unethical activities. In a sense, he

---

advertising. Testimony of Mervyn Field, President of the Field Institute, San Francisco, California, before the Fair Political Practices Commission, March 23, 1982.

[3] One of the underlying causes of the Watergate scandal ten years ago was the fact that many persons who had engaged in unethical campaign practices were subsequently appointed to high positions with the federal government. Having crossed over the official line during the campaign, they continued their questionable activities while members of the White House staff.

is like the novice shoplifter who, having successfully purloined his first trinket, is far more likely to shoplift again—and this time for something more valuable.

WHY UNETHICAL CAMPAIGN CONDUCT IS ON THE INCREASE

Although there are many reasons why the use of false and misleading campaign advertising is on the increase, the single most important one is that such advertising, when professionally prepared and appropriately timed, is highly effective. Such advertising can break a candidate "out of the pack" in a primary election, rapidly erode the lead of a forerunner, catapult an unknown candidate into the limelight, and severely undercut the public's respect for a tested incumbent. There are, of course, certain risks, including the possibility of a voter backlash against a candidate whose misstatements or distortions are effectively exposed. Unfortunately, the risk of a backlash can be minimized through the use of modern technology, particularly computerized mass mailings.

Several factors have combined to make ads which contain false and misleading statements or which attack an opponent's integrity, character, or private life particularly effective. First, as a whole, the voting public has come to be bored by the overabundance of political advertising, especially the run-of-the-mill variety. Political advertisements are now cluttering the mails and saturating the airwaves. Thus, the attention given to any one political advertisement has declined proportionately. More important, however, is the fact that political ads must compete with a rising crescendo of aggressive and slick commercial advertisements. Consequently, in order to be effective, political ads must "grab" an audience emotionally. Unfortunately this often translates into political advertisements which contain personal attacks or other irresponsible or sensational charges. The more effective political ads also take advantage of or play upon the voter's general disenchantment with officeholders and candidates. The "trick" is to personalize that general disenchantment by affixing it to one's opponent.[4] Running negative advertising against one's foe is the best way to accomplish this objective.

---

[4] Historically, this phenomenon is similar to what occurred during the 1952 and 1954 congressional elections. In those election campaigns many candidates sought to personalize the public's fear of communism by creating significant doubt about their opponent's loyalty. See Stanley Kelly, Jr., *Public Relations and Political Power* (Baltimore: John Hopkins University Press, 1956) pp. 107–143.

The continuing decline in party strength and party loyalty is another reason why ads which distort or attack a candidate's personal integrity or record are increasingly effective. A Democratic or Republican label on a candidate no longer symbolizes a clear or recognizable set of values, commitments, or support or opposition to major government programs. Rather, candidates must increasingly develop and advertise their own personal proposals and their own individual stands on issues. In a sense, today's candidates must write on a blank slate devoid of any clear ideological matrix supplied by their party. And although a candidate is freer to campaign on his own record, if he has one, and to enunciate positions different from those of his party, he is also more vulnerable to false statements about his stands on issues and to attacks against his character.

A final factor contributing to the greater use of false and misleading advertising is the growing dependence by candidates on professional campaign firms. Such firms have motivations and agendas that in many instances differ from those of the candidates who retain them. Today, almost all candidates for election to the United States Congress, major state legislatures, and visible local offices employ professional campaign firms to manage their campaigns: to develop overall strategy, select issues for the campaign (and often the candidate's stand on those issues), and create an appropriate image for the candidate. These campaign management firms, however, also possess a distinct and pecuniary interest in the outcome of elections quite separate from that of their candidates. Not only does their own win-and-loss record affect the number of future clients they will attract, but many firms—particularly those which represent challengers or lesser known candidates—operate on a contingency fee basis. Although they may receive only a small payment "up front," they can expect a large bonus if their candidate proves successful. And, since the nature of campaign firms is to operate behind the scenes and out of the limelight, it is solely the candidate's reputation and not theirs which is on the line during a campaign.

Because campaign firms have more to gain than to lose by engaging in false and misleading advertising, many tend to push candidates to the limit. In some instances, if the candidate is reluctant or hesitates, a campaign firm will simply take action on its own. The candidate will discover what ads have been distributed only after the fact. Such occurrences are more likely in larger campaigns in which, because of the amount of advertising being produced and the hectic pace of the campaign, candidates simply cannot personally edit or approve all copy. Of course, the impact upon an opponent's reputation or on the election process as a whole is the same regardless of whether the campaign firm or the candidate himself is personally responsible for distributing the false, misleading, or slanderous advertisement.

The only real deterrent to this type of political advertising has been the fear of a voter backlash. In order for a backlash to occur, however, the false statements must be discovered, their lack of truthfulness demonstrated, and responsibility for the advertisement pinned on the offending candidate. All three of these tasks have been made more difficult by the use of computerized mailings[5] and last-minute television and radio spots. Political mailings can now be carefully targeted to select audiences. Through the use of computers and carefully honed mailing lists, such mailers arrive in the privacy of the home and can convey a variety of different and, if desired, contradictory messages to respective voters.[6] Further, because their messages can be tailored to the recipient's specific interests, it is unlikely that one homeowner will discuss the content of the political mailings he receives with his neighbors. Thus, campaign advertisements sent to individual voters through the mails can effectively skirt public exposure. And where there is no exposure there is also no sunlight to serve as a disinfectant. Even more important, false statements in targeted mailings may go undetected by the sender's opponent for a substantial and critical period of time. This is particularly true when mailings are sent on the very eve of an election. Even if detected, such mailings cannot be effectively countered.

Last-minute television and radio spots can create the same problems. The candidate who is attacked may be unable to correct any misinformation either because he lacks funds to purchase time for rebuttal or because it is too late to do so. Appeals for media support to set the record straight may also fall on deaf ears, especially if the victim is campaigning for a less visible office. During the week before the election the press focuses attention exclusively on the larger or more significant contests. There simply is no media time to devote to smaller campaigns. At the same time,

[5] In California over 50% of campaign expenditures in an average legislative race are now made for the preparation and distribution of mass mailers. *Campaign Costs: How Much Have They Increased and Why?* FPPC, January, 1980.

[6] The following excerpt from the *Direct Mail and Mail Order Handbook*, Dartnell Services, 2nd ed. (1974), p. 469, emphasizes the "audience selectivity" of mass mailings: "Direct mail is the most selective of all mass media. . . . Where radio or TV coverage might be too broad, direct mail can be pinpointed to selected areas of the state, or town—of even a ward or precinct. And it can let you talk about specific issues to people you know in advance will be most interested in those issues. . . . The possibilities are as wide as your imagination for using direct mail's unique selectivity to appeal to the individual interest of individual voters."

the press is likely to be swamped with charges and counter-charges and reluctant to make snap judgments shortly before an election.

Frustrated candidates who not only detect falsehoods but are actually able to generate press interest find it increasingly difficult to convince voters either that a challenged ad is false or that retribution should be taken at the polls against the purveyor of the false advertising. The fact that there exists no forum for resolving whether or not any particular ad is false or misleading is a crucial flaw in efforts to clean up the political arena. In the absence of any such forum (or adjudicatory body) there is no effective way to affix a label of unethical conduct on an unscrupulous opponent. A cynical public has been so heavily deluged with charges of dirty campaigning that one more candidate claiming he has been wronged by his opponent is likely to elicit no more than a bored yawn and a "So what?" from the voters. To a certain extent the public has become immunized to regularly administered doses of exaggerated, distorted, or spurious campaign charges.[7] All the factors considered, there are now few if any practical restraints on the type of advertising which can and does occur during political campaigns.[8]

CONCEPTUAL FRAMEWORK FOR ASSIGNING ETHICAL RESPONSIBILITIES TO CANDIDATES FOR PUBLIC OFFICE

In developing a conceptual framework for assigning ethical responsibilities to candidates, it is necessary to consider the purposes meant to be served by political campaigns, the type of candidates who should emerge victorious after an election, and the composition of the audience to which campaigns are addressed.

Little thought was given by the founders of our system of representative democracy to the proper role or function of political campaigns. It was simply assumed that qualified candidates for public office would step forward and that an educated electorate would select its representatives from such candidates on the basis of their public reputation. It was certainly not envisioned that candidates would make campaign speeches

---

[7] In fact, most campaign strategists now advise candidates not to waste time defending charges, but rather always to stay on the attack against their opponent. See footnote 32.

[8] At the same time there is growing financial pressure upon candidates to do whatever is necessary to win, including the issuance of false and misleading advertisements. In many states and localities holding public office has become a profession. As salaries and other perquisites of public office have increased, the income derived from public service has become the main source of livelihood for more and more officeholders. Thus the loss of an election may have come to mean unemployment for the defeated officeholder.

or solicit votes. Indeed, as late as 1836 when William Henry Harrison became the first presidential candidate actually to stump for votes by making campaign speeches, many reacted with shock and scorn.[9] Times have clearly changed. Today's voter not only finds himself subjected to an endless barrage of campaign speeches and political advertising, but officeholders must now devote a substantial portion of their time to campaigning actively or planning their next campaign.

The Purposes Served by Campaigns

Distributing Accurate and Relevant Information

The most obvious purpose of modern political campaigns should be to convey information to voters which will assist them in making intelligent choices between competing candidates.[10] For this purpose to be served, however, the information conveyed must be both accurate and relevant, and individuals who choose to run for office must assume an ethical responsibility to provide such information. If the information supplied is not accurate, wrong choices may be made and the public will be defrauded. If the information conveyed is not useful in determining how candidates are likely to perform in the office, then it is irrelevant and should be discouraged.

Five different, although interrelated, categories of information about candidates appear to meet the relevancy test. Certainly, information on a candidate's past record is important for assessing his likely performance in office. Similarly relevant is information about a candidate's stands on issues or decisions which he will have to debate, resolve, or make should he be elected.

A third category of relevant information is that which pertains to the character of a candidate, particularly if such information provides insight into how a candidate is likely to exercise the power of his office and whether he can be trusted to follow through on the stands taken or promises made during the campaign. Even if information on a candidate's

---

[9] "Electioneering for the Presidency has spread its contagion to the President himself. . . . One of the most remarkable peculiarities of the present time is that the principal leaders of the political parties are traveling about the country from State to State, and holding forth, like Methodist preachers, hour after hour, to assembled multitudes, under the broad canopy of heaven." John Quincy Adams quoted in Alexander Heard, *The Costs of Democracy* (Chapel Hill: University of North Carolina, 1960) pp. 400–401.

[10] Stanley Kelley succinctly describes this purpose as the "informing function" of campaigns. See Kelley, *Political Campaigning*, p. 80.

character does not provide such direct insight, it may nevertheless be considered relevant if it pertains to a candidate's overall integrity, veracity, and fitness to serve.

Fourth, information concerning to what persons or interest groups a candidate is likely to be responsive if elected to office is clearly relevant. Included in this type of information would be an accurate list of major campaign contributors as well as the financial holdings and other investments owned by the candidate.[11]

Finally, information concerning a candidate's skills and ability to perform competently once in office is clearly relevant. Can he articulate and argue a position or assimilate facts and draw appropriate conclusions? Is he sufficiently forceful? Can he compromise? How does he react under stress? These are all legitimate questions which can and should be properly addressed in campaign literature and advertisements. The answers to many of these questions, however, can be accurately discerned by voters only by observing how a candidate reacts to various incidents on the campaign trail, his demeanor in public, his conduct during face-to-face encounters with his opponents, his off-the-cuff comments, and his responses to tough questions from members of the press corps. A candidate's actions in public will also obviously provide insight into his overall character. Indeed, the informational purpose of a campaign cannot be fully met unless a candidate assumes an obligation to appear at public events where his character and skills may be displayed and judged.

Involving the Public in Issue Debates

Political campaigns should also serve the purpose of involving the public in periodic debates over important issues as well as the overall direction of government.[12] Mechanisms for involving citizens in government decision making are not required in a truly participatory democracy, but in a representative democracy mechanisms for involving voters in

---

[11] Forty-two states require candidates for state office to disclose major campaign contributors before the election. Twenty-four states require candidates to disclose their financial holdings when they become candidates. *The Blue Book: A Compilation of Campaign Ethics and Lobbying Reform Laws*, Council on Governmental Ethics Laws, 1981.

[12] Paul Lazersfeld, in his many studies of elections and voter attitudes, identifies three major effects which political campaigns have on voters: reinforcement of previously held beliefs, conversion to modified views, and activation of voter interest in issues and in their government. See discussion of Lazersfeld's works in Key, *Politics, Parties and Pressure Groups*, pp. 482–485. In *The Cost of Democracy* pp. 426–427, Alexander Heard discusses how issue debates which occur during campaigns serve to "organize agreement or disagreement on public matters" or "put [them] on the shelf" and to develop a "unity of community."

policy debates are essential. It is through the campaign and election process that the public's feeling of participation in and control over its government—so necessary to the continued legitimacy of that government—is nurtured.

Rather than being passive observers of such periodic debates, candidates should be expected to play a leadership role, suggesting and defining issues, articulating positions, arguing the pros and cons. However, it should be recognized that the advent of sophisticated public opinion polls has somewhat complicated this task for candidates. There is now the temptation to take a poll, assess where the sentiments of the voters lie, and then adjust one's own position to reflect that of the voters.[13] Fortunately, the point has not yet been reached at which reliable polls can be taken on each and every issue of importance to a campaign,[14] and it would be wrong for a candidate, from both the ethical and the strategic standpoints, to confine his campaign to those issues upon which opinion surveys can be or have been taken.[15] Rather, candidates have an affirmative obligation to express themselves on all major issues which evolve during a campaign, including those which may be of importance to only an isolated segment of the voting public.

On the other hand, candidates should not be unduly criticized for doing extensive polling. This is because a third important purpose of political campaigns should be to provide officeholders with a means for assessing the public's views and for receiving critical feedback and guidance. In this regard, it is appropriate that some credit (or tactical advantage) be given to candidates who are best able to discern the views of their constituents or who are at least able to ask the right questions. To a significant degree a candidate's ability to represent his district depends on his ability to read the collective mind of his constituents.

---

[13] A candidate's wisdom in relying exclusively on public opinion polls is questionable. All a poll really tells a candidate is where the public may be on any given issue at the time the poll is taken. As the weeks of a campaign pass, public opinion polls quickly become dated as new issues arise, concerns are focused, and events beyond the control of the candidates alter the campaign's agenda.

[14] There are many issues upon which polls cannot be taken, e.g., issues that arise spontaneously from a campaign, pertain to only a minority of voters, or are relevant only to the narrow office sought.

[15] General public opinion surveys are clearly no substitute for the more formal referendums on the issues which take place through campaigns and elections for public office. Opinions which are voiced on issues in response to public opinion surveys may well be quite different from those expressed by voters following a spirited debate among the candidates and in the thoughtful privacy of the voting booth.

Providing Feedback and Guidance to Elected Officials

The function of providing feedback to elected officials is important regardless of whether elected officials are properly viewed as followers of their constituents' views or as independent thinkers and leaders. Even officials who place themselves in the independent leader category must at least consider the views of their constituents in formulating their own stands. And, it is rare for any official to hold strong personal views on all issues which fall within his purview. Thus, there are always many issues on which even the most ardent of officeholders willingly defers to his constituents.

A campaign can best provide feedback and guidance if the candidates, in addition to polling, participate in events where they can listen to citizen concerns and assess the depth of those concerns. Public exposure of this kind is almost ensured in competitive races where it is strategically important for candidates to appear particularly attentive to their constituents' views and perceptions. It is more problematical in campaigns in which one candidate is considered a "shoe-in." Even safe candidates, however, have an obligation to make themselves available to the voters (symbolically to press the flesh) if only to underscore their status as elected representatives.

Accentuating the Public's Watchdog Role

Campaigns for public office also provide an effective means for voters to exercise their watchdog role over their government. This is a fourth major purpose which should be served by political campaigns. In order for this purpose to be fulfilled, it is important that campaign information be dispersed, and debates on issues conducted, in a manner which will attract public interest and attention. In this regard, advertisements which are dramatic, humorous, hard-hitting, or which otherwise rivet the public's attention on campaigns and candidates should not be unduly criticized, provided, of course, that they are truthful.

It is also important that challengers do a credible job of exposing and commenting on the record of incumbents—detailing their voting records as well as their services (or lack thereof) to various constituent groups. Aggressive campaigning by challengers provides an important way for voters to maintain vigilance over elected officials.[16]

---

[16] Given the fact that such a high percentage of incumbents generally win reelection it would be unwise, however, to view election campaigns as simply a mechanism for either validating or rejecting an officeholder's performance.

Desirable Characteristics in Successful Candidates

A second consideration in developing ethical guidelines for candidates is the type of candidate who should, in an ideal sense, emerge as a winner from an election campaign. Again, the founders of our democratic system of government gave little thought to the candidate selection process; they simply assumed that dedicated members of the landed and educated aristocracy would present themselves for election. For a host of reasons it can no longer be assumed—if indeed it ever could—that political office will attract the "best and the brightest." It is appropriate, therefore, that some consideration be given to the characteristics of candidates who should emerge victorious from political campaigns. Certainly, we do not wish to impose standards of conduct which would result in "undesirable" or "wrong" candidates being elected to office.

Obviously, honesty and integrity are traits we not only want but expect in our elected officials. But we also want competent officials and *competence* is a difficult term to define. There is a variety of skills and qualities which render an official competent, and the relative importance of each such skill or quality may differ greatly from one office to another. Some general characteristics which appear relevant to almost all elective offices, however, are intelligence, good health, perseverance, an ability to get along with others, the capability of working under pressure, and a willingness to compromise when necessary.

Although campaigns may help voters to assess certain of these traits, others may not be revealed or accentuated during the campaign. Although unfortunate, this is an intrinsic shortcoming of the campaign process. A much more important problem, however, is presented by campaigns that place a premium on characteristics which either have no bearing on a candidate's likely competence in office or which are opposite from those desired. The more often campaigns are won by those who most effectively manipulate the media, deceive the voters, pull surprises on their opponents, or hire the least ethical campaign firms, the less likely it is that competent and ethical individuals will end up in office. Few if any of these characteristics translate into competent performance in office. Thus, a key goal of any standards or procedures developed for encouraging ethical campaigns should be to heighten the importance of qualities which relate to public service and to deemphasize those which are unrelated or antithetical.

Composition of the Campaign Audience

The third task which must be completed before proposing ethical standards or procedures for candidates is to analyze the characteristics, interests, and attention span of voters who comprise the audience for political campaigns.

One assumption underlying representative democracies is that a significant portion of the public will actually vote in elections. A corollary assumption, at least for modern democracies, is that a core group of voters will be attentive to campaigns and will take the information distributed during campaigns into account in casting their ballots. If these two assumptions are not correct, then nothing that goes on in a political campaign is of any real significance, and officeholders could just as well be chosen by lot, seniority, or any other scheme which would not entail the expense and time now devoted to campaigns for public office.

Although the level of attentiveness and interest in election campaign by individuals who comprise this core group of voters varies widely, it is hoped that this group, as a whole, will determine the ultimate outcome of elections. But this is where assumptions begin to collapse, for it is increasingly clear that it is not an informed core of voters that determine the outcome of elections but rather those voters, who, having paid little attention to the campaigns or candidates, nevertheless choose to cast ballots. It is also this nonattentive and ill-informed group which is the most vulnerable to manipulation through false and misleading advertising or last-minute sensational appeals.[17]

In past years, it was safer in a sense for voters who had not followed campaigns to go ahead and vote on all candidates. When the labels Democratic or Republican legitimately stood for a firm matrix of philo-sophical beliefs or governmental programs, voting a party ticket was less likely to result in significant distortions. Similarly, in nonpartisan races voters were once relatively comfortable voting for all incumbents. The public's growing distrust of government officials, however, has resulted in a growing uneasiness over voting for incumbents as a class. Finally, as a result of more and more positions' being made elective, the typical election ballot has grown so long and unwieldy that it is almost impossible for even the most thoroughly informed voter to exercise an intelligent choice for every office.

---

[17] It is true that fewer and fewer people are voting in elections. Although this phenomenon may pose a problem for theoreticians, a far greater problem may be presented by the fact that so many people who are voting do not understand for whom or for what they are voting.

As a result of all these factors, the votes of an ever increasing proportion of the electorate can be easily swayed by false and misleading advertising or other unethical campaign practices. This is an important fact which must be considered in developing any standards or procedures to control unethical campaign conduct. It is also a fact which underscores the importance of such an undertaking.

STANDARDS AND PROCEDURES FOR ENCOURAGING ETHICAL CAMPAIGN CONDUCT

Before attempting to develop standards and procedures for encouraging ethical campaigns, one must understand both the legal limitations and practical restraints involved.

There are justifiably severe restraints upon what any government agency can or should do to regulate political advertising. Although the constitutional limits placed upon government regulation of "campaign" speech have not been precisely defined by the courts,[18] there is general agreement that the United States Constitution provides its broadest protection for speech which occurs during political campaigns.[19] Campaign advertising has always been afforded the broadest possible protection from government intrusion in order "to assure (the) unfettered exchange of ideas for the bringing about of political and social changes desired by the people"[20] and to enhance the nation's "profound commitment to the principle that debate on public issues should be uninhibited, robust and wide-open."[21] Put in layman's terms, we as a nation have always thought that there is inherent danger whenever the government seeks to censor (or otherwise regulate) the statements of candidates competing to lead our government.

In line with this thinking, courts have consistently held that the government may impose sanctions against candidates for false and misleading advertisements only in very limited circumstances such as when a candidate has promised to commit a clearly illegal act,[22] has

---

[18] See, generally, L. Tribe, *American Constitutional Law*, secs. 13–26, at 798–799 (1978); "Developments in the Law," 88 *Harvard Law Review*, 1111, 1272, 1298 (1975).

[19] Monitor Patriot Co. v. Roy, 401 U.S. 265, 272 (1971); Alderman v. Philadelphia Housing Authority, 496 Fed. 2d 164, 168 (3d Cir., 1974), cert. denied 419 U.S. 844 (1974).

[20] Buckley v. Valeo, 424 U.S. 1, 14 (1976); see also Roth v. United States, 354 U.S. 476, 484 (1957).

[21] New York Times Co. v. Sullivan, 376 U.S. 200, 270 (1964).

[22] Brown v. Hartlage, 102 Sp. Ct. 1523, 1529–31 (1982).

libeled his opponent with actual malice,[23] or has knowingly published false statements which have materially affected the outcome of an election.[24] None of these after-the-fact remedies are particularly effective, and consequently very few law suits seeking redress are ever brought. At the same time, courts have ruled that the government may not exercise any prior restraint over campaign advertisements.[25]

More relevant to our discussion, courts have struck down statutes which have imposed mandatory fair campaign practices codes on candidates prohibiting the personal vilification of one's opponent or the misrepresentation of a candidate's position or party affiliation.[26] Laws requiring candidates to disclose the contents of their political advertisements to their opponents prior to distribution have met with a similar fate.[27]

In the absence of any meaningful regulation by the government, we must look to standards and procedures which will win the voluntary support and cooperation of candidates. There are two ways to accomplish this objective. First, a group of persons whose reputation for fairness, nonpartisanship, and knowledge of the campaign process is unquestioned can be assembled to establish ethical standards, arbitrate disputes, and render public judgments on unethical campaign conduct. Several entities have attempted to fulfill this role over the years. None has been able to gain the trust and confidence of sufficient numbers of candidates to make a difference.[28]

---

[23] New York Times v. Sullivan, 376 U.S. 200 (1964).

[24] Gertz v. Robert Welch, Inc., 418 U.S. 323 (1978); Vanasco v. Schwartz, 401 F.Supp 87 (E.D.N.Y. 1975) aff. 423 U.S. 1041 (1976); Menekevich v. LeFebvre, 303 N.W. 2d 462 (1981).

[25] Lower state courts in California have upheld an Orange County initiative empowering a government commission to receive and adjudicate complaints alleging false or misleading campaign advertisements in county elections. Although the commission can impose no fines or other sanctions, it assumes jurisdiction over disputes whether or not the affected candidate consents and makes its findings prior to the election. For a discussion of the Orange County Commission and the use of adverse publicity as a restraint on false campaign advertising see NOTE:—"The Use of Adverse Publicity to Regulate Campaign Speech," 12 *Pacific Law Journal* 811 (1981).

[26] Vanasco v. Schwartz, 401 Supp. 87, 97 (E.D.N.Y. 1975), aff. 423 U.S. 1041 (1976).

[27] Commonwealth v. Wadzinski, 422 A. 2d 124 (1980).

[28] Perhaps the best known and most successful group attempting to regulate unethical campaign advertising was the Fair Campaign Practices Commission based in Washington, D.C., which operated from 1965 to 1979. Presidents Truman and Eisenhower served as honorary chairmen of the commission, whose membership included respected political leaders and high-ranking government officials. The commission developed a generalized fair campaign practices code and encouraged candidates to sign it. The commission was also available to arbitrate disputes concerning false or misleading advertisements when-

The second approach is to encourage competing candidates to agree upon a statement of fair campaign principles as well as procedures for processing or resolving specific complaints against advertisements. The advantage of this approach is that the candidates themselves devise the rules and procedures and hence become committed to their own system.[29]

It is relatively easy to draft a set of fair campaign standards for inclusion in an agreement. Most candidates would agree that the following general obligations should be assigned to candidates in any fair campaign practices agreement: (1) that the candidate himself assume personal control and accountability for the conduct of his campaign; (2) that he provide accurate and relevant information on his and his opponent's past records, stands on issues, character, and competency; (3) that he participate in debates over issues relevant to the office sought; (4) that he appear at public forums and other events where his skills for office can be demonstrated and where he can receive commentary and feedback from his constituents; and (5) that he disavow and repudiate support deriving from any group which distributes false or misleading campaign materials.[30]

Although these broad standards may win ready acceptance from

---

ever both candidates agreed to the arbitration. Although the commission's code was subscribed to by many candidates, the commission's arbitration proceedings were seldom used. Few candidates were willing to trust their political fortunes to the judgment of a commission—even a prestigious one—headquartered in distant Washington, D.C.

[29] It would be naive, however, to assume that competing candidates, particularly those embroiled in active campaigning, will initiate the necessary negotiations on their own. Some prodding from outside groups, as well as the preparation of a "model" code or agreement to serve as the starting point for negotiations, is required. The best entity to fill this role is not a government agency but rather a nonpartisan citizen's group such as the League of Women Voters, Common Cause, or the like. The press, of course, can also play an important role in encouraging candidates to negotiate fair campaign agreements. More important, the press can be invaluable in enforcing any fair campaign agreements which are successfully negotiated, by threatening to publicize any breaches which occur.

[30] The obligation to repudiate support from unethical or overzealous third parties was included in recognition of the growing problem of false and misleading campaign materials distributed by "independent" political action committees such as the National Conservative Political Action Committee (NCPAC). While such groups generally concentrate on attacking an opposing candidate's record, performance, or character rather than on supporting a specific candidate, their activities pose both practical and ethical problems for their intended beneficiary. Independently produced ads may not only interfere with the campaign strategy of a candidate but may also result in a backlash against an innocent candidate. Because of these dangers, most candidates seek to dissociate themselves from the advertising presented by independent groups. From an ethical standpoint, any candidate who knows or has reason to know that such advertising is false or misleading has a duty both to dissociate himself from the group publicly and to repudiate their specific ads.

I.   FAIR CAMPAIGN PLEDGE

We pledge to conduct our campaigns for public office openly and fairly. We will discuss the issues and participate in fair debate with respect to our views and qualifications. We will not engage in, or permit, defamatory attacks upon the character of our opponents; nor shall we engage in unwarranted invasions of personal privacy unrelated to campaign issues. We also will not use or permit the use of any campaign material or advertisement which misrepresents, distorts, or otherwise falsifies the facts regarding any candidate. Finally, we will publicly repudiate support deriving from any individual or group whose activities would violate this Fair Campaign Pledge. In signing this pledge we assume personal control and responsibility for the conduct of our campaigns.

II.   SPECIFIC AGREEMENTS

We further agree to the following specific conditions:

Direct Mailings

1. We will clearly identify ourselves (or our campaign committees) as the sender of all our campaign mailings.
2. During the last 14 days preceding the election, we agree to provide the other candidates with a copy of all campaign mailings at least 48 hours before they are placed in the mail.

Submission and Review by Independent Panel

We agree to sumit a copy of all campaign advertisements to an independent panel at least 48 hours before they are placed in the mail, broadcast, or otherwise published. Each candidate shall pick one person for the panel, and an additional member will be agreed upon by the other panelists. The panel will review the advertisements for any statements which are clearly false or misleading. The panel shall be guided by the Fair Campaign Pledge in making its determinations.

Following its review of an advertisement, the panel may take no action or it may recommend changes to the candidate. If changes are suggested, the candidate affected may either accept the changes, amend the advertisement in some other way to make it acceptable to the panel, or forego the advertisement. Should he or she elect, however, to proceed with an advertisement despite an adverse panel recommendation, the panel shall immediately make its recommendation public. All recommendations made and actions taken by the panel must be done by majority vote.

Any expenses incurred by the panel or panelists will be borne equally by the candidates.

Signature_____   Signature_____

Figure 1. Model Fair Campaign Practices Agreement.

candidates, the real challenge is in developing acceptable procedures for ensuring that the standards are followed in practice. From our prior discussions it is clear that any such procedures must address those campaign techniques or technologies which permit candidates to engage in unethical conduct, focus on time periods during a campaign when the opportunity and temptation to engage in campaign chicanery are greatest, and provide a means for making timely and binding judgments concerning false campaign advertisements.

The model Fair Campaign Practices Agreement (see Figure 1) was developed by the California Fair Political Practices Commission (FPPC) in an attempt to take these three considerations into account. It incorporates the five ethical obligations discussed above[31] and embodies procedures for ensuring that candidates have a full opportunity to respond to all ads produced by their opponents and for establishing candidate-appointed panels to resolve disputes over individual advertisements.

The clear focus of the agreement is upon deterring the preparation and distribution of false and misleading advertising rather than providing for retractions or other after-the-fact remedies. Imposing sanctions against candidates for unethical conduct, particularly after an election, does little to aid the candidate who has been unfairly attacked or to build public confidence in the electoral process. Retractions also seldom reach the same audience and are almost impossible to secure in the heat of a campaign.[32]

The model agreement's most important procedural feature[33] is the

---

[31] Although the model agreement does not specifically require face-to-face debates during a campaign, it is anticipated that all candidates who sign the agreement will commit themselves to public debates. This was the experience with the vast majority of California candidates who signed the agreement before the 1982 general election.

[32] In a handbook to congressional candidates distributed by the National Republican Party for use in the 1982 election campaigns, the following advice to candidates was provided: "In most campaigns, especially challenger campaigns, it is going to be necessary to attack the opponent in order to win. Negative campaigning has a bad name, but so do a lot of things that work. . . . The key to a successful attack, however, is this: Once it is made you cannot back down. To do so is an admission of having made an unfair attack and that is a very bad position in which to be put."

[33] Several other procedural provisions were considered but ultimately rejected for inclusion in Section II of the model agreement. One would have prohibited candidates from entering into "contingency" payment agreements with campaign management firms. This section was rejected on the basis that it discriminated against lesser known or less well financed candidates, who are able to secure professional campaign help only on a contingency basis. Another provision discarded would have banned the introduction of any new issue relating to a candidate's character, qualifications, or personal life during the last week of the campaign except in direct response to a new issue raised by the opponent. The words

requirement that all campaign mailings[34] be shared with the opposition forty-eight hours before they are placed in the mail. As several professional campaign consultants put it, "The mere thought that you will have to show your advertisement to your opponent will generally deter misleading advertising." Add to this deterrent the fact that the forty-eight-hour rule affords an opponent ample time to prepare a rebuttal ad or to make the proposed mailing a campaign issue of its own. The predisclosure requirement applies only during the last two critical weeks of the campaign in order not to interfere unduly with the timely and public distribution of most campaign advertisements.[35]

In order to secure the fullest possible cooperation from candidates, the agreement calls for the candidates themselves to appoint the members of the reviewing panel. The agreement also requires all advertisements to be submitted to the panel so that the panel may have a complete picture of the campaign, its ebbs and flows, the strategies being utilized, and how any one ad may fit into an overall pattern or practice. Again, the panel's primary mission is to deter the preparation of false and misleading ads and not to censor ads. Although the panel may suggest that an ad be changed or pulled, its only recourse against a candidate who refuses to follow the panel's recommendation is to publicize its findings. Such an event is likely to be rare. Should it occur, however, the affected candidate, having

---

new and *direct response* proved too difficult to define. A third proposal would have required candidates to discharge employees engaging in false or misleading advertising. This was adjudged inconsistent with the candidates' pledge to assume personal responsibility for their campaigns. Finally, a provision requiring candidates to disclose the identity of major campaign contributors was eliminated since most states and many localities already require such disclosure.

[34] Oral statements made on the campaign stump or during press conferences are not covered by any of the agreement's provisions. Any attempt to control oral communications could unduly interfere with spontaneous and robust debates. In addition, oral statements are often made on the spur of the moment without the benefit of a deliberative process during which a candidate can consider what is being communicated to the voters. Finally, disputes over what was actually said, and in what context, could unnecessarily embroil the candidates in endless controversy.

[35] In order to police the forty-eight-hour predisclosure rule, as well as to ensure that voters can identify the senders of all campaign mailings, the agreement requires candidates clearly to identify themselves on all their campaign mailings. While several states, including California, have enacted statutes which require candidates to identify themselves on all campaign mailings, such laws may now be in question as a result of Schuster v. Municipal Court, 109 Cal. App. 3d 887 (1980) cert. denied 450 U.S. 1042 (1980). In *Schuster* the court struck down, on First Amendment anonymity grounds, a statute requiring all groups producing campaign literature (including handbills) to identify themselves on all such literature.

appointed the panel's membership, will have a difficult time disowning or disputing the panel's findings.

THE MODEL AGREEMENT IN OPERATION

The results of the FPPC's efforts to promote the model Fair Campaign Practices Agreement during California's 1982 general election campaign were generally favorable.[36]

In almost all campaigns in which both candidates signed the model agreement, they met in publicized face-to-face debates on the issues. Campaign advertisements were personally screened and cleared by the candidates and the forty-eight-hour predisclosure requirement was complied with in most instances. Although some of the advertisements were clearly negative in tone, no ad was publicly repudiated by a panel for being false or misleading. Finally, when ads were criticized by opponents, candidates took personal control of their defense rather than attempting to shift responsibility or blame to their campaign managers. Almost all of the candidates whose campaigns were governed by the agreement viewed the agreement as a positive aspect of their campaigns and stated that they would sign the agreement in future election campaigns.

The FPPC's effort to market[37] the model agreement aggressively also produced two major side effects. First, it served to focus public and media attention on the problem of false and misleading advertising. Second, in those races where in only one candidate chose to sign the agreement the opponent's refusal to sign became a major campaign issue. Candidates

---

[36] Competing candidates signed the agreement in one statewide race (superintendent of instruction), in 8 out of 100 contests for state legislative seats, and in 4 out of 43 congressional races. The agreement was also used officially in numerous local and judicial contests. In three of the five other major statewide races (including those for governor, lieutenant governor, and attorney general), and in an additional ten contests for state legislative or congressional seats, at least one candidate signed the agreement.

[37] As part of the commission's overall efforts to promote utilization of the model agreement, the commission's chairman visited the editorial boards of all the state's leading newspapers. Press conferences were held at various locations throughout the state in order to generate television and radio coverage for the model agreement's provisions. A letter signed jointly by the commission's chairman and the president of the California League of Women Voters was mailed to all statewide and legislative candidates urging them to sign the agreement. Copies of the letter were also distributed to the media, generating yet another round of publicity. Locally, presidents of county League of Women Voters chapters publicly volunteered to serve on any review panels established by candidates. Finally, information packets were mailed to political reporters and commentators throughout the state suggesting that they ask candidates their stand on the model agreement.

who balked at the agreement received negative publicity and their ads were subjected to increased scrutiny by the press. And although some observers believe that controversy over the signing or nonsigning of fair campaign agreements may have unnecessarily distracted public attention away from other important issues, the FPPC was pleased with the overall result—a general decline in the level of false and misleading campaign advertising. Although the model agreement is clearly no panacea, it can play an important role in reducing unfair political ads and in focusing public attention on unethical campaign practices.

5

Lobbying and Legislative Ethics

JAY H. HEDLUND

Our system of representative democracy gives elected officials the responsibility of taking power granted to them by the voters and balancing the competing interests and demands of 230 million people to fashion public policy for the common good. For the public to have confidence in the integrity of its elected officials and government policies it must be able to trust that elected officials will freely vote their consciences while earnestly pursuing the best interests of the country and responsively listening to the concerns of their constituents. That goal, however, is threatened in the United States Senate and House of Representatives by the pervasive and often invisible influence of special interest money and the lobbyists who direct its flow in Washington. Campaign contributions from political action committees (PACs), speaking fees from organized interest groups, and the often undisclosed multimillion-dollar lobbying efforts of those interests are increasingly undermining the integrity of Congress.

The elected officials we send to Washington to represent our interests there are not expected to carry out their task while blind and neutral like Justice. We expect them to be accessible to countless constituents and interest groups while being informed and articulate about complicated national problems and the intricate legislation needed to deal with those problems. We ask them to be open to all points of view but to be forceful advocates for specific legislation and policies. We yearn for statesmen who will show leadership and stay above petty political bickering and yet elect our leaders in a process that demands that they be partisans who will

JAY H. HEDLUND ● Common Cause, 2030 M Street, N.W., Washington, D.C. 20036.

wade into the churning competition among political parties and ideologies.

The people elected to do this job reflect the collective qualities of their constituency. By and large more gregarious and ambitious than a typical constituent, members of Congress rise out of the diverse values, backgrounds, strengths, weaknesses, and expectations of the more than one-half million people in each House district or the larger population represented by Senators. From this constituency a member is placed on a fast track in a heady atmosphere of a powerful world capital. They lead a life of impossible demands on time, energy, and patience that few citizens would willingly choose in their own professions.

Former Congressman William Brodhead (Democrat, Michigan) describes the pressures in this life:

> What kind of life do I have? How do I live? Well, I don't live very well. I'm subject to tremendous ethical conflicts all the time. Pressure all the time. A declining standard of living, traveling, working nights, on weekends. . . .The main thing is that this is a very difficult job.[1]

Members of Congress are generally honest, open, and accessible while faced constantly with making large and small value judgments in gray areas. Congressman Thomas Downey (Democrat, New York) says, "Most issues here are not issues of conscience or morality—they are questionable calls."[2] Each day they face basic decisions that can require the balancing of ethical choices: "Where should I be?"—back home in the district, in Washington, on a fact finding tour; in committee, on the floor listening to debate, back in the office; "Whom should I see?"—constituents, the Cherry Blossom Queen, experts from an executive agency, campaign contributors, lobbyists, the press; "How should I act on public policy?"—on which issues of all those before Congress to take the time needed to become expert, with whom to align, where and how to compromise; "How should I move politically?—to balance party loyalty with personal philosophy, to be an insider or a maverick, to seek higher office or greater institutional influence.

In this human, hectic, informal, and often unobserved give-and-take of political and legislative process, stakes are enormous for members of Congress, for interest groups, and for the country. A $700 billion annual budget, tax policy that determines the distribution of several hundred billions of dollars, regulations that can mean millions of dollars to a single

---

[1] Julie Kosterlitz and Florence Graves, "A Congressional Rising Star Calls It Quits," *Common Cause*, June 1982, p. 25.
[2] Elizabeth Drew, *Politics and Money: The New Road to Corruption* (New York: MacMillan, 1983), p. 79.

company or billions to the economy all become battlegrounds for competing philosophical, regional, economic, and political interests. In this intense and complicated arena legislators develop a unique relationship with and often a reliance upon lobbyists for private interests to further their objectives in both the legislative and political process.

A typical lobbyist—though clearly not all—is a white male lawyer. He often comes to the profession after working the other side of the street, perhaps as a former elected official, staff member on Capitol Hill, or campaign worker. Their number and scope of activity are unknown with any precision because of an ineffective 1946 federal lobby disclosure law. Only about 5,500 of the estimated 16,000 lobbyists in Washington are even registered with the House of Representatives. Moreover, the amount of money spent by any one lobbyist or by all lobbyists can only be estimated.[3] Nonetheless, lobbying in all its forms exceeds a billion dollars in cost annually.

A main function of all lobbyists is informative—to provide expertise to a member and his staff on some of the more than 10,000 bills and resolutions that are filed in a Congress. No single member nor his staff can be expert or even reasonably well informed on more than a relative handful of these issues. The lobbyist aims to fill this information void as his legislation makes its way through committee or to the floor of the House and Senate.

In this role of information trader the lobbyist represents his clients' interests, not a vaguely defined broader public interest. Although a lobbyist may often invoke higher purposes for his legislative goals, his persuasive power is designed to further the narrow interest of his client or organization. The lobbyist's role, influential in Washington, is largely unnoticed by the public. In noting the need for the public disclosure of lobbying activity the Supreme Court 30 years ago said:

> Otherwise the voice of the people may all too easily be drowned out by the voice of the special interest groups seeking favored treatment while masquerading as proponents of the public weal.[4]

A lobbyist is often valued by potential employers or clients for the political contacts he has with key people in Congress who are in a position to effect their legislative interests. This qualification for the job can help form relationships between legislators and lobbyists that give the appearance of normal social or personal friendships but are often shallower

---

[3] David Shribman, "Lobbyists Proliferate—So Do the Headaches," *The New York Times,* 25 July 1982, p. E5.
[4] U.S. v. Harriss, 347 U.S. 612, 625 (1954).

relationships of mutual professional convenience. Former Congressman Brodhead noted how the personal relationships between legislator and lobbyist are exploited:

> [You have] very superficial relationships. . . . I've never been to a social occasion in this town, ever, where somebody wasn't trying to hustle me to vote for or against some piece of legislation.[5]

The Washington Post in March, 1982, reported on how the desire for a lobbyist with good political contacts can be taken to an extreme when stakes are high. It cited the case of a lobbyist hired by the Milliken Research Company to lobby a single senator on an antitrust bill in the Senate Judiciary Committee that would save Milliken more than $14 million:

> When William A. Meehan, lobbyist, marched into the office of Sen. Arlen Specter (R-Penn.) . . . no round of introductions was necessary. Meehan does not cut much of a swath in Washington; he's never lobbied here before. But in Specter's hometown of Philadelphia, Meehan has been the Republican Party boss for the last two decades, and he's the closest thing Specter has to a political godfather. . . . "He's the only one on the committee I've approached because he's the only one I know," the Philadelphian explained.[6]

Given the barrage of issues and the countless interests contending for the attention of a legislator, a lobbyist's fundamental task is to make sure he has a chance to plead his case. He must overcome the political, policy, personal, or other barriers raised by legislators and staff that stand in the way of garnering majority support for legislative goals. Toward this end it is a truism in lobbying that "access is everything."

Political contributions from special interest groups play a crucial role for many lobbyists in gaining access to key legislators. Washington correspondent for *The New York Times* Steven V. Roberts has reported that many congressmen feel taking a campaign contribution creates an obligation that must eventually be repaid. Roberts observed further:

> In one sense, power in Washington can be equated with access—the quicker your phone call gets returned, the more influence you have. And when a lobbyist calls a lawmaker who has taken his money, the return time is reduced considerably.[7]

Legislators understand this relationship and some are open about how it works. Congressman Tony Coelho (Democrat, California) is

---

[5] Kosterlitz and Graves, "Rising Star," p. 25.

[6] Paul Taylor, "One Man, One Vote, One Lobbyist," *Washington Post*, 9 March 1982, p. A8.

[7] Gordon Adams, *The Iron Triangle: The Politics of Defense Contracting* (New York: Council on Economic Priorities, 1981), p. 112.

chairman of the Democratic Congressional Campaign Committee responsible for raising funds for Democratic candidates for the House. He describes what he holds out to the larger contributors to his committee:

> Access. Access. That's the name of the game. They meet with the leadership and with the chairman of the committees. We don't sell legislation; we sell that opportunity to be heard.[8]

Increasingly, lobbyists have become a major conduit of political campaign funds for candidates for Congress. This phenomenon is directly related to the extraordinary growth in the last decade of the importance of PACs in campaigns. Since 1974, the number of PACs has increased from 608 to over 3,400. PAC contributions have risen dramatically as well, going from $12 million in 1974 to $80 million in 1982. The growth of PAC giving has surpassed even the rapidly increasing costs of campaigns. While the amount of money raised by Senate general election candidates increased roughly 180 percent from 1978 to 1982, PAC receipts increased 250 percent. The dependence of congressmen on PAC funds has also risen sharply. Although in 1974 PAC money accounted for only 14 percent of the funds for the average House candidate, in 1982 candidates for the House received fully one-third of their funds from PACs.[9] Those funds are an essential part of many lobbyists' strategies for gaining access to members after they are elected.

Although lobbyists and interest groups have always sought special legislative treatment, the extent to which organized campaign giving has dominated the political process is relatively new and arose, in part, from earlier election law changes. In 1974, Congress passed major reforms of the presidential campaign financing system as a result of the Watergate scandal. With those reforms Congress provided for presidential elections to be financed primarily with public funds while rejecting a similar system for Congressional elections. Congress also enacted new limits of $1,000 on the size of personal contributions to candidates for Congress as well as to candidates for president. At the same time that the role of private contributions was minimized, Congress also removed an existing restriction in the election law that had prohibited interests with government contracts from donating to any federal candidates through a political action committee. With the role of special interests curtailed in presidential campaigns, with no public financing of congressional races, and with

---

[8] Drew, p. 49.

[9] Unless otherwise noted, figures used in this article are based on Common Cause analyses of campaign finance disclosure statements filed with the Federal Election Commission or personal financial disclosure statements filed by representatives or senators with the Clerk of the House of Representatives or the Secretary of the Senate.

restrictions removed on the establishment of PACs, a growing number of special interest groups turned their efforts toward increasing their influence in Congress.

For many lobbyists the campaign financing role is the single most important part of their lobbying efforts. One has said, "99 percent of lobbying in this city is now fund raising."[10] Some top lobbyists refuse to represent a client unless it has a political action committee to give contributions to candidates. One of those, Robert McCandless, has explained: "Corporations can't get the attention of a congressman pulled in a thousand directions unless they go to that member and say, 'We care about your re-election.'"[11]

This activity constructed around our system of campaign financing where by political action committee contributions become a primary tool for the Washington lobbyist to achieve his client's or organization's legislative goals is the Achilles heel for legislative ethical standards. The threat is widely perceived. *Time* magazine goes so far as to say, "Today the power of PACs threatens to undermine America's system of representative democracy."[12]

Elizabeth Drew, a careful observer of the interrelationships of legislators, lobbyists, and PAC contributions, suggests how the democratic process is being threatened:

> The acquisition of funds has become an obsession on the part of nearly every candidate for federal office. The obsession leads the candidate to solicit and accept money from those most able to provide it, and to adjust their behavior in office to the need for money.[13]

Legislators have an even better view of how this system works. Congressman Henson Moore (Republican, Louisiana) has said:

> If he [the member of Congress] knows you aren't politically active, he may be polite to you, but if you really want to see him perk up and be interested in what you say, let him know you represent a political action committee that is going to be active in the next election.[14]

The results of PAC giving are reflected in congressional action, whether it is specific policy decisions such as Federal Trade Commission regulations or broader policy areas of government spending and taxation.

[10] Drew, p. 58.
[11] Alvin P. Sanoff, "PAC Spells More Than a Game in Politics," *U.S. News and World Report*, 25 October 1982, p. 37.
[12] Walter Isaacson, "Running with the PACs," *Time*, 25 October 1982, p. 20.
[13] Drew, p. 1.
[14] Jack Wardlaw, "Moore: Business Lobby Should Turn National," (New Orleans) *Times-Picayune/ States-Item*, 4 December 1981, p. 20.

PACs are permeating the Congressional process. Here are a few examples of the relationships Common Cause found in the Ninety-seventh Congress between campaign contributions and legislative outcomes:

1. An analysis of a 1981 House vote on dairy price supports and contributions from the three largest dairy PACs showed that representatives who voted for higher dairy price supports had received on the average nearly six times as much from those PACs in 1978–80 as did representatives who voted against the dairy lobby on that vote.

2. On May 18, 1982, by a vote of 69 to 27, the Senate approved S. Con. Res. 60, which struck down the proposed Federal Trade Commission used-car rule. National Automobile Dealer Association (NADA) PAC contributions to senators in their most recent campaigns equalled $435,560. The 69 senators who voted for the veto resolution received, on the average, twice as much in campaign contributions from the dealers as the 27 senators voting against the resolution.

NADA PAC contributions to House members equalled $848,846 (1979 through the first four months of 1982). The 286 House members who voted for the veto resolution received an average of five times as much from the Auto Dealers PAC as did the 133 House members who voted against the resolution. In the House, 82 percent of those who received contributions from the Auto Dealers PAC voted for the veto resolution. Of those House members who received no NADA PAC contributions, 32 percent voted yes and 63 percent voted no.

3. During the 1979–80 and 1981–82 election cycles, the PACs of the American Medical Association (AMA) and the American Dental Association (ADA) contributed more than $3 million to House members who served in the Ninety-seventh Congress. In December, 1982, the House voted to exempt the business practices of state-licensed professionals from Federal Trade Commission jurisdiction. The 208 representatives who voted for the AMA/ADA-backed position received more than two and a half times as much from these PACs as the 195 members who voted against the professionals.

During six years from 1977 through 1982, the AMA PACs gave a total of $6,266,015 to all congressional candidates. Of that amount, $3,845,141 was contributed to candidates now serving in Congress—$3,233,656 to representatives and $611,485 to senators.

4. The 215 representatives who voted for the automobile domestic content bill in December, 1982, received $1.3 million in PAC contributions from the United Auto Workers during the last two congressional elections, eighteen times as much as the $72,000 received by the 188 representatives who voted to defeat the bill. Among House Democrats, the recipients of most of the UAW's PAC contributions, the 171 members

who voted for the UAW-backed legislation received an average of $7,700 per member in UAW PAC contributions, or more than six times as much as the $1,240 per member average received by Democrats who voted against the bill.

It is not necessary to have hard evidence—a "smoking gun"—that campaign contributions actually buy votes for serious questions to be raised in the public's mind about the integrity both of individual members of Congress and of the House and Senate as institutions. PAC money has become the primary building block of a relationship that eases access for lobbyists to members of Congress and too frequently squeezes out the average citizen. As Congressman James Leach (Republican, Iowa) sees it:

> You see a breakdown in citizen access. Not that a constituent isn't going to get in the door, but the guy who gave the money is going to get in first. So what you really see is a breakdown in constitutional democracy, which is supposed to be based on citizen access and constituency access. We're seeing regional politics become national. National groups determine outcomes, whereas local constituencies used to provide the crucial role. This is new.[15]

PAC contributions, moreover, are distinctly different from most individual contributions in that PACs make their decisions about who will receive their contributions as part of their long-range sophisticated Washington lobbying strategies.

> A gift from an individual citizen is a contribution from a kind of one-person multiple source: consumer, employer or employee, family member, man or woman, a certain age, experience or education. Most citizens who do contribute have more than a single interest or objective. Too often the same cannot be said of the narrow-based PACs. Typically, the PAC to Preserve the Upper Great Lakes Widget Industry cares only how the legislator votes in the subcommittee on widgets. Little if any attention is given to the legislator's vote on widows, orphans, veterans, MXs or 14Bs. Individuals generally have wider interests than PACs.[16]

But individuals generally do not have the elaborate lobbying apparatus and the Washington representatives that PACs have. In this environment there is enormous pressure on legislators to vote with the special interests even if that may be contrary to the broader but less intense public interest.

Elected officials are increasingly open about the dilemma this system of financing poses to the integrity of the legislative process:

Former Congressman Barber Conable (Republican, New York):

---

[15] Drew, p. 34.

[16] "Staying Even with the PAC," *Washington Post,* 2 December 1980, p. A18.

I'm scared. These new PACs not only buy incumbents, but affect legislation. It's the same crummy business as judges putting the arm on lawyers who appear before them to finance their next campaign.[17]

Senator Thomas Eagleton (Democrat, Missouri):

The current system of funding congressional elections is a national scandal. It virtually forces members of Congress to go around hat in hand, begging for money from Washington-based special interests, political action committees whose sole purpose for existing is to seek a *quid pro quo*.[18]

Senator Robert Dole (Republican, Kansas):

When the political action committees give money they expect something in return other than good government. It is making it much more difficult to legislate.[19]

The impact of this system of campaign financing is pervasive and poses a constant and overriding ethical dilemma for each individual member of Congress as well as the House and Senate as institutions. As Elizabeth Drew writes:

We have a system in which even the best intentioned politicians get caught up in actual or apparent conflicts of interest, in which it is difficult to avoid in effect selling votes for campaign contributions. We have a system in which even the best people do these things, not because they want to but because they are trapped.[20]

Political action committee contributions are not the only tools lobbyists use to gain access to members of Congress and to influence legislation. In both 1979 and 1980 special interests gave $2.3 million and in 1981 more than $3.4 million to members of the House and Senate, particularly the most influential members in those bodies, in large payments that went directly into their pockets. In 1982, senators alone received more than $2.4 million in such payments.[21] Those payments—honoraria for speeches—although legal under present provisions of law and legislative codes of conduct, raise serious concerns about real or apparent conflicts of interest.

Lobbyists who control honoraria can use them to gain an advantage in the legislative process. It is logical for groups concerned about issues

---

[17] Mark Green, "Political PAC-Man," *The New Republic,* 13 December 1982, p. 18.

[18] Testimony before the United States Senate Committee on Rules, by Senator Thomas Eagleton (D-Mo.), 26 January 1983.

[19] Albert R. Hunt, "Special-Interest Money Increasingly Influences What Congress Enacts," *The Wall Street Journal,* 26 July 1982, p. 1.

[20] Drew, pp. 96–97.

[21] Special Report of the Democratic Study Group, U.S. House of Representatives, 16 June 1982, p. 5.

that affect them to invite legislators who are expert on those issues to speak to them. Yet this creates the potential conflict of interest. Significant sums of money paid for speeches can often represent an investment by that group to develop unique access to those legislators most critical to their legislative agenda.

Senator Lowell Weicker (Republican, Connecticut), an opponent of such payments, says they "create a situation where a very small segment of the population enjoys a special relationship that is not enjoyed by the population as a whole."[22] In addition, this pursuit for personal financial gain from honoraria may detract from the time and attention representatives and senators need for official duties. The speeches, moreover, are likely to be written by congressional staff during working hours at taxpayer expense.

The problems created by honoraria are growing. The Democratic Study Group of the House of Representatives in 1982 found that

> members of Congress are not only becoming increasingly dependent on special interests to finance their election campaigns, they are also becoming more dependent on them as a source of personal income to supplement their official pay.[23]

Evidence of the increased reliance on honoraria is seen in the fact that Senators received 47 percent more in such payments in 1982 than in 1981.

This growing dependence on outside sources of income has come less than five years after the House and Senate recognized that members relying on honoraria and other earned income beyond their official salaries posed a dangerous threat to public confidence in the integrity of Congress. In 1977, along with a substantial congressional pay increase, the House and Senate each adopted strengthened codes of conduct that included limitations on outside earned income to 15 percent of their official salary, to become effective in 1979.

The House has abided by a limitation on earned income since 1979, although raising it to 30 percent in 1981. The Senate, at the beginning of 1979, postponed the implementation of its limit for four years before finally repealing it outright late in 1982. With no overall limitation in the Senate code of conduct, the sole restriction on outside earned income for Senators in recent years was a 1976 statutory $25,000 annual cap on honoraria. After Congress repealed this sole restriction in October, 1981, no limitation at all existed on how much a senator could earn in 1981 and 1982 in outside income in addition to his official salary.

---

[22] Martin Tolchin, "Perils Presented by Outside Income," *New York Times,* 10 January 1983, p. A16.
[23] Democratic Study Group, p. 5.

In the summer of 1983 Senator Henry Jackson (Democrat, Washington), terming the honoraria situation in the Senate "a scandal waiting to happen,"[24] forced through a 30 percent limit on honoraria in exchange for a $9,000 pay raise for senators that would bring salaries to $69,000, the same level of their House colleagues. A similar proposal had been rejected by the Senate in 1982. The salary increase was effective July 1, 1983, although the cap on honoraria was delayed until January 1, 1984. There was a predictable dramatic increase in Senate honoraria for 1983, up more than 35 percent to $3.3 million, as Senators capitalized on the unlimited system before the cap would go into effect in 1984. Recent history, however, should forewarn of efforts to amend or repeal the cap so that senators could continue to supplement their official salaries with extensive speaking fees.

The lifting of the limitations on outside earned income that were adopted in 1977 has raised questions of credibility, integrity, and public confidence in Congress. Congressman James Jeffords (Republican, Vermont) has called the practice of lobbying groups' giving honoraria to legislators "legalized bribery. When a special interest group pays $1,000—let alone $2,000—for a short speech, it is clear that the payment is made for the purpose of influencing legislation."[25]

Lobbyists, using honoraria as a tool for access to those members of Congress who can most directly influence their legislative interests, direct the heaviest amount to members of the majority party and, more specifically, to those in leadership positions. Republican senators in 1981, the first year of their new majority status in the Senate, received nearly double the honoraria as in 1980—$1.1 million compared to $600,000. Their 1981 amount was nearly twice as much as that received by Senate Democrats. In 1981 in the House, where Democrats maintained a majority, members of that party received nearly one-quarter of a million dollars more than their Republican counterparts.

Surveying the 1981 Senate honoraria the New York Times found:

> Only one Democrat was among the top 19 earners, indicating that the party in power, and its committee chairmen, enjoy a special advantage in obtaining lecture fees, and that it was a senator's power rather than his speaking ability that really earned those fees. Most of the senators received a large share of their speaking fees from organizations over which the chairman had jurisdiction.[26]

---

[24] Julie Kosterlitz and Florence Graves, "Is Congress Underpaid?", *Common Cause,* July/August 1983, p. 16.

[25] John S. Lang and Robert A. Barr, "New Furor Over the Ethics of Congress," *U.S. News and World Report,* 19 July 1982, p. 29.

[26] Tolchin, p. A16.

Such observations fuel a growing public perception that favoritism and self-interest are more important in the legislative process than merit and the public interest. The correlation between a legislator's position of influence and the speaking invitations he receives from lobbying groups is as obvious to insiders as it is troubling to a skeptical public. Congressman Henry B. Gonzalez (Democrat, Texas) clearly describes a situation any veteran of Congress would recognize:

> After I became Chairman of the Housing Subcommittee, certain people from the industry wanted to invite me to speak—for an honorarium, of course. I'd ask them how come they never wanted to hear me when I was chairman of the International Finance Subcommittee, and they don't have any answer. But you know the answer: Now I'm in a position they think can help them.[27]

Honoraria, like campaign contributions, often are a part of an elaborate strategy developed by lobbying groups to have closer access to decision makers in Congress. Efforts by lobbyists to maximize that access and to get the undivided attention of their legislative targets also frequently lead to free trips for members of Congress. A trip to a trade association convention or a meeting with corporate executives, either to give a speech for an honorarium or to do "fact finding," may also provide the member and spouse with a holiday of sorts while giving the lobbyist who arranges the trip the undivided attention of his most important legislative targets.

A House Ways and Means Committee staffer says about that time together for lobbyists and legislators on trips:

> I would say, knowing what I do about politics, that an awful lot of business is done between people like that whether it's on the fifth green or a plane trip down to whatever it is. . . . An hour on a plane trip together, that's as significant as their spending 20 days together in Washington.[28]

Unfortunately the "fee" to create such an efficient working environment can be so high—travel, lodging, meals, gifts, entertainment—as to be beyond the reach of nearly all but the well-financed Washington-based lobbying operations. Some members of Congress spend so much time on the road with lobbying groups that obvious questions are raised not only about the propriety of such trips but also about the adequacy of their attention to duties in Washington.

Congressman Dan Rostenkowski (Democrat, Illinois) is chairman of the House Ways and Means Committee. He is responsible for shepherd-

---

[27] Lang and Barr, p. 29.
[28] Ted Gup, "Golfing No Handicap for Chairman of House Ways and Means Committee," *Washington Post*, 6 June 1982, p. A12.

ing through his committee and the House legislation that may be worth millions of dollars to any single interest group. In the first two years of the Reagan Administration, his committee, among other important issues, acted on the largest tax cut bill in history and the country's largest peacetime revenue bill. Access to Rostenkowski, and his good will, is a precious commodity to the thousands of lobbyists who follow the work of his committee.

Rostenkowski is willing in the extreme to accept the lavish hospitality of some of these lobbyists. In five months spanning the winter of 1981–82, the Washington Post reported, he spent 30 percent of his time as a guest of various corporations, trade associations, and individuals at resorts in Florida, California, and Hawaii. The *Post* found that hotel and transportation costs for those trips, exceeding $10,000, were paid for by the sponsoring groups. He also received in the first three months of 1982 $10,000 in honoraria and more than $15,000 in campaign contributions from these same groups or their affiliates. In addition, his hosts gave him hundreds of dollars worth of gifts including a watch, radio, golf clothes and equipment, luggage, and other merchandise.[29]

Although Rostenkowski's actions are among the most blatant, it is not at all unusual for other members to have trips provided for them by lobbyists. In October, 1981, prior to action on the defense appropriations bill, the lobbyists for Hughes Helicopter, Inc., which was concerned about funding for the production of the trouble-plagued AH64 helicopter, arranged a three-day hunting trip to Montana for two members of the House Appropriations Committee.[30] The National Association of Broadcasters in 1981 and 1982 treated thirty-two members to all-expenses-paid trips to their conventions in Las Vegas and Dallas. Of the thirty-two, seventeen were on the House and Senate Commerce Committees, which were considering legislation to deregulate the broadcasting industry.[31] Similar examples abound.

Lobbyists do not neglect showering similar attention on important staff members with whom they will work on a day-to-day basis as their legislation moves through the Congress. Key staff members watch over the drafting of bills and amendments, develop committee reports and floor statements for members, and are in an ideal position to advocate positions with their bosses at crucial points in the legislative process. Lobbyists

---

[29] Ibid., p. A1.

[30] Walter Pincus, "Helicopter Maintenance on the Hill," *Washington Post*, 14 March 1982, p. A2.

[31] Jack Anderson, "Lobbyists Offer Junkets, Parties Liberally on Hill," *Washington Post*, 25 January 1983, p. C13.

constantly aim to make staff people advocates for their legislative interests. A senior staff member of an important money committee like Finance or Appropriations, in fact, may receive more attention and favors from lobbyists than junior members of Congress who have not yet risen to positions of influence.

Again, the Ways and Means Committee provides some of the clearest examples of lobbyists courting favor with key staff. The *Washington Post* points to a trip to New Orleans in March, 1982, for two top aides to Congressman Rostenkowski and a lobbyist for Nevada casino and off-track betting groups:

> It was the beginning of a three-day weekend of door-to-door limousine service, a luxury hotel, elegant restaurants, and seats in the governor's box in the Superdome for the NCAA basketball semifinals. In between was a day's visit to offshore mining operations and talk of minerals. The trip—costing more than $1,000 a person, including comparable air fare—was paid by Freeport-McMoRan Inc. Pending legislation could have a multimillion-dollar impact on the company's tax liability.[32]

Such trips although barely disguised whirlwind vacations paid for by special interests, are allowed under the present enforcement of the code of conduct of the House as long as a claim can be made that it is related to official duties. Although subsidized trips by members must be reported, trips by staff generally are not reported publicly unless those involved are among the relative handful of top-paid congressional staff who are required to make annual public statements of financial interest.

The examples cited may seem flagrant but they are rooted in an attitude expressed by an aide to Rostenkowski: "Washington is a casual sort of 'let's-have-lunch, let's-go-to-New-Orleans' kind of town. It's all done informally. There is a steady sort of nodding of heads here."[33] It is an attitude that exacerbates the public's suspicion that decisions affecting their lives are made more on a basis of favors and cronyism than on merit. The unchecked abuse of the relationship between lobbyists and legislators and their staffs, particularly when exploited by leaders in the House or Senate, establishes a minimal standard for what is acceptable for the institution in this area. At present it is a standard that inevitably erodes public confidence in Congress.

On a long-term basis the isolated, dramatic, and illegal violation of ethical standards by a few in Congress—as in the Abscam scandal—may be less destructive to the integrity of the institution than the failure of the

---

[32] Ted Gup, "Life in the Tax Lane: Staff Gets Trips, Too," *Washington Post,* 7 June 1982, p. A1.
[33] Ibid., p. A2.

House and Senate to establish and enforce appropriately high standards of conduct to guide the actions of all members during their service in office. The individual gross violation of a member trading on his office for personal gain can create a crisis for the institution. As in the case of Abscam, however, it is likely to create the impetus necessary for the Congress to address such a crisis directly and responsibly.

The more subtle deterioration of ethical standards posed by campaign money, honoraria, and excessive travel and gifts gradually reinforces a public perception that the whole legislative process is influenced more by lobbyists and special interest money than by merit. It is a perception that to the degree that it reflects reality it threatens public trust in our system of representative government.

With so much at stake in the legislative arena for interest groups and for elected officials, it would be naive to suggest that strengthened institutional standards of integrity would stamp out avarice or excessive self-interest. Indeed, draconian restrictions that hindered the vigorous competition of ideas and interests necessary in the legislative process would not be healthy. It is not too hopeful to expect, however, that progress can be made to establish standards that can maintain public confidence in the integrity of the Congress and to help assure the ethical accountability of individual representatives and senators in the face of special interests that too often have driven out ideas and competition with political money.

In fact, substantial progress has been made in recent years in elevating congressional ethical standards. In the wake of Watergate, reform-minded legislators and a concerned public teamed up to help pass open-meeting rules, campaign finance disclosure laws, and strengthened codes of conduct with improved enforcement by the House and Senate ethics committees. Additional reforms are needed, however.

First, the system of financing congressional elections must be changed. The Congress, which enacted significant and successful reforms to deal with the corruption of the financing of presidential campaigns, must set its own system of financing campaigns in order.

Comprehensive reform of campaign financing would include a system to increase the role of the small-sum, individual contributor to congressional campaigns. A system of public financing—where small private contributions to qualifying candidates would be matched with federal funds—would increase the importance of the individual contributor and lessen the role of PAC contributions. Establishing a new source of campaign funds would give a candidate an alternative to accruing the compromising obligations that are created by going "hat in hand" to the PACs.

At the same time, campaign finance reform should establish new limitations on PAC contributions. The Federal Election Campaign Act limits contributions to a candidate from a PAC to $5,000 in a primary and $5,000 in a general election. At present there is no overall limit on how much a candidate may receive from all PACs. Thus there are no checks on the aggregate influence of PACs.

In 1979 the House passed—but the Senate did not consider—a measure that would have limited the total amount of PAC contributions a House candidate could receive in any election. Such a limitation for both the House and Senate should accompany a public financing package in order to curb the growing dependence of congressional candidates on PAC contributions and to lessen the special advantage lobbyists who control those PAC contributions have in the legislative process.

Second, tight new restrictions must be placed on honoraria. Representatives and senators ought to be expected to rely on their official salaries, not payments from lobbying groups, as their principal source of earned income. To make it easier to do so, members should be supported in efforts to establish pay levels that fairly reward the demanding nature of the job and that reasonably can be expected to keep pace with inflation and to minimize the economic sacrifices demanded of those in public service.

The limited honoraria, if any is allowed, should be insulated to the greatest degree possible from a member's legislative activity. Acceptance of honoraria from any source that has legislative interests before the member's committee should be prohibited.

Third, travel and gifts provided by interest groups for members and staff should be more clearly circumscribed by the codes of conduct of the House and Senate and enforced strictly. The presumption should be that travel necessary for effective government performance should be paid for by the government. Any staff travel paid for by outside groups should be publicly disclosed. To eliminate the abuse of turning such trips into thinly disguised vacations for members or staff paid for by lobbying groups, expenses for family members, extended stays beyond the time necessary to complete government-related business, and extravagant "expenses" should be strictly and clearly prohibited.

Finally, a new, effective, and enforceable federal lobbying disclosure law should be passed. In a democratic system of government, lobbying should be a positive influence, encouraging the public's participation in political issues and congressional awareness of public opinion. Congress should ensure that such lobbying is done openly. Just as there are requirements for open congressional meetings, disclosure of elected officials' financial holdings, and disclosure of campaign contributions, a suitable lobby disclosure law should satisfy the public's right to know how organized interests are trying to influence Congress. This is consistent with the principle that the governmental process and all significant factors that affect it must be open to public scrutiny to warrant public confidence in the integrity of governmental actions and policies.

At this point neither the public nor members of Congress can determine which interests are spending how much money on lobbying for legislative goals. In late 1982 and early 1983, the banking industry spent—but did not fully disclose—millions of dollars in a successful grassroots campaign to repeal tax withholding on interest and dividends. The insurance industry spent more than $1.8 million—much of it undisclosed—in a four-month period in 1983 in a nationwide grassroots effort against legislation that would prohibit insurers from discriminating on the basis of sex with respect to premiums, benefits, and availability of coverage. The natural gas industry has also undertaken a million-dollar grassroots lobbying campaign to secure deregulation of natural gas, and the securities industry has initiated a more modest effort to repeal a new Social Security provision relating to tax-exempt bonds. These are just part of grassroots lobbying campaigns that—apart from the money spent on salaries for lobbyists in Washington, campaign contributions, honoraria, and entertainment costs—are estimated to cost lobbying groups well over $1 billion annually, with most of it never publicly reported.[34]

In the words of former Senator Abraham Ribicoff (Democrat, Connecticut), effective lobbying disclosure is needed "so that the voice of the few and the money of the few do not make it impossible to hear the voice of the many."[35] To improve the present inadequate lobby disclosure, the Congress should consider three major changes to the current lobby disclosure law.

First, the provisions that designate who must register as lobbyists should be tightened. The disclosure law could be amended to include a time and dollar expenditure threshold which, when crossed, would require an individual or organization to register.

Second, the provisions that designate what must be disclosed should also be tightened. The law should be amended to define explicitly and include grassroots lobbying as a covered lobbying activity.

Finally, Congress should consider amending the enforcement provi-

---

[34] "The Swarming Lobbyists," *Time*, 7 August 1978, p. 14.
[35] Common Cause, *The Tip of the Iceberg: The Case for Full Disclosure of Lobbying* (Washington, D.C.: Common Cause, 1977), p. 5.

sions of the law, which are currently widely ignored. Because the existing criminal penalties are perceived by many as being so harsh that they inhibit enforcement efforts, Congress should consider adding less severe civil enforcement provisions to the lobby disclosure law. It should also consider granting specific authority to an oversight agency, such as the General Accounting Office, to audit disclosure reports and conduct preliminary investigations of suspected violations.

Richard Bolling represented the citizens of Kansas City, Missouri, in Congress for over thirty years, rising to the chairmanship of the powerful House Rules Committee. When he retired in 1982 he was widely regarded not only as a legislative giant but also as one of those members who cared most about the institutional integrity of the Congress. He warned of the growing danger of PAC contributions, honoraria, and sophisticated grassroots lobbying campaigns threatening Congress's integrity and its ability to govern:

> The explosion in PAC funds and other forms of special interest money is undermining public confidence in the institution of the Congress, and for good reason. It may sound idealistic, but I know from experience that Congress must have and must appear to have integrity in order to retain the public's confidence. But the public increasingly suspects that at least a portion of Congress is no longer *pure*. Because, increasingly, what the public sees is legislation that looks like special interest wish lists. What the public increasingly discovers is that interest groups are buying the sort of access that they as voters could never dream of.[36]

Members of Congress who have been successful in the present system may have an incentive to maintain it. The lobbyists' direction of PAC money to their campaigns will help assure their reelection. It is safer politically to take thousands of dollars in honoraria for speaking before special interest groups than it is to justify voting for a pay raise at election time. Trips to resorts paid for by lobbying groups offer a welcome respite from the rigors of a demanding job.

The personal interest a member of Congress has in maintaining the present system is in direct conflict with the broad public interest in reforming a system in which public trust in government is corroded by the lopsided influence that special-interest money gives organized lobbying groups in Washington. One Washington insider, in comments on the campaign finance system, makes the case for members acting against self-interest to curb the influence of special interest money:

---

[36] Speech by Congressman Richard Bolling, O'Neill Professor of American Politics, Boston College, September 21, 1983, pp. 8–9.

My view is that if the money represents an unfair advantage it ought to be eliminated. Where is the ethics or morality in saying the system ought to be maintained because it benefits you, if the advantage is inherently unfair?[37]

There is a special ethical responsibility for members of Congress to vote against their own self-interest and to put new checks on special-interest money. They have a moral obligation to rebuild the integrity of the Congress and reassure the public of that integrity. No one could put the need to do so more strongly than House veteran Bolling: "We can control the pernicious influence of money in politics. . . . It is essential to the survival of our democracy."[38]

[37] Drew, p. 156.
[38] Bolling, p. 13.

6

Socialization and Ethics in Congress

ROGER H. DAVIDSON

Ethical—or unethical—conduct does not take place in a vacuum. Although popular or journalistic accounts still take the customary Calvinistic view that divides the political world into the elect and the damned, careful observers of politics sense that life is not so simple. Ethical purposes can be advanced by politicians whose styles are rough or profane—the names of Lyndon Johnson, Richard Daley, and Phillip Burton spring immediately to mind. On the opposite side, countless legislators of exemplary behavior achieve little of substance; many, like the proper people who passed by on the other side of the road in the story of the Good Samaritan, are insensitive to human needs that could be served by the legislative process. In other words, members' propensities for getting in trouble with the law or with ethical expectations are an imperfect measure of their worthiness as legislators.

Legislators, moreover, move in a social and institutional context. Elected officials face certain dilemmas—intellectual, social, moral, financial—that inhere in their jobs. Lawmakers borrow ideas and deliver speeches prepared by others. They receive campaign assistance from interests they may find abhorrent. They may concede certain issues in order to gain leverage on issues they deem more important. Being an elected official, in short, is a frustrating business in which behavior may be dictated by the situation and therefore less than ideal. Most thoughtful

The views expressed in this paper are those of the author and do not reflect those of the Congressional Research Service.

ROGER H. DAVIDSON ● Congressional Research Service, United States Library of Congress, Washington, D.C. 20540.

participants and observers of the legislative process have commented on the situational ethics involved in legislative life.

If behavior occurs in context, then it is presumably learned behavior. Elected officials are probably neither more nor less moral than the rest of society; they ingest their notions of morality from the families and communities that nurtured them, and no doubt they reflect the standards of the regions they represent.

The institution of Congress also exerts a powerful influence. Newly elected senators and representatives do not enter a fragmentary and pliable institution; on the contrary, they enter chambers brimming with history, traditions, and unwritten rules of the game. Although there is ample room for individuality in acting out roles within each chamber, new members discover that they must pretty much accept the institution on its own terms. These institutional imperatives are communicated to new members through internal communications networks. This learning takes place in ways that intrigue students of Congress.

Political scientists know a good deal about how new members learn the institution's norms and folkways. A flurry of studies appeared in the late 1960s and early 1970s; and although the work has flagged in recent years, a number of insights have entered the literature. Some scholars have also examined congressional ethics, although this topic has been conceded mainly to journalists and so-called public-interest lobbyists. But the topic of legislative ethics remains a live one.

The link between legislative ethics and the institutional learning process is, however, virtually unknown territory. Earlier studies of socialization covered basic legislative bargaining rules but devoted little attention to broader questions of ethics. And the students of ethics have paid little heed to the degree to which ethical precepts may be fostered and communicated within the institution. In this chapter we endeavor to examine and speculate on this connection.

NORMS IN THE POSTWAR CONGRESS

Not so very long ago, the behavioral norms of Congress were strongly articulated and forcefully conveyed by senior legislators to newcomers and observers alike. Former Senator Joseph S. Clark (Democrat, Pennsylvania), first elected in 1956, recounts that he was counseled on the subject for an hour and a half by his friend Hubert Humphrey. Once in Washington, he and the five other freshman Democratic senators were treated to a luncheon hosted by the majority leader, Lyndon B. Johnson (Democrat, Texas). Beside each plate was a copy of William S.

White's *Citadel: The Story of the U.S. Senate,*[1] autographed not only by the author but by the majority leader as well. During the luncheon, Johnson urged his new colleagues to consider the book—a "love affair" with the postwar Senate—as "a sort of McGuffey's Reader from which we could learn much about the 'greatest deliberative body in the world' and how to mold ourselves into its way of life."[2] Along with a few of his colleagues, Clark managed to resist these blandishments; but it was clear that they had encountered a powerful system of standards, or norms, that were associated with success as a legislator.

White's study of the Senate was impressionistic and biased; but Donald R. Matthews' *U.S. Senators and Their World,* which appeared three years later, was a scholarly approach to the "world's most deliberative body" that has not been matched to this day.[3] The "effective Senator," Matthews found, was one who took to heart a series of informal "folkways" that were promulgated by, and served the interests of, the conservative coalition that ran the chamber during the 1950s. These folkways included: (1) specialization, (2) legislative work, (3) reciprocity and comity among senators, (4) courtesy, (5) apprenticeship and deference to elders, and (6) institutional loyalty. Although senators were free to choose alternative standards of behavior (Clark and others increasingly did so), Matthews lent weight to the establishment view that influence within the Senate was associated with compliance with these norms.

The postwar House of Representatives was a more steeply structured body which relied on seniority as its organizing principle. The norms of the body were reflected in what Richard F. Fenno, Jr., termed its "seniority–protégé–aprenticeship system."[4] This code of behavior was forcefully impressed upon new members by their elders, especially by the "old bulls" on both sides of the aisle who ran the standing committees. Typically, years passed before members could chair a subcommittee, manage a piece of legislation, or serve on a conference committee. There were exceptions, however. Senior chairmen and party leaders occasionally singled out promising newcomers, giving them important tasks and sponsoring their careers. Speaker Sam Rayburn cultivated a number of newcomers, among them Lyndon Johnson and Richard Bolling. Other "youngsters" were given heavy responsibilities. But for the majority of

---

[1] (New York: Harpers, 1957).

[2] Joseph S. Clark, *Congress: The Sapless Branch* (New York: Harper & Row, 1964), p. 5.

[3] (Chapel Hill: University of North Carolina Press, 1960), especially Chap. 5.

[4] Richard F. Fenno, Jr., "The Internal Distribution of Influence: The House," in *The Congress and America's Future,* ed. by David B. Truman (2nd ed.; Englewood Cliffs, N.J.: Prentice-Hall, 1973), pp. 84–86.

members, adherence to the folkways and the long wait for seniority were the only route to power.

These norms were not neutral or disinterested codes of behavior. On the contrary, they reflected the Capitol Hill power structure of the day, whose needs they served and whose duty it was to convey them to newcomers. The rise of this network of norms coincides roughly with the ascendancy of the so-called conservative coalition, which dominated the House and Senate from the mid 1930s through the mid 1960s.

During these years, it often appeared that Congress was ruled by a relatively small coterie of powerful senior members, many of them committee chairmen and ranking minority members. Of course, not all of these leaders were blessed with extraordinary talent or skill, the vagaries of the seniority system being what they were. To a remarkable degree, however, the two chambers came to be dominated by the personalities, resources, and philosophies of these individuals. The conservative coalition was bipartisan in scope. The Democrats controlled Congress for all but four years (1947–1948 and 1953–1955), and on the Hill the party took a distinctly southern and conservative cast. Well into the 1950s, Southerners outnumbered Northerners among Democrats of both chambers. Lacking vigorous two-party competition, southern and border states had the habit of repeatedly returning their incumbents to Washington–making those members winners in the seniority game. Even when the conservative Democrats' ranks dwindled, or when the GOP captured Congress, plenty of conservative Republicans were on hand to uphold the alliance.

This conservative establishment was aided by the rules and procedures of the two houses. Bills were typically referred to a single committee, remaining in perpetuity within that panel's jurisdiction. Within the committee, the chairman typically controlled the flow of legislation, hired and fired the staff, allocated time in hearings, monitored the flow of paperwork, and made subcommittee appointments and adjusted workloads. In the House, tightly controlled floor procedures underscored seniority leaders' grip on measures emanating from their committees. The Rules Committee often granted leaders' request for "rules" limiting amendments or waiving points of order against committee-reported bills. Unrecorded teller votes on amendments in the committee of the whole discouraged non-committee members from remaining on the floor to argue and vote against committees. The final stages of the process were tightly controlled, with membership on conference committees normally reserved for the most senior committee members.

These rules and procedures were in turn buttressed by organizational folkways of the type we have already described. Coming from safe one-party areas that allowed them freedom to master their committee's subject matter and the chamber's traditions, leaders of the day encouraged specialization and respected others who did the same. Within their committees, they instructed their flocks on the intricacies of policy matters familiar from years of review; younger members were urged to follow suit and to select certain issues they could call their own. Norms of specialization, reciprocity, and deference discouraged legislators outside the committee from meddling, even during floor debate. During this era, then, the power structure of the two chambers paralleled the growth and dissemination of a compatible set of ethical norms. In turn these norms facilitated and perpetuated the existing system of arrangements.

Though pervasive, these establishment norms were not the only ones available to legislators in the post–World War II years. There existed also a set of counternorms, not dominant but nonetheless well defined and for some members more congenial than the establishment norms. These prescriptions stressed constituency or public outreach rather than legislative work; within the chambers they dictated aggressiveness rather than deference, wide-ranging policy interests rather than specialization, quest for leverage and publicity rather than apprenticeship, and responsiveness to outside constituencies rather than exchanges of cues. The old-style "statesman," representing a safe one-party area, could afford to specialize and play the workhorse role. Not so those members from competitive districts (which came to include most senators and increasing numbers of representatives) or those who aspired to higher office. They could not afford such a leisurely approach to their legislative duties. In rejecting the conventional norms of behavior, not a few of them were rebuffed by senior members and told their legislative careers were doomed.

Those who accepted these counternorms, whether from necessity or choice, nonetheless found colleagues who were in the same boat. Because these members were normally excluded from wielding influence within the chamber—from becoming, for example, one of Matthews' "effective Senators"—they were cast into the roles of outsider or maverick. If they could not exert influence *within* the institution, they would attempt to exert influence *upon* it; or they would leave to pursue other goals outside the institution. While abandoning temporarily their chance to scale the heights of power within the two chambers, such members could and did follow role models provided by more senior mavericks and banded together to exchange information and give moral support.

In the House of Representatives, counternorms were promoted by the Democratic Study Group (DSG), one of the best known and most successful of the so-called informal caucuses on Capitol Hill. The DSG started in December, 1956, when a young Minnesota representative named Eugene J. McCarthy circulated among a group of his friends a statement of aims that became known as the Liberal Manifesto. Early the following year Representative Frank Thompson, Jr. (Democrat, New Jersey) inserted the program into the *Congressional Record,* and the number of signers stood at 80. These liberal Democrats, many from urban areas, at last had found a way to express their impatience with the conservative leadership and to air their own ideas about what measures Congress should be considering. Known initially as "McCarthy's Mavericks," the group soon acquired an informal whip system and eventually a staff assistant.

Over the next two decades the DSG provided information, guidance, and organization for newly elected liberal Democrats in the House. Buoyed by Democratic electoral gains in such years as 1958, 1964, and 1974, the DSG came to embrace a sizable majority of House Democrats; it was a force representing the emerging mainstream of the Democratic party. As such it played a major role in discarding the old rules and folkways and substituting new ones. The DSG organized a series of floor amendments that pumped life into the Legislative Reorganization Act of 1970; and with the start of new Congresses in 1971, 1973, 1975, and other years, DSG leaders prepared agendas of proposed rules changes for action by the Democratic Caucus and even by the House itself.[5] It therefore provided the information and organization that mobilized new waves of Democratic members during this period. The mavericks, at first viewed with suspicion or at best bare tolerance, became eventually the leaders of the new order.

In the Senate, the story was similar although the particulars were different. Prior to 1958, liberals of both parties found themselves relegated to outsider roles, attempting to appeal to public opinion over the heads of Senate elders. Notable among the outsiders of the 1950s were such Senators as Wayne Morse of Oregon, Paul H. Douglas of Illinois, and Joseph S. Clark of Pennsylvania. Even when their ranks were augmented with newcomers, their influence over Senate procedures lagged behind their numbers. The notion of a tight, conservative ruling clique, or "inner

---

[5] On the DSG's history and contributions to the reform movement, see: Kenneth Kofmehl, "The Institutionalization of a Voting Bloc," *Western Political Quarterly* 17 (June 1964), 256–272; Norman J. Ornstein, "Causes and Consequences of Congressional Change: Subcommittee Reforms in the House of Representatives," *Congress in Change: Evolution and Reform,* ed. by Norman J. Ornstein (New York: Praeger, 1975), pp. 88–114; and David W. Rohde, "Committee Reform in the House of Representatives and the Subcommittee Bill of Rights," *Annals of the American Academy of Political and Social Sciences,* 411 (January 1974), 39–47; and Roger H. Davidson, "Subcommittee Government: New Channels for Policy Making," in *The New Congress,* ed. by Thomas E. Mann and Norman J. Ornstein (Washington D.C.: American Enterprise Institute, 1981), pp. 99–133.

club,'' became an obsession for senators who perceived themselves on the outside looking in.

Slowly the picture changed. An informal policy of assuring each new senator at least one major committee assignment—the so-called Johnson rule, initiated by Lyndon Johnson—eventually brought more equitable distribution of desirable committee seats. As the seniority system worked its inexorable way, many of the "young Turks" of the 1950s became the "old Turks" of the 1960s and 1970s; meanwhile, the older generation of conservative leaders passed from the scene. Most notably, Johnson's departure and the accession of Mike Mansfield (Democrat, Montana) as majority leader dramatically changed the atmosphere of the Senate. "We've had a dispersal of responsibility," Mansfield explained. "I'm not the leader, really. They don't do what I tell them. I do what they tell me."[6] Later Senate floor leaders have echoed these sentiments. Mansfield summarized his philosophy for dealing with his colleagues:

> Senators realize that they are treated as I'd like to be treated—as mature men. Their independence is not infringed upon. They know that everything is on the table. They know all about our moves ahead of time. There are no surprises.[7]

The young activist liberals of the Mansfield era were unimpressed with old rules about the sanctity of seniority. "We don't feel there's time to waste on that old seen-and-not-be-heard business," one of them explained. "After all, if a man manages to get to the Senate, he must have something to contribute."[8] The vocal outsider, Clark, finally concluded: "The old times have changed. The Senate establishment is gone. Democracy is now pretty much the rule in the Senate."[9]

In the Senate as in the House, alternative role models were available for new senators who balked at the establishment way of being a senator. Senator Clark, who railed against the "Senate establishment," was one leader among the outsiders. So was Douglas, who was so frustrated with the obstruction of Senate leaders that once upon leaving the Senate chamber and calling for an elevator, he turned to an aide and said bitterly: "Let's ring three times [the signal to the operator that a senator was waiting] and pretend we're a senator."

Therefore, when William Proxmire (Democrat, Wisconsin), a loner

---

[6] Quoted in *The New York Times*, 17 July 1961, p. 11.

[7] Andrew J. Glass, "Mansfield Reforms Spark 'Quiet Revolution' in Senate," *National Journal* (March 6, 1971), p. 509.

[8] Quoted in Dan Cordtz, "The Senate Revolution,"*Wall Street Journal*, 6 August 1965, p. 8.

[9] U.S. Congress, Senate, *Congressional Record* 111, 89th Cong., 1st sess., September 13, 1965, p. 111, 22636.

and an activist, entered the Senate in 1957 to take Joseph R. McCarthy's seat, he had role models to follow. As Huitt recalls the story, Proxmire waivered between outbursts of self-assertion and periods of quiet frustration.[10] Finally, when he could no longer stand the strictures imposed by the traditional folkways, he decided that he would "be a senator like Wayne [Morse] and Paul [Douglas]." Huitt pointed out that, whereas the traditional inner-club role might be useful for preserving the status quo, it would hinder those seeking change:

> The behavior associated with the Outsider may be functional for protest groups seeking a spokesman, dysfunctional for groups needing leverage inside the legislative body.[11]

In other words, insider's and outsider's norms sprung from different roots and served quite different functions.

HOW MUCH LEARNING? HOW ETHICAL?

Reflecting on these events, scholars of the past generation examined the content of these legislative norms. Several questions are pertinent to the present inquiry. How widely were these norms accepted by members? How did members learn these norms? And to what degree did the norms embrace ethical concepts? The findings have considerable intrinsic interest but offer somewhat inconclusive answers to the questions we have posed.

The content of post–World War II Senate folkways is well established, thanks to Matthews' persuasive findings. Matthews identified six folkways that he argued were enforced in many informal ways: (1) new senators should serve an apprenticeship; (2) senators should concentrate on Senate work rather than on gaining publicity (that is, they should be "workhorses" and not "showhorses"); (3) senators should specialize on issues within their committees or affecting their home states; (4) senators should show courtesy toward colleagues; (5) senators should extend reciprocity to colleagues—that is, they should provide willing assistance with the expectation that they will be repaid in kind one day; and (6) senators should loyally defend the Senate, "the greatest legislative and deliberative body in the world."[12]

How extensively were these norms, or folkways, communicated

---

[10] Ralph K. Huitt, "The Outsider in the Senate: An Alternative Role," *American Political Science Review* 55 (September 1961), 566–575.

[11] Ibid., p. 575.

[12] Matthews, Chap. 5.

within the body from senior members to newcomers? Because of the nature of the Senate—its heavy reliance on staff and the difficulty of measuring senators' own interactions—there is little evidence from other studies to corroborate or extend Matthews' analysis. However, it appears to be clear that the norms were forcefully disseminated to newer members, at least during the Johnson period. The testimony of senators, especially those who resisted the conventional norms, is too persuasive to dismiss. Even Huitt, although arguing that the traditional norms were not the only ones extant, did not dispute their existence or wide dissemination.

The ethical content of the folkways was quite limited in scope. As we have observed, it reflected the power structure of the day and served its purposes. No doubt it also had the effect of smoothing the legislative process, facilitating the kind of bargaining and exchange behaviors that are endemic to processing legislation. These norms did not, however, address larger questions of ethical behavior for elected officials—campaign tactics, for example, or relationships between elected officials and private interests. In other words, the norms were largely procedural and institutional in nature, focusing upon relationships among fellow legislators.

The House of Representatives, of course, relied less upon informal norms and more on formal channels of power. From interviews in the early 1970s, however, Herbert B. Asher uncovered seven norms: (1) friendly relationships are desirable; (2) the important work of the House is done in committee; (3) procedural rules of the House are essential; (4) members should not personally criticize colleagues on the House floor; (5) members should be prepared to trade votes; (6) members should be specialists; and (7) freshmen members should serve apprenticeships.[13] Table 1 shows the proportions of senior and freshmen members articulating these norms. Asher's interviews cast doubt on at least one norm which had been regarded as crucial in the post-World War II era: neither freshmen nor senior members appeared to believe strongly in the apprenticeship norm. Otherwise, the precepts uncovered by Asher roughly paralleled those found in the Senate at the same time.

Interviews with House members, however, cast doubt on the importance of learning among freshmen, or between freshmen and more senior members. Although he identified several widely held norms, Asher found little norm *learning* going on. Because freshmen and nonfreshmen exhibited close agreement on most of the precepts, it was likely that newcom-

[13] Herbert B. Asher, "The Learning of Legislative Norms," *American Political Science Review* 67 (June 1973), 501–503.

Table 1. Norms Expressed by House Members: 1968

	Expressed in interviews with	
Norms	Nonfreshmen	Freshmen
Friendly relationships are important	97%	100%
Important work is done in committee	95	90
House rules are important	82	100
Don't personally criticize members	82	71
Trade votes if necessary	81	72
Specialization	80	73
Apprenticeship	38	57
Spend time on the House floor	—	73

Note: Reprinted, by permission of the publisher, from Herbert B. Asher, "The Learning of Legislative Norms," *American Political Science Review* 67 (June, 1973), 503.

ers knew these norms even before they arrived on the scene. Perhaps the newcomers' prior experiences in state assemblies, city councils, and the like had served to inculcate such values. Perhaps they were values learned in a wide variety of political activities. Whatever the explanation, Asher was not able to verify a process of norm learning.[14]

As with the Senate folkways, the House norms carried a discernible though limited ethical content. In the House, the precepts reflected a body that adhered to fairly strict rules and worked through a strong committee system. Yet, like norms in the Senate, House norms carried few implications for the broader ethics of public officeholders or policy makers.

Recent research makes clear that Senate and House norms have faded in importance (see Table 1). In the Senate, members now participate early and often in all phases of deliberations.[15] Many senators, especially those with an eye on the White House, work tirelessly to attract national publicity and personal attention. Committee specialization, though still apparent, is far less rigid than it used to be because senators have numerous overlapping committee assignments and are expected to hold views on a wide range of issues. Courtesy and reciprocity are still maintained, but institutional loyalty—in this era of cynicism about government—wears thin.

[14] Ibid., 512.
[15] Norman J. Ornstein, Robert L. Peabody, and David W. Rohde, "The Contemporary Debate: Into the 1980s," in *Congress Reconsidered,* ed. by Lawrence C. Dodd and Bruce I. Oppenheimer (2nd ed.; Washington,D.C.: Congressional Quarterly Press, 1981), pp. 16–19.

Even the loose network of House norms has been diluted.[16] New members, impatient with the notion of apprenticeship, plunge into the work of the House as soon as they learn their way around. Leadership comes earlier to members than it used to. Specialization still occurs—more so in the House than in the Senate—but many members dip into unrelated issues. Nor are committees the only forums for influencing legislation. Looser norms for floor participation and voting have expanded members' chances for shaping bills outside their own committees' jurisdictions. Relaxation of such norms as specialization and apprenticeship reflects the decentralization of Capitol Hill.

THE CURRENT SITUATION

The traditional norms and folkways of the two chambers have weakened and changed. More stress is now placed on following one's constituencies. Whereas Speaker Sam Rayburn enjoined new members to "go along" if they wanted to "get along" in Congress, hardly anyone gives that kind of advice anymore. More prevalent is Representative Phil Gramm's (Texas) explanation of his independence from his party: "I'm going to dance with them that brung me"—meaning his conservative Texas constituents.[17] (When disciplined by Democrats for passing caucus secrets to the Republicans, Gramm resigned his seat, switched parties, and was then elected as a Republican.) Less premium is placed on comity, compromise, or bargaining exchanges. Institutional loyalty has suffered in the wake of public restlessness with legislative products and the performance of government itself.

Not only have the norms themselves changed, but the structures that support and foster them have shifted as well. As more members have come from previously unrepresented social groupings, the shared attitudes and values of the older and more homogeneous generation of members have become diluted and diverse. Inasmuch as today's members follow more varied paths to Capitol Hill—fewer having served in state legislatures, for example—they share fewer values derived from prior political socialization. Within Congress, fewer senior members are on hand to instruct and advise newcomers; those who remain hesitate to offer advice. At any rate, senior members' formal powers for backing up such advice are far less formidible than they were in the post–World War

---

[16] Burdett A. Loomis and Jeff Fishel, "New Members in a Changing Congress: Norms, Actions, and Satisfaction," *Congressional Studies* 8 (Spring 1981), 81–94.

[17] Quoted in the *Washington Post,* 21 November 1982, p. A2.

II era. Face-to-face relations among legislators are probably fewer than they once were.

These shifts have profoundly altered Congress, both as a human organization and as a representative assembly. Whereas members used to deal with one another directly on a daily basis when Congress was in session, today they interact through layers of staff aides and complex organizational arrangements. Informal relationships have been replaced by extensive rules, procedures, and precedents. In the House of Representatives, members know few of their colleagues well, or even at all in some cases. Close associates tend to be those who are brought together in committees or other workgroups. Even more frequently, members and staff aides working on a given problem are unaware of what others are doing. In short, Congress has shifted perceptibly from a unified, corporate body to a bureaucratic one—with all its trappings of size, complexity, specialization, and routinization. In a slightly different context, Senator Howard Baker has called today's legislators "elected bureaucrats."[18]

Today's procedures and norms, in turn, are supported and transmitted by a complex institutional network. While these norms are different in content, and differently disseminated, from those of yesterday, there is by no means a situation of ethical anarchy. On the contrary, institutional control of behavior is probably stricter today than ever before. Observers may disagree over the utility or propriety of contemporary rules of the game, but there can be little argument that they exist.

For one thing, everyone elected to Congress has been exposed to the fact that politics is now a highly regulated industry. Those who run for federal office are subject to the provisions of the Federal Election Campaign Act Amendments of 1976 (P.L. 94-283), which mainly cover campaign finances. Certain controls are exerted over sources and amounts of campaign contributions, and indirectly over how funds are spent. Reports must be filed periodically and are publicly available. The Federal Election Commission (FEC) serves as the regulatory agency for campaign finance, issuing rulings and undertaking enforcement. Other agencies have a role in receiving campaign reports, certifying proper elections, and hearing complaints. These include the Clerk of the House and the Secretary of the Senate, the housekeeping committees (House Administration, Senate Rules and Administration), and the House and Senate ethics panels (House Standards of Official Conduct, Senate Select Ethics). Few candidates, then, conduct federal campaigns without law-

---

[18] *Congressional Record* 129, 98th Congress, 1st session, June 14, 1983, daily edition, p. S8374.

yers and accountants at hand, and financial administration has become a major campaign chore.

During and even prior to campaigns, candidates profit from seminars and workshops conducted by political parties and other groups. Campaign literature is also supplied by such groups. Most of this material is directed to conducting successful campaigns, and its ethical content may be suspect. However, candidates are given heavy doses of "dos and don'ts" of campaign practices, whatever their effects.

Newly elected members encounter plenty of people and groups eager to advise on the conduct of members of Congress. I myself have participated in a number of such orientation sessions, the subjects of which ranged from substantive issues and parliamentary procedures to the details of hiring staff, moving to Washington, and organizing the congressional office. Such sessions tend to focus on relentlessly practical issues, but they embrace implicit ethical considerations and challenge members-elect to define for themselves what kind of lawmakers they wish to be. Hill offices—including the housekeeping committees and fiscal officers of the two chambers—orient members and their staffs in numerous matters which contain ethical issues—for example, staff salaries, office allowances, the franking privilege, and so forth. A major purpose of such sessions is to help members and their staffs avoid running afoul of federal statutes or chamber rules.

Congressional agencies are available to instruct and answer questions at all times, not merely when members and staffs are newcomers. Most of these contacts are at the staff rather than the member level, although occasionally members themselves make the inquiries. The Congressional Research Service, for example, stands ready to advise members and staffs on matters concerning legislative and office practice. Although CRS does not offer personal legal advice, it serves as a sort of "institutional memory" for Congress by reviewing, explaining, and interpreting statutes and congressional rules. It organizes institutes and briefings for members and staffs and offers advice upon request.

Other sources of ethical instruction are the House and Senate ethics codes, adopted in 1968 and substantially tightened in 1977. The codes apply to members and key staff aides. They require extensive financial disclosure, restrict members' outside earned income to 15 percent of salaries, prohibit unofficial office accounts once used by members to supplement official allowances, and impose standards for using the congressional franking privilege. The two ethics committees (House Committee on Standards of Official Conduct, Senate Select Ethics Committee) have been created to implement the codes, investigate charges against members, and issue advisory opinions. The panels have in fact heard allegations against members, and occasionally have recommended censure or expulsion. But their major ongoing task is to respond to inquiries (usually at a staff level) and give advisory opinions concerning given courses of conduct. The staff director of the House panel estimates that three-quarters of the committee's staff time is devoted to giving advisory opinions. The Senate committee estimated that some 2,500 telephone inquires were received during 1982.

The franking privilege—the right of members to send out mail under their signatures without cost to them—also attracts controversy and special regulatory action. The existing franking law, passed in 1973, confers wide mailing privileges but forbids using the frank for mail "unrelated to the official business, activities, and duties of members." It also bars the frank for "mail matter which specifically solicits political support for the sender or any other person or any political party, or any vote or financial assistance for any candidate for any political office." Personal references to, and photos of, the legislators are also covered. In addition, as mentioned already, House and Senate rules touch on use of the frank—for example, forbidding mass mailings sixty days before a primary or general election. The Senate prohibits mass mailings to "postal patrons" (directed to postal addresses but not specific individuals). Such matters are the province of the Senate Rules and Administration Committee and the Committee on House Administration. There is also a Congressional Mailing Standards Commission in the House, charged with recommending changes in franking guidelines.

As a result of all this activity, today's lawmakers are at no loss for help in conducting themselves and running their offices. In posing the question of ethical learning, then, it is essential to recognize the institutional growth that has transformed Capitol Hill in recent years. Norms are learned less through interchanges of members than through the work of a large, layered collection of staff bureaucracies. In actuality, most day-to-day decisions having ethical consequences are made and transmitted by staff aides.

These observations serve to underscore a relatively new dimension of the ethics of lawmaking. That is, today's member of Congress is less a sole proprietor than an employer, manager, and coordinator of other people. Aside from the few who have had careers as owners or managers of businesses, lawmakers are poorly trained in personnel skills. Yet this is an important aspect of legislative performance in Congress inasmuch as the ability to obtain, keep, motivate, and utilize staff can make the difference between effectiveness and ineptitude. Legislators continue to argue that they need freedom in hiring and firing staff aides because of the sensitive political nature of the work. Yet for most public jobs Congress has recognized the desirability of a merit system with safeguards against discrimination and procedures for handling grievances. This principle has been applied to congressional support agencies such as the Congressional Research Service and the General Accounting Office. The unregulated status of congressional hiring remains a live issue that will undoubtedly persist. In the meantime, a voluntary employment mediation committee is available to hear grievances that arise under the present system.

Another unresolved issue has to do with legislators' reliance upon material prepared by staff aides. Members exhibit ambivalence on this subject. On the one hand, all of them rely heavily upon staff-prepared speeches, statements, reports, and other materials. Rare indeed are the legislators who write their own utterances—an inevitability in view of the number and complexity of issues with which legislators are expected to deal. On the other hand, many members are not entirely comfortable relying on secondhand materials, and some cling to the notion that they personally conduct all their legislative business. There is persistent laxness in acknowledging staff contributions, and periodic efforts to reverse the dependency upon staff. For example, both chambers strictly limit the number of staff aides allowed on the floor during sessions, and a 1983 reform proposal—submitted by two former senators but never acted upon—suggested that senators refrain from delivering written speeches in the Senate chamber.[19]

Staff activism enlarges the ethical focus to include staff aides as well as members. Like the legislators they work for, key staff aides are subject to ethical guidelines embodied in statutes and the rules of the two houses. Occasionally there have been reports of staff misconduct which has resulted in distorting the legislative process. It was once disclosed that an entire hearing was fabricated by a committee staff member—who was dismissed after the story surfaced. More recently, a staff aide was thought to have rewritten transcripts from a House hearing, to the disadvantage of the minority-party members. The Committee on Standards of Official Conduct was called upon to investigate the situation.[20] In addition to these public reports, there have been private reports of staff members' overstepping their authority. Their authority is usually ill-defined, with ultimate responsibility remaining with lawmakers. It is therefore hard to know where the fault lies. Clearer delineation of the metes and bounds of

[19] Former Senators James B. Pearson and Abraham A. Ribicoff, "Draft Report of the Senate Study Group" (April 5, 1983), pp. 18–19.
[20] Charles Fishman, "Printed Record Inverts Words of House Members," *The Washington Post*, 18 June 1983, p. A3.

staff duties may be a way of fostering learning about ethics at the staff level.

A larger concern is the extent to which staff members should perform the duties of elected officials. One study of congressional staff is entitled *Unelected Representatives*.[21] It has been established that staff members cannot cast votes for the lawmakers who employ them, either in committee or on the floor. Nor are staff members supposed to conduct hearings, although upon occasion they do, and there have been serious proposals that they do so on a regular basis.[22] Staffs are pivotal in every branch of government: the modern presidency is in large part a staff structure, and revelations make it clear that Supreme Court clerks do far more than look up citations in law books. However, formal recognition of the staff's place in representative government has been slower to develop, perhaps because of the unique role that elected officials are supposed to play in speaking for their electorates. This would seem to be an underdeveloped aspect of legislative ethics.

A tangential issue, though by no means a trivial one, is the place of families in the scope of lawmakers' ethical behavior. In particular, what formulas or guidelines might clarify conflicts between legislators' official duties and their personal duties as spouses, parents, or whatever? In the past, this question was rarely accorded such attention, but in recent years members and their families have become vocal in speaking about it. New member briefings emphasize the problems families have in fitting themselves into legislative schedules and demands. Congressional spouses' groups offer counsel and support for family members. Whereas it was once regarded improper for members to relocate their families to the nation's capital, it is now regular practice. Congressional schedules these days are more congenial to family and school cycles than they once were. Even so, some members have retired from office because they decided that office-holding was incompatible with the demands of raising a family. It is a problem that bears examining, not only in the legislative branch, but elsewhere in government where jobs are physically or psychologically demanding.

Finally, today's Congress is—perhaps more than ever before—constrained by other people's standards and behavior. Members of Congress are often led to act in anticipation of—or in fear of—reactions from those outside the body. In particular, actions of voters, journalists,

---

[21] Michael J. Malbin, *Unelected Representatives: Congressional Staff and the Future of Representative Government* (New York: Basic Books, 1980).

[22] S. Res. 15 93rd Congress, 1st session. See *Congressional Record*, 93rd Congress, 1st session January 11, 1973, daily edition, pp. S 460–462.

potential or real opponents, courts, and executive agents can impinge upon legislators' actions. Of course, Congress was designed to be a reactive institution, open and permeable to outside influences. But its vulnerability to contemporary outside forces is probably unique. These forces are more numerous and powerful then ever before, and their demands are transmitted quickly and forcefully. At the same time, Congress's own institutional defenses are stretched thin. Senators and representatives are well aware that, no matter what their popularity at the polls, they belong to an institution that is deeply distrusted by the general public.[23] No doubt this is a major reason why institutional loyalty has sagged in recent years, as we have already noted.

The press is a powerful force in shaping public attitudes about Congress and in limiting the actions of members themselves. Indeed, the press is more obtrusive and critical than probably at any time since the early nineteenth century, when fiercely partisan newspapers routinely pilloried their enemies in print. Michael Robinson, a scholar who has studied the links between Congress and the press, concluded in 1980 that "the *overall* image coming out of the nationals—papers and networks combined—is more stark, more serious, more intrusive, and more investigative . . . than it has ever been."[24] Comparing a bribery scandal involving Representative Daniel Flood (Democrat, Pennsylvania) with a similar case ten years earlier, Robinson concluded that the press gave greater play to the more recent scandal.

Looking askance at governmental institutions is natural for men and women of the fourth estate. Cynicism pervades the journalistic profession, at least at the national level. Prizes and honors tend to go to those who expose wrongdoing. The muckraking tradition of reform-minded journalism dates from the early days of the twentieth century; scandalmongering and sensationalism go back much further, to the very beginnings of mass-circulation papers. This tradition is kept alive by investigative reporters like Jack Anderson, whose preoccupations include congressional "perks" and junketing trips abroad. Investigative reporting gained new respectability in the 1970s, when dogged and skillful reporting uncovered scandals surrounding Watergate and the conduct of the Vietnam War. As a result, matters of legislators' behavior that would have been hushed up a generation ago—not only bribery or abuse of

---

[23] For a review of major findings concerning the public image of Congress, see Roger H. Davidson and Walter J. Oleszek, *Congress and Its Members* (Washington, D.C.: Congressional Quarterly Press, 1985), pp. 158–162.

[24] Michael J. Robinson, "Three Faces of Congressional Media," in *The New Congress*, ed. by Thomas E. Mann and Norman J. Ornstein (Washington, D.C.: American Enterprise Institute, 1981), p. 75.

office, but personal matters like sexual harassment, homosexuality, or alcoholism—are these days broached openly. Sometimes, press enthusiasm to "get" public officials becomes excessive. Observers conclude this occurred when Representative Allen T. Howe (Democrat, Utah), charged with soliciting two police-decoy prostitutes in his home town, was repeatedly castigated by Salt Lake City newpapers.[25]

Another source of guidance for individual legislators is the network of specialized interest groups. Such groups do a thorough job these days of tracking the voting records of individual senators and representatives. More than seventy such groups compile indexes of votes which "grade" legislators according to the standards and goals of the given interest group. These records are disseminated to group members through specialized modes of communication; often they materialize in the form of campaign contributions from the group's political action committee—or the withholding of such contributions. The result is that few votes are truly "invisible" to the public: no matter how trivial, there is always the possibility that some interest, representing some segment of the legislator's constituency, will be on the lookout.

The inability of Congress to resolve the matter of its members' salaries and outside earnings illustrates the power of the outside forces to define and propel an issue, for good or ill. Setting their own compensation has never been a comfortable task for senators and representatives. Extensive press coverage and editoral comment, not to mention constituent reaction, exacerbated this task during the inflationary 1970s. A couple of automatic mechanisms for adjusting salaries were adopted; but neither could be satisfactorily applied to legislative pay because of the likelihood of media reaction. In 1982 the Senate declined to raise its salary while retaining an unlimited level of outside earned income (mainly honoraria from speaking to lobby groups). The situation was open to misinterpretation; and when reports of annual speechmaking income were subsequently released, editorial writers lost no time pointing out the ethical problem. Yet after the Senate narrowly voted to limit such income and raise salaries as the House had done, the *Washington Post*'s headline read: "Senators Raise Own Pay."[26] In such a context it is not surprising that the two chambers often seem not to know which way to turn.

The new press activism as articulator and purveyor of legislative morals, in other words, has been a mixed blessing. There is little question that it has made legislators more careful of actions—and appearances—

---

[25] Milton Hollstein, "Congressman Howe in the Salt Lake Media: A Case Study of the Press as Pillory," *Journalism Quarterly* (Autumn 1977), pp. 454–458, 465.

[26] *The Washington Post*, 17 June 1983, p. A 1.

than ever before. Members and their staffs are on the lookout for actions that might be interpreted negatively. A common rule of thumb on Capitol Hill, articulated by members and staff alike, is, "If there's any doubt, then *don't.*" By the same token, a greater forthrightness in dealing with allegations is seen on the part of individual members and such official bodies as the ethics panels. Voluntary resignations have occurred, as well as formal disciplinary proceedings against members. Even when the allegations proved farfetched and false, as in the 1982 charges involving sex and drugs among members and pages, the congressional response was prompt and, on the whole, salutary.

At the same time, the press has proved to be an imperfect guide to contemporary legislative ethics. First, the press still tends to focus on narrow questions of what it labels as "scandals"—for example, junkets, salaries, perquisites, and personal brushes with the law. Second, the local press—which especially in the case of House members prints much of what constituents read or hear about elected officials—is far less prepared or willing to criticize than is the Washington press corps, who spend less time focusing on individual legislators. Third, reporters' narrow definitions of legislative ethics lead to very little thoughtful or accurate reporting on the stewardship of individual lawmakers or the efficacy of the legislative process. Such inquiries would require an expenditure of time, research, and reflection beyond the resources of most news organizations. (In the early 1970s the Ralph Nader organization launched a series of in-depth reports on every member of Congress. The venture proved a disappointment and in any event was not repeated.) The average voter is left, then, with inadequate means of evaluating the performance of individual representatives. Finally, to the extent that outside forces, such as reporters and interest groups, are guiding legislators' behavior, the result may be more one of timidity or acceding to external demands than purposeful pursuit of political objectives.

SUMMARY

The theme of this chapter has been the shift in congressional ethics from an informal network of norms or folkways to a formal network of statutes, rules, and precedents. In the former case, ethical principles were learned through experience and personal, face-to-face contact with senior members. The norms were enforced by hierarchical distribution of power in the two chambers. Although these norms failed to address the larger questions of legislative behavior, they helped facilitate the operations of the post-World War II Congress, an institution that relied on specialization and exchanges of influence to produce results.

Today's Congress has forfeited the face-to-face relationships of the past but is marked by institutional proliferation of committees, subcommittees, partisan and informal caucus groups, and multiple staff support systems. If denied informal face-to-face socialization, today's members of Congress are exposed to a wide variety of advice through briefings, orientations, staff advice, and the ongoing availability of information. Ethical learning for today's legislator is vastly different, but probably no less effective, than the simpler learning process of an earlier day. However, ethical standards and learning processes continue to raise fundamental questions about the nature of legislative ethics and the ability of voters to know and evaluate these standards.

7

Legislative Ethics in the New Congress

DAVID E. PRICE

A glance at recent books on Congress—*Congress in Change, Congress Reconsidered, The New Congress*—suggests a preoccupation with how the institution is changing. Although such an emphasis risks underestimating the regularities and stabilities of congressional behavior, it is a useful point of departure for an examination of the dilemmas of role and value confronting contemporary legislators. What are the dominant features of the current congressional environment, and what implications do they have for the ethical obligations of individual members and groups of members?

In asking this question, I conceive of ethics quite broadly, encompassing not merely the minimal standards of probity which members should observe but much farther-reaching questions as to how they define and carry out their responsibilities. I will begin with a brief characterization of the congressional setting—a setting that increasingly leaves members "on their own," ethically and otherwise. I will then highlight several dilemmas of role definition and institutional responsibility which arise within this setting. I do not mean to suggest that the answer to the legislature's problems lies entirely or even mainly in a heightened sense of personal responsibility on the part of its members. But individual responsibility is an irreducible element of congressional performance and one that has been given increased importance by the decline of the norms and structures that formerly ordered members' behavior.[1]

---

[1] Although this article focuses explicitly on the U.S. Congress, many of the trends and dilemmas described are present at the state level as well. I am drawing in part on my

DAVID E. PRICE ● Department of Political Science, Duke University, Durham, North Carolina 27706.

THE CONGRESSIONAL SETTING

The picture leading students of Congress paint of members in their institutional environment has shifted significantly in the past twenty-five years, from an emphasis on their *adaptation* to well-defined norms and procedures, to a portrayal of them as purposive *agents* in a fluid organizational setting. This shift is partially a function of changing fashions in social-science research—with economic or rational-actor modes of analysis supplanting "sociological" or functionalist approaches[2]—but it also owes much to changes in the institution being examined: Congress is now shaped more by the ambitions and interests of individual members and less by party and committee and other institutional systems than was the case in the 1950s.

Richard Fenno's landmark studies of the appropriations committees drew heavily on concepts from functionalist social science—role, function, integration, and adaptation—terms which suggested that members conformed to the institutional environment more than they shaped it:

> The study conceives of the House Committee (and the Senate Appropriations Committee) as a *political system*—having certain identifiable, interdependent, *internal parts,* existing in an identifiable *external environment,* and tending to *stabilize* both its internal and external relationships over time. . . . In the description of internal relationships, the emphasis on normative expectations is expressed via the idea of *norms.* . . .In a reasonably stable system, patterns of behavior tend to coincide with patterns of expectations. People usually do what they are expected to do.[3]

Similarly, Donald Matthews' 1960 study of the Senate stressed the "folkways" of the institution, "its unwritten rules of the game, its norms of conduct, its approved manner of behavior." Members were expected to serve a proper period of apprenticeship, to carry their share of the legislative workload, to specialize in their committee's policy areas, to reciprocate the favors and assistance of colleagues, to defend the Senate as an institution—and they paid a price in esteem and effectiveness if they did not. "There is great pressure for conformity in the Senate," an influential member told Matthews. "Its just like living in a small town."[4]

"Ethics and Legislative Life: Thoughts on Representation and Responsibility" (Denver:LEGIS/50), a working paper prepared in 1979 for the Center for Legislative Improvement.

[2] See Brian Barry, *Sociologists, Economists, and Democracy* (London: Collier-Macmillan, 1970), Chaps. 1, 6.

[3] Richard F. Fenno, Jr., *The Power of the Purse: Appropriations Politics in Congress* (Boston: Little, Brown, 1966), pp. xviii, xxi.

[4] Donald R. Matthews, *U.S. Senators and Their World* (New York: Vintage Books, 1960), p. 92.

The leading studies of the decade that followed, however, differed considerably in their approach. When Fenno turned from the "self-contained" world of appropriations to more loosely structured and permeable committees like Education and Labor and Foreign Affairs, he found the "conceptualization of the social-systems literature" less useful and turned to more "individualistic" modes of analysis.[5] His comparative study of six House committees thus treated the goals of individual members (reelection, influence with the House, good public policy) as a major explanation of committee performance. David Mayhew, in his influential 1974 essay, *Congress: The Electoral Connection,* made a more decisive break from the functionalist frameworks of the past. "I have become convinced," Mayhew wrote, "that scrutiny of purposive behavior [of individuals] offers the best route to an understanding of legislatures—or at least of the United States Congress."[6] Mayhew thus posited the assumption that members of Congress were "single-minded seekers of reelection," and found a close fit between the behavior such an assumption led one to predict and actual congressional performance.

A number of developments made such an individualistic portrayal an increasingly plausible one. Fenno was impressed by variations among the committees he studied and by the evidence that, on many committees, the system-maintaining norms so pervasive on appropriations had little chance to develop because of the influence of client-group, executive, and other external forces. In the meantime, a number of scholars found the more general folkways of the House and Senate to be changing and/or declining in their influence on member behavior.[7] Particularly significant was the fading of the expectation that one would serve an extended period of apprenticeship before taking an active role in committee or on the floor;

---

[5] Fenno, *Congressmen in Committees* (Boston: Little, Brown, 1973), p. xvii. For further discussion, see the review by David E. Price, *American Political Science Review,* 71 (June 1977),701–04.

[6] David R. Mayhew, *Congress: The Electoral Connection* (New Haven: Yale University Press, 1974), p. 5.

[7] See Nelson W. Polsby, "Goodby to the Inner Club," *Washington Monthly,* August, 1969, pp. 30–34; David E. Price, *Who Makes the Laws?* (Cambridge: Schenkman Publishing Co., 1972), pp. 7–8, 266–68, 313–17; Randall B. Ripley, *Power in the Senate* (New York: St. Martin's Press, 1969), chapters 3, 7; Herbert B. Asher, "The Learning of Legislative Norms," *American Political Science Review,* 67(June, 1973),499–513; Norman J. Ornstein, Robert L. Peabody, and David W. Rohde, "The Contemporary Senate: Into the 1980s," in *Congress Reconsidered,* ed. by Lawrence Dodd and Bruce Oppenheimer (2nd ed; Washington: Congressional Quarterly Press, 1981), chap. 1; and Burdett A. Loomis, "The 'Me Decade' and the Changing Context of House Leadership." in *Understanding Congressional Leadership,* ed. by Frank Mackaman (Washington: Congressional Quarterly Press, 1981), chap. 5.

as Congressman John Brademas, the Democratic Chief Deputy Whip, observed, "1976 is not 1966 and it's not 1956. I don't think, given the changes in American society, that intelligent and highly motivated young men and women will sit back and wait for a few years before speaking out."[8] While members still valued subject-matter specialization and expertise, they became less hesitant to become involved in areas beyond their committee assignments. The introduction of bills and issuing of pronouncements on a wide variety of subjects, formerly the hallmark of a few "mavericks," became widely engaged in and tolerated, and members became less concerned to maintain a facade of committee or party unity as they took their causes and their amendments to the floor.

These changes accelerated among the Democrats after the 1958 elections sent large numbers of liberal, non-Southern partisans to both houses. The formation of the Democratic Study Group in the House (1959) and the legislative activism of "policy entrepreneurs" like Hubert Humphrey, Paul Douglas, and Joseph Clark in the Senate represented a challenge to senior party and committee leaders and gave a foretaste of the pressures for a dispersal of authority and resources that would be felt in both chambers during the next two decades. The changes among Republicans were more gradual but no less pronounced: the GOP had a few individualistic entrepreneurs of its own (Senator Jacob Javits being the prototype), and the desires of (generally younger) members for a more distinctive and less accommodating minority policy role were an important element in the successive replacement of Joseph Martin (1959) and Charles Halleck (1965) as House minority leaders. The years preceding (and culminating in) the 1980 election then witnessed the advent of another sort of policy-oriented individualist, particularly among Senate Republicans, more doctrinaire than the activists of the Javits–Humphrey stripe, less seasoned politically and less inclined to compromise, more radically critical of the legislative institution, more single-mindedly determined to "go public" with symbolic issues such as school prayer and busing. It is perhaps among this group, of whom Jesse Helms is the prototype, that allegiance to the traditional folkways such as apprenticeship, specialization, legislative comity, and institutional patriotism has reached its lowest ebb.[9]

---

[8] Quoted in James L. Sundquist, "The Crisis of Competence in Our National Government," *Political Science Quarterly*, 95(Summer 1980),198.

[9] See Albert R. Hunt, " 'Popsicle Brigade': New GOP Legislators Impress Their Seniors, Though Not Favorably," *Wall Street Journal*, 14 December 1981, p. 1.

THE ELECTORAL SETTING

These changes are rooted to a considerable extent in the altered context in which members are elected and seek reelection. Of primary importance is the decline of the political parties, both as shapers of electoral choice and as organizations controlling critical campaign resources. Members are increasingly on their own electorally and less dependent on the parties. They face electorates less inclined to vote for them on partisan grounds alone and a public largely unaware of and unconcerned about their party regularity once they are in office. They are generally nominated not by party caucuses or conventions but by direct primaries, and the number of districts with party organizations strong enough to control the nomination process has declined substantially. Candidates must raise their own funds and build their own organization at the primary stage and often for the general election as well. National partisan swings have become less and less determinative of election outcomes in most congressional districts, and ticket splitting has become endemic. Understandably, members are inclined to see the services they render to their districts and the visibility they maintain there as more crucial to their electoral fortunes than their ties to the organized party, either at home or in Congress.

The electoral environment has changed in other ways as well. Both senators and representatives face larger, more heterogeneous districts; better educated and/or more demanding constituencies, with expanded expectations as to the role and obligations of government; and electorates less easily reached through traditional friends-and-neighbors or clubhouse politics. Television has become the dominant campaign medium, with far-reaching consequences for candidate and congressional behavior. It places a premium on highly visible posturing in Washington—"showhorse" behavior of the sort the folkways proscribed. By promising to reach voters directly and persuasively, it further reduces member dependence on party organizations. It requires huge outlays of money, thereby increasing candidate dependence on groups with money to give and on direct-mail technology. Members may respond to this complex of environmental forces in a number of ways: some may stake out roles as champions of cancer research or as defenders of agricultural subsidies, others may hold widely publicized hearings on various outrages and abuses, and others may offer anti-abortion or balanced-budget riders to bills, smoking out the good guys and the bad guys for fund-raising and campaign purposes. But these responses are all entrepreneurial in character, more readily understandable in terms of the profit-and-loss calculations of individual political agents than in terms of the established norms of the legislative institution.

This campaign environment has proved quite congenial to interest group influence. Campaigns cost more, party support counts for less, and political action committees (PACs) have proliferated—a response both to the increasing impingement of government on the interests of business, labor, and the professions and to the complex of campaign finance laws enacted during the 1970s.[10] While members of Congress no longer can rely on huge contributions from a few dominant sources, they must scramble for a much larger total amount from a bewildering array of PACs. The share of House candidates' receipts coming from PACs has increased in a step-by-step fashion, from 16 percent in 1972 to 28 percent in 1980 and 30 percent in 1982. Despite the fund-raising successes of the Republican party, the share of candidate receipts contributed by the parties has declined by 50 percent (to a level of 6 percent) over the same period.[11]

Such an electoral context, volatile and structurally fragmented, can increase members' sense of vulnerability, but it also puts a premium on personal electoral entrepreneurship and makes it easier for members to insulate themselves from national partisan trends. The result, at least in the House, has been an enhancement of the electoral advantages of incumbency. Typically, about 90 percent of House incumbents seek reelection in a given year, and more than 90 percent of these win. Even in years when the party's fortunes are in decline, its members of Congress generally do very well: 89 percent of Democratic House incumbents survived the Reagan election in 1980, and 85 percent of Republican incumbents prevailed over their challengers in the midst of the Democratic comeback in 1982. Senate incumbents also enjoy a decided advantage, though not as great as that of their House counterparts: senate races are better publicized, more heavily influenced by issue considerations and media images and less by constituent service and simple name familiarity. But they are no more party-oriented than House races; they are simply less "safe," with the entrepreneurial efforts of challengers more likely to match those of incumbents in effect.[12]

To some extent congressional incumbents are "the accidental bene-

---

[10] See the discussions in Michael J. Malbin, ed., *Parties, Interest Groups and Campaign Finance Laws* (Washington: American Enterprise Institute, 1980), Pts. I and II.

[11] Computed from data in Federal Election Commission releases of March 7, 1982, and May 2, 1983; and Roland McDevitt, "The Changing Dynamics of Fund Raising in House Campaigns," in *Political Finance*, ed. by Herbert Alexander (Beverly Hills: Sage Publications, 1979), pp. 141–49.

[12] See the discussion in Gary C. Jacobson, *The Politics of Congressional Elections* (Boston: Little, Brown, 1983), especially chap. 5.

ficiaries of behavioral changes they had no part in creating or fostering . . . an unraveling of party allegiance among voters and a resulting shift to the incumbency cue in voter decisions."[13] But members have hardly been passive participants in this process. We have already noted the prevalence of what Mayhew calls "position-taking"—making speeches, introducing bills and amendments, assuming postures designed for maximum electoral appeal. Members also find it profitable to "advertise"—building name familiarity and a favorable image through newsletters, media reports to the district, and huge volumes of mail—and to "claim credit," performing favors for constituents and publicizing their own role in securing funds and projects for the district.[14] The quest for electoral security by means of position taking, advertising, and credit claiming helps explain the kind of staff increases, district-office allowances, and franked mail privileges members of Congress have voted themselves in recent years. It also helps explain another important feature of congressional change: the widening dispersal of authority and resources.

Increasingly impatient with the norms of apprenticeship and deference, and anxious to gain visibility and leverage earlier in their congressional careers, members pressed during the 1960s and 1970s for a further decentralization of the committee system. The result was a proliferation of subcommittees—senators are currently spread among 113 subunits and House members among 154—and a series of rule changes, mainly in the House Democratic Caucus, mandating a high degree of subcommittee autonomy. Although many members found this reduction in the power of full committee chairs and the spreading around of legislative resources quite serviceable in terms of their desire for a piece of policy "turf," organizational fragmentation has posed certain problems for Congress as an institution. It has heightened the tendency toward "particularism," the servicing of narrowly based interests with limited regard for broader considerations, as members have gravitated toward subcommittees in whose jurisdictions they and their districts have a particular stake. It has complicated congressional policy making by making mobilization of the chamber more difficult and by providing numerous checkpoints for those who wish to oppose new departures in policy. It has, in fact, helped prompt another sort of congressional reform—the new budget process,

---

[13] See Albert Cover and David Mayhew, "Congressional Dynamics and the Decline of Competitive Congressional Elections," in *Congress Reconsidered,* ed. by Dodd and Oppenheimer, 2nd ed., p. 77; and Walter Dean Burnham, "Insulation and Responsiveness in Congressional Elections," *Political Science Quarterly,* 90(Fall 1975),412–15.

[14] See Mayhew, *Electoral Connection,* pp. 49–77.

for example, and the increased powers over committee assignments, scheduling, and other processes granted to the party leadership—which represents a partial corrective to those changes that have decentralized power. But the net effect of congressional reform has been to put more resources in the hands of individual members while making Congress as a whole more difficult to manage and to mobilize.[15]

DILEMMAS OF REPRESENTATION AND RESPONSIBILITY

Thus does a quick survey of members in their legislative and electoral settings point up the emergence of an organizationally fragmented, almost atomistic, Congress: members on their own in a fluid electoral environment; a decentralized institutional setting, with many of the norms and structures that formerly ordered behavior in a weakened state; particularistic pulls from constituency groups and PACs, increasingly unmediated by party; increased opportunities for electoral and policy entrepreneurship, but in a volatile environment that requires constant attention and offers few reliable mechanisms of support; weakened inducements to committee or party solidarity or to institutional patriotism. There is indeed much that is new about this Congress, much that alters the incentives and opportunities, vulnerabilities and constraints facing individual members, and much that alters Congress's proclivities and capacities as a policy-making institution.

Here I consider these developments by reflecting on the ethical dilemmas they pose for the responsible legislator. I do not assume that it is possible or desirable for politicians to eschew the profit-and-loss calculations related to the maintenance of their electoral viability or to the preservation of their power base within the institution. I do assume, however, that a broad range of legislative strategies and involvements are compatible with, and indeed can be supportive of, self-interest in these senses. Agonizing choices must sometimes be made. But most members of Congress, most of the time, have a great deal of latitude as to how they define their roles and what kind of job they wish to do. If they do not have the latitude they can often create it, for they have a great deal of control over how their actions are perceived and interpreted. I thus conceive of these ethical dilemmas as choices a politician makes *within* the bounds of political "necessity."

1. *To what range of values and interests should I be responsive?* It is

---

[15] See David E. Price, "Congressional Committees in the Policy Process," in *Congress Reconsidered,* ed. by Dodd and Oppenheimer, 3rd ed. (1985), chap. 7.

tempting to believe that one is being properly representative and responsive if one gives a respectful hearing to those groups that present themselves on a given issue and then reaches a reasonable accommodation among them. Congressman Timothy Wirth (Democrat, Colorado) has taken this logic a step further, suggesting that taking contributions from the communications groups over which his subcommittee has jurisdiction is unlikely to compromise him because of the plurality of these groups and the disagreements they have among themselves: "The telecommunications types have all kind of different interests, and they're a diverse group."[16] It is a common and all too convenient assumption that fairness or even "neutrality" consists of being an honest broker among such contending interests. Such an assumption, of course, finds some support within the pluralist school of political science. Cannot we expect the most directly affected and intensely interested groups to make their voices heard on a given matter? "Normally," Braybrooke and Lindblom write, "people are not slow to protest when a policy looks like worsening their condition."[17] Politicians, such analysts conclude, will generally feel constrained to be attentive to such groups and to strike some sort of balance among them. Perhaps that is an acceptable operationalization of representative government under contemporary conditions.

But perhaps not. A number of analysts have argued persuasively that the politically active organizations or constituencies prepared to press their views on a given question are likely to be a highly selective sample of those whose interests and values are affected.[18] One cannot assume that all affected interests will find ready access to the political arena. Some lack the organizational or other resources to make their voices heard. Others may be frozen out by virtue of the ties that exist between dominant groups and clientele-oriented committees and agencies. And broader and more diffuse interests will generally have more difficulty mobilizing their constituencies and developing effective organizational structures than will those more narrowly based interests whose stakes are more immediate and tangible.

A responsible legislator will take the initiative in looking to those

---

[16] Quoted in Elizabeth Drew, "Politics and Money," Part I, *The New Yorker,* 6 December 1982, p. 127.

[17] David Braybrooke and Charles E. Lindblom, *A Strategy of Decision* (New York: Free Press, 1963), pp. 185–86.

[18] See, for example, E. E. Schattschneider, *The Semi-Sovereign People* (New York: Holt, Rinehart and Winston, 1960), chapter 2; Theodore J. Lowi, *The End of Liberalism* (2nd ed. ; NewYork: W. W. Norton, 1979), chap. 3; Robert Paul Wolff, *The Poverty of Liberalism* (Boston: Beacon Press, 1968), chap. 4; and Mancur Olson, Jr., *The Logic of Collective Action* (New York: Schocken Books, 1968), chap. 5.

poorly organized or deviant interests that the system might exclude, and to broad, shared public interests which are inadequately mirrored in the "pressure system." Many of the developments we have surveyed promote an uncritical particularism: the fragmentation and clientele orientations of subcommittees, the increased campaign role of PACs, the decline of parties as institutions mediating between organized interests and public officeholders. But taking a broader view of one's representative role need not be seen as self-sacrificial behavior, at least most of the time. Legislators often find it politically profitable to cultivate new constituencies, or to appeal over the heads of contending groups to a broader public concerned with one issue or another. Such strategies do not succeed automatically: legislators must *work* at increasing the salience and attractiveness of their policy stances. To transcend the "brokering" role and to make such moves politically viable and attractive to their colleagues, members must shore up supportive groups, cultivate the media, and otherwise attempt to "broaden the *scope* of conflict."[19]

Responsible representation does not require a dark view of any and all collaboration with "the interests." But neither does it permit a sanguine view of representation as a mere balancing of pressures, or an expectation that the competition of the interests organized and active in a given area will insure an equitable outcome. It is important to take account of the biases and exclusions of the group system and to face environmental pressures toward particularistic accommodation with a degree of scepticism and fortitude.

2. *To what extent and in what fashion will I contribute to the work of the legislature?* Members of the modern Congress, it has often been noted, are very thinly spread, a condition substantially worsened by the proliferation of subcommittees and the escalating demands of electoral entrepreneurship. The institution suffers, however, not simply from the overextension of its members, but from the erosion of the inducements to engage seriously in the *work* of Congress. Pulling one's weight in committee and developing a substantial area of expertise are still serviceable strategies for members who would gain the esteem of their colleagues. But the weakening of the norms of apprenticeship and specialization, together with the pressures for self-promotion created by the new electoral environment, have made showhorse behavior more profitable and less costly than it was in the past.[20] Members have stronger incentives

---

[19] The phrase is Schattschneider's; see *Semi-Sovereign People,* chaps. 1–2.

[20] For an attempt to operationalize the showhorse–workhorse typologies and to discuss the conditions of their occurrence, see James L. Payne, "Show Horses and Work Horses in the United States House of Representatives," *Polity* 12 (Spring 1980),428–56. Payne finds

to latch onto a piece of policy "turf," to gain control of a subcommittee, and to cultivate an image of policy leadership. But their incentives to engage in the painstaking work of legislative craftsmanship, coalition building, and mobilization may actually be weaker. Such activities are more difficult under conditions of organizational fragmentation, and the pressures to do one's homework are less compelling. Moreover, as Mayhew stresses, the electoral payoffs for merely taking a position or introducing a bill may be just as great as those that reward more extensive or conscientious efforts:

> When will [members of Congress make a concerted effort to] mobilize? They will do so when somebody of consequence is watching, when there is credit to be gained for legislative maneuvers. The most alert watchers are doubtless representatives of attentive interest groups. . . .They may be able to detect whether or not a congressman can "deliver". . . .Yet scrutiny has it limits. On matters where the audience for congressmen's activities is not a closely scrutinizing one, the incentive to mobilize diminishes. Mobilization, after all, requires time and energy; it may require the trading away of valued goods. Congressmen always have other things to do—such as making speeches, meeting constituents, looking into casework. To put too much into mobilization would be to misallocate resources. For members who make the motions or [introduce] the bills there may be a value in winning, but how much of a value? A congressman can hardly be blamed if there are not enough right-thinking members around him to carry his motions. He's fighting the good fight. . . .Would Senators Hatfield and McGovern have been any the more esteemed by their followers if their antiwar amendment had won rather than lost?[21]

Part of the problem is the dimensions that political self-promotion has assumed in the modern Congress: members are more and more distracted personally (the average House member now goes home three weekends out of four) and the bulk of the new staff and other resources that members have voted themselves have gone into constituent communication and services. This is not to say that casework and the legislator's ombudsman role are unimportant. Indeed, as Fenno argues, the member's multifaceted interactions with his constituents—communicating, explaining, assisting, responding—may be more important to their sense that he represents them than any simple congruence between his and their

---

that the orientations are indeed distinctive, with few members ranking high on both "legislative work" and "publicity" indices. He also finds evidence that "being a show horse pays off electorally," and is far less costly than it once was in terms of advancement within the House.

[21] Mayhew, *Electoral Connection*, pp. 115–17.

policy views. Moreover, time spent at home and otherwise cultivating constituent relations can be crucial in giving the member the kind of leeway he needs for flexible and cooperative legislative activity.[22] But alterations in both the electoral environment and the congressional ethos have made it thinkable, perhaps even profitable, for a number of members to engage almost exclusively in constituency-cultivating activities to the detriment of Congress's legislative and oversight tasks. And even when members do turn their attention to policy, their involvement is too often superficial and fleeting.

This sort of "position-taking" can be just as deceptive and manipulative as other forms of self-promotion. "Appearing to do something about policy without a serious intention of, or demonstrable capacity for, doing so," as Fenno stresses, "is a corruption of the representative relationship."[23] And of course such behavior robs the legislative institution of the energy and persistence needed to make it work, at precisely the time when the tasks of coalition building and mobilization have become appreciably more difficult. Dedicated and skilled legislators are still to be found in Congress, and some have managed to make of their legislative power and productivity a substantial electoral asset. The institution still depends on members' assuming such roles and adopting such priorities, but this behavior is more dependent on the choices and proclivities of the members themselves and less on institutional pressures and constraints than was formerly the case.

3. *What responsibilities do I bear for the functioning of the committee and party systems?* "Public duty," wrote Edmund Burke, "demands and requires that what is right should not only be made known, but made prevalent; that what is evil should not only be detected, but defeated":

> When a public man omits to put himself in a situation of doing his duty *with effect,* it is an omission that frustrates the purposes of his trust almost as much as if he had formally betrayed it.

Such a demand for seriousness of purpose speaks directly, of course, to the superficial and symbolic gestures that too often pass for policy making in the contemporary Congress. But what Burke specifically had in mind was the need for members of parliament to associate, to cooperate under the standard of a party:

> No man, who is not inflamed by vain-glory into enthusiasm, can flatter himself that his single, unsupported, desulatory, unsystematic endeavors, are of

---

[22] Richard F. Fenno, Jr., *Home Style: House Members in Their Districts* (Boston: Little, Brown, 1978), pp. 240–44.

[23] Ibid., p. 243.

power to defeat the subtle designs and united cabals of ambitious citizens. When bad men combine, the good must associate; else they will fall, one by one, an unpitied sacrifice in a contemptible struggle.[24]

Public duty, Burke argued, gives powerful ethical support to party fidelity. He was profoundly skeptical of the tendency of politicians to tout their own independence or to portray themselves as motivated by conscience; too often, he suspected, this was a cover for the pursuit of private advantage. Party operations, Burke believed, could and should leave room for occasional dissent, but the desire for concord and for effectiveness would properly nudge fellow-partisans toward agreement:

When the question is in its nature doubtful, or not very material, the modesty which becomes an individual and that partiality which becomes a well-chosen friendship, will frequently bring on an acquiescence in the general sentiment. Thus the disagreement will naturally be rare; it will be only enough to indulge freedom, without violating concord, or disturbing arrangement.[25]

Such a view, of course, squares imperfectly with the individualistic notions of moral autonomy to which Americans typically repair. Former Senator Jacob Javits no doubt anticipates his readers' applause as he declares: "In this clash of loyalties—loyalty to constituents, loyalty to party, and loyalty to myself—my constituents and I had to prevail."[26] But we should beware of imputing ethical superiority to the "loner." If the committees and the parties play a legitimate and necessary role in developing and refining measures, in aggregating interests, in mobilizing the chamber, should not there be a burden of proof on the member who would violate the comity and the discipline necessary to their successful functioning? This is neither to endorse mindless party regularity nor to deny that members should sometime resolve conflicts with party or committee solidarity in favor of personal convictions regarding constituency interests or the public good. But such choices should be difficult and not arrived at lightly.

Party voting has displayed a long-term decline in both houses over the course of this century, although in recent years the decline has leveled off and the average member's party-support score has slightly increased.[27] For this, the increased role of the Republican party in recruiting and

[24] Edmund Burke, "Thoughts on the Cause of the Present Discontents," in *Works* (London: George Bell and Sons, 1893), I, pp. 372–73. Emphasis added.

[25] Ibid., p. 378.

[26] Jacob K. Javits, *Javits: The Autobiography of a Public Man* (Boston: Houghton Mifflin, 1981), p. 134.

[27] See David E. Price, *Bringing Back the Parties* (Washington, D.C.: Congressional Quarterly Press, 1984), pp. 51–57.

supporting candidates may bear some responsibility, as may various measures that have enhanced the role of the House leadership. But neither constituency nor chamber pressures constrain most members to support or work within the party; how closely they do so is largely a matter of individual choice. The same is increasingly true of work on committees, most of which have seen their ability to maintain a united front on the floor and to command the deference of the parent chamber decline. Although many members may welcome the reduced hold of these systems on them, they also have reason to reflect on the price the *institution* has paid in its reduced capacity to act in an orderly and concerted fashion. It will not do simply to revel in one's status as a free agent; an adequate ethic will give substantial weight to the need to maintain mechanisms of *collective* action and responsibility.

4. *How should I present myself in relation to the legislature's practices and performance?* Every member of Congress, former Congressman Bob Eckhardt (Democrat, Texas) suggests, performs three functions: lawmaker, ombudsman, and educator.[28] This latter function, as we have seen, may be closely related to the first: any lawmaker who wishes to do more than simply defer to the strongest and best-organized interests on a given matter must give some attention to explaining his actions and educating his constituents, helping them place the issue in broader perspective or perhaps activating alternative bases of support. The extent to which a member is willing and able to undertake such explanations, I have suggested, is ethically as well as politically significant.[29]

Here I turn to another facet of the legislator's educative role: his portrayal of Congress itself. Richard Fenno describes as his greatest surprise, upon traveling with House members around their districts, the extent to which each one "polished his or her individual reputation at the expense of the institutional reputation of Congress":

> In explaining what he was doing in Washington, every one of the eighteen House members took the opportunity to picture himself as different from, and better than, most of his fellow members in Congress. None availed himself of the opportunity to educate his constituents about Congress as an institution— not in any way that would "hurt a little." To the contrary, the members'

---

[28] Norman J. Ornstein, ed., *The Role of the Legislature in Western Democracies* (Washington, D.C.: American Enterprise Institute, 1981), pp. 96–97.

[29] For discussions of various techniques—and difficulties—of "explanation," see John W. Kingdon, *Congressmen's Voting Decisions* (2nd ed.; New York: Harper & Row, 1981), pp. 47–54; and Fenno, *Home Style,* chap. 5.

process of differentiating themselves from the Congress as a whole only served, directly or indirectly, to downgrade the Congress.

"We have to differentiate me from the rest of those bandits down there in Congress," Fenno heard a member say to a campaign strategy group. " 'They are awful, but our guy is wonderful'—that's the message we have to get across."[30]

So much for the norm of institutional patriotism! Opinion polls regularly reveal Congress to be among the lowest-ranking American institutions in the public's esteem, an evaluation not unrelated to the ethical and structural failings we have already described: individual grandstanding, particularism, obstruction, and deadlock. Every indication is that members then compound the problem by distancing themselves from any responsibility for the institution's functioning. And they are phenomenally successful, matching the 10 percent approval rating for Congress with a 90 percent reelection rate for themselves.

The point is not that a member should defend whatever the legislature does. But it is deceptive and irresponsible perpetually to play the outsider, carping at accommodations reached as though problems could simply be ignored, costless solutions devised, or the painful necessities of compromise avoided. The responsible legislator will communicate to his constituency not only the assembly's failings, but also what it is fair and reasonable to expect, what accommodations they would be well-advised to accept, and so forth. In the past, institutional patriotism has too often taken an uncritical form, assuming that whatever the process produces must be acceptable. But self-righteous, anti-institutional posturing is no better. The moral quixotism to which reelection-minded legislators are increasingly prone too often serves to rationalize nonproductive legislative roles and to perpetuate public misperceptions of the criteria it is reasonable to apply to legislative performance.

Thus, although it may be politically profitable to "run *for* Congress by running *against* Congress," the implications for the institution's effectiveness and legitimacy are ominous. As Fenno concludes,

> The strategy is ubiquitous, addictive, cost-free, and foolproof. . . .In the short run, everybody plays and nearly everybody wins. Yet the institution bleeds from 435 separate cuts. In the long run, therefore, somebody may lose. . . .Congress may lack public support at the very time when the public needs Congress the most.[31]

---

[30] Ibid., pp. 164, 166.
[31] Ibid., pp. 168, 246.

LEGISLATIVE STRUCTURES AND LEGISLATIVE ETHICS

Although the American founders regarded public virtue, a willingness to forego private advantage for the sake of the commonwealth, as essential to the health of the new republic, they were unwilling to trust human nature to its own devices. On the contrary: government must be *structured* in such a way, not only to anticipate self-serving behavior but to turn it to good account. "Ambition must be made to counteract ambition," wrote James Madison in *The Federalist* (no. 51).

> This policy of supplying, by opposite and rival interests, the defect of better motives. . .[is] particularly displayed in all the subordinate distributions of power, where the constant aim is to divide and arrange the several offices in such a manner as that each may be a check on the other—that the private interest of every individual may be a sentinel over the public rights.

It can be argued, analogously, that certain of Congress's organizational features have structured the pursuit of political advantage and turned it to the institution's account. The committee system, for example, accommodates the aspirations of disparate members but also represents a corrective of sorts to congressional individualism—a means of bringing expertise and attention to bear on the legislature's tasks in a more concerted fashion than the free enterprise of individual members could accomplish. The committee system channels members' desires for leverage and status into activity that serves the *institution's* needs and builds its policymaking capacities.

Such an institutional-maintenance function is even more obvious in the case of Congress' powerful "control committees"—Appropriations, Ways and Means, and, now, Budget—and the party leadership. Mayhew argues that the willingness of members to defer to these control mechanisms and to reward those who operate them with power and prestige can be understood as the "purchase" of a collective good—the preservation of the institution against the consequences to which unchecked individualism and particularism could otherwise lead.[32] But members do not make these calculations in a vacuum; they come into an institution where these structures and the norms and patterns of authority that support them are already in place. If members are to function effectively they must, to a significant degree, honor these patterns and direct their own initiatives through approved channels.

It is important to subject such institutional structures and norms to ethical scrutiny. Despite Madison's expectation that the checking and

---

[32] Mayhew, *Electoral Connection*, pp. 141–58; see also Price, "Congressional Committees," pp. 170–75.

balancing of power would protect the public interest, we know that in fact the constitutional system has historically given advantages to certain types of interests at the expense of others. Similarly, the norms and structures that gave inordinate power to Congress's committee chairmen in the 1950s had a distinctive policy impact, inhibiting overdue changes in civil rights and other areas. As Roger Davidson argues in Chapter 6, that period's folkways were "promulgated by, and served the interests of, the conservative coalition that ran the chamber during the 1950s." There were powerful ethical arguments for modifying this particular pattern of institutional maintenance. I do not mean to suggest that the directions in which Congress has moved and the policies it has adopted in the ensuing years represent some sort of ethical decline. Indeed, the contrary case could convincingly be made.

What I do mean to suggest, however, is that congressional behavior has become less structurally and normatively constrained in the past twenty-five years, and that this loosening, rooted mainly in the electoral incentives facing individual members, poses serious problems for the functioning of Congress as an institution. Both Congress's capacity to produce coherent policy and the quality of its policy product are at stake.

These dilemmas demand renewed attention to congressional organization and structure. Of particular importance are current efforts to strengthen party organs and to devise a budget process that facilitates policy coherence and control without completely submerging the representative and innovative capacities of the committee system. But the strengthening of the structures and norms by which the legislature "supplies the defect of better motives" and protects its institutional capacities will not gainsay the need for individual responsibility.

In examining Senate policy making in the 1960s, and particularly in attempting to account for the emerging phenomenon of "policy entrepreneurship," I recognized the necessity of incorporating individual purposes and values into any adequate account of legislative behavior.[33] That necessity is even more apparent today. In the new Congress members increasingly find themselves on their own—in dealing with the pressures and pulls of particularism, in deciding what kind of contribution they will make to the work of the legislature, in making the party and committee systems work, and in shaping citizen perceptions and evaluations of the institution. Such dilemmas will continue to be central to legislative life, questions of value which members cannot help addressing in one way or another. How they deal with them will decisively shape the capacity of Congress for leadership and the quality of its performance.

[33] Price, *Who Makes the Laws?*, pp. 306–11.

III

TOWARD A NEW FRAMEWORK FOR LEGISLATIVE ETHICS
THEORY AND PRACTICE

8

Legislative Ethics and Moral Minimalism

BRUCE JENNINGS

The last decade has been marked by a growing concern with ethical issues in American society. In a host of public policy decisions—environmental protection, affirmative action, abortion, busing, foreign aid, and more—the moral and social values at stake have been identified and debated. Across the broad spectrum of the professions—from business and engineering to law and social work—there has been a renewed awareness of the complex moral dilemmas and hard choices that abound in professional life. Concomitantly, many philosophers, political theorists, and other scholars have turned their attention to the study of "applied ethics" in an attempt to bring various normative theories of ethics and politics to bear on these practical social issues.

Thus far in the study of government ethics (one branch of applied and professional ethics), the moral responsibilities of public administrators, policy makers, and civil servants have received the most concerted attention, whereas legislative ethics has been relatively neglected.[1] This is unfortunate because legislative representatives play a unique role in our constitutional system. Legislators have special ethical obligations, which should be given careful, systematic analysis in their own right.

As the study of legislative ethics develops, it will be necessary to mark out its appropriate boundaries and scope and to reflect upon the

[1] Cf. Joel Fleishman, Lance Liebman, and Mark H. Moore (eds.), *Public Duties: The Moral Obligations of Government Officials* (Cambridge,Mass.: Harvard University Press,1981); and Peter A. French, *Ethics in Government* (Englewood Cliffs, N.J.:Prentice-Hall,1983).

BRUCE JENNINGS ● The Hastings Center, Hastings-on-Hudson, New York 10706.

broader intellectual and civic purposes that may be served by this mode of analysis. New fields have a way of developing their own internal research programs and agendas, of course, and it is pointless to attempt to stipulate these in advance. But it is not too early to raise general questions about the scope and purpose of legislative ethics—in part because the field has already shown a tendency to concentrate on fairly narrow issues and in part because legislative ethics raises important background questions concerning the theory and practice of legislative representation. These questions must be addressed before the study of legislative ethics can develop a firm sense of its own proper direction.

Accordingly, in this essay I propose to set out and analyze what I take to be the most important critical questions that have been and should be raised about the scope, goals, and effects of the study of legislative ethics. The way these questions are answered will ultimately affect both the content of legislative ethics—that is, the range of issues it discusses, the types of ethical principles it invokes, the modes of legislative conduct it prescribes and proscribes—and the relationship between the theory of legislative ethics and its practice, including particular ethics regulations and reforms in Congress and the state legislatures.

TOWARD A BROAD CONCEPTION OF LEGISLATIVE ETHICS

In American political thought there is a long-standing tradition of ethical norms surrounding governmental service. Notions such as the pursuit of the public interest, the exercise of a morally and legally obligatory public trust, and democratic accountability have always informed our expectations about the proper use of governmental authority and power by our elected and appointed public servants. In the last few years, however, a distressing series of scandals—Watergate, Koreagate, Abscam—involving the abuse of authority and the misuse of office for personal financial gain have abruptly brought these notions out of the textbooks and into the headlines. The ensuing public debate has been anguished and tangled enough to show that, as a citizenry, we are more than a little uncertain about the proper function and scope of ethical standards in political life. Our traditional canons of political ethics seem rusty from lack of use and require substantial elaboration and clarification if they are to serve as effective directives for the conduct of public officials facing new kinds of institutional, electoral, and ideological pressures. At the same time, current public attitudes about standards of political ethics are inconsistent and extremely volatile, oscillating between cynicism and moral outrage.

Scandals and persistent evidence of declining public confidence have provoked governmental institutions at both the federal and state level to set up a variety of new ethics laws, codes, and enforcement mechanisms. In the last few years, for example, approximately thirty states have passed new conflict of interest or financial disclosure requirements and have established ethics committees or commissions to oversee and enforce them. At the federal level the Ethics in Government Act of 1978 imposed a variety of new restrictions and requirements on certain classes of government employees, with a special emphasis on high-level officials of the executive branch. In 1977, the House and the Senate addressed some of the special problems of legislative ethics by adopting new codes of conduct for members and staff and by establishing permanent ethics committees.[2]

In the debates surrounding these new ethics codes and enforcement procedures, the scope of legislative ethics has been very narrowly defined. Financial disclosure and conflict of interest are virtually the only issues given much attention in these discussions, and the prohibition against the use of office for personal financial gain is the only ethical principle that has been clearly defined.

But surely there is more—much more—to legislative ethics than that. To limit our ethical concern to matters of financial misconduct is to blind ourselves morally to richer and more nuanced traditional understandings of political corruption. Without a broader perspective on legislative ethics, we shall fail to see the moral significance of the myriad pressures and influences in the ordinary course of legislative life that tend to subordinate the good of the political community as a whole to the private interests of particular groups. These pressures are ever present and systemic; they stand on a different level from intermittent scandals like Koreagate or Abscam, and they are woven much more deeply into the fabric of legislative politics than is the venal financial misconduct that has received so much attention lately. Finding the moral thread that ultimately holds that fabric together despite those pressures requires a more complete theory of legislative ethics than the reformers of the 1970s have given us.

Taking a broader view of the ethical duties of legislators in a democratic society quickly shows us a legislative world filled with difficult choices and tensions between ethical duty and political self-interest. For example, if (as Amy Gutmann and Dennis Thompson argue in Chapter 9[3])

---

[2] For a detailed account of these reforms, see Congressional Quarterly, Inc., *Congressional Ethics* (2nd ed.; Washington: Congressional Quarterly, 1980).

[3] "A Theory of Legislative Ethics," Chapter 9 of this volume. For further discussion of

legislators have a duty to be autonomous, accountable, and responsible, then many routine facets of legislative conduct must come under closer ethical scrutiny. An autonomous legislator is one who does not permit any particular interest group unduly to influence his or her judgment on policy issues, and who takes special care to attend to the needs and interests of relatively powerless and voiceless constituents. From this point of view, the ways in which legislators spend their time, grant access, and make contacts with constituents become significant ethical as well as political issues. Similarly, an accountable legislator is one who provides constituents with the information and understanding they need in order to fulfill their obligations as democratic citizens. A responsible legislator is one who works to enhance the proper functioning of legislative institutions and the legislative process. These considerations, in turn, raise serious ethical questions about the failure of legislators to serve as political educators and to deepen their constituents' understanding of the merits of policy issues and of the strengths, as well as the shortcomings, of the legislative process. For example, nearly all legislators at one time or another indulge in the political expediency of "running for the legislature by running against the legislature." Few, however, seem to perceive that they are violating important ethical duties and eroding the democratic legitimacy of our legislative system by doing so.[4]

Considerations of this sort provide a relatively straightforward rationale for analyzing a very wide range of legislative and representational activity from a moral point of view. But, arguably, these considerations alone are not sufficient to demonstrate the value of a mode of inquiry designed to get legislators to interpret their own activities in moral terms and to take moral principles (and the specific obligations derived from those principles) seriously in their decision making.

Hence, because it so directly involves the interconnection between moral and political imperatives, legislative ethics remains a problematic subject, continually in need of reassessment and defense. This is not due merely to the fact that substantive ethical claims made about legislative and representational activity are (as the philosophers say) "essentially contestable," for claims made in all other areas of moral and political

---

these principles see *The Ethics of Legislative Life: A Report by The Hastings Center* (Hastings-on-Hudson, N.Y.: The Hastings Center, 1985).

[4] Cf. Richard E. Fenno, Jr., *Home Style: House Members in Their Districts* (Boston: Little, Brown, 1978), pp. 168, 244–247. For further discussion of the legislator's moral responsibility to the legislature as an institution, see David E. Price, "Legislative Ethics in the New Congress," chap. 7 of this volume.

discourse have this feature as well.[5] Of course, there are no definitive answers to many of the moral and political questions raised by legislative ethics but that does not mean that reasonable discussion and analysis of these issues is impossible.

Nor do the difficulties we face in getting a handle on legislative ethics come solely from the fact that we lack any universally accepted, overarching theory of good and right conduct in general from which specific ethical judgments about legislative conduct could be derived. For again, experience drawn from other areas of moral and political discourse indicates that substantial progress can be made toward clarifying concrete ethical issues and establishing standards for practical decision making, even though many conceptual and philosophical problems remain unresolved at the level of normative ethical theory.[6] Rather, the problematic nature of the study of legislative ethics comes from the peculiar nature of legislative activity in our political system, the functions that system calls upon legislators to perform, and the widely held belief—among many political scientists, journalists, and legislators themselves—that the effective, and indeed the democratically proper, functioning of legislative politics requires what I shall call a "moral minimalism" vis-à-vis the demands that citizens place upon their legislative representatives, and vis-à-vis the demands legislators place upon themselves. These factors have led many to conclude that ethical analysis should be limited to a fairly narrow range of legislative conduct and that a hard and fast line should be drawn between those areas of legislative behavior to which moral considerations of obligations, virtue, and principle properly apply and those areas where non-moral considerations of political self-interest and prudence must hold sway.

---

[5] For a discussion of essentially contestable concepts see William Connolly, *The Terms of Political Discourse* (2nd ed.; Princeton: Princeton University Press, 1983).

[6] In saying this, however, I do not mean to suggest that legislative ethics is an autonomous domain of inquiry, wholly divorced from more general modes of moral and political theory. On the contrary, as I shall argue at various points throughout this chapter, many of the substantive claims one makes about the ethical responsibilities of legislators do depend upon a more general understanding of what a legislature should and can do, the legislature's proper function in the political system, and the legislator's proper role in the process of liberal democratic governance. All I want to suggest here is that a serious analysis of legislative ethics need not be postponed until these more general normative questions have been settled independently. Indeed, the study of legislative ethics can incorporate these questions and press the discussion of them forward in new ways. In the end, I would hope that stimulating a more widespread public conversation about the ethical responsibilities of representative legislators would lead to an even more thoroughgoing conversation about the public purposes of representative government itself and about the capacity of our existing institutional structures to embody those purposes.

LEGISLATIVE ETHICS AND ITS DANGERS:
THE CASE FOR MORAL MINIMALISM

The problem of the scope of legislative ethics, as I am construing it here, involves this distinction. Where should the line between moral principle and political prudence be drawn? Broadening the scope of legislative ethics involves asking ethical questions about—and requiring ethical justifications or excuses for—many aspects of legislative conduct and decision making that are now analyzed largely in nonmoral terms.[7] Resistance to this and the strong impulse to maintain the status quo division of labor between moral and nonmoral discourse (or to alter it very gingerly at the margins) are rooted in the fear that systematically injecting explicit ethical considerations into public discourse about legislative activity—supplementing our usual idiom of political interest, power, and advantage with an idiom of moral obligation, principles, and responsibilities—would not benefit either legislators or society as a whole.

These fears, and their backlash against the wide-ranging application of ethical analysis in political contexts, were forcefully expressed in a recent *Wall Street Journal* editorial:

> We are going to have to kill ethics before ethics kills us. . . .We seem to have invented a new form of government. Probably it should be called government by character assassination. Policy debates are won or lost not by besting your opponent on the merits, but by suggesting he has done something unethical. Once the ethical issue is raised, everything else stops until the last entrail of morality has been examined. . . .It is as deluding and as self-destructive as any other obsession, and we risk going down in history as the first civilization to strangle itself in a frenzy of ethics. . . .The point is that there's a kind of ethical absolutism that no human and no human institution can sustain. It's not necessary to abandon ethics to recognize that the real world will always be full of cut corners and uneasy compromises. If you set out to destroy a person or cripple an institution by dredging up every possible ethical question, you will always be able to find ammunition. Yet this kind of assault has become the common coin of our discourse. . . .At some point the untrammeled pursuit of virtue becomes irresponsible. . . .This is something we need to think about.[8]

Now, it is not difficult to point out the confusions and slippery logic that abound in this commentary:

First, legislative ethics need not be absolutist in either theory or

---

[7] "Model Code of Ethics for the United States Senate," *Hastings Center Report*, Special Supplement, Vol. II, No. 1 (February 1981), pp. 19–27.

[8] "Ethicsgate," *Wall Street Journal*, 15 July 1983, p. 26.

practice; on the contrary, the carefully reasoned weighing and balancing of conflicting principles and obligations are its primary concerns.

Second, ethical considerations need not detract from attention to the merits of political debates; on the contrary, ethical notions are inherently involved, explicitly or implicitly, in our basic judgments about what those merits are in the first place.

Finally, one need not defend the partisan or ideological misuse of ethical argument in order to conclude that ethics has an important and necessary place in our public discourse about legislators and legislative politics. Indeed, strengthening the analytic capacity of legislators and their constituents to reason clearly about ethical issues is the best way—perhaps the only way—we have of protecting our political institutions against sophistry, character assassination, and hypocritical moralism. The *Wall Street Journal's* worries about the latter are certainly well founded, but its case against ethics, and *mutatis mutandis* against broadening the scope of legislative ethics, suffers from its inability to distinguish between moral sophistry and genuine ethical analysis. If moral talk by and about legislators is used deceptively to conceal less noble motives and purposes, then we surely need more, not less, systematic analysis and criticism in the area of legislative ethics so that we can better detect phony and inconsistent ethical arguments when they are made.

However, if views such as those expressed in this editorial fail to make a convincing case against broadening the study of legislative ethics, they nonetheless deserve to be taken seriously for at least two reasons: first, they can serve to remind us that injecting ethical analysis does make a difference in politics. Moreover, underlying these worries about expanding the scope of legislative ethics there is a more complex, theoretical argument for moral minimalism in legislative ethics.

Those who are wary of applying ethical analysis in legislative or other political contexts are correct in their (somewhat jaundiced) perception that ethics does make a difference in politics. Too often in the past, those who have promoted applied ethics in professional settings have tried to make the enterprise seem as nonthreatening as possible by contending that ethical analysis merely provides a technique for clarifying previously held implicit values or "intuitions," and a set of conceptual tools and skills that is itself "value-neutral" in the sense that it is compatible with a comfortable plurality of different moral beliefs and attitudes. Critics have been quick to point out the problems contained in this peculiar notion of value-free ethics.[9]

[9] Cf. Mark T. Lilla, "Ethos, 'Ethics,' and Public Service," *The Public Interest,* No. 63

The future study of legislative ethics must start with a clear acknowl-edgment that the moral arguments and the moral convictions engendered by those arguments do not leave the world just as it is. Injecting moral discourse into a complex social practice like doctoring or lawyering or legislating and representing has important consequences for that practice: it restructures perceptions, limits defensible options, and imposes new burdens of self-explanation and self-justification on practitioners. In the long run it can change the way a practice and practitioners are evaluated and the public demands that are placed upon them. Even though, as I argued above, ethical analysis need not and usually does not involve the assertion of absolutist principles or obligations, it does place a strain on institutions by supplementing—and often challenging—their customary norms, internal idioms, and ethos. As Max Weber, a much more powerful and nuanced critic of political ethics than the editorial writer quoted above, aptly put it, a commitment to moral principle is not "a cab, which one can have stopped at one's pleasure."[10] In political life, moral discourse competes with other languages of interpretation and self-understanding that political agents frequently employ; in particular, it trumps considerations of expediency, strategic or partisan advantage, and political self-interest. In American legislative life, there is no gainsaying the fact that moral discourse—I mean rigorous ethical argumentation, not moralistic rhetoric—would be a new, and in many ways disruptive, guest at the table.

This brings me to the second reason why those who resist broadening the scope of legislative ethics are indeed on to something that we as a society need to think about. If moral discourse does compete with alternative conceptual schemes in political, and especially legislative, life, then it is not self-evident that the moral point of view is always and everywhere the most valuable and beneficial perspective for political agents to adopt.

It is no accident that explicitly moral concerns do not occupy a primary place in the everyday self-consciousness of legislators, for traditional theories of representative democracy have taught our political culture to understand politics in terms of power, competition, and struggle. Increasingly in the twentieth century we have adapted our political concepts and imagery to a system of "adversary democracy" in

---

(Spring 1981), pp. 3–17; J. Peter Euben, "Philosophy and the Professions," *democracy*, Vol. 1, No. 2 (April 1981), pp. 112–127; and Arthur L. Caplan, "Mechanics on Duty: The Limitations of a Technical Definition or Moral Expertise for Work in Applied Ethics," *Canadian Journal of Philosophy*, Supplementary Volume VIII (1982), 1–18.

[10] Max Weber, "Politics as a Vocation," in *From Max Weber: Essays in Sociology*, ed. by H. H. Gerth and C. Wright Mills (New York: Oxford University Press, 1958), p. 119.

which the role of the individual legislator is to compete with other legislators on behalf of the particular interests of his or her constituency.[11] In this view, the legislative process becomes a microcosm reflecting the economic, social, and ideological cleavages of society as a whole. It is an arena wherein political advocates strategically compete within a minimal structure of rules, rather than a forum in which political representatives assemble to deliberate cooperatively in pursuit of a common social good.

The language of moral obligation fits uneasily in the general conception of adversarial legislative politics, for it betokens a more constrained legislative space, one in which the imperatives of competive advantage and political prudence so essential to adversarial representation—pass the bill, strike a deal, deliver the goods, cultivate the right image, get reelected—are hemmed in by moral imperatives of a more general and fundamental nature. If considerations of moral duty retain a place in this conception of legislative representation at all, they do so only as a reminder that the legislative advocate's primary responsibility is to win on behalf of his constituents. T. V. Smith, a philosopher and former legislator, articulated this position clearly:

> The legislature itself is a problem-solving place where men (and women) gather who owe little to one another but much to persons not there—persons, indeed, who seldom come there. We legislators owe only deference to one another, but both duty and victory to constituents back home.[12]

If we pursue the logic of this conception of the legislator's duty, we quickly arrive at the position I have referred to as moral minimalism.

A CRITIQUE OF MORAL MINIMALISM IN LEGISLATIVE ETHICS

We are now in a position to reconstruct the argument of moral minimalism and to formulate it in its most general and strongest form. Broadly stated, the argument goes something like this:

> Those who advocate broadening the scope of legislative ethics contend that the ultimate goal of a broad-ranging study of legislative ethics is to formulate specific moral ideals and principles to govern the institutionalized practice of legislative representation. It aims to

---

[11] Jane J. Mansbridge, "Living with Conflict: Representation in the Theory of Adversary Democracy," *Ethics*, Vol. 91, No. 3 (April 1981), pp. 466–476.

[12] *The Legislative Way of Life* (Chicago: University of Chicago Press, 1941), p. 4, quoted in Roger H. Davidson, *The Role of the Congressman* (New York: Pegasus, 1969), p. 27.

stimulate a public conversation about these ideals and principles—a conversation that will eventually move us toward a new civic consensus regarding the norms of politically acceptable conduct—and it encourages opinion makers, journalists, citizens, and legislators themselves to evaluate legislative conduct and decision making in moral terms. But if these goals were realized, they would alter our political culture in ways that would make it harder rather than easier for democratic legislators to represent their constituents responsibly. And they would undermine the effective functioning of the legislative process, making it harder rather than easier for legislative assemblies to construct programs of governance that could work in our highly complex, interdependent, and pluralistic society.

Expanding the scope of legislative ethics would dangerously blur an important boundary line between the realm of "ethics" and the realm of "politics." That fragile boundary line has been established with considerable difficulty during the course of American political history in order to preserve an ethically unemcumbered legislative space within which political representatives can engage in the prudential, instrumental give-and-take of bargaining, compromise, and coalition building. Ethical encroachment on that space must be minimal and limited to matters directly related to the prohibition on the use of office for personal financial gain. Beyond that, the democratic legislator's only responsibility is to work as effectively as he or she can within the pluralistic legislative process, guided primarily by the political reward system institutionalized in the electoral process.

Standing behind the argument of moral minimalism are several basic concerns rooted in the history of liberalism and modern democratic theory. In order to assess the challenge it poses for the study of legislative ethics, we should begin by noting these concerns.

As *The Federalist Papers* make clear, the American political system was designed to solve one long-standing problem of political theory: namely, the problem of how to make the self-interest of the rulers coincide with the interests of at least a majority of the ruled, while at the same time protecting the fundamental interests or rights of the minority.[13] In his defense of the Constitution's institutionalization of Congress, Madison suggested a variety of reasons why even the legislature (particularly the less democratically responsive Senate) would contain built-in

---

[13] Cf. *The Federalist,* ed. by Jacob Cooke (Middletown, Conn.: Wesleyan University Press, 1961), Nos. 10 and 51, pp. 56–65, 347–353.

protections against the serious and systematic violations of minority rights and interests. Among them were the sense of justice and civic virtue of individual legislators. But these considerations were ancillary to his argument; Madison was not one to place much faith in the enlightenment and virtue of political elites. In the final analysis, the main protection for minority interests lay in the intragovernmental checks among executive, legislative, and judicial powers and not in the checks internal to the legislative branch itself. On the other hand, and precisely for this reason, Madison was greatly concerned that Congress (especially the House) remain responsive to the will of the majority of the electorate in order to keep the overall balance of power in the republic from tipping in an antidemocratic direction.

Thus, like other republican theorists before him, Madison's main concern about legislative politics focused on maintaining democratic accountability and warding off the personal corruption of legislators by constructing an artificial identity of interests between legislator and constituent, ruler and ruled.[14] Somewhat later, James Mill made an even clearer, albeit more simplistic, argument to the same effect in his *Essay on Government.* Both Madison and Mill assumed, on the basis of their theories of natural human egoism, that legislators would be primarily self-interested in their motivation and that their basic goal would be to retain power through reelection. Hence, their theories of legislative politics led readily to a conception in which the electoral system works very much like Adam Smith's market where the public interest (i.e. democratically responsive, nondespotic governance) would be produced by an invisible hand if legislators acted like political entrepreneurs and attempted to maximize their own self-interest.[15]

Clearly, in this line of analysis, the role of legislative ethics is limited and extremely problematic. If political entrepreneurs need any sense of ethical responsibility at all to supplement their basic calculus of prudential self-interest, that ethical sense should be constrained within narrow and specific bounds. At most it should proscribe the misuse of office for personal gain and reinforce legislators' sense of themselves as the servants of their constituents. Just as some broader, non-profit-oriented moral convictions purportedly lead to economically "irrational" behavior

---

[14] *The Federalist,* Nos. 52–58, pp. 353–397.

[15] I need hardly add that the most influential schools of contemporary political science—pluralism and Downsian economic theories of democracy—have largely followed this line of analysis. For suggestive discussions, see Sheldon S. Wolin, "The American Pluralist Conception of Politics," in *Ethics in Hard Times,* ed. by Arthur L. Caplan and Daniel Callahan (New York: Plenum Press, 1981), pp. 217–260; and Brian Barry, *Sociologists, Economists, and Democracy* (London: Collier-Macmillan, 1970).

in the marketplace and threaten to undermine the workings of the invisible hand, so too do moral convictions held by legislators threaten to undermine democratic responsiveness. This line of analysis and this stream of liberal democratic theory provides, I think, a powerful underpinning for moral minimalism in legislative ethics; and it reinforces our current worries about stirring up any motivations, whether ethical or otherwise, that would distract legislators from their primary focus on their own political self-interest.

Moreover, there is an inherent tension in the practice of political representation that has always been worrisome to liberal democratic theorists. This is the tension between the normative expectation that a representative should represent the subjective preferences (or self-defined interests) of the constituents and the normative expectation that a representative should represent the objective needs (or enlightened interests) of the constituents. For a variety of reasons (e.g., constitutent apathy on most issues, significant electoral advantage for incumbents), representative democracy pulls in the direction of the latter. Or, more precisely, it pulls in the direction of the representation of the needs of constituents as those needs are defined and *perceived by the representative*. This is troubling for liberal democrats who hold that, in the final reckoning, each person is the best judge of his or her own good. Trying to keep legislators primarily sensitive to political pressures above all has been seen as the most practical solution to this problem. This political focus keeps legislators democratically honest. To moralize their self-conception of their role too much might exacerbate their tendency toward a kind of antidemocratic paternalism.

Finally, behind the argument of moral minimalism stands a tradition of social theory that grew out of the political turmoil of the sixteenth and seventeenth centuries.[16] According to this tradition, moral discourse is socially polarizing and devisive. When human beings define their often competitive relations in terms of fundamental ethical or religious principles, they lose the capacity to compromise and come to blows. Following the terrible religious warfare that devastated Europe in these centuries, political theorists systematically tried to cordon off ethical discourse in the private realm and redefined politics in terms of material rather than spiritual interests. The argument of moral minimalism shows the legacy of

[16] Cf. A. O. Hirschman, *The Passions and the Interests: Political Arguments for Capitalism Before Its Triumph* (Princeton: Princeton University Press, 1977); and Nannerl O. Keohane, *Philosophy and the State in France* (Princeton: Princeton University Press, 1980), pp. 83–150.

this tradition's wariness about the polarizing effects of ethical discourse in political life.

How then can a broad-ranging conception of legislative ethics be defended against moral minimalism? Would injecting wide considerations of moral principle and obligation into public evaluations of legislative conduct hamper the effective functioning of the legislative process? And would it undermine the practice of responsible democratic representation? In a moment I shall take up these issues directly. Before doing so, however, I want to mention two more specific considerations that undermine the force of the minimalist argument.

One obvious way to short-circuit the argument of moral minimalism is to point out that it is itself dependent upon a general theory of legislative ethics. That is, it is a rule-utilitarian theory that stipulates a tacit ethical obligation for legislators to remain politically oriented in most of their activities, on the basis of the claim that this particular dividing line between ethics and politics maximizes the political good and creates the process necessary for effective governance in a system like ours. Thus, this argument does not really cut against expanding the study of legislative ethics *per se*. Instead, it offers one already quite general theory of legislative ethics and simply argues against other competing general theories of the subject.

In addition, many of the worries expressed, particularly by legislators themselves, about broadening the scope of legislative ethics are based on a failure to distinguish between the question of what should be included in the general study of legislative ethics and the question of what should be included in a code of legislative ethics. Some legislators, like Senator Howell Heflin (Democrat, Alabama), vice-chairman of the Senate Select Committee on Ethics, have strong—and I think well taken— reservations about including all ethical considerations that are arguably pertinent to legislative conduct in an institutionally enforced black letter code.[17] They therefore tend to resist talking about the whole range of legislative activity in explicitly ethical terms because they fear that such talk will eventually lead to a sweeping written ethics code that would produce a myriad of political and procedural headaches.

Certainly, in order to allay this fear, the distinction between the scope of a code and the scope of legislative ethics *per se* will have to be argued for. After all, intuitively one might doubt that the distinction should be made: "If X is a genuine moral obligation incumbent on a

---

[17] U.S. Congress, Senate Select Committee on Ethics, *Hearings,* 96th Cong., 2nd sess., *Revising the Senate Code of Official Conduct* (Washington, D.C.: Government Printing Office, 1981), pp. 83–93.

legislator, why shouldn't the legislature state and enforce it as a moral rule?'' But this sentiment does not appear to me to be decisive. Just as there are compelling practical and moral reasons not to subsume all ethical obligations under legal obligations in society, similarly within an institution like a legislature there are compelling reasons not to codify all ethical norms. The question of what should be included in a code, or even the question of what should be written into some set of ethical guidelines, turns largely upon issues of enforceability, equity, and clarity of interpretation. It is logically separate from the question of what range of legislative activities should be evaluated and debated publicly in ethical terms. We may or may not want to include more rules, and different kinds of rules, in legislative ethics codes than they now contain. But nothing about the scope of legislative ethics *per se* follows from that decision, and saying that the scope of legislative ethics should be broadened does not entail that the codes should be broadened.

However, neither pointing out that moral minimalism represents a particular theory of legislative ethics nor distinguishing between the study of legislative ethics and codes of legislative ethics really gets to the heart of the matter. We must turn, finally, to the core issues of the minimalist position mentioned above.

Moral minimalism rests, as we have seen, on an adversarial conception of the legislative process, one in which effective political activity depends upon maximal freedom of maneuver and compromise within a minimal structure of moral and legal restraints.

The first problem with this account is that it is not sufficiently attentive to the indeterminacy of even the most competitive and interest-oriented political activity. On one level, legislators surely are appropriately viewed as advocates. However, their advocacy is always multiple—they must select which battles to fight and set priorities in their use of political influence. Equally important, they must ordinarily choose among a variety of potentially winning strategies, no one of which is clearly superior from a purely political point of view but each of which may have significantly different moral costs or institutional implications. A minimalist framework of moral and legal norms proscribing the abuse of office for personal financial gain is simply insufficient to guide this choice of roles and strategies.

Even adversarial legislators must make ethical decisions and face moral dilemmas in the practice of politics. About that, they have no choice. But they do have a choice about whether or not to recognize those moral dilemmas clearly and to make moral decisions on the basis of sound reasoning and careful weighing of consequences. Political considerations alone do not dictate the outcome of this choice; political effectiveness does not entail moral indifference. Indeed, legislators who patently lack any moral sensibility or vision concerning their station and its duties eventually lose the respect and trust of their colleagues and supporters and consequently lose their political influence as well. Thus even if legislative politics is legislative warfare carried on by other means, there is still room for—and a telling need for—a comprehensive understanding of legislative ethics in legislatures and in the political culture at large to help maintain an essential legislative *jus in bello*.

But, in fact, the legislature is not such a Clausewitzian world. The second problem with moral minimalism's account of the legislative process is that its stress on adversarialism is one-sided and self-defeating. Moral minimalism tacitly presupposes that individual legislators will adhere, as a matter or course, to some important ethical norms. If legislators did not routinely recognize and obey certain ethical obligations—e.g., truth telling, promise keeping, commitment to procedures— the legislative space to which the argument for moral minimalism appeals would not be the scene of an orderly, if competitive, bargaining and coalition-building process; it would be a self-defeating war of all against all. The contemporary environment within which legislators must operate is highly decentralized and has multiple decision-points. Legislatures are peculiarly fragile organizations, biased toward negative decision making and prone to institutional paralysis. These tendencies are exacerbated when legislators carry their adversarial pursuit of individual self-interest too far and forget that democratic representation is a fundamentally collective process made possible only by a principled—and not solely prudential—commitment to mutual accommodation and cooperation. At times in the past, Congress and most state legislatures have had reasonably well functioning, if tacit and imperfect, ethical socialization processes and institutionalized, structural brakes on the atomizing, centrifugal forces at work within them. Today those structures and informal codes are far weaker than they once were, and the brakes are largely moral ones operating within each legislator's own understanding of his or her public and institutional responsibility. Without those moral brakes, without an understanding that there is more to democratically responsible representation than the duties of pure adversarialism, the political flexibility moral minimalism seeks to preserve would be self-defeating.

In short, the notion of a firm boundary line between ethics and politics is actually quite misleading. Legislative ethics and legislative politics do not stand in a zero-sum relationship to one another by any means; they can be mutually reinforcing and symbiotic. The danger arises when the tacit, informal norms of legislative ethics visibly break down or, worse, quietly and imperceptibly erode. Under these circumstances, broadening the study of legislative ethics and developing a more rigorous systematic analysis of its basic norms and role obligations may be essential to preserving the democratic integrity of the legislative process.

Thus, to emphasize the evaluation of legislative conduct from a moral point of view, or to seek ways to reinforce the ethical integrity of that conduct is neither to adopt an antipolitical stance nor to disregard the value of the political world legislators inhabit. Rather, the ethical scrutiny of legislative life can and should be based on a thoughtful, balanced appraisal of the opportunities as well as the limitations that political realities create.

One way of doing this is to analyze carefully the perceived tensions and dilemmas to show that in some cases that perception is mistaken because it rests on a misunderstanding of what ethical integrity requires or a miscalculation of what political effectiveness demands. Another is to call attention to the many ways in which politically effective representation—and indeed the political self-interest of individual legislators—is enhanced by, or even depends upon, ethically responsible conduct. Legislators who are blind to the ethical obligations of their role or who carelessly disregard those obligations do sooner or later lose the respect of their colleagues and the trust of their supporters. Having lost that respect and trust, they lose their political effectiveness and influence as well.

It is no less important to understand the current institutional pressures and political forces that tend to increase the tension between ethics and politics and from there to seek to devise countervailing measures to mitigate these pressures. As I mentioned earlier, an array of such measures has been undertaken in recent years, such as disclosure requirements, ethics codes, committees, and commissions. Others, such as further campaign finance reform, changes in the way campaigns are conducted, and moves to reform the internal functioning of legislative bodies are presently being debated. Whatever the merit of particular reforms, none of them will work well unless standing behind them is a movement in our political culture toward a more thoughtful and discriminating understanding of the ethical duties legislators ought to fulfill. Whether legislative ethics and legislative politics reinforce one another or conflict in any given political system is a function of the demands legislators place on themselves and the expectations citizens have about their representatives. Far from undermining democratic stability, as the moral minimalists fear, important and ultimately quite concrete and practical democratic values will be served by beginning a new and much broader public dialogue about legislative ethics among legislators, among commentators, educators, and journalists who influence public opinion, and among the citizenry as a whole.

At the end of the day, our attitude toward the desirability of broadening the scope of the study of legislative ethics and our assessment of the argument for moral minimalism will depend upon both a normative and an empirical evaluation of the functioning of the legislative process. In an ideal democratic world—a world of better information, an informed, participating citizenry, and social justice and equality—a minimalist conception of legislative ethics might be enough, although it would probably not have much cultural appeal. In a different, imperfect political world—in what I believe is our political world—democratic citizens must make principled arguments in public about the ethical responsibilities of legislators, arguments about their duties as political leaders and educators, and arguments about the limits of what political self-interest can justify. This is one of the ways (not the only way, but one of the ways) we have of making American democracy work.

9

The Theory of Legislative Ethics

AMY GUTMANN and DENNIS THOMPSON

Even in their most practical moods, legislators make arguments and proposals that presume the truth of certain political theories. When Senator Lowell Weicker and others proposed that an ethics code requiring only financial disclosure should replace the current elaborate set of rules about conflicts of interest, gifts and outside income, they implied that such a code would be more democratic; it would make representatives answerable to their constituents rather than to a legislative committee.[1] The democratic appeal of the proposal is its apparent deference to a delegate theory of representation.

But if we begin to analyze its implicit theoretical assumptions, we can see that the proposal is more problematic than it appears at first. A delegate theory does not entail that only constituents in one district or state should control the conduct of the representative from that district or state. On a delegate theory, constituents in *any* state or district may quite properly instruct their representative to seek standards to govern the conduct of *all* representatives. The idea that disclosure alone is sufficient thus turns out to be theoretically misconceived. It may be suitable for representation in a convention (what Burke called a "congress of ambassadors from different and hostile interests"),[2] but it hardly seems appro-

[1] Congressional Quarterly, *Congressional Ethics* (2nd ed.; Washington, D.C.: Congressional Quarterly, 1980), p. 57.
[2] Edmund Burke, *Burke's Politics*, ed. by Ross Hoffman and Paul Levack (New York: Knopf, 1959), p. 116.

AMY GUTMANN and DENNIS THOMPSON ● Department of Politics, Princeton University, Princeton, New Jersey 08544.

priate for an ongoing institution that, like the United States Congress, should hold its members to common standards.

Politicians, then, like the rest of us, are theorists whether or not they recognize it. By uncovering the theoretical confusion on which a practical reform rests we can begin to see its practical inadequacy as well. We can escape theory only by leaving our theoretical assumptions unexamined—and thereby leaving our practical proposals unfounded.

One may grant that theory is important, or at least unavoidable, but still wonder why a special theory of legislative ethics is necessary. Why not simply use a general theory of ethics or politics to guide the conduct of legislators and assess the structure of legislatures? It is true that a theory of legislative ethics at root must be consistent with a general theory of ethics. But the principles of legislative ethics are not the same as the principles that follow directly from ordinary ethics. The requirements of the role of a legislator distinguish the content of legislative morality from that of ordinary morality. The duties of this role may actually conflict with the duties of citizens.

Legislative ethics is both more permissive and more restrictive than ordinary ethics. It is more permissive because it allows legislators to place particular interests ahead of the general interest. A legislator is sometimes expected to vote in the interest of his constituents even if the vote is contrary to the public interest. The justification for such permission is a moral one: a system in which individual representatives advocate the interests of their constituents is more likely to yield the general interest in the long run. Furthermore, given such a system, a legislator who always neglects his constituents to serve nobler causes may actually betray his trust; after all, he promised his constituents to look after their interests. But these justifications do not eliminate the conflict between legislative ethics and ordinary ethics. Rather, they help clarify the nature of that conflict by showing that the problem of legislative ethics is a problem of the duties of role in a system.

The same conclusion emerges when we consider how legislative ethics may be more restrictive than ordinary ethics. Legislators may be held to standards that, if enforced against ordinary citizens, would violate their rights. Legislators may be required, for example, to disclose more about their personal lives than citizens are expected to disclose even to their employers. The justification is, as before, a moral one. First, because legislators have significant power over us and act as our agents, we need to know more about them than about our fellow citizens. Second, legislators take office well aware of the burdens of public office and of the norms that govern the conduct of officials. Legislators can reasonably be said to consent to these more stringent demands. Here again the justification for special duties of a legislator underscores the distinctive problem of legislative ethics—the effect of the legislative role on the moral duties of persons.

This general problem will be considered in two parts. The first part of this essay discusses the ethics of legislators. It examines the duties of the legislator within a given legislative structure. It argues from certain general features of the role of the legislator to particular duties of that role. The second part of the essay discusses the ethics of legislatures. It explores general ways in which structures of legislatures and other institutions can support the duties of legislators and considers how particular political reforms can serve as the structural supports.

THE ROLES OF THE REPRESENTATIVE

The natural place to look for instruction about the role of the legislator is in theories of representation, specifically in trustee and delegate theories.[3] But when political scientists have tried to apply such theories to the behavior of legislators they have not met with much success. Most legislators see no relevance in these theories and deny the conflict the theories pose between the role of delegate and the role of trustee. They think as their constituents, or at least want to assume that they do, and therefore refuse to distinguish between exercising their own judgment and following the desires of their constituents. One political scientist who asked members of Congress whether they should act as delegates or trustees received responses such as, "Who dreamed up these stupid questions?" and "I refuse to answer these high-school questions."[4]

It is not surprising that these questions should elicit such responses. The questions suppose a far too simple way of understanding the role of the representative. Theories of representation, at least sophisticated ones such as those of Burke and Mill, hold much more complex views of the

---

[3] Burke, *Burke's Politics*, pp. 114–20; John Stuart Mill, *Considerations on Representative Government*, in *Collected Works*, vol. XIX, ed. by J. M. Robson (Toronto: University of Toronto Press, 1977), especially chap. XII.

[4] Thomas E. Cavanaugh, "Role Orientations of House Members: The Process of Representation," paper prepared for delivery for the 1979 annual meetings of the American Political Science Association (Washington, D.C., 1979), p. 25. When members are asked more concrete questions about their roles, they are more likely to give informative responses. See, e.g., Roger H. Davidson, *The Role of the Congressman* (Indianapolis and New York: Pegasus, 1969), pp. 110–142; and John W. Kingdon, *Congressmen's Voting Decisions* (2nd ed.; New York: Harper & Row, 1981), pp. 29–71, 110–176.

representative's role, recognizing that the role must be placed in the context of a process of representation that itself occurs within a larger political system. If we heed these more complex theories, we shall notice two characteristics of the role of the representative that should be taken into account by any theory of legislative ethics. The role should be regarded as (1) multidimensional and (2) system-dependent.

First, a representative must choose among several aspects of his role or (we may say) several different roles. Burke emphasized that a representative owes allegiance to many different principles and groups of people, and in our time the number and variety of those principles and groups have expanded significantly. We can identify at least three dimensions of the representative's role. First, there is a distinction that corresponds to the traditional one between trustee and delegate. We distinguish trustees from delegates according to the reasons for their decisions—whether they decide according to expressed preferences of the persons they represent or according to the representative's judgment about the interests of the persons they represent. Since preferences and interests may coincide, delegates and trustees may in fact act in the same way some of the time. But when preferences and interests do not coincide, then we face the problem that resembles the problem of paternalism in professional ethics.[5] Under what conditions and for what reasons may an agent act beyond or even contrary to the wishes of his principal? As in professional ethics, we should maintain a strong presumption against overriding the preferences of principals, but we would not want to deny that the presumption could be rebutted in some circumstances.

We should consider not only how citizens should be represented, but which citizens should be represented. Along with the traditional categories of nation and district, we take note of others that complicate the life of the legislator. Sometimes legislators owe allegiance to their party, either because they owe their election to the party label more than anything else or because they need the party's support for their own legislative programs. And some legislators properly see themselves partly as spokespersons for groups such as blacks and women who are underrepresented in the legislature. The obligation to the district is also more complex than has usually been supposed. Because a representative's electoral constituency is a majority of the electorate in the last election, he faces the question of how much he owes to other groups, including

---

[5] Cf. Dennis F. Thompson, "Paternalism in Medicine, Law, and Public Policy," in *Ethics Teaching in Higher Education*, ed. by D. Callahan and S. Bok (New York: Plenum Press, 1980), pp. 245–72.

those who voted against him, and even those who would compose the current electoral majority. Furthermore, many legislators find themselves bound to local elites whose interests may diverge from those of other groups in the district. Yet one can imagine that representing such an elite could sometimes be justifiable—for example, when the elite promotes economic development that would benefit the poor in a district.

So far, then, we have not just two theories of representation, as is commonly suggested, but at least eight theories, even if we consider only nation, party, district, and district majority in combination with delegate and trustee conceptions. And even this simplifies the representative's role. A more accurate account would add a third dimension, indicating the types of issues with which a representative must deal. We may wish to say, for example, that a particular legislator should act as a delegate on welfare issues that would allocate funds to the poor in his district but that he should act as a trustee on issues of foreign policy, especially if his constituents are both impoverished and bellicose. And if he then decides to follow the district majority on civil rights, we begin to see the complexity of the role (or roles) among which he must choose.

Even if we were able to spell out all the possible roles a legislator might legitimately adopt, we would not yet have a theory of representation, because we would not have indicated which role a representative ought to adopt. Such a theory, however, is probably not possible in face of the manifold conditions that affect the choice of roles. General principles instructing legislators on which role to adopt usually prove inadequate. Two recent philosophical efforts will illustrate the difficulties of establishing such principles.

John Rawls argues that the "rational legislator is to vote his opinion as to which laws and policies best conform to principles of justice. No special weight is or should be given to opinions that are held with greater confidence, or to the votes of those who let it be known that their being in the minority will cause them great displeasure."[6] Under the "ideal conditions" to which Rawls explicitly refers, this principle may be eminently acceptable. But under most actual conditions, where citizens take positions that they think will support their own interests, the legislator may be justified in taking intensity into account. One could argue that in these circumstances citizens who have a greater stake in the outcome should have greater influence on it. As Brian Barry points out, on many matters there is no "common good" in a strict sense, only a

---

[6] John Rawls, *A Theory of Justice* (Cambridge, Mass.: Harvard University Press, 1971), p. 361.

"clash of interests," and the issue for the legislator is "which interests should prevail."[7]

Yet, as Barry himself recognizes, we do not want to say that all issues should be treated in this way. He suggests that on "issues of general public morality," such as the abolition of the death penalty, intensity of preference should not count.[8] But he does not offer any rationale for singling out these issues, or even a criterion for recognizing them. When philosophers try to provide such rationales or criteria, they usually turn to the distinction between utility and rights. Alan Goldman, for example, suggests that in serving their constituents representatives may not violate the "negative rights" of citizens.[9] (Rights are "interests of individuals important enough to be protected against additions of lesser interests across other persons." Negative rights are claims not to be treated in certain ways, whereas positive rights are claims to have certain goods.[10]) When negative rights are not in question, the legislator may consider only the utility of his constituents. Goldman concludes that representatives should follow the preferences of a majority of their constituents in such cases, although he allows exceptions for intense minorities and for paternalistic judgment by the legislator.

The problem with this approach is that the very definition of what is to count as a right is itself a question that, at least in part, should be determined in the political process, including the deliberations and votes in the legislature. A principle that tells legislators not to violate negative rights is not much help when they are considering whether to support legislation that would establish new rights. It is possible that we may be able to justify some distinction between rights and utility that is relatively independent of the political process, but it is doubtful that any distinction between positive and negative rights can be so independent. The growth of the welfare state has often been explained and defended as a progressive recognition that the government should provide certain benefits (positive rights) in order to prevent harm being done to citizens (negative rights). Yet its opponents claim that the welfare state violates the negative rights of other citizens (property owners, for example). We expect legislators, among others, to resolve such disputes, and in doing so they sometimes create, rather than follow, our distinctions between positive and negative rights.

[7] Brian Barry, *The Liberal Theory of Justice* (London: Oxford University Press, 1973), p. 150.

[8] Ibid.

[9] Alan H. Goldman, *The Moral Foundations of Professional Ethics* (Totowa, N.J.: Rowman and Littlefield, 1980), pp. 76, 88–89.

[10] Ibid. p. 24.

The second general characteristic of the role of the representative—that it is system-dependent—helps explain why theorists have failed to produce plausible principles specifying which role a representative should choose. The choice seems indeterminate not only because there are so many roles from which to choose, but also because the choice depends on what else is happening in the legislative system. In an ideal system, we could assume that each legislator does what he ought to do and that the system as a whole functions as it should. But under actual conditions neither of these assumptions holds. In choosing how to fulfill the duties of his role, therefore, a legislator must take into account the actual conduct of other legislators, as well as that of other agents and the general features of the political system as a whole.

Traditional theorists of representation recognize that representation is not simply a one-to-one relation between constituents and legislators but a collective process involving systematic interaction among many people holding different roles.[11] It is this pattern of conduct in the representative system as a whole that should ultimately determine our moral and political judgments about legislative ethics. When Mill served in Parliament he refused to be the spokesman merely for his constituents or even for his party, but instead took a more visionary stance, advocating causes such as female suffrage well before they had any chance of enactment. Yet he did not think that every representative should be as independent as he was. In fact, according to his own theory of representation, legislators should follow the wishes of their constituents at least on matters involving "fundamental convictions."[12] Some legislators should play the role Mill himself did, but most should not. What we should seek, Mill suggests, is a representative assembly that is well balanced among various kinds of representatives. The duties of any single representative depend on what other representatives do or fail to do, and thus the proper role of a representative cannot be determined without reference to the state of the legislative system at a particular time.

These two general characteristics of the role of representative have important implications for legislative ethics. Because legislators must choose among many different roles, and because the rightness of that choice depends on the state of the system in which they make it, legislative ethics cannot specify in advance a particular set of duties for a representative. Legislative ethics cannot tell the representative whether to act as a trustee or delegate, even on a given issue, and certainly cannot

---

[11] Hanna Pitkin, *The Concept of Representation* (Berkeley: University of California Press, 1967), pp. 221–24.
[12] Mill, chap. XII, p. 510.

tell him what position to take on the issue. It follows that legislative ethics will grant considerable discretion to legislators in their choices of role and their decisions on policy. To this extent, theorists who with Burke would give scope to the independent judgment of legislators are correct. But it does not follow that legislative ethics is reduced to the study of the character of legislators. We do not simply say, as Burke sometimes implied, that citizens should seek the best men and permit them to exercise their best judgment. The very fact that so much discretion is necessary implies that the conditions under which the discretion is exercised are crucial. The primary focus of legislative ethics thus becomes the legislative process itself, and the chief ethical duties of legislators concern making legislative discretion conform to political democracy. In this way, the ethics of legislators ultimately derives from the theory of democracy.

THE DUTIES OF LEGISLATORS

If legislative ethics concentrates on the circumstances of legislative discretion, it must address three aspects of the context in which legislators make judgments: the nature of the influence on individual legislators, the public knowledge of the activities of legislators, and the way the legislature as a whole functions. Each of these implies a set of duties for legislators in a democracy, and together they exhaust the range of those duties.

The first duty, that of legislative autonomy, requires that representatives deliberate and decide free from improper influence. Citizens often cannot assess whether their representatives' decisions are correct, but they certainly should be able to judge whether their representatives reached those decisions in a process that could reasonably be expected to produce legislation that is not biased or corrupt. We assume that legislation is less likely to be just if legislators make decisions in an atmosphere of improper influence. The difficulty is to determine what kinds of influence are improper. We should not demand, even as an ideal, a wholly unencumbered legislator, one who acts utterly unswayed by political pressures and partisan loyalties. Legislators, after all, are representatives engaged in a democratic politics and should often be persuaded by the views of constituents and party leaders. But legislative judgment should not be determined by influences that are irrelevant to the merits of the legislation. That a representative's constituents favor a particular policy is usually a relevant consideration, but the representative's reelection alone is not. (Reelection would be a legitimate reason if the representative's defeat could be shown to affect adversely legislation or the legislative process.) This criterion of relevance excludes only very few kinds of influence *per se*. It would rule out bribery and extortion since a legislator who accepts a bribe may be assumed to act for reasons more related to the money he receives than to the content of the legislation he supports. Beyond these clear instances, we cannot say that any type of influence will always violate or will always satisfy the duty of autonomy. We can, however, identify certain types that deserve special scrutiny because they strongly suggest excessive dependence or pressures irrelevant to the merits of the legislation.

A standard that prohibits the influence or motive of personal gain underlies the traditional approach to legislative ethics, as exemplified in most codes of ethics. Codes typically devote more attention to preventing conflicts of financial interest than to anything else. The idea of conflict of interest in democratic representation, however, is paradoxical. To avoid a conflict of interest, legislators are not supposed to do anything that would appear to further their own interests. Yet, as Madison emphasized, a legislator must share a "communion of interest with his constituents."[13] He cannot adequately represent the interests of constituents without also representing some of his own. The most common way of resolving this paradox has been to say that a conflict of interest exists only when a representative would personally benefit from some piece of legislation in a way or to a degree that other people would not.[14] Applied to voting on bills, virtually the only conduct that this stipulation has excluded is a member's voting on a controversy about his own seat in the legislature.

Certainly we can say, following the codes, that a legislator should not support legislation, with the principal purpose of furthering the "pecuniary interest" of himself, his family or friends.[15] Personal financial gain, of course, is a particularly suspicious sign that a legislator may not be judging matters on their merits, but other kinds of motives may be even more pernicious and probably more common. First, the motive need not be directly personal. The influence of campaign contributors does not necessarily corrupt legislators, but when legislators must rely chiefly on a few large contributors, they begin to lose their independence of judgment. They become more like lobbyists than legislators. Second, the motive

[13] *The Federalist*, ed. by Jacob Cooke (Middletown, Conn.: Wesleyan University Press, 1961), No. 57, pp. 586–87.

[14] Robert S. Getz, *Congressional Ethics: The Conflict of Interest Issue* (Princeton, N.J.: Van Nostrand, 1966), pp. 57–58.

[15] U.S. Senate, Committee on Rules and Administration, *Standing Rules of the Senate*, 96th Cong., 2nd sess. (Washington: U.S. Government Printing Office, 1980), Rule XXXVII, pp. 46–49.

need not be financial either. The influence of groups—even groups that espouse principles the legislator himself accepts—may be undesirable when it overwhelms other considerations in the mind of the legislator. The legislator permits considerations that are relevant to one issue to determine his positions on other issues for which they are irrelevant. A representative who always uses his office zealously to pursue the legislative goals of some single-issue movement thus may be abandoning the autonomy of legislative judgment as much as the representative who sells out to special interest groups. In American culture money is no doubt the most common enemy of legislative autonomy, but ideology is as potent and may be more insidious.

Thus the problem is neither personal gain nor financial inducement as such. Since many different kinds of influence can erode legislative autonomy, the patterns of pressure rather than the types of pressure must be our central concern. We should be most disturbed about the legislator who consistently supports bills that mainly benefit his campaign contributors or the legislator who exclusively serves the aims of a special interest group. There is of course a larger problem of patterns of influence on the legislature as a whole. Although the duty of autonomy does not reach this problem, a duty of responsibility to the institution explicitly attends to it. A legislature of autonomous representatives would be an improvement over most actual legislatures, but it would fall short of being an ethical legislature.

A second set of duties of legislators concerns accountability. Because representatives may legitimately assume many different roles, we cannot stipulate that they should have to answer to any particular group about any particular decision they make. But for the very same reason we can insist that they take special care to ensure that all citizens have sufficient information to assess their decisions. The more discretion they have, the more the public must know about their decisions and the factors that influence them. What the public must know is thus likely to be more extensive than what legislators at present disclose. This is true both of legislative activity and of personal conduct.

The information that citizens should have about legislative activity is not confined to the speeches and votes on bills on the floor of the legislature. Much significant legislative activity takes place in caucuses, closed committee sessions; many votes in committee and on procedural matters are at least as significant as the final debate and vote on bills in the full legislature. Although the essential compromises of democratic politics cannot always be struck in the glare of publicity, decisive deliberations cannot be kept from the public without violating the duty of accountability.

Violations are less often the consequence of an attempt to conceal the machinations of sinister interests than the result of a failure to recognize the need for public debate of an issue. The discussion of difficult issues may go on for many years behind the scenes, with the result that the legislation finally adopted does not reflect the views of most citizens and in fact may be seriously misconceived. This was the case with debate and policy on public financing of treatment for kidney disease. According to one account, the debate was conducted *sotto voce*. It was "carried out mainly within the inner councils of the medical-scientific community and the political-governmental system. . . . Both opponents and proponents were reluctant to have this issue fully considered in a public debate, fearing that it was too divisive for the polity to handle."[16] In the legislation it finally passed, Congress committed far too many resources to one kind of disease and one group of victims, at the expense of diverting funds from programs that could have helped more people who suffered from other kinds of diseases. There is no guarantee that if the debate had been more public the legislation would have been more rational. But citizens would have had a better understanding of what their legislators had done and would have been in a stronger position to call for changes in the policy in the future had they believed such changes necessary.

Unlike citizens, legislators usually cannot complain that their privacy is violated by exposure of their private lives. Public officials exercise power over us on our behalf, and we must know a great deal about them if we are to trust them with the discretion their offices confer. In their relations with colleagues, constituents, lobbyists, administrators, members of the press, perhaps even with their friends, legislators are engaging in the representational process. We may need to learn quite a lot about these associations if we are to judge the propriety of their conduct as representatives. They know that this is one of the burdens of public life, and they consent to it when they accept public office. This is not to say that there are no limits to what the public may know about legislators. Only information relevant to the performance of their legislative functions should be open to scrutiny. But this principle may entail disclosure of a wide range of quite intimate information, such as the medical condition or even the psychological state of legislators. It would, for example, encourage journalists to report, as for many years they did not, cases of alcoholism that caused members to neglect their duties. Furthermore, the principle requires different kinds and degrees of disclosure for the

[16] Richard A. Rettig, "The Policy Debate on Patient Care Financing for Victims of End-Stage Renal Disease," *Law and Contemporary Problems*, 40 (Autumn 1976), 212–30.

different roles that representatives play in the legislative process. A member of the Banking and Currency Committee, for example, should expect to have his personal finances more closely examined than those of a member of the Committee on Administration (although since both vote on the same issues on the floor, both should expect to disclose much more than ordinary citizens). A congressman who acts as a spokesman for various religious organizations should anticipate public inquiries about his own religious beliefs and activities. And if a candidate makes his personal life a campaign issue by portraying himself as a "good family man," he can hardly complain if the press writes about his wife and children.[17]

The third duty of legislators involves responsibility to the legislature itself. Representatives are responsible not merely for their own legislative activities but also for the state of the institutions in which they act. Lawmaking in the modern legislature is a complex business requiring the cooperation and contribution of many. The achievements of Congress depend on all members doing their share in holding hearings, mobilizing support, administering staffs, floor-managing bills, overseeing administrative agencies, and performing all the other tasks that keep the institution and government functioning for the benefit of all.

But the duty of responsibility goes beyond doing one's fair share of the collective chores of the institution. A more extended idea of responsibility appropriately applies to public office. In ordinary moral life, we are not usually held responsible when other people fail to do their duty; we assume only limited obligations to prevent or correct wrongs that others commit. We are not generally expected, for example, to prevent other parents from neglecting their children or to undertake the care of the children ourselves. Responsibility in public life is more demanding. Officials may be held responsible for preventing or correcting the failures of others—first, because officials have voluntarily accepted a public office for which citizens in advance have specified the scope of responsibility; and, second, because in office they have greater capacity (more power and knowledge) than ordinary citizens have to prevent and correct the wrongs that others commit. Both of these reasons apply with special force to the role of the representative since that role is system-dependent. What any single representative should do depends on what other representatives are doing, or failing to do. This extended notion of responsibility imposes on legislators a more extensive duty than most have assumed in

---

[17] See Dennis F. Thompson, "The Private Lives of Public Officials," in *Public Duties: The Moral Obligations of Government Officials*, ed. by J. Fleishman *et al.* (Cambridge, Mass.: Harvard University Press, 1981), pp. 221–47.

the past. Three kinds of conduct that the duty of responsibility would proscribe illustrate its implications.

First, there is the common practice of running *"for* Congress by running *against* Congress." As Richard Fenno points out,

> It is easy for each congressman to explain to his own supporters why he cannot be blamed for the performance of the collectivity. . . . The beauty of the strategy is that everybody can use it and nobody will be called to account by those under attack. . . . In the short run everybody plays and nearly everybody wins. Yet the institution bleeds from 435 separate cuts. In the long run, therefore, somebody may lose.[18]

This practice would become less common if legislators accepted the duty of responsibility to the institution. Incumbents would not pretend that they are blameless for the poor legislation that Congress passes or for the failure of Congress to enact good legislation. They would have to show at least that they made good faith efforts themselves to do something about the failures of the institution they are criticizing.

Second, legislators would not be so reluctant to criticize and penalize their colleagues for transgressions of institutional standards. Although in recent years the Senate and the House have been somewhat more inclined to act against their colleagues who are guilty of gross violations of legislative ethics and the criminal law, neither body has shown much enthusiasm for establishing and enforcing stringent standards of conduct for its members. Many observers believe that in 1977 it took the threat of no pay raise to win the passage of the tougher rules in the present code, and since then some of these have been relaxed. Most individual legislators assiduously strive to avoid service on the Senate Ethics Committee and the House Committee on Standards of Official Conduct. Legislators rarely report improprieties of their colleagues or even of the members of their colleagues' staffs, and they even more rarely criticize colleagues in public for neglecting their legislative duties.

Finally, and most importantly, legislators who accept the duty of responsibility would recognize that they should take steps to correct structural defects in the legislature itself and more generally in the process of democratic representation. A persistent defect of liberal representative systems is the neglect of the interests of citizens who either cannot press their claims at all or cannot do so as effectively as citizens who possess greater resources.

It is hardly reasonable, of course, to blame a legislator for the fact that some citizens or groups never express their views in the political

[18] Richard F. Fenno, Jr., *Home Style: House Members in Their Districts* (Boston: Little, Brown, 1978), pp. 167–68.

process. Even a legislator who with the best intentions looks for these silent groups may have trouble finding them. From the perspective of the legislator traveling in his district, "the people" are hard to find, although "certain people" are not. As one Congressman observed,

> You go where people meet. That means you spend more time talking to groups like the Chamber of Commerce than you do to people who live along the road here. The great mass of people you can't reach. They are not organized. The leadership, the elite, runs along the top of all institutions, and you can reach them, but not the people generally.[19]

But the very difficulty of locating "the people" makes it all the more important that the duties of a representative be understood to include the pursuit of the interest of the unorganized, seeking them out and helping them formulate their fair claims on government. The legislator's responsibility, then, goes well beyond making the representational process as it exists work smoothly; it extends to making that process work more democratically.

It might be objected that the legislative duties we have described conflict with each other. In fulfilling their duty of accountability, legislators, it may be said, necessarily sacrifice their autonomy. Or: When legislators assume more responsibility for pursuing the interests of the unorganized, they become less accountable to their organized constituents. The idea behind these objections rests upon a theoretical confusion. The duties of legislators, commonly derived from democratic theory, are in principle mutually compatible. The duty of autonomy does not require legislators to act only on their independent judgment on a particular issue despite any opposition they face from their constituents. Autonomy is a duty to make decisions free from *improper* influences. Some electoral pressures surely must count as proper influence. We would need to deploy a broader democratic theory to determine the precise conditions under which electoral pressures count as fair or proper influence. But insofar as accountability contributes to a well-informed citizenry, it helps satisfy a necessary condition of fair electoral influence on legislators. As for the alleged conflict between accountability and responsibility, we should remember that accountability only requires legislators to inform their constituents of their political activities. It does not require them to act generally as delegates or trustees of their constituents' interests. In serving the interests of the unorganized, legislators therefore do not violate their duty of accountability unless they refuse to publicize their actions.

Although the theory of legislative duties is not inconsistent in theory,

---

[19] Ibid., p. 235.

legislative duties may conflict in practice. The specific means by which legislators are expected to fulfill one of their duties may make it more difficult for them to fulfill another. For example, opening committee sessions to the public in order to further accountability may increase the pressure of organized interests on legislators and thereby make it harder for them to fulfill their responsibility to help the unorganized. In devising structures that support legislative duties, we should try to minimize such conflicts. But some are likely to be unavoidable. We should resolve these by reference to the democratic theory from which the three legislative duties are derived. For each conflict among duties we must consider what will strengthen the democratic process over time. Since a fundamental democratic principle is popular sovereignty, accountability ultimately must take priority over autonomy. But a specific means of furthering accountability may not trump responsibility or autonomy if it risks undermining the long-term prospects of popular sovereignty. Although this method does not provide a simple set of priority rules for resolving conflicts among duties, it does rule out certain arguments as inconsistent with democratic theory. We cannot, for example, give priority to autonomy on grounds that legislators are generally more likely than citizens to make the correct decisions.

THE STRUCTURES OF LEGISLATURES

To fulfill their responsibility in office, legislators must understand not just what their duties are but also what sorts of structural reforms could improve the ethics of legislatures and thereby the democratic process. It would take a comprehensive theory of democracy to determine how to change that process to give groups that are now underrepresented a greater voice in politics. A theory of legislative ethics can make only a more modest contribution to a legislator's understanding or structural reform: it can explain the ways in which structures can be used to support the duties of autonomy, accountability, and responsibility.

One might suppose that a concern for the ethics of legislature is misplaced in a society that is unjust in more fundamental ways: why bother with the misconduct of legislators when the basic needs of citizens are unmet and opportunities to participate in the democratic process are unequal? But the need to find structural means of supporting the duties of legislators is even greater in such a society. The less we can count upon the procedural justice of the democratic process itself, the more we must count upon the ethics of legislators for serving the poor and underrepresented, and resisting the many pressures upon them to serve those who are already privileged.

We need not presume that politicians are, as the conventional wisdom holds, "a good deal worse, morally worse than the rest of us" to think it important to look for ways in which institutional rules, customs, codes, and laws can aid legislators in fulfulling their duties.[20] We need only assume that they are, like the rest of us, not angels. If they are less than angels, then structural supports are necessary.[21] Furthermore, even angels could benefit from structural supports for supplying the defect of perfect knowledge and coordination of their collective activities.

Structures can serve in three ways to support legislators in carrying out their duties. First, structures can create specific duties that would not otherwise exist. Some duties do not exist unless we can expect that they will be enforced or we can trust each other to perform them. Although this is not true, as Hobbes believed, for all our obligations (such as the duty not to injure others), it probably is true for those duties the social purpose of which cannot be achieved unless compliance is widespread. Even Kant argued that certain duties (such as the duty to respect private property rights) are contingent in this sense.[22] Duties that are intended to ensure the fairness of a competitive process, such as elections, are most clearly contingent on mutual guarantees, because their very purpose, procedural justice, depends on compliance by (nearly) all the competitors. Such duties, to use Hobbes's terms, bind us *in foro interno* "to a desire they should take place," but not *in foro externo* "to putting them in act" without enforcement or mutual guarantees.[23]

This argument does not depend on accepting Hobbes's views of human nature. If we presume, contrary to Hobbes, that many people are public spirited, or even altruistic, structural guarantees will still be necessary to create certain duties. We do not want only altruists to handicap themselves in the race for public office. For them to do so would be not only self-defeating but also against the public interest of organizing a process to maximize the possibility that the best people win.

A second way that structures can support duties is by improving

---

[20] Michael Walzer, "Political Action: The Problem of Dirty Hands," *Philosophy and Public Affairs* 2, No. 2 (Winter 1973), p. 162.

[21] See *The Federalist*, No. 51, p. 349.

[22] "No one is bound to refrain from encroaching on the possession of another man if the latter does not in equal measure guarantee that the same kind of restraint will be exercised with regard to him." *The Metaphysical Elements of Justice*, ed. by John Ladd (Indianapolis: Bobbs-Merrill, 1965), § 42, p. 71.

[23] *Leviathan*, ed. by C. B. Macpherson (Baltimore: Penguin Books, 1968), Pt. I, chap. 15, p. 215.

moral character. "A good and sound constitution," Rousseau argued, "is one under which the law holds sway over the hearts of the citizens; for, short of the moment when the power of legislation shall have accomplished precisely that, the law will continue to be evaded. But how to reach men's hearts?" The key to reaching the hearts of citizens, according to Rousseau, is educating them when they are young "through institutions that . . . develop habits that abide and attachments that nothing can dissolve."[24] Institutions can improve moral character by reaching not only the hearts but also the minds of citizens, teaching them to think systematically and critically about how to fulfill their duties. In the case of public officials, institutions can improve moral character without actually changing anyone's character simply by attracting better people to office. Although in a democratic society we cannot, as Plato imagined, "compel the best natures . . . to see the good" and then to take their turn in the drudgery of politics,[25] we can try to arrange political offices so that they attract as many of the best people as possible, while still maintaining a fair democratic process.

The third general way in which institutions can support duties is by offering what social scientists have called selective incentives (more commonly known as rewards and punishments) to individuals to make their behavior, regardless of their character, conform more closely to their duties.[26] This institutional method of making self-interested calculations correspond to dutiful actions, "the principle of the artificial identification of interests,"[27] finds its most comprehensive expression in Bentham's political theory. But it was Hume who provided the best reason for using institutional incentives in this way to support legislative duties: "It is a just *political* maxim *that every man must be supposed a knave,* though at the same time . . . [it] is false in *fact.*" If we do not assume politicians to be self-interested and we do not find institutional means to make them, "notwithstanding [their] insatiable avarice and ambition, cooperate to public good," then, Hume concluded: "We shall in vain boast the advantages of any constitution and shall find in the end

---

[24] *The Government of Poland*, ed. by Willmoore Kendall (Indianapolis: Bobbs-Merrill, 1972), p. 4.

[25] *The Republic of Plato*, ed. by Allan Bloom (New York: Basic Books, 1968), Bk. VII (519d, 540b), pp. 198, 219.

[26] See, e.g., Mancur Olson, Jr., *The Logic of Collective Action* (New York: Schocken Books, 1968), pp. 51, 133–35.

[27] Elie Halevy, *The Growth of Philosophical Radicalism* (Boston: Beacon Press, 1955), pp. 17–18.

Means of:	Structural supports for:		
	Autonomy	Accountability	Responsibility
Creating duties	Limitations on contributions and honoraria	Laws requiring disclosure	Rules against filibustering
Improving moral character	Primary education (including character) Secondary and higher education (critical moral resoning)	Habits of honesty	Legislative customs and codes of ethics
Supplying incentives	Explusion for bribery and extortion Public financing Raising salaries	Sunshine laws responsible and competitive journalism Public hearings in bureaucracies	Publicizing and punishing absenteeism Public financing (paradox of legislative reform)

Figure 1

that we have no security for our liberties or possessions except the good will of our rulers; that is, we shall have no security at all."[28]

One could turn the tables on Bentham and Hume and argue that even with the most highly developed system of selective incentives we shall boast in vain of the ethics of our legislatures if all our legislators are insatiably greedy and ambitious. There always will be ways for the unscrupulous to benefit from shirking their duties. But this argument tells us only that it would be a mistake to concentrate exclusively on any single way in which structures can support legislative duties, not that moral character is the key to legislative ethics.[29]

The analysis that follows examines specific institutional means for furthering each legislative duty—autonomy, accountability, and responsibility—in each of these three ways: creating specific obligations to support that duty, improving moral character, and increasing compliance with the duty regardless of moral character (see Figure 1). The analysis is by no means exhaustive. It only demonstrates ways of reasoning from the general duties of legislators to some specific structures of legislatures. A much more detailed empirical investigation would be necessary to defend conclusively any specific institutional reform.

[28] "Of the Independency of Parliament," *Essays: Moral, Political, and Literary* (London: Oxford University Press, 1963), p. 68.

[29] Cf. Joel Fleishman, "Self-Interest and Political Integrity," in *Public Duties*, p. 82.

STRUCTURAL SUPPORTS OF DUTIES

The duty of legislative autonomy itself does not depend upon institutional enforcement, since the social benefits of autonomous judgment and behavior do not disappear with partial compliance. Legislators who find themselves surrounded by colleagues controlled by special interest groups still have an obligation to use specific means "to avoid all conflicting interests and influences that might undermine, or appear to undermine, independent judgment on behalf of the public interest."[30] The more specific obligation to limit the size of campaign contribution, however, is contingent on well-enforced rules that define such an obligation. Legislators are not obligated to limit the size of campaign contributions that they receive from individuals or organizations unless they are assured that their challengers are similarly bound or that they are not thereby unfairly disadvantaged in electoral competition. It would defeat the purpose of imposing the obligation if the electoral fortunes of only public-spirited politicians suffered.

It is also true that large contributions, gifts, and honoraria do not necessarily cause legislators to disregard the merits of legislation. Yet to preserve autonomy we are justified in placing limitations on these sources of income because of their potential for corrupting the judgment of legislators. Although we often cannot say that a particular contribution has corrupted the judgment of a particular congressman, we can say that a pattern of contributions to a congressman or a group of congressmen is likely to do so. If the members of the Committees on Banking, and Energy and Commerce predominantly receive contributions from the industries they regulate, we may reasonably suspect that the influence of these industries on these congressmen is greater than the merits of their cases would warrant.

Citizens not only need to know about improper influences in the legislature but also must seek to eliminate them if possible. Disclosure alone is inadequate because legislators on these committees are responsible for designing bills in the general interest. But some ways of overcoming the dependence of legislators on special interests create new problems. A rule requiring members of these committees to divest themselves of all financial holdings and not accept any campaign contributions from the industries that they regulate could create excessive dependence on opposing interests. In the absence of public financing of elections it might also unfairly disadvantage them compared to their

[30] "Model Code of Ethics for the United States Senate," *A Hastings Center Report Special Supplement*, ed. by Carol Levine and Joyce Bermel (February 1981), p. 19.

challengers. It is impossible to solve the problem of excessive dependence without public financing, but rules limiting the size of honoraria and contributions alleviate it and do so without creating worse problems in its stead. Congress now limits the size of a single honorarium to $2,000 and campaign contributions to $1,000 for an individual and $5,000 for a political action committee. Raising the limit for individual contributors up to that for PACs, as Gary Jacobson suggests,[31] might reduce further the disparity of influence between organized groups and individuals. Determining where to set the ceiling on contributions requires calculating the effect of different ceilings on the electoral competition between incumbents and challengers. One cannot expect politicians to make these calculations individually and arrive at similar estimates. This is another reason why laws that represent a collective judgment are necessary to establish and enforce such an obligation.

Since its primary requirement—a capacity to act on relevant reasons—is a faculty that legislators acquire before entering office (if they acquire it at all), the duty of autonomy is especially dependent upon the moral education provided by nonlegislative institutions. Two forms of moral education support autonomy: basic character training and training in critical reasoning. Both are necessary; neither alone is sufficient. The basic moral education that legislators receive as children undoubtedly has a profound effect on their moral character. But in a democracy, primary schools should provide a general education for democratic citizenship. They cannot, as in aristocratic societies, provide an education in political leadership for one class of citizens and an education in political deference for another. However successful our basic moral education is, therefore, the habits that it inculcates and the precepts that it teaches will not directly constitute a morality for public office.

Courses in political ethics can contribute to developing the autonomy of legislators, teaching them how to think systematically, critically, and publicly about the special moral problems that are routinely encountered in public life. Discussion and debate in caucuses and committees as well as on the floor continues moral education in the legislature itself. We should recognize that this kind of cognitive moral education is not a substitute for early character training. But we should not therefore decide to "send the philosophers home . . . and admit that moral education will take place, much as it always has, through examples and even a bit of

---

[31] See Gary C. Jacobson, *Money in Congressional Elections* (New Haven: Yale University Press, 1980), p. 243.

'indoctrination' in the virtues of democracy.''[32] Without a trained capacity for moral deliberation, legislators will be ruled only by habit and tradition; they will be incapable of criticizing or defending bills on moral grounds, unable to persuade their colleagues through rational argument when controversial issues arise. The same point Michael Walzer has made about the inadequacy of our cultural ideal of the "strong, silent hero" applies, perhaps with greater force, to legislators who cannot engage in moral discourse:

> One would not want Humphrey Bogart to stop in the middle of *Casablanca*, say, and deliver a lecture on just and unjust wars. But it is important to understand that his gut feeling and his instinct for the good are parasitic on other people's lectures, on a whole tradition of moral discourse. It is also important to understand that his silence is at least in part inauthentic and historically false. For in war, men and women face hard choices, and have to think about them. And since those choices are not only personal but also collective, they have to think out loud, to argue, to criticize, to persuade. On these occasions it is not all that helpful to be heroic but inarticulate.[33]

But we cannot count on moral education to support the duty of autonomy. First, because we simply do not know how to educate people who always act autonomously despite pressures to do otherwise. Even people of high moral character occasionally succumb to temptation, and the risks of the misuse of power are greater in politics than in most other pursuits. Furthermore, citizens sometimes have good reason not to choose the candidate who has independent judgment, even if they have sufficient information to determine who that is. When they disagree with the independent candidate on an issue of fundamental moral importance, voters might reasonably choose a challenger who endorses their position on this issue. This is one exception that Mill recognized to his general rule that citizens should defer to politicians of superior character and intellect:

> A people cannot be well governed in opposition to their primary notions of right, even though these may be in some point erroneous. A correct estimate of the relation which should subsist between governors and governed does not require the electors to consent to be represented by one who intends to govern them in opposition to their fundamental convictions.[34]

We must therefore also look to structures that will supply the defect of better motives to legislators who are not predisposed to act autonomously. Although we cannot enforce the duty to exercise independent

---

[32] Mark Lilla, "Ethos, 'Ethics', and Public Service," *The Public Interest*, No. 63 (Spring 1981), p. 17.

[33] "Teaching Morality," *The New Republic*, 10 June 1978, p. 13.

[34] *Considerations*, chap. XII, p. 510.

judgment, we can establish certain rules that prevent or at least decrease the need for legislators to depend excessively on certain interests.

The most obvious negative incentives for violating the duty of autonomy are criminal laws against bribery and extortion. But criminal punishment is not enough since conviction for bribery or extortion does not always result in defeat at the polls. Moreover, autonomy is a duty owed not only to a legislator's constituents but also to those groups that are least well represented electorally and financially. Legislatures therefore should as a rule expel congressmen who flagrantly violate the duty of autonomy through bribery or extortion.

Another set of reforms would increase the public funds legislators receive so as to decrease their dependence on private interests and thereby increase their freedom to judge legislation on its merits. Public financing of elections probably would be the most effective (and costly) means of freeing legislators from excessive dependence upon financial interests to whom they do not want to be beholden. The degree of freedom of course would vary with the level of financing. But any level of financing that reduces the time legislators must spend raising money increases the time they can spend deliberating and responding to those groups whose views are relevant to the merits of legislation. Public financing also might improve the character of legislators, since people who wish to dedicate a significant part of their lives to public service are less likely to seek or to stay in office if the "disgusting, degrading, demeaning experience"[35] of raising campaign funds interferes significantly with their ability to exercise their judgment (or act responsibly) while in office.

Increasing the salaries of legislators is a less costly (though probably less effective) means of increasing their autonomy by decreasing their dependence on special interests. Those states that still have part-time "citizen-legislators" might consider making representation a full-time, full-paying job, which it probably should be in any case given the quantity and complexity of legislation that now comes before state legislatures.[36] Congress and full-time state legislatures might pay their members higher salaries. Increasing salaries also would make legislative office more attractive for people who are not independently wealthy, thereby expanding the pool of qualified candidates. Furthermore, as long as we cannot eliminate all the influences that bias the independent judgment of legisla-

[35] Hubert Humphrey, quoted in Jacobson, *Money*, p. 170.
[36] See the Citizens Conference on State Legislatures, *State Legislatures: An Evaluation of Their Effectiveness* (New York: Praeger Publishers, 1971).

tors, we should prefer legislatures composed of a wider rather than a narrower range of socioeconomic interests.

The idea of increasing the salaries of legislators is, for many reasons, unlikely to be popular. But citizens should realize that their unwillingness to spend enough to permit congressmen concurrently to live on their salaries and up to the standards expected of them almost invariably results in legislatures disproportionately composed of the independently wealthy. The premise of a common argument against raising legislators' salaries—that we do not want our representatives to lose touch with the common person—is sound, but the conclusion—that we therefore should not pay them higher salaries—is not.

Like autonomy, the duty of accountability exists without specific means of enforcement simply by virtue of our democratic system of government. But unlike autonomy, almost every means of achieving accountability requires mutual guarantees in order to become a specific legislative duty. This is because the major purpose of accountability is for citizens if they wish to make fully informed choices among the candidates running for office. For candidates of one party to reveal to voters all the relevant facts about themselves, whether favorable or unfavorable to their electoral fate, makes relatively little sense, except as a tactic to win the favor of the electorate and apply pressure to their challengers to do the same. Voters would still not know whether the information they received was complete or accurate. They would have good reason to be suspicious, since it is not likely that politicians, just for the sake of furthering accountability, would freely admit facts that they believe will harm them at the polls. With certain exceptions (like murder or insanity) disclosure is not obligatory unless most competitors comply, because only then would disclosure not defeat the major purpose of accountability.

In addition to supplying information that voters can use to hold legislators accountable, laws requiring financial disclosure also place an additional burden of justification upon legislators who back bills that serve their own financial interests and thus may discourage legislators from flagrantly subordinating their political judgment to their financial interests. Some congressmen have complained that disclosure makes it more difficult to vote their conscience on bills that also benefit them financially. It is true that only in extreme cases, when a legislator's position blatantly violates the public interest or seems inconsistent with his voting record on similar issues, can we conclude with any certainty that his judgment is not autonomous. That it can be misleading and an obstacle to autonomy is not an argument against disclosure, only against its misuse, since the alternative is clearly worse: permitting legislators to use the power of public office secretly to further their personal interests. Surely it is better to burden legislators with the task of convincing us that they have good reasons for supporting those bills that also benefit them financially.[37] As Mill argued, "even the bare fact of having to give an account of their conduct is a powerful inducement to adhere to conduct of which at least some decent account can be given."[38]

Far from being too great a burden, the present disclosure rules of the House and Senate do not ask enough of congressmen. The rules do not require disclosure of loan guarantees that legislators have made to businesses, even though legislators may act to aid those businesses. And they leave some important details of reporting to the discretion of individual members, such as whether to identify the nature of their holdings with a brokerage firm, or in a trust or partnership.[39] The most serious deficiency of present disclosure laws is that they do not provide for a congressional committee or an independent agency to check the accuracy of disclosures. Without a provision for random audits, the requirement of disclosure, according to Senator William Roth, "is a paper tiger." The effect of disclosure without any check on its accuracy in some instances may be worse than no disclosure at all, because citizens may be led to have a "false sense of confidence" in their representative's judgment.[40] To guard against this misplaced trust is a large part of the purpose of disclosure laws.

Beyond trying to teach all citizens the virtue of honesty, social institutions offer no specific educational means to promoting accountability by improving moral character. The duties of autonomy and accountability radically differ in this respect as well. The willingness to make independent judgments is in general a virtue, but the willingness to publicize facts about one's life is not.[41]

Abuses of accountability occur not only when individual politicians lie or conceal information to improve their electoral fortunes but also when legislators collectively act in secret, sometimes even when they act

---

[37] See Jeremy Bentham, "On Publicity,"*Essays on Political Tactics*, Vol. 2 in *The Works of Jeremy Bentham,* ed. by John Bowring (Edinburgh: W. Tait, 1843), 310–17.

[38] *Considerations*, chap. X, p. 493.

[39] *Congressional Quarterly*, September 5, 1981, p. 1678.

[40] Brooks Jackson, "Congress Is Disclosing Less Than Meets the Eye," *The Wall Street Journal*, 12 August 1982, p. 3.

[41] Sissela Bok makes a similar point in comparing lies and secrets: "Whereas every lie stands in need of justification, all secrets do not. Secrecy may accompany the most innocent as well as the most lethal acts; it is needed for human survival, yet it enhances every form of abuse." *Secrets* (New York: Pantheon, 1982), p. xv.

in good faith to further their conception of public, party, or constituent interest. Sunshine laws that open floor proceedings, committee hearings, and caucuses to some form of public scrutiny promote accountability and simultaneously increase the incentives for legislators to act responsibly.[42]

The major difficulty in designing sunshine laws is determining what kind of publicity is most appropriate. Whether proceedings on the floor, in caucuses, and committee hearings should be televised, open to the press, the public, or reported only by detailed minutes depends on the effect of each form of publicity on the purposes of the particular proceedings and the importance of immediate and broad dissemination of the information. Television coverage might be appropriate for floor proceedings but not for committee hearings that involve the testimony of private persons or for caucuses that must facilitate bargaining and compromise.

Laws requiring that legislators make more information available to the public, however, are only a partial solution to the problem of accountability. Depending on how it is processed, more information may make accountability more difficult. Citizens may have access to a great deal of information that they cannot possibly use to good effect. The more information that is available for public scrutiny, the more newspapers, journals, and public interest groups must take as one of their primary responsibilities presenting information in a form that interested citizens can use.

One risk of increasing publicity of legislative action is that more controversial decisions may be delegated to bureaucratic agencies, thereby defeating the very purpose of publicizing legislative activity. One way of decreasing this risk is to open more of the proceedings of bureaucratic agencies to the public. Since it is virtually impossible (and probably undesirable) for legislators themselves to formulate all the policies necessary to govern a complex society, we already have good reason to institute procedures that increase public scrutiny of bureaucratic agencies.

Many of the specific obligations that comprise the general duty of responsibility exist independently of enforceable regulations. Doing one's fair share of institutional chores, not running for Congress by running against it, not protecting congressional colleagues from due criticism, and taking steps toward structural reform of the institution are examples of largely noncontingent duties. But at least one part of the duty of

---

[42] "Secrecy can diminish the sense of personal responsibility for joint decisions and facilitate all forms of skewed or careless judgment." Bok, *Secrets*, p. 109.

responsibility is contingent upon institutional enforcement: the duty not to obstruct legislative procedures. In the partisan process of legislation it is unlikely that all legislators will exercise sufficient self-restraint over their discussion to permit expeditious lawmaking. And if only those legislators who restrain themselves do not filibuster, debate on the merits of a bill suffers from the absence of those voices that might have contributed the most to its substance. Without uniform enforcement we would bear the costs of a rule against filibustering—restricting freedom of debate—without realizing the benefits of a more efficient process of legislation. Since partial compliance may produce worse results for the legislative process than no compliance at all, the duties of legislators with regard to activities such as filibustering are best viewed as contingent on the existence of well-enforced rules that clearly define what constitutes unacceptable obstruction.

The means of educating legislators to be more autonomous in their judgment is bound also to make them more willing to accept many of their institutional responsibilities. However, legislative institutions themselves can do more by way of education to further the responsibility of their members than they can to further their autonomous judgment. Customary practices are one essential part of an education in legislative responsibility: congressional party leaders and committee heads have in the past taught new members what is expected of them; members informally distribute honors and dishonor among themselves according to traditional understandings of what constitutes responsible behavior. Codes of ethics may be another part of the moral education of legislators. Unlike many customs, codes make the mutual standards of responsibility explicit and therefore help ensure that all legislators are informed of those standards, even if they are not convinced by them.[43] The educative effects of institutional customs and codes are especially important in supporting unenforceable responsibilities, such as the duty to attend to under-represented interests, which are not likely to be fulfilled unless they become part of a constitutional morality.

But customs and codes are not enough so long as electoral pressures deflect congressmen from fulfilling their institutional responsibilities toward spending their time raising campaign funds and promoting their own reelection. Selective incentives can ameliorate this problem either by increasing the extent to which institutional responsibility pulls legislators away from electioneering or decreasing the extent to which electioneering pushes legislators away from institutional responsibility.

---

[43] Dennis Thompson, "The Ethics of Representation," *A Hastings Center Report Special Supplement*, p. 11.

Punishing congressmen for dereliction of duty is a means of increasing the pull away from electioneering. Mike Mansfield, then the Senate majority leader, suggested an indirect form of punishment for absenteeism:

> How we can work in a situation like this [where Senators do not even appear to vote] I don't know. But I am at the end of my wits. I do not know any way to keep them here, unless perhaps the local newspapers start publicizing the absenteeism of their Senators.[44]

Congress itself has used a more direct incentive in the past. Despite lack of enforcement and an attempt by the Senate to repeal it in 1976, a law (passed in 1856) still on the books provides for docking the salaries of congressmen. Its standards of negligence may be too strict, but the claim that such a law has "no contemporary meaning" because "a senator's absence from Washington and the Senate floor at no time separates him from the continuing responsibilities of his office any more than when . . . the Supreme Court justices are away from the court on recess" is unconvincing.[45] The more appropriate analogy is to justices who are regularly away from the Court during oral arguments or when their fellow justices are deciding cases.

Although the principled objections to docking pay and withdrawing perquisites are not cogent, the practical objections may be compelling. Such penalties are not likely to have much deterrent effect if the alternative to being irresponsible is not getting reelected. The most direct and least costly means of furthering legislative ethics are not always the most effective. Public financing of elections would be more effective: it has the potential of significantly reducing the electoral pressures on legislators that push them away from their institutional responsibilities, and attracting more people to office who want to serve the public dutifully and have the freedom to do so once in office.

THE PARADOX OF LEGISLATIVE REFORM

When we seek structural supports for the most extended and important notion of responsibility—the duty to try to correct the structural defects of the institution—we encounter a general paradox of legislative reform. We need good structures to create responsible legisla-

---

[44] David R. Mayhew, *Congress: The Electoral Connection* (New Haven: Yale University Press, 1974), p. 142.

[45] Francis R. Valeo, quoted in *Congressional Ethics* (2nd ed.; Washington, D.C.: Congressional Quarterly, 1980), p. 73.

tors, but we also need responsible legislators to build good structures. So, who shall legislate for the legislators?

An ideal legislator was Rousseau's response to a similar paradox: by what means can an unenlightened people institute an enlightened system of laws? To invoke the ideal legislator—"a superior intelligence beholding all the passions of men without experiencing any of them . . . yet ready to occupy itself with [our happiness]"—is to admit that the cause of significant structural reform is hopeless in a democracy.[46] Is there any other way of legislative reform? Despite the Rousseauean paradox, reform is not impossible. It may be possible even if we can only count upon incumbents to regulate themselves in what they perceive to be their own interests, because some of the reforms that we need are in their interests. Higher salaries and some changes in campaign financing are examples. That this is so should not make us complacent about achieving even these reforms. Although legislators may consider a salary increase in their financial interest, most believe (whether accurately or not) that an increase is not in their electoral interest. Consequently, most salary raises have been passed retroactively, surreptitiously, or automatically.

The use of campaign finance reform to strengthen the electoral advantages of incumbents is a more serious and complicated problem. Whatever the advantages of public financing for supporting the ethics of legislators, we should oppose such reform if it undermines the competitive democratic process by giving incumbents an overwhelming chance of reelection. Not all schemes of campaign finance would have this consequence, and the interest of legislators in supporting challengers from their own party mitigates against adoption of schemes that create an unfair competitive advantage for incumbents. (This is one among many reasons to find ways of shoring up our declining party system, perhaps by channeling campaign funds through the parties.[47])

If these efforts were all we could expect from legislators' calculations of their interest, we might well despair of legislative reform. But we can reasonably hope that citizens and nonlegislative institutions will exert pressure on legislators to adopt a more enlightened view of their interest—to recognize the necessity of maintaining public confidence in the integrity of democratic legislatures and the democratic process more generally. The press may be the single most important institution for these purposes. But not just any press will do. We need journalists who accept as part of their duty to provide citizens with information relevant to

---

[46] "The Social Contract" in *The Social Contract and Discourses*, ed. by G. D. H. Cole (New York: E. P. Dutton, 1950), Bk. II, chap. 7, p. 37.

[47] G. Jacobson, *Money*, pp. 170–75.

holding representatives accountable. The theory of legislative ethics therefore requires a companion theory of journalistic ethics.

The prospects for the practice of legislative ethics, even more so than that of journalistic ethics, depends ultimately upon the active support of citizens. The theory of legislative ethics can guide legislators who, independently of popular preferences, wish to act dutifully to improve democratic institutions. But it would be foolish to anticipate that the ethics of legislators or the ethics of legislatures will be radically improved before democratic citizens demand improvement. The theory of legislative ethics can serve to advise not only legislators but also citizens. Both the theory and practice of legislative ethics in these ways rely on the theory and practice of democracy.

ACKNOWLEDGMENTS

For comments on earlier versions of this essay, we are grateful to Douglas Arnold, Daniel Callahan, Gary Jacobson, and Bruce Jennings. We also benefited from discussions with members of the Hastings Center Project on Legislative Ethics.

10

The Scope of Legislative Ethics

JOHN D. SAXON

Few readers would dispute the notion that well-publicized scandals such as Abscam[1] have sullied the reputations of our legislatures. Where agreement is less likely to be found, however, yet where it is critically needed, is with regard to the myriad issues subsumed under the rubric of "legislative ethics." These issues go to the very foundations of American democracy. They involve theories of legislative representation, questions of the definition and scope of ethics, the standards against which legislative conduct is judged, the question of by whom legislative conduct should be judged, the role of legislative disciplinary committees, and the wisdom and efficacy of codes of conduct.

WHAT IS LEGISLATIVE ETHICS?

The first issue on which there is little consensus[2] is the most fundamental: What is legislative ethics? How do we define it, and what is

---

[1] For a history of the Department of Justice investigative operation which came to be known as Abscam, see U.S. Congress, Senate Select Committee on Ethics, *Report of the Select Committee on Ethics, U.S. Senate, Investigation of Senator Harrison A. Williams, Jr., to Accompany S. Res. 204, September 3, 1981*, Rept. No. 97–187, 97th Cong., 1st sess. (Washington, D.C.: Government Printing Office,1981) p. 23. For an analysis of the benefits and deficiencies of Abscam as an undercover operation see U.S. Congress, *Final Report of the Select Committee to Study Undercover Activities of Components of the Department of Justice to the U.S. Senate*, Report No. 97-682, 97th Cong., 2nd sess., December 15, 1982 (Washington, D.C.: Government Printing Office, 1982), pp. 1–22.

[2] It is necessary to refer to consensus, as this essay does repeatedly, because *ethics* refers

---

JOHN D. SAXON ● Director of Corporate Issues, RCA Corporation, and former counsel, Select Committee on Ethics, United States Senate, Washington, D.C. 20006.

its proper scope? One obvious parameter which helps define legislative ethics is that legislators should not break the law. They should not engage in bribery. They should not sell, or trade on, their office. But to define ethics by reference to the criminal law is to provide only a floor of minimal standards of conduct; "serve, and break no laws" as an aspirational norm for legislators addresses questions of criminal procedure and rules of evidence more than it does conduct befitting the dignity of legislative institutions.

Legislative ethics obviously means more than simply break no laws, more than avoid going to jail. Many would suggest that ethics is defined in terms of a "higher standard"—higher than the aspirational norms against which we measure the conduct of the average citizen. Having said this, though, what does it mean? What is this higher standard which gives meaning to legislative ethics and practical guidance to legislators?

It is often expressed by the maxim, traceable to Plato, that "public office is a public trust."[3] Perhaps better than any single statement, this

to *shared* values and principles, not purely subjective or individualistic ones. In seeking consensus, we are elevating to a level of mutual recognition, and affirming, certain principles we hold in common (shared values) but which previously we may not have so clearly recognized as being shared. By *ethics,* then, in this essay, the author refers to a "shared moral consensus."

The need for consensus in the field of legislative ethics was repeatedly recognized in recent hearings to revise the U.S. Senate's Code of Official Conduct. Ethics Committee Chairman Senator Howell Heflin concluded his opening statement by asking, "Finally, and perhaps most fundamentally, is there consensus in our society at large as to what constitutes ethical behavior among elected officials?" U.S. Congress, Senate Select Committee on Ethics, *Hearings, Revising the Senate Code of Official Conduct Pursuant to Senate Resolution 109,* 97th Cong., 2nd sess. (Washington, D.C.: Government Printing Office, 1981), p. 2. Senator Heflin later cited agreement among his colleagues on certain ethical goals but a lack of consensus regarding how those goals should be met: "Those of us in the Senate fully recognize, and fully accept. . .that the maintenance of high standards of conduct among elected officials is paramount. Where we perhaps lack consensus, and we seek answers through means of these hearings, is how best to meet the challenge of preserving the integrity of the institution and its Members." Ibid., p. 133. Vice Chairman Senator Malcolm Wallop, comparing the Senate attempting to revise its ethics code in 1980 to the Senate which adopted that code in 1977, lamented, "I don't think we are any closer in consensus as to what it should be now as we were at the time that took place. . . .I wish that something could float down from heaven on the chairman and myself and we could come to the kind of consensus that would satisfy not only our ethical needs but the public's perception of what we are doing." Ibid., pp. 125–126. Dr. Daniel Callahan, Director of The Hastings Center, testified, "In studying the experience of various professional groups with their own codes of ethics, we have found that they do not function well unless they are firmly rooted in an underlying ethical consensus among members of the professions." Ibid., p. 79.

[3] Association of the Bar of the City of New York, *Congress and the Public Trust* (New York: Atheneum, 1970), p. xix.

concept captures the essence of ethics in public service. It is succinct, simple, even eloquent, but in many ways it is nonetheless fundamentally unhelpful. In numerous matters arising in the course of service in state legislatures and the Congress, it provides little real guidance for those who seek to do what is ethical.

Consider the practical shortcomings of this seemingly appropriate precept: "public office is a public trust" means, we might agree, that at all times a legislator will do what is in the interest of the public, as opposed to what is in his personal interest. But *which* public? The American public in general, or the public in that legislator's home district or state? There is no problem if the two coincide. Often, however, they do not. For example, suppose a United States senator represents a grain-producing state and the president proposes a grain embargo against an adversary in retaliation for that adversary's aggression against a third nation. Clearly, the *national* interest would require support of the embargo. But if the senator's constituents vigorously opposed it, the senator arguably would be breaching his public trust, violating his sacred covenant with the people of his state, if he voted against their wishes.[4] (Consider, too, the related question of how many of his constituents opposed the embargo, and with what intensity.)

This example obviously raises the issue of whether one subscribes to the trustee or delegate theory of representation.[5] Although this dichotomy is not a new one, it does have an ethical dimension if as a component of legislative ethics we include the notion that service in legislative bodies means that at all times one will serve the interests of the public.

If the concept "public office is a public trust" includes the requirement that a legislator serve the interests of the public, it logically follows that there is a concomitant *ethical* obligation to ascertain what those "interests" are. The extent of this requirement, however, is equally unclear. To be ethical, to what lengths must a legislator go in determining the views of his constituents? At least theoretically a case could be made that if he sends no questionnaires to his constituents he is guilty of a breach of ethics. Of course, if he were a member of Congress, he could

---

[4] Such a hypothetical case, in fact, was offered by Senator Heflin in the Senate code revision hearings. U.S. Congress, Senate Select Committee on Ethics, *Revising the Senate Code,* p. 84. Heflin admonished his witnesses that the notion of referring to something as in the national interest versus merely state or local interest was risky because it was "putting dangerous labels onto traditional legislative perogatives." Ibid., p. 85.

[5] It has been suggested that the delegate–trustee dichotomy does not readily lend itself to "any very helpful general principles or ethical standards." Dennis F. Thompson, "The Ethics of Representation," *Hastings Center Report,* Special Supplement, Vol. II, No. 1 (February 1981), p. 12.

send, by means of franked mail,[6] a questionnaire to each constituent four times a year. We might then want to ask if it mattered that in the process he possibly enhanced his name identification at taxpayer expense. Would we then examine *motive*[7]—franked questionnaires, for example, are permissible, even with an incidental political benefit, but *only* if sent with the intention of soliciting constituent input and not of deriving political benefit? If so, the question of how, and by whom, motive is determined is problematic. Motive could, and probably would, be mixed—part solicitation of constituent views, part taxpayer-funded political advertising. Relatedly, we might ask if the questionnaire were worded—which we know can be done—so as to contaminate the response data. Is this unethical?

A panoply of similar definitional problems abounds. Consensus probably exists for such abstract propositions as: legislators should not accept gifts from parties with an interest in legislation which might improperly influence them in the discharge of their official duties; they should do nothing which would compromise their independence or autonomy of judgment; they should not conduct themselves in a manner which reflects discredit on the institution; and they should avoid even the appearance of impropriety. Each of these statements helps give definition to legislative ethics. Applied to specific circumstances, however, it is unclear what these arguably vacuous statements really mean.

It could be argued that any gift from a lobbyist, even a simple lunch, would appear improper to some people. Yet few state representatives could realistically be expected to "sell out" for a club sandwich and a beer.

Succumbing to pressures to vote along party lines could also be said to compromise one's autonomous judgment;[8] yet most observers would

---

[6] The vice president, each member or member-elect of Congress, the elected officers of both houses, the legislative counsels of each house, the Senate legal counsel, and certain other persons are authorized to send as "franked" mail matter relating to the "official business, activities, and duties" of their office. 39 U.S.C. § 3210 (b) (1). The term *frank* is derived from the latin word *francus*, meaning "free," *Black's Law Dictionary* (Rev. 4th ed.; St. Paul: West, 1968), p. 787, and denotes the autograph or reproduced facsimile signature of the person authorized to send matter through the mail without prepayment of postage charges. 39 U.S.C. § 3201.

[7] It is necessary to distinguish at least two senses of motive. One, the actual state of mind of a person (or legal *mens*), is likely to be impossible to discover and arguably irrelevant to evaluating conduct; second, the aim or purpose that could reasonably be ascribed to an observable action, is a more objective standard and is more directly relevant to understanding legislative conduct and its consequences.

[8] For a discussion of the "threat to the autonomy of legislative judgment," see Thompson, "The Ethics of Representation," p. 12.

be reluctant to conclude that it is unethical *per se* to vote along party lines. Perhaps party line voting would be unethical if a legislator did so without reflection on the merits of the issue. But again, someone would have to determine motive.

It may be that these are not ethical issues at all, but merely questions of political judgment. But they logically flow from abstract propositions generally accepted as within the scope of legislative ethics. How that scope is delimited is but a variation on the question of what is legislative ethics, and it is equally as elusive.

THE SCOPE OF LEGISLATIVE ETHICS

Consensus likely exists for the proposition that legislators should not engage in conflicts of interest. Conflict of interest is usually defined in *financial* terms—that a legislator will not undertake an official act in return for a thing of value which redounds to his personal financial benefit.[9] The philosophical justification for the avoidance of conflicts of interest is legislative autonomy: a legislator should be free to exercise his independent judgment on behalf of his constituents. But many things could compromise one's independence of judgment. Party affiliation, already alluded to, is one. So is geography. It would be difficult to believe, for example, that in Sunbelt–Frostbelt battles over the formulae used in dispensing federal grant dollars each member of Congress reached his decision after careful, objective reflection on the merits, divorced from considerations of from which region he comes and into which region the federal spigot flows.[10]

Or religion. It is inconceivable to me that religion has played no part whatever in voting on issues involving prayer in public schools, abortion, aid to parochial schools, or support for Israel. The argument, however, is not that if it did this was improper. Rather it is to demonstrate the difficulty in defining ethical conduct in such broad and abstract terms as avoiding influences which compromise autonomous legislative judgment.[11] On the other hand, definitions of legislative ethics or delimitations

---

[9] Thompson has criticized "the exclusive—almost obsessive—focus of the [U.S. Senate ethics] code on conflicts of *financial* interest," contending that financial conflict of interest alone cannot provide an adequate basis for a code of ethics for legislators. Ibid., pp. 11–12 (emphasis in original).

[10] For a discussion of the impact of regional groups and caucuses on the congressional policy-making process see Richard E. Cohen, "Regionalism Playing an Increasing Role in Shaping Congress's Policy Debates," *National Journal*, 15 (May 21, 1983), 1053–1057.

[11] Perhaps it is unrealistic to suggest that such influences can be avoided entirely. As a

upon its scope which address conflicts of interest only in financial terms only get at corruption or "near-corruption," not bias or prejudice, which may be not only more pervasive but also more pernicious.

In addressing the scope of legislative ethics it is possible that we have placed too much emphasis on money. Perhaps the *least defensible* influence which can compromise autonomous legislative judgment is money. The harm flows, though, not from money itself, but from the likelihood that the influence it has is disproportionate to that which it should have. Yet overzealous grassroots lobbies operating on shoestring budgets can exert an influence disproportionate to their numbers, just as can lobbyists who generously spread money around in the form of gifts, meals, beverages, entertainment, travel expenses, honoraria, and campaign contributions. Perhaps the scope of legislative ethics should extend to influences which are unnaturally disproportionate or have an unhealthy effect on the political process whether for reasons of money or numbers of people. No broad consensus exists, however, for determining which influences are disproportionate or have an unhealthy effect on the process, although it would be necessary to consider the balance of influences in the system as a whole, not just those of an individual legislative representative, or even one branch of government.

The notion of proportionate influence raises a further question regarding scope: if certain ethnic groups are not represented in legislatures in numbers proportionate to their incidence in the general population, the question of how well legislators represent the underrepresented becomes, for some, an ethical one. In addition, the argument can be taken one step further: that legislators have an ethical, and affirmative, obligation to ferret out and serve *any* group which is unrepresented or underrepresented.[12]

It has been suggested that aspects of the legislative process itself should also come within the scope of legislative ethics.[13] For example,

---

practical matter, they often cannot. What should, and perhaps can, be avoided is the compromising of autonomous judgment to which contact with such influences can lead.

[12] The need to broaden the scope of legislative codes of ethics to address the "exclusion of interest" so as to include the obligation to represent those citizens traditionally underrepresented has been advanced by Thompson, "The Ethics of Representation," pp. 12–13.

[13] Thompson, for example, believes we should broaden the scope of legislative ethics to encompass abuse of legislative process, which can "frustrate the process of arriving at just laws." Ibid., p. 12. Callahan has testified that abuse of the advise and consent power by the U.S. Senate has an effect far more serious than if a senator were to violate the franking laws. U.S. Congress, Senate Select Committee on Ethics, *Revising the Senate Code*, pp. 81–82. Senator Heflin cautioned, however, against what he called the danger of "trying to put ethical standards into. . .legislative functions". Ibid., p. 91. For a

consensus would likely exist for the proposition that in their official acts, legislators should be fair, objective, and forthright. Yet it is not unheard of for a legislator to "stack" a hearing or "slant" a hearing record. To some, this is a legitimate use of the legislative process; to others, it is "just politics"; to still others, it is unethical conduct. The relationship between scope and enforcement, developed below, is illustrated if we take the latter view. How would a broad ethical prohibition on abuse of the legislative process be enforced? To prevent stacking a hearing, would we require a "pro" witness on a given issue for every "con" witness testifying? But some witnesses are neither pro nor con, and some issues do not lend themselves to such simplistic categorizations. The difficulty in making such a judgment, as with determining when a hearing record is slanted or when a nominee's confirmation is stalled for purely political reasons, should be evident.

We might also agree, as an abstract ethical proposition, that legislators should conduct themselves on the floor with civility and regard for the dignity of the institution. Accepting this, how are we to characterize an *ad hominem* attack? What if, for example, in the House of Representatives, a member from a heavily industrial state referred on the floor to a colleague from a largely rural state as a "redneck"? Perhaps such behavior is merely crude and ungentlemanly. Some, however, might argue that it is not befitting the dignity of the institution, and therefore is unethical. Such a position perhaps confuses congressional *etiquette* with congressional *ethics*. Maybe, though, they differ only as a matter of degree. If you think not, consider your response if during a heated House floor debate on abortion a pro-life member were to call a pro-choice member a "baby killer."

It should be clear from the foregoing that attempts to define the scope of legislative ethics are difficult, to a large degree, because of a lack of consensus on such questions as who is the "public" whose interest a legislator should serve. Which theory of representation one adopts suggests certain things about the ethical obligations which follow. If one adopts the view that subjects, as a consequence of their social contract, authorize action on the part of the sovereign, then it would arguably be unethical for the sovereign to act without their authorization. This notion breaks down in contemporary application when one considers that on most, if not all, issues on which legislators vote some constituents clearly favor their vote, whereas others clearly oppose it. There would be no one

---

discussion of the notion of ethics versus politics in the context of broadening the scope of legislative ethics see Callahan, "Revising the United States Senate Code of Ethics," *Hastings Center Report,* Special Supplement, p. 3.

left to serve in our legislatures if we disciplined all legislators guilty of the theoretically unethical conduct of voting without the authorization of all the represented.

In truth, no one theory of representation is the correct one. Legislators alternate between roles as delegate and trustee. The dichotomy, however, is not a false one; it is simply that there are certain decisions which are more appropriately made with regard to the national interest, irrespective of constituent views, whereas others may be made on a more parochial basis. Yet no one has been able to delineate which decisions universally fit the former category and which fit the latter, making it difficult, when operating from the assumption that as a proposition of legislative ethics legislators should seek to serve the public interest, to determine whether a legislator is being ethical when sometimes he votes in the national interest and sometimes not. One can be quite troubled by the difficulty of this analysis and yet not be ready to state unequivocally that whether one votes in the national interest as a member of the House or Senate or the state interest as a member of a state legislature is not a question with an ethical dimension. For some, the answer may be that a legislator should *always* vote in the *public* interest, but how the *public* is defined is a matter of discretion left to the individual legislator. If so, there is something at least confusing, and perhaps disturbing, about the possibility on a given vote in the Congress of 535 different definitions of the public interest, which notion would perhaps also suggest that uniformity is not a necessary ingredient of legislative ethics. Nor, if the broad goal is representativeness, is it altogether clear that our legislatures would ultimately be more *representative* were they comprised solely of priests, rabbis, or angels.

Definitional problems are also presented by differing views as to the obligations and allegiances of legislators. At any given moment, they owe allegiance to the public at large, their constituents, the voters who elected them, the institution of the Congress or their state legislature, the United States government or the government of their state, their party, their colleagues, their staff, the committees and caucuses of which they are a member, the ad hoc policy coalitions to which they belong, their families, and themselves (their conscience, their physical health, their political well-being). As should be obvious, these allegiances frequently conflict. To require, therefore, as an abstract proposition that a legislator not breach his allegiance to one of these groups lest he be guilty of ethical misconduct is both purposeless and unfair. It is difficult—perhaps impossible—to rank in priority those to whom legislators owe allegiance, yet the definition of legislative ethics would be clearer could consensus be achieved on such a ranking.

How a legislator views his official duties affects determinations of whether they have been ethically discharged, yet consensus as to what one's official duties are is difficult to achieve. If a legislator neglects his official duties, he is guilty, we might agree, of misconduct; some might suggest the most serious form of misconduct. If a legislator misses a crucial roll call vote, we could reason, this is misconduct—a neglect of duties, an abdication of the solemn responsibility to represent one's constituents on an important matter of public policy. But before we discipline for such misconduct, surely we would require more than one vote to be missed. But how many? Perhaps we would want to examine the *nature* of the vote. If so, what standards would we apply for judging the nature? Some might want to know *why* the legislator missed the vote. What if the legislator were giving a political speech at a campaign fund-raiser? What if it were a nonpolitical speech, but for which he received an honorarium? What if he were conducting field hearings on unemployment in his state or district? Would it matter whether unemployment were a serious problem among his constituents, or whether he were up for reelection? Perhaps it all comes down to motive, but if it does, we are once again presented with the difficulty of how, and by whom, motive is determined.

Official duties, like allegiances, can both vary and conflict. Some are more important than others. But determinations of importance must also vary from legislator to legislator. There is a place for Mr. or Ms. Outsider, Righteous Cause, Educator, Maverick, and Institution. There is a legitimate place for the legislator who masters parliamentary procedure. It is difficult to say such a legislator is guilty of misconduct if he neglects meeting constituents in order to be on the floor. It is also difficult to label as being guilty of misconduct a legislator who ignores committee work if he believes it more important to raise public consciousness regarding the burning issues of the day. Yet, in a broadened scheme of legislative ethics, we would likely agree that committee work and constituent contact are important components of legislative duties, the neglect of which constitutes unethical conduct.

The ultimate legislative act is the vote, for which legislators arguably should be held most accountable. But there exists little consensus for how this is to be done. Presence for a roll call vote may actually mean neglect of other duties. In fact, a strong case could be made that voting is the *easiest* of legislative duties. Assuming discharge of the obligation to vote is our standard, what then? Surely we would not require 100 percent attendance. Would it be 75 percent? 51 percent? Suppose our standard were 95 percent, and a legislator made 98 percent of all roll call votes.

Many might find it curious if the two percent missed were because the legislator dodged the controversial issues of busing, abortion, gun control, and school prayer. Our legislator could have made 100 percent of all roll call votes (a fine example, we would all agree!) but each time could have taken her guidance from her party leader, or her largest campaign contributor. Or she could have voted *for* an issue, but worked behind the scenes to insure its defeat. From these simple examples, it should be evident that the act of voting as a duty of legislative office does not give rise to an easy consensus for delimiting the scope of legislative ethics.

One way in which consensus could be found regarding the scope of legislative ethics is to suggest that although allegiances, theories of representation, and concepts of official duties may vary from legislator to legislator, or from situation to situation, whatever one's particular theories, allegiances, or roles, they are not to be neglected for personal gain, either financial *or* political, which neglect would constitute ethical misconduct. There are, no doubt, legislators whose primary goal is political survival,[14] and recent structural and normative changes in the Congress and some state legislatures have given rise to a form of destructive individualism or enterpreneurship whose emphasis on electoral consciousness raises serious ethical questions.[15] Such behavior often manifests itself in otherwise legitimate legislative acts (the holding of hearings, franking of newsletters, or exchange of information and views with lobbyists) which are only unethical—if at all—when the motive for their undertaking is exclusively or primarily personal advancement and not the serving of desirable legislative ends. How such determinations of motive are made, and what standards are thus employed, have yet to be agreed upon, but these questions must be addressed.

WHAT STANDARDS SHOULD APPLY?

The matter of the standards to be employed in evaluating legislative conduct appears at first blush to be unrelated to the question of the proper scope of legislative ethics, yet it raises two questions which bear in a direct and significant manner upon the issue of scope: that of the proper

[14] David R. Mayhew writes that "congressmen must constantly engage in activities related to reelection" and identified three kinds of activity which members find it electorally useful to engage in: advertising, credit claiming, and position taking. *Congress: The Electoral Connection* (New Haven: Yale University Press, 1974), pp. 49–73.

[15] Mayhew, as much as a decade ago, began to see evidence of this. Ibid.

balance between specificity and generality and the relationship of procedural due process to this balancing equation.[16]

The question of a proper balance concerns how to make the standard
general enough to approximate the desired higher standard without being
vague and thereby presenting legislators faced with allegations of misconduct with a procedural due process "notice" problem.[17]

It is axiomatic that ethical determinations involve line-drawing, often
in grey areas. In a politically charged climate in which incumbent
legislators are scrutinized with frequency and intensity by both challengers and the media,[18] the least we can do is prospectively to give them the
benefit of our collective wisdom as to the specific conduct we expect of
them.

To provide legislators no more guidance than the admonition to do no
wrong and reflect no discredit could lead, on the one hand, to the
disciplining of legislators who admit to the commission of acts which they
never conceived a given ethics committee using a particular *after the fact*
standard would deem improper; on the other hand, it could breed timidity
on the part of legislators who, given such vague guidance, are afraid to do
anything.

The desire for specificity should not be misinterpreted. A legislator is
not relieved of responsibility for the propriety of his conduct by requiring
that allegations of misconduct be measured against precise standards.
Legislators must still make individual judgments. What we must guard
against is that we do not leave them hanging; that is, that we fail to tell
them, as specifically as possible, what behavior is expected of them other
than "do not reflect discredit on the institution"[19] but afterwards inform
them that in a particular area of greyness they made the wrong decision,
for which they are to be disciplined.[20]

---

[16] The relationship between the scope of an ethics code and its enforcement is discussed by
Thompson, "The Ethics of Representation," p. 13.

[17] Imposing sanctions for the violation of general, aspirational norms raises what Senator
Heflin called the "question of vagueness and uncertainty and the issue of the rule of law."
U.S. Congress, Senate Select Committee on Ethics, *Revising the Senate Code*, p. 2.

[18] Senator Heflin believes the media have a tendency to overstate the extent of unethical
conduct in our legislatures. The media, he stated, "takes [sic] a violation and sometimes
blow it out of proportion," Ibid., pp 58–59. For a discussion of the impact of the media
regarding the debate over ethics versus politics in the context of broadening the scope of
legislative ethics see Callahan, "Revising the United States Senate Code of Ethics," p. 3.

[19] The damage an individual legislator can do to the reputation of the institution as a whole
is discussed by Thompson, "The Ethics of Representation," p. 13.

[20] It has been suggested that the congressional power to discipline by expulsion is restricted
to certain improprieties such as violations of criminal law and official misconduct. There
appears, however, to be little credible support for this view. See "Bowman v. Bowman,

Going too far in the direction of specificity, though, presents its own problems. First, if all situations are covered by a body's internal standards, the individual legislator ends up making no ethical judgments himself, which surely cannot be desirable.[21] Second, legislators predisposed to misconduct arguably would be encouraged to engage in improper acts on the theory that they were not expressly forbidden by such specific standards.

The quest for specificity also takes us away from concern for a higher standard in that adherence to a higher standard obviates the necessity for, and makes the disciplinary process impervious to, attempts to apply formal requisites of due process.[22]

The argument goes like this: since we are not talking about the criminal process, we do not have to meet the constitutional requirements which obtain for criminal defendants. Instead, we are concerned about whether the conduct complained of is exemplary, or whether it tarnishes the integrity of the institution and its members.

Even in a legislative disciplinary proceeding, however, allegations of misconduct must meet some minimal (though perhaps unstated) requirement as to form. They are presented by someone, as is evidence, which must meet tests of admissibility. The allegations are evaluated by someone, against certain standards. Burdens of proof must be met and presumptions overcome. Standards of fairness and impartiality must be observed. Although not a criminal proceeding, a legislative disciplinary proceeding is, at a minimum, quasi-judicial. Surely the procedural due process rights of notice, the opportunity to be heard, and to confront and examine witnesses should be afforded the accused.[23]

Article I, Section 5: Congress' Power to Expel—An Exercise in Self-Restraint,'' 29 *Syracuse L. Rev.* (1978), 1072, 1092–1102; McLaughlin, "Congressional Self-Discipline: The Power To Exclude and To Punish," 41 *Fordham L. Rev.* (1972), 43, 48–51.

[21] Senator Wallop referred to his fellow Senators who rely on the Select Committee on Ethics to interpret the Senate Code of Official Conduct, thereby insulating them from criticism, as "colleagues who come to us to receive their cocoon." U.S. Congress, Senate Select Committee on Ethics, *Revising the Senate Code*, p. 29.

[22] Callahan contends the dilemma over the specific versus the aspirational exists within every profession or discipline which has sought to regulate the conduct of its members, and that to date none has found "the ideal balance," Callahan, "Revising the United States Senate Code of Ethics," p. 4.

[23] For a discussion of what procedural safeguards should be afforded the accused in a congressional disciplinary proceeding, see the discussion between Senator Heflin and Victor H. Kramer, U.S. Congress, Senate Select Committee on Ethics, *Revising the Senate Code*, pp. 72–73. Current procedural rules within the Senate are set out in U.S. Congress, Senate Select Committee on Ethic, *Rules of Procedure*, adopted February 23, 1978, revised July, 1982 (Washington, D.C.: Government Printing Office, 1982). Current House procedural rules are set forth in U.S. Congress, United States House of

Disciplinary proceedings also have within them the potential to be charged with emotion. Given the low esteem in which legislators are held by the public, the tendency of allegations to have greater attendant publicity than subsequent findings of exoneration, and the tendency of misconduct charges—once made—to haunt public officials throughout their careers, however unfounded they may prove to be, it is at least arguable that highly visible public officials should be afforded *greater* procedural due process than "common criminals" who do not operate within such an environment.

A case can be made for such a view, especially given what some observers see as an American public, informed by cynical media, which believes all officeholders to be "on the take." Such a public would believe that all against whom charges are brought are guilty and, upon the criminal conviction or legislative disciplining of a legislator, that their suspicions about all legislators have been confirmed. Perhaps there are legislators who would hide behind the shield of procedural due process. If such protections are deemed worthy for the innocent, however, it is inconsistent with our historic conception of fairness to argue that it would be unethical for them to be used by the guilty.

The question of standards and the tension between the desire for a higher standard and the needs of procedural due process have been insufficiently examined. Perhaps the courts may delineate the requisites of due process in legislative disciplinary proceedings; given their past pronouncements, however, it is extremely unlikely that they would cast aside what they have asserted are constitutional obstacles to such a ruling.[24] The whole matter is an important one, however, for the question

---

Representatives, Committee on Standards of Official Conduct, *Rules of Procedure*, 98th Cong., 1st Sess., January 27, 1983. For an excellent overview of the procedural rights of individuals in Congressional hearings in general see James Hamilton, *The Power to Probe* (New York: Random House, 1976), Chapter 8.

[24] The reluctance of the courts to interfere with, or define the procedural safeguards necessary for, congressional disciplinary proceedings is grounded largely in the separation of powers doctrine. See, e.g., Williams v. Bush, 81-2839 (Dist. Ct., D.C., 1981). In *Williams*, former Senator Harrison A. Williams, Jr., brought suit in federal district court to enjoin the Senate from debating the resolution recommending his expulsion from the Senate for Abscam-related violations of federal criminal law and Senate rules until such time as the court specified, among other things, the due process rights to which he was entitled. Judge Gerhard A. Gesell, in an oral ruling denying Williams' motion for a temporary restraining order (Hearing on Motion for Temporary Restraining Order, November 27, 1981, Transcript, pp. 26–28), and Judge Louis F. Oberdorfer, in an unreported written opinion dismissing Williams' suit (Unreported Memorandum Opinion, February 3, 1982, pp. 2–3), both cited separation of powers reasons for refusing to delineate Williams' procedural due process rights.

of standards and the needs of due process both affect, and are affected by, the scope of legislative ethics.

WHO SHOULD DECIDE THESE QUESTIONS?

Implicit within this discussion has been the notion that in judging legislative conduct *someone* would do the judging. But who? The obvious answer is the public at large, but insuring uniformity of judgment is difficult (assuming, as some might, that uniformity is desirable), to say nothing of whether the public is sufficiently well informed to understand these questions fully. If not, we could rely upon the media to inform them, although some may find unsettling the notion of an ethics regulatory scheme which depends for its success on an enlightened public and responsible media.

If legislators misbehave, their constituents can always "unelect" them, but not until the end of their terms. If a senator, for example, misbehaves during his first year in office, we would have to wait five years for discipline at the polls. Even then, the public can always choose not to "unelect" him. In fact, if a legislator is convicted of a felony, a significant body of political theory would support his constituents' right—conviction notwithstanding—to return him to office. Having that right, the question then becomes whether *should* they return him.

The view has been expressed that perhaps we should have no specific prescriptive or proscriptive standards, but rather require extensive public financial disclosure, that is, to disclose publicly all financial dealings—gifts, honoraria, assets, business endeavors, and affiliations—and then let the voters decide whether their legislator's conduct has been proper.[25] Aside from the obvious deficiency that not all ethical problems are financial ones and hence would not be disclosed, one must also question

---

[25] At the U.S. Senate code revision hearings, Senator Malcolm Wallop stated, "I would submit that the vast majority of the provisions of the present Code of Official Conduct could well be rendered unnecessary by a meaningful system of public financial disclosure." U.S. Congress, Senate Select Committee on Ethics, *Revising the Senate Code*, p. 149. Former Committee Vice Chairman Senator Harrison Schmitt testified that he favored a scheme which combined the Senate's existing public financial disclosure statement with publication of the preceding year's tax return, in large measure because such a scheme would be "basically self-enforcing." Ibid., p. 36. For an explanation of one such full disclosure scheme see the testimony of Senator Lowell P. Weicker, Jr., ibid., pp. 94–98, 153–155. The limitations of such a full disclosure model have been pointed out by Thompson, "The Ethics of Representation," pp. 13–14, and by Joel L. Fleishman, "The Disclosure Model and Its Limitations," *Hastings Center Report*, Special Supplement, pp. 15–17.

whether the voters would have the proper sensitivity to evaluate certain types of conduct. The chairman of a legislative energy committee, for example, should probably have at least minimal contact with energy companies. Were there no such contact between legislators and lobbyists with expertise in the legislators' area of jurisdiction, the legislators might be put in fewer compromising positions. But they also would know less. As one observer put it, we would find ourselves with legislators on white horses wearing white hats, but the white hats would be sitting atop empty heads.[26] The more cynical members of the public, however, would nonetheless view such contact as inherently suspect. The greater question, of course, is how much contact is too much?

The uniformity question, related to the earlier question of national versus local interest, is similarly problematic. Assuming we seek to guarantee autonomous judgment, it might be said that if a legislator receives gifts, honoraria, and campaign contributions from oil companies and then votes the producer line on every vote, he is "in bed with big oil" and his independence of judgment has been compromised. Yet voting with big oil may be exactly what the voters of his state want and therefore what he ethically should be doing, if he is from an oil-producing state. Permitting the voters to decide questions of ethics could lead to the arguably anomalous result that receiving gifts or honoraria from oil companies, for example, is ethical for legislators from Louisiana, Texas, and Oklahoma but not for those from Michigan or Massachusetts; tobacco money would be ethical in North Carolina but not in Vermont; cattle ranch money would be okay in Montana but not in Delaware.

Problems of who should do the judging are not eliminated simply by making the judges members of legislative ethics committees.[27] Little consensus exists on the question of what is the proper role of such a committee. Some argue that it is merely to receive and investigate complaints of wrongdoing (reactive); others say that it is to initiate investigations (aggressive) and to counsel legislators (preventive). Per-

---

[26] Testimony of Florida State Senator Jack Gordon, U.S. Congress, Senate Select Committee on Ethics, *Revising the Senate Code,* p. 116.

[27] Getting legislators to serve on ethics committees—generally viewed as a thankless task—is quite difficult. As Senator Wallop bluntly put it: "What I worry about is that we already have a situation in which people snicker about 'Oh, you poor bastards are on the Ethics Committee, I am going to lay this on somebody who hasn't seniority enough to say no, or hasn't been around long enough to say no.' We want to get the Committee and the Senate to change its mind about the Committee, to see that assignment as a singular affirmation of trust on the part of the leadership; and get the Senate to think better of itself in terms of its ability to make its own reputation." Ibid., p. 145. For a general discussion of the problem of enlisting members for service on legislative ethics committees see Callahan, "Revising the United States Senate Code of Ethics," p. 2.

haps it should be all of these. If the committee views its role as merely reactive, many serious dilemmas may go unresolved. If, on the other hand, it adopts an activist posture, then threshold judgments of a more subjective nature must be made about whom and what to investigate, judgments which some legislators would be understandably reluctant to make.[28]

Excessive reliance on ethics committees creates an additional problem. With no consensus on many of these questions, and with legislators operating within a fish bowl with their conduct subject to close scrutiny, it is only natural to expect them to seek answers to ethical questions from their ethics committees. In one sense, this is desirable—better to ask and avoid improper conduct than to act blindly or without certainty. Yet this approach could ultimately lead to determinations of ethics *by committee*. Individual members could delegate, even abdicate, their responsibility for individual ethical judgments. Ethics committees would become a substitute for individual integrity, a form of legislators' "security blankets," with legislators' attitude being that "if *they,* the members of the committee, determine that it's ethical, I'll do it. If they determine that it's unethical, I won't." Such a system raises a fundamental philosophical question about who should be making such decisions.[29]

If the problems with such a system of "ethics by advisory opinion" proved too great, they could be alleviated by abolition of ethics committees or their authority to render advisory opinions. But this raises a problem equally as troublesome: that a public official, whose every act is magnified and examined by a critical press, the general public, and eager challengers, would be left with no concrete guidance in deciding upon the proper course of action in instances which are unprecedented, subjective, or unclear.[30]

---

[28] At the U.S. Senate code revision hearings, Senator Wallop suggested the Select Committee on Ethics broaden its role to include the counseling of members. He defined the Committee's proper role as follows: "I suggest the implementation of a full-ranging ethics program which offers counseling and guidance to Members, contains a minimum of outright regulation, provides a meaningful financial disclosure of interests rather than wealth, and maintains the jurisdiction and authority of the Ethics Committee to actively investigate any allegations of misconduct which, if true, would reflect discredit upon the Senate." U.S. Congress, Senate Select Committee on Ethics, *Revising the Senate Code,* p. 148.

[29] Senator Wallop referred to it as "substituting the ethical judgment of a commission for those broader ethical judgments that an individual should make on his own behalf." Ibid., p. 118.

[30] The problem with any ethics regulatory scheme which relies in substantial measure on the public as judges of legislative conduct must resolve the difficulty Fleishman cited regarding the full disclosure model: how to guarantee that relevant information necessary

ARE CODES OF CONDUCT THE ANSWER?

Codes of conduct exist for most professions and many legislative bodies.[31] Although helpful as a means of providing general guidance, they are not without their limitations.

The first problem, that of determining a code's purpose, is the fundamental one.[32] It can narrowly, precisely circumscribe behavior by use of proscriptive or prescriptive norms. It can set a higher standard by means of aspirational norms. It can be written largely for the prospective guidance of legislators; to satisfy cosmetically (or appease) the public; or to serve as a standard against which allegations of misconduct are judged after receipt of a complaint. It can be enforced in its entirety, or like the Ethical Consideration–Disciplinary Rule distinction in the recently modified Code of Professional Responsibility of the American Bar Association, only the minimal standards could be enforced with the higher standards being merely aspirational.[33] If a code exists for the prospective guidance of legislators, its drafters must ascertain whether it should attempt to be dispositive of all questions of ethics. As with many other questions addressed herein, there is insufficient consensus regarding the purpose of codes.

There is also insufficient consensus regarding the *scope* of codes. Legislative codes of conduct presently are confined to such matters as financial disclosure, gifts, conflicts of interest and disqualification, outside earned income, franking, political activity, campaign finance, travel, defrayal of official expenses, and employee discrimination.[34] Questions

---

for wise decision making is widely disseminated. "The Disclosure Model and Its Limitations," p. 17.

[31] The process of formalizing and standardizing in a procedural way specific rules of conduct for public officials has been appropriately referred to as "the institutionalization of ethics in government." Bruce Jennings, "The Institutionalization of Ethics in the U.S. Senate," *Hastings Center Report,* Special Supplement, p. 5.

[32] For an excellent discussion of the various purposes which legislative codes of conduct can serve see Callahan, "Revising the United States Senate Code of Ethics," p. 2.

[33] The Model Code of Professional Responsibility was adopted by the ABA in 1969 but was viewed as having become outdated as the practice of law changed dramatically during the 1970s. In 1977, the Association leadership established a Commission on Evaluation of Professional Standards to evaluate the Model Code and recommend appropriate revisions. The commission discarded the code format, with its confusing ethical consideration–disciplinary rule distinction, and developed a new code in traditional legal "restatement of the law" format with explanatory comments. The new Model Rules of Professional Conduct were approved by the ABA House of Delegates at their 1983 annual meeting. "A New Ethics Code," *American Bar Association Journal* (January 1984), p. 13.

[34] Such is certainly the case with the present codes in the United States Senate and House of Representatives. The Senate code comprises rules XXXIV–XLII of the Standing Rules

such as duties of office, obligations to constituents, access to the institution, and abuse of its processes are not usually covered.[35]

Codes are also affected by the lack of consensus in the standards debate over specificity versus generality. The difficulty is in drafting a code *specific enough* to provide concrete, prospective guidance to legislators without removing their individual responsibility and without legitimizing those things not expressly included as prohibited, yet *general enough* to contain aspirational norms without being so vague as to subject legislators to charges of unethical conduct by political enemies. If we adopt norms of aspiration, do we enforce them? If so, we have the problem of determining *prospectively* what is meant by such a norm as not "reflecting discredit on the institution." If we adopt aspirational norms but do not enforce them, there seems something a bit curious about the admission we make to the public: that we know, and can agree upon, what the highest attainable standard of conduct *should* be, but will not enforce it; that we will only *enforce* a standard lower than what we really know to be befitting the dignity of our legislatures. If a legislature adopts only aspirational standards—not to be enforced—the question arises whether its ethics committee would still entertain complaints. If so, we might be faced with the lack of the due process requirement of before-the-fact

---

of the Senate. U.S. Congress, *Standing Rules of the Senate,* Doc. No. 98–10, 98th Cong., 1st sess. (Washington, D.C.: Government Printing Office, 1983). The House code is found in Rule XLIII of the Rules of the House. U.S. Congress, *Code of Official Conduct, Rule XLIII of The Rules of the House of Representatives,* Committee on Standards of Official Conduct, United States House of Representatives, Washington, D.C., 97th Cong. For an explanation of the House rules see U.S. Congress, Committee on Standards of Official Conduct, *Ethics Manual for Members and Employees of the U.S. House of Representatives,* (Washington, D.C.: Government Printing Office, 1981). For a brief history of the existing House and Senate codes, see Jennings, "The Institutionalization of Ethics in the U.S. Senate," pp. 7–8; for a fuller history of the earlier evolution of ethics codes in the House and Senate, see Association of the Bar of the City of New York, *Congress and the Public Trust,* pp. 216–221.

[35] An excellent statement on the need to broaden a legislative ethics code to these and other subjects was offered by Daniel Callahan at the U.S. Senate's code revision hearings: "[A] Code of Ethics ought to serve a broader purpose than that of simply attempting to cope with corrupt behavior and abuse of the office of Senator. . . We think a code should define the broadest purpose and function of the office of Senator. It should encourage a full reflection on all the roles of a Senator, and it should embody positive obligations as well as negative injunctions. The Code should be broad enough to provide Senators with a general framework to reflect upon the moral responsibilities that come with their place in our society. . . . It should, most importantly, provide a clear statement to the American people reaffirming the Senate's commitment to honor its public trust." U.S. Congress, Senate Select Committee on Ethics, *Revising the Senate Code,* p. 76.

notice.[36] If not, public confidence in the integrity of our institutions may be further eroded as our ethics committees will be viewed as being unresponsive to public charges of impropriety. If we adopt specific prescriptive or proscriptive norms, it is possible legislators might concentrate only on those provisions of the code.[37] The cumulative effect may cause us to ask if we truly want a situation, which several of these possibilities would permit, of a risk-free legislator.

Codes of ethics should never be permitted to substitute for the exercise of individual judgment. They can never cover every conceivable circumstance, nor can they provide every possible answer. They are for general guidance, and yet there exists a tendency to view them as all-encompassing, as if a code were dispositive of every question. If something is not prohibited by the code, we reason, it is not unethical. If something is not addressed by the code, we conclude, it does not involve a question of ethics.

Codes of conduct are necessary for professions and public officials. But if ethical determinations are inherently subjective, from the moment the pen is first put to paper and the first ethical canon begins to take shape, we have already made arbitrary decisions about scope, about definition, about reach, about degree—all matters on which consensus is less than sufficient.

Codes do an especially poor job of resolving dilemmas.[38] How would a code strike a proper balance, for example, which permits legislators at the federal level to serve their legitimate informing function by means of franked mail but stops them short of using the frank as political propaganda? How would a code strike a balance which permits legislators to have legitimate, substantive, ongoing contact with representatives of so-called special interests, yet prevents them from developing over time such a cozy relationship that their autonomy is compromised?

---

[36] For a fuller exposition of this problem, see the statements by Senator Heflin, ibid., pp. 26, 52.

[37] This problem has been cited by Senator Wallop as cause for some concern: "[W]hat is disheartening is that their [his colleagues'] ability to make honest judgments is obscured by a Code which narrows the scope of their consideration to the prohibitions found within that Code." Ibid., p. 12. For further statements by Senator Wallop on the problem of narrow specificity and the presumed propriety of that which is omitted, see ibid., p. 28.

[38] While legislative ethics codes "may have some value in terms of compliance by legislators, they are not a complete solution, perhaps not even a significant one, to the problem. . . . There is a need for the sensitizing of legislators to basic values and to their difficulties in balancing these values in resolving ethical dilemmas." James C. Kirby, Jr., "The Efficacy of Legislative Ethics Codes: The Congressional Experience," The Center for Legislative Improvement, *LEGIS/50 Working Paper Series on Legislative Ethics*, No. 4 (1979), p. 8.

Codes also have inherent limitations. In theory, a code would not only *prohibit* misconduct, but also *encourage* ethical conduct. But it is unclear what incentives to good conduct are capable of being institutionalized. If one goal of codes is to change the behavior of legislators, it is also unclear how we measure their efficacy,[39] how we would know when misconduct has been deterred by reason of a code rather than by something else.[40] And if a code by its nature represents a visible effort at self-regulation, given the low esteem in which our legislatures are held, such codes could be inherently suspect in the eyes of the public.

CONCLUSIONS

In addressing legislative ethics, once the scope is broadened beyond "don't steal" and "don't take bribes" we lose much of the consensus necessary for an effective ethics regulatory framework. As has occurred recently in the field of bioethics, we now confront vexing problems, often new and often in the form of dilemmas, to which solutions are not easily found.

My thesis has been very simple. The scope of legislative ethics, at present, is too narrow, confined largely to notions of financial conflict of interest. That scope should be broadened. Yet idealistic notions about the scope of legislative ethics, and equally idealistic notions about the efficacy of codes of conduct, are ill-suited for complex legislative environments in which there have been vast institutional changes; theories of representation vary; consensus on what constitutes official duties is nonexistent; obligations and allegiances often conflict; and legislatures operate in the glare of attendant publicity which has a profound, and often both undesirable and unfair, effect.[41]

---

[39] The efficacy of congressional ethics codes is treated in Association of the Bar of the City of New York, *Congress and the Public Trust*, pp. 221–225.

[40] There is considerable sentiment that ethics codes do not deter legislative misconduct. As former Committee Chairman Adlai Stevenson told the U.S. Senate Select Committee on Ethics during its 1980 code revision hearings, "If there are culprits in our midst, they are very unlikely in my judgment to be deterred by ethics codes." U.S. Congress, Senate Select Committee on Ethics, *Revising the Senate Code*, p. 137. Senator Wallop concurred: "Nothing within the present Code would have led to the discovery of, or prevented the past activities of Senators which were not consistent with the high standards we must demand of ourselves as United States Senators. No amount of regulation or disclosure will prevent a person, Senator or not, from knowingly committing an illegal or unethical act." Ibid., p. 149.

[41] One example of unfairness which involves publicity concerns the availability of legislative ethics committees as a convenient forum for political challengers to bring unfounded or

The import of these thoughts is not to suggest that legislative ethics, like obscenity, is something which cannot be defined but rather is recognized only when seen. It is to suggest that there will be little consensus on the definition of legislative ethics, and the broadening of its scope, until there is better consensus on the issues of official duties, allegiances, and theories of representation and until we further examine questions of political values, legislative priorities, incentives for proper behavior, incentives for reelection, institutional changes and forces, the role of the media, and the degree to which the citizenry is enlightened.

Moreover, the goal of legislative ethics is arguably itself unclear.[42] Perhaps we seek solely to preserve autonomous judgment by policy makers. Perhaps it is better policy we desire. Perhaps better representation. Some might argue that we simply want to affect legislators' conduct; others would argue that we are after their hearts and minds. Beyond not wanting legislators to steal or to be bribed, it is open to question whether the American public even cares about these more abstract questions on which consensus is so elusive.

Not only must we come to the realization that legislative ethics is more complicated than perhaps previously thought, that consensus is lacking in many critical areas, but also that many questions may be unanswerable. For example, which better insures proper conduct: aspirational or prescriptive norms? What standards best enhance the image of a legislature in the eyes of the public? Is there a distinction between individual and institutional propriety? What moral obligations does one assume upon election to Congress or a state legislature? What are the traits and attributes of an ethical politician? Can we say with certainty how a legislator of high moral character should act in every circumstance? Fundamentally, what are the ethical implications of the fact that our representative democracy, designed over two centuries ago, must now operate within a pluralistic, technical, complex postindustrial society?

Arbitrary standards and codes of conduct, regardless how well-

---

speculative charges against an incumbent, all with considerable attendant media coverage. Incumbents, it should be noted, have no comparable forum. For a discussion of the extent to which this has plagued the U.S. Senate, see U.S. Congress, Senate Select Committee on Ethics, *Revising the Senate Code*, pp. 46–47, 86–87, 91–92.

[42] Perhaps as good a statement of the goal of legislative ethics codes and regulatory schemes as can be found exists in the Preamble to the Model Code of Ethics for the United States Senate developed by a panel assembled by The Hastings Center: "[I]n order to maintain the integrity of representative government and to sustain the confidence of citizens in their representatives." "Model Code of Ethics for the United States Senate," *Hastings Center Report*, p. 19.

intended or well-drafted, ultimately will not answer the unanswerable. The solution is not to resort to the old saw "You can't legislate morality" and throw up our hands. It may be, however, morality and ethics being inherently subjective, the standards for ethical judgment must similarly be subjective. In the final analysis, it may be the individual public servant's inner voice which determines the scope of matters with an ethical dimension, and it is that inner voice which must guide him. Although many factors—public opinion, media scrutiny, peer pressure, institutional forces, party doctrine, likelihood of reelection, codes of conduct—can influence that voice, legislative ethics must ultimately be a matter of individual conscience and the covenant established in the electoral context between electors and the elected.

Critics may suggest that we cannot rely on individual good will. In the final analysis, we may have no choice. Legislative ethics, ultimately, is a question of motive. There are too many legitimate governmental, even political, needs to be served to prohibit certain conduct or activities just because if carried out with less than noble intent there is the possibility of either impropriety or its appearance. Once we go beyond "break no laws," what remains of the parameters of propriety is fuzzy, subjective, and difficult to delineate.

Ultimately legislators will be left with little specific guidance, and yet the arena in which they operate subjects them to intense scrutiny. Such is perhaps an occupational hazard. Codes of conduct, although helpful, serve ultimately as a crutch. The best standard, and the best definition of the scope of legislative ethics, may, after all, be the simplest: *Public office is a public trust.* This means nothing should be permitted, no conduct engaged in, which would infringe on the ability of a legislator to exercise autonomous judgment in discharging that public trust. It means that to serve one's fellow citizens is life's highest and most honorable calling; that no thought of personal gain—financial, political, or otherwise—should dictate the decisions entrusted to legislators on behalf of others. It means they neither profit from, nor trade on, their positions. It means that when entrusted with the power to make decisions affecting the lives and livelihood of others, *their* best interest is a legislator's sole justification for official acts. It means, one could hope, that legislators would avoid even the slightest appearance of impropriety.[43]

---

[43] This concept is in keeping with that of a "higher standard" espoused by Chairman Heflin and Vice Chairman Wallop of the U.S. Senate's Select Committee on Ethics. Heflin, affirming that the "maintenance of high standards of conduct among elected office holders is a matter of great priority," concluded, "[T]he American public has every right to demand nothing less than the utmost in integrity from those elected to positions of public trust. This expectation is firmly woven into the fabric of the American experience." U.S.

Such a standard is, admittedly, subjective. Consensus could not be found in defining every term. But in a vast sea of subjectivity, it is perhaps the best we can do. I leave it to the individual judgment of each legislator to give it meaning, with this admonition: define the scope of what constitutes legislative ethics broadly and the range of questions which permit an ethical dimension liberally.

Perhaps we will fail in this task. But try we must. As John W. Gardner reminded us recently, "The capacity of humans to achieve the exalted goals they conceive is limited at best; but their insistence on trying is sacred."[44]

Congress, Senate Select Committee on Ethics, *Revising the Senate Code,* p. 1. Wallop stated, "In the final analysis, we all recognize that we are keepers of the public trust and must hold ourselves to an inherently higher standard of conduct than might otherwise be required." Ibid., p. 150.

[44] John W. Gardner, *Morale* (New York: W. W. Norton, 1978), p. 120.

11

Legislative Codes of Ethics

DANIEL CALLAHAN

For reasons both lofty and lowly, legislative reform efforts in recent decades have focused almost exclusively on the devising or revising of codes of ethics. *Reform* and *codes* have seemingly been understood as synonymous, as if no other route to improved moral behavior existed. The lofty reason behind that emphasis has been the belief that codes provide a particularly effective means by which to shape behavior and articulate acceptable standards of conduct. A more mundane reason may be that it is far easier to devise codes than it is to change those structural or institutional conditions that provide the occasion for misuse of public office in the first place.

No doubt it is that combination of high and low motives that accounts for the characteristically mixed public attitude toward codes. A great deal of effort usually goes into their formulation, they are readily invoked when needed—and yet they are often looked upon with skepticism and jaded amusement. As Charles S. Levy has noted:

> Codes of ethics are at once the highest and lowest standards of practice expected of the practitioner, the awesome statement of rigid requirements, and the promotional material issued primarily for public relations purposes. They can embody the gradually evolved essence of moral expectations, as well as the arbitrarily prepared shortcut to professional prestige and status. At the same time, they are handy guides to the legal enforcement of ethical conduct

DANIEL CALLAHAN ● Director, The Hastings Center, Hastings-on-Hudson, New York 10706.

and to punishment for unethical conduct. They are also the unrealistic, unimpressive, and widely unknown or ignored guides to wishful thinking.[1]

Levy's characterization, perhaps overdrawn, nonetheless brings out the ambivalence that ought to be felt toward codes and their potential efficacy. Legislative codes of ethics ought to be taken seriously, in their formulation, their publication, and their implementation. Yet it would be naive to expect that a code, however well formulated, can alone carry the burden of improved individual or insitutional behavior. If it would be a mistake to place the entire burden of moral hope on a code, it would be no less an error to think that a legislative body can get by without a written statement of its higher values and the ethical requirements of office. An unarticulated and unwritten "gentlemanly code" may have worked well enough in Congress and state legislatures in the nineteenth century. But it will not work any longer. Nor is a financial disclosure provision an adequate substitute for a code. Such disclosures are often not easily accessible to the public or very informative about potential financial conflicts of interest; and they do not even touch upon a wide range of other ethical issues or upon the ethical standing and reputation of legislatures as a whole. Yet a reform effort that encompassed only an effort to change or improve upon a code would inevitably be inadequate, implicitly failing to take account of all those other determinants of moral thoughts and behavior that will and must work their influence. Nonetheless, the writing of a code and the continuing seriousness with which it is taken will be an important index of moral commitment.

Any effort to write a legislative code of ethics must begin with the basic question of the purpose of a code. Surprisingly, it is practically impossible to find any general discussions (much less a theory) about their purposes. To judge from present codes, the tacit answer seems to be that a code is meant to specify and to curb unacceptable behavior; and such behavior is for the most part taken to be that which bears on financial conflicts of interest or the misuse of office for personal financial gain. The scope of the present code of the United States Senate is not untypical, focusing on eight topics only—the acceptance of gifts, outside earned income, financial conflict of interest, unofficial office accounts, foreign travel, use of the franking privilege, political fund activities, and employment practices.[2] It appears to be no less commonly assumed that if an

[1] Charles S. Levy, "On the Development of a Code of Ethics," *Social Work* 19 (March 1974), p. 207.
[2] A number of the ideas developed in this article were first explored in a project carried out by The Hastings Center on revising the U.S. Senate Code of Official Conduct. The results of that project—and a model code developed as part of it—can be found in "Revising the

elected representative observes the (narrow) standards specified in the code, no other grounds would then exist for passing a negative judgment on his or her moral behavior as a public official.

One might in fact guess that another tacit purpose served by a narrow, financially oriented code is that of defusing and delimiting the sphere of ethics, putting as much as possible outside of it and into the more plastic and permissive realm of politics and corrigible public opinion. Far from welcoming a strong public consensus on proper moral standards of a broad and positive kind, legislators may well prefer its absence. They may on occasion be unfairly judged in the absence of such a consensus, but it is more likely that they will benefit from uncertainty and ambiguity.

Moral questions are, in short, generally disliked by legislators. They evoke public indignation, grass-roots revolt, and the formation of fractious, single-minded coalitions. The fewer issues that can be labeled "moral" the better. In saying that I am not implying that legislators do not want to act in moral ways. With others in this volume, I believe that most legislators are ethically serious and responsible. But that predisposition is not incompatible with a wariness toward the rhetoric of morality, or a suspicion of efforts to place the label of "ethics" on a wide range of practices and behaviors thought to be part of the ordinary give-and-take of political life. More than most other people, legislators know that as much harm as good can on occasion be done by a high-minded brandishing of the sword of morality. It is as easily used by fools and knaves as by saints and sages.

I believe it is important to keep this background in mind when thinking about legislative codes of ethics. It helps to explain the narrowness of present codes and the likely resistance of proposals to devise different kinds of codes. Despite those difficulties, it is important that legislative codes be approached in a more open, imaginative way. If intelligently and sensitively devised, they could actually help legislators in their relationship with the general public, make their own role a bit easier, and offer a modest contribution to the more effective functioning of democratic representation.

Before addressing specifically the issue of legislative codes it might be worth asking some general questions about the concept of codes in general, about the experience of other groups with codes, and about the different possible roles that they can play. Consider, for a start, some of the general questions that can be asked. Ought a code to have as its goal

United States Senate Code of Ethics," *Hastings Center Report,* Special Supplement (February 1981), pp. 1–28.

that of shaping behavior toward positive ends, or should one be satisfied with only curbing unacceptable behavior? Ought a code to set out aspirational ideals, high hopes only, or ought it to be written in a way that allows minimal achievement by all at all times? Should a code try to resolve particular moral dilemmas, or should the final moral judgments be left up to the individual conscience? Ought codes to provide guidance only to those affected by them, or ought they also to be designed to educate the general public about what they can rightfully expect of those who are covered by them? Should a code be written in the formal language of the law (as is now the case with most legislative codes), or in more ordinary language? Can a code be credible if it does not provide for a specific enforcement mechanism, or are informal peer and public pressures sufficient? Should codes be written and enforced by legislators only (as is now the case with Congress), or should there be a public representation in both processes?

That is a long list of questions and it would be difficult to discern any consensus on proper answers in either the scanty theoretical literature on codes or in the practices of the various professional and other groups that have devised codes. The 1970s saw a great deal of reform activity in the professions, much of it centering on the devising or revising of codes. The American Medical Association (AMA), the American Bar Association (ABA), the National Association of Social Workers, and the American Association for the Advancement of Science, among others, all undertook code revisions; and numerous corporations and other groups have done the same.

Yet there were some striking differences among those efforts. At one extreme, the new AMA code, officially called "Principles of Medical Ethics," consists of seven propositions, each no longer than one sentence and each aspirational in character (no enforcement mechanisms are prescribed). At the other extreme, the newly adopted code of the ABA is (although an improvement upon the old one) lengthy, detailed, and highly legalistic in character. It not only sets out in great specificity the expected standards of behavior but also provides solutions to a number of common dilemmas. By contrast, the AMA code gives no guidance at all on particular dilemmas.

Some professional codes go to considerable lengths to spell out their philosophical and moral foundations, whereas others do so briefly or not at all. In some fields the code is a central and important document; in others most practitioners seem unaware of its existence. A few major and traditional professions have no general codes of ethics at all—education, the ministry, and the military, for example; and one would be hard pressed to find evidence that those fields are comparatively more lacking in moral clarity than those that have codes. In sum, there is no consensus about the nature and purpose of codes, nor is there any useful evidence that one type of code is more illuminating, or credible, than another. Yet this curious babble of tongues may reveal less than meets the eye and afford more opportunities than might be expected. The lack of agreement on codes does not, as might initially be guessed, indicate a failure to achieve one. There have, on the contrary, been no serious attempts among the various professions to work together in thinking about codes and no theoretical efforts to fill that gap. The picture that emerges is that of a variety of parallel efforts, rarely informed of like efforts by others, and just as rarely tutored by any systematic effort to analyze the purposes to be served by codes. That situation, however, provides the opportunity to learn from the pooled experience of various codes and to glean from a wide range of possibilities those that might best serve legislative ethics.

A beginning can be made by asking first whether there is any established distinction between a code of ethics for a profession and a code for legislators. There is no allusion in the small literature on codes to that problem at all. In the American political tradition, legislators are not professionals in the conventional sense of that term. They may be professional lawyers, or accountants, or business persons, but as legislators they are elected as citizens and to represent citizens. The Constitution specifies only minimal requirements for senators and representatives, and none of them turns on the possession of professional credentials. Does that mean, then, that a code for legislators ought to be different than one for professionals? Not necessarily, except that such a code will not specify norms of technical competence as is the case with most professional codes.

Yet legislative codes as presently written at both the federal and state level are in fact significantly different from most existing professional codes. In general, they are narrow in scope and short on aspirational statements, and they fail to deal with the full range of legislative or representative functions. It is clear that the states have imitated each other to a considerable extent, but far less clear where the model for the original imitation originated. Literary and internal evidence, however, would suggest that ethical codes were designed to become part of parliamentary and other manuals of rules designed for the management and good order of legislatures. Most appear within the body of such rules or, if published separately, follow them in style and format. In most other fields and professions, codes are entirely discrete documents, independent of other rules and procedures.

The present code of official conduct of the United States Senate is typical of legislative codes. It has been incorporated as part of the

"Standing Rules of the Senate," comprising Rules 32–42—one set of rules among many. It is not preceded by a preamble (hence, neither its purposes nor foundations are alluded to) and focuses as mentioned above on a narrow range of essentially financial issues. It is the task of an ethics committee to supervise the implementation of the code, to issue interpretations on unclear or disputed aspects, and to deal with charges or accusations brought under the code. That committee has reported its task to be tedious and burdensome and the details often petty.[3]

A code of that kind is entirely inadequate. It does not do full justice to even a minimal range of the ethical issues that confront legislators. It does not place their moral duties within the context of their other duties. It does not identify the moral customs or traditions or reasoning that would provide a rationale for the specific provisions of the code. From the wide range of other codes in other fields it is possible to imagine some richer possibilities for legislative codes. I will lay out and try to defend some of those possibilities.

A legislative code ought to contain both general aspirational elements (espoused ideals) and precisely codified rules of conduct, principally negative prohibitions. It should encompass the equivalent of what the earlier code of the American Bar Association referred to as "ethical considerations" and "disciplinary rules."[4] A code that contains only the former (as is customary with legislative codes) will lack bite and the possibility of adequate enforcement. A code that contains only the latter will fail to set high enough standards, too severely narrowing the scope of ethics. In distinguishing between aspirational principles and specific rules, it may be necessary to think of some parts of a code as permanent and others as changeable according to shifting circumstances. The aspirational parts should be written in a way that can stand the test of time. Rooting of them in history and tradition will be a means to that end. By contrast, some or most of the more specific (what lawyers term "black-letter") rules and regulations will possibly require frequent revision. The purpose of the more changeable rules is not only to clarify and modify specific points where necessary but also to make certain that those items that are in principle enforceable are stated in such a way that they can be acted upon. A code with a number of unenforceable aspirational elements will be far more credible if it also contains many elements that are enforceable.

---

[3] Cf. "Hearing Before the Select Committee on Ethics, United States Senate," 96th Cong. (Washington, D.C.: Government Printing Office, 1981), *passim*.

[4] *Code of Professional Responsibility and Code of Judicial Conduct* (Chicago: American Bar Association, 1975).

A legislative code ought to lay out the moral obligations of individual legislators and of the legislature as an institution. The moral obligations should be stated in positive as well as negative terms. The predominance of the latter in present codes often leaves utterly up in the air the positive moral goals of legislative ethics, suggesting that the mere avoidance of a few specified evils constitutes the fullness of the legislative moral life. But just how full and extensive is that moral life? Although a legislative code may not be able to touch on everything, it should try to encompass the most important parts of a legislator's varied roles.

Legislators are public officials. It is their duty to see that laws are upheld and enforced, particularly those bearing on the integrity of the legislature. As public officials, they have a special obligation to promote the public interest. To use their office for private gain is the most obvious betrayal of that role. A code should express the broad and positive obligation to promote the public interest and the negative obligation to refrain from using the office for private gain.

Legislators are also representatives. They are elected to act as the agents of those they represent and are accountable to them for their performance in office. On occasion there may and probably will be a conflict between their duty to the public interest and their duty to their constituents; and there may be no readily available solution to that kind of dilemma. No code can resolve that old and inherent dilemma (referred to elsewhere in this volume as the tension between the delegate and the trustee theories of representation). But at the least a code should make clear how basic and inescapable are the obligations of responsible representation. That means a protection of the interests of constituents, accessibility to them, and a special regard for those who might have the most difficulty in making known their needs and interests.

Legislators are also legislators. The purpose of noting this self-evident point is to underscore the collective duties of legislators. Those collective duties are toward the institution of the legislature, toward its customs and rules, and toward those parliamentary and other procedures designed to promote both healthy debate and mutual cooperation. It is not enough that individual legislators be men and women of integrity. No less important is their credibility as a collective whole, a decisive determinant of the extent to which the public respects the legislative process and representative democracy as fundamental institutions for the common good. Responsible attention to legislative duties will be minimal condition for a discharge of the duties of the legislative role, whether they encompass attention to routine commitee assignments, the gathering of information on critical issues, legislative oversight, or honorable committee hearings and investigations and sensible expenditure of public funds.

Legislators, particularly in Congress, are also employers. They have personal staff members, oversee the duties of committee employees, and are responsible for the research, clerical, and other personnel necessary for the efficient operation of the legislature. As employers, legislators have the ordinary duties of fairness and of insuring their employees' compliance with pertinent rules and regulations, particularly those bearing on the carrying out of duties for which they were legitimately hired. On the whole, the duties of legislators as employers have been greatly neglected, in great part because the state legislators are still woefully understaffed in the first place, but also because large personal staffs and legislative support staffs are still a relatively recent phenomenon in Congress. But with the rapid growth of what one observer has called the "unelected representatives," and of their increasingly important role, it is an area that not only needs more stress in codes but also greater study and thought.

Legislators are, finally, often candidates for office. The fact that legislators are elected for limited terms of office means that they are likely to want to continue in the same office or to seek other offices. The use of the privileges of office as a means of continuing in office are well known. There is an inevitable advantage for incumbents merely in holding office, and the temptations to improve that advantage by skillful political use of its perquisites are well known. A code ought to address both the larger ethical issues about the misuse of the advantages of incumbency and the detailed issues (e.g., a franking privilege, personal use of campaign funds) that constitute its substance.

Although there are no doubt other possible ways of classifying the roles and duties of legislators, those suggested here cover most of their activities and also allow for distinctions among the roles they play. A failure to make such distinctions can render general statements about the moral duties of legislators too thin and lacking in contextual specification to have much bite, and no less fail to distinguish among the different kinds of moral dilemmas or problems that can confront legislators, problems that go well beyond financial conflicts of interest.

Yet even if agreement can be reached about the practical range of roles and issues pertinent to legislative ethics, and about the appropriate moral duties, a code should be something more than a set of bald moral assertions and commands. It should seek to commend itself to legislators and the public by articulating the philosophical, political, and ethical premises upon which it rests. It should show itself to be not so much a set of isolated rules trying self-consciously to superimpose virtue and rectitude on the workaday political world as a set of standards integral to a competent and responsible discharge of office. A promising way to do that would be an articulation of the basis of the guiding principles and an explanation of how they are expressed in specific code provisions. Individual rules should be well grounded in their underlying principles, should fit together in a coherent way, and should be accompanied by an explanatory rationale. The history and traditions of legislatures, democratic principles, and political convictions central to American life (and, in the state, regional life) provide the obvious and necessary ingredients for the general principles and the more explicit rules meant to exemplify them.

I have now made a number of general proposals about legislative codes. Is it possible to encompass all of them? Of course it would be, but a code that tried to do too much could fail as effectively as one that tried to do too little. A code should not be so short and general as to create ambiguity and invite uncertainty about its meaning and implications. Nor should it be so detailed and legalistic as it invite its readers to overlook its foundations, its spirit, and its positive aspirational aims. A legislative code should be one that is easily read and comprehended by legislators, staff members, and, no less important, by the general public. An excessively detailed and legalistic code would not effectively serve that public purpose.

No impression should be conveyed that the code is meant to provide an exact prescription of correct behavior for any and all circumstances. No code of ethics can offer a resolution of all moral dilemmas. In many cases there will be a conflict of duties, and no perfect resolution will be possible. On other occasions, it will be difficult to understand exactly how a principle or rule ought to be applied. Problems of this kind militate against great precision in a code and equally against conveying the illusion of precision. A code of ethics should have as its fundamental goal the general guidance of the behavior of legislators, not the provision of moral solutions to be mechanically applied. Prudence and individual judgment will always be needed—a point as important to make to the general public as to the legislators themselves.

It was earlier noted that most legislative codes are now incorporated as parts of standing legislative rules. I think that is a mistake, conveying the idea that moral rules as just so many more rules, of no greater importance than others. But they are. For unless legislators display more integrity and a respect for ethical virtues and principles, their entire credibility as public servants, and as representatives, will be fundamentally compromised. A legislative code ought, ideally, to be a document that precedes, and is meant to animate, all the other rules and procedures of a legislature. A code should set the basis for the legislative and representative process in its entirety, providing the basic stimulus for the observance of other legislative rules and procedures and serving, most vitally, to set forth the higher spirit of legislative action and behavior.

That approach should make obvious a point that my general strategy presupposes: a code should not have as its primary and only purpose the curtailing of misbehavior. That seems to be the premise of existing codes. Instead, a code should provide those general moral principles that can guide the individual judgments of legislators, remind them collectively of their public duties and purposes, and provide the general public with a reasonably full and compelling picture of what a legislature believes to be its moral duties and how it is prepared to pursue them.

There are two critical conditions that are bound to affect the understanding and implementation of a code—the way it is created and the way it is enforced. On the first point, it appears to be long-standing custom at both the state and federal level that codes are devised by legislators for legislators, with practically no public contribution or comment at all. Yet codes of ethics could have considerably more credibility, and possibly be better in their provisions, if the public were invited to comment on them. The Constitution provides that the House and Senate shall establish their own rules and regulations, but it does not preclude a public role; there is thus no legal reason why the public cannot voluntarily be called upon to help in the devising, modifying, or reforming of codes. At present, there is a great deal of public discussion of the behavior of legislators, considerable widespread cynicism (much of it actually ill founded), and periodic intense media interest—just the combination of circumstances that invites a more active effort on the part of legislators to seek a more positive public interest in their problems. The creation of special public commissions to devise or revise codes, a more active public participation in hearings on code reforms, and similar familiar devices (in most other areas of legislative life) would represent significant progress.

As matters now stand, legislators are often their own worst enemies. In response to particular scandals and public outcries, intense, often precipitate, code revisions and reforms are undertaken. But between those outbursts, nothing much is done at all; and, to make matters worse, various positive actions may be taken that seem self-serving and designed to erode the adopted codes. The most flagrant example of this would be the way in which pay raises or provisions concerning outside honoraria have been adopted in Congress—usually in a hurry, with a minimum of debate, little or no public participation, and a frequent use of unrecorded voice votes. For a group of men and women who go to extraordinary lengths in most of their activities to be sensitive to a public relations viewpoint, it is uncommonly clumsy. That it regularly brings the media down upon them should hardly be a surprise. Only a larger public role, and one more integrally a part of the process, is likely to reduce those avoidable difficulties.

The issue of enforcement is no less important. Legislators and the general public must believe that violations of a code, at least those "disciplinary" and black-letter aspects of it, will be promptly, fairly, and effectively enforced. That may not always be easy to accomplish, in great part because of the requirements of due process or because of jurisdictional complications with certain kinds of violations. Nonetheless, the public is far more likely to be tolerant of those complications (and not dismiss them as mere evasions) if there are mechanisms to see that all charges are speedily investigated, that serious charges are pursued with diligence, and that an efficient and expeditious procedure exists for dealing with violations of the code.

Once again, as in the developing or revising of a code, it would be most helpful for legislators to have the services of outside members of the public. Their role could be that of assistance in the development of investigations, in the evaluation of charges, and in the oversight of general procedures. A place for the public as advisors, counselors, and observors of procedure would not usurp the centrality of self-enforcement of codes; it would simply be a means of assuring the public that legislatures use acceptable means of enforcement and proceed with due vigor in their utilization.

Is what I have argued for so far an exercise in fantasy, far removed from anything likely to be accepted by legislators? Not necessarily. First, a number of other fields and professions have in the past couple of decades significantly expanded their thinking about the scope, range, and depth of ethics. A general trend has, in fact, been discernible: from codes that were narrow in scope and self-protective to codes of considerable breadth and avowed accountability to the public interest. There is no reason why legislatures cannot become part of this trend; and it is actually surprising that it has taken so long to arrive. Second, it is no less regressive to have codes that say nothing about ideals and emphasize only a short list of prohibitions—codes that read more like penal codes than codes of ethics. Every field and profession of any significance now has codes willing to express high aspirations, even if difficult always to achieve and even more difficult to enforce. None has suffered any notable harm from that development, and the very process of debating such changes has had a useful educational impact.

Third, many of the points I have encompassed are drawn from ideas and procedures now actually in place, though erratically so. Both the Senate and the House of Representatives have well-developed proce-

dures for investigating charges, answering inquiries, and observing suitable requirements of due process. The same situation is not uniformly the
case in state legislatures. Hence, the problem is not the total absence of
procedural or other ingredients, but of making them more widespread,
refined, and consistent. Neither is the public now wholly absent. But its
role is so haphazard and sporadic that it neither satisfies the public nor
helps the legislators.

Fourth, many of the present obstacles to richer and more potent
codes are what I would term psychological and sociological. By that I
mean that they stem from general anxieties about change and from the
persistence of outdated and poorly based habits and practices. The
principal anxiety, I believe, is not so much that a potent code will in fact
curb dubious activities that legislators want to sustain (although there
may be some of that) but that it will complicate and make more difficult
their existing problems. They worry that much of what is now called
"political," and thus is already controversial enough, will now be tagged
"moral," with all of the self-righteous, judgmental, and pompous rhetoric
too often now associated with public discussions of ethics. As a study
carried out in the South Carolina Assembly notes, a bit anxiously: "Based
on research. . .in other states. . .legislation must be drawn in a manner to
prevent [its] use. . .for political purposes or to maliciously damage the
reputations of elected public officials and public employees."[5] They
worry that the inclusion of aspirational language—the language of broad
principles and high ideals—will create a legal morass, admitting neither of
great precision nor of fair enforcement. They worry about criticism by the
media. Narrow codes, with precise probibitions, seem the safer course
from a procedural (and public relations) point of view.

They seem to worry, finally, that too much attention paid to ethics,
too subtle and elegant a code, will simply serve as a distraction from the
actual business of representation and legislation, that it will superimpose
an additional layer of volatile considerations (and thus confusion) on what
is already an excessively complicated and overburdened system. In a
word, ethics is important, but only if taken as an occasional purgative in
times of severe illness and not as a dominant part of a daily diet.

It is possible that public agitation could induce, or force, legislatures
to take codes more seriously, not simply in the sense of more rules better
enforced, but in the sense I have been suggesting here—that of fuller,

---

[5] *State of South Carolina State Ethics Act: A Comparative Analysis* (Columbia, S.C.:
Dennis Building, Suite 545, 1981), p. 1. Senator Howell Heflin expressed similar sentiments in the 1981 Senate Code Revision Hearings, "Hearings Before the Select Committee," p. 86.

richer, and more sophisticated codes. The problem with a reliance upon external pressure (which might not work anyway) is that it would fail to take account of the fact that legislators are bound to be significant gatekeepers of legislative ethics. They will always retain a considerable degree of discretion, procedural control, and peer pressure and accountability.

Externally imposed standards are not likely, then, to be effective. Moreover, since an important aim of an emphasis on ethics is self-discipline, externally imposed standards and procedures could be self-defeating, reducing rather than enhancing internal regulation. At the same time, it is necessary that there be continuing pressure on legislators to take ethics seriously—gently and persistently on a daily basis, sharply and dramatically when serious scandals erupt. The upshot of those reflections is that a format, scheme, and theory for a code must be presented that would be attractive to legislators, promising both to enhance reflection on ethics but not to overburden the system in the process—pressure, but of a manageable kind and degree.

If legislators could come to see that a code need not be only a potential weapon for criticizing or attacking them, they might be open to possibilities other than those customarily envisioned. It can be, as Charles S. Levy has noted, an "enabling rather than intimidating medium of influence."[6] A code can represent a common standard that can be appealed to by a legislator when he or she justifies an unpopular act of conscientious judgment to colleagues or voters. Put positively, a code can embody a standard that a legislator can legitimately claim to be seeking and a standard that transcends private values. Put negatively, a code could provide protection to those who might feel compelled to take unpopular stands or to criticize the behavior of their colleagues. What those possibilities suggest is supportive of the most persuasive reason for having a code in the first place: the need for a commonly agreed upon set of ethical standards.

Moral pluralism is a cherished part of our cultural and political life, and many of those skeptical of codes believe they can be a hazard to pluralism. They would prefer to leave moral issues up to the private judgment of legislators and the popular judgment of voters. But it should be evident that the public is not all that morally permissive. They judge legislatures collectively and not just the behavior of individual legislators, and their judgment can be swift and harsh. They are outraged when moral principles are violated. Moreover, some common moral discourse is necessary for legislatures to function at all. There are limits to moral

[6] Levy, p. 208.

pluralism, which in any event is as possible to use against legislators as in their defense. And quite beyond the needs of legislators, and legislatures, is that of public education. Unless the public can be persuaded that legislators are accountable to some known and evident moral standards and that those standards are taken seriously, the public will be unable to frame realistic expectations by which to pass their own judgments.

Legislators will surely not profit from a system for which, in the absence of any consensus whatever, the public will invent ad hoc and capricious standards. Legislators often feel unfairly used, by the public and by the media. In part that is because they feel they are being judged by standards beyond their control and unreasonable in their substance. There is considerable validity to that reaction. But it is naive to except anything better if legislators do not take the lead in trying to educate the public and the media about the appropriate standards by which they might be more fairly judged. Yet that could hardly be accomplished in the absence of such standards.

12

Enforceable Standards and Unenforceable Ethics

JOHN M. SWANNER

A Rule of the United States House of Representatives provides that when a committee issues a report and any member of that committee is in less than complete agreement, that member may file supplemental, minority, or additional views. Certainly what I have to say is not a minority or dissenting view; it is thus in the spirit of suggesting additional or supplemental comments that I offer the following comments in response to Daniel Callahan's chapter.

The term *code of ethics,* when applied to elected bodies, has appeared to take on meanings beyond the term itself. In the passion for demanding systems of moral behavior for elected public servants, the schematic rationale for either all moral conduct or for the narrower "code" has not been clearly distinguished. I view my assignment here to be to provide a fairly narrow framework for constructing a code—or codes, as it will turn out. But before that, I will define a broader context into which the code fits logically.

As Callahan has said, the aim of a code is improved moral behavior. Ideally, each legislator would be motivated internally—by conscience and a sense of duty—to act ethically. If this were the case, there would be little need for codes, official sanctions, or means for enforcing those sanctions. But pending the millenium, these external mechanisms are necessary because our system of government is not so durable that it can

JOHN M. SWANNER ● U.S. House Committee on Standards of Official Conduct, United States House of Representatives, Washington, D.C. 20515.

withstand every self-seeking effort. It becomes a simple matter of providing managed restraints, or else chaos will ensue.

How then do we construct the machinery, the general attributes of which have been very well covered in Callahan's paper?

First, we must particularize legislative codes lest we be tempted by misleading analogies. Unlike the assumption underlying professional codes, in drafting codes for legislators the competence of the practitioner is not relevant. From one perspective of the ideal, legislators ought to be "average" if they are to be "representative." Of course we hope for much more, but we achieve no ideal results, from any perspective. Legislators generally are from the upper levels of the group that elected them, but they by no means have to be. Thus the kind of "competence" that we would demand of practitioners of professional or associational groups is simply not relevant to legislative bodies.

Similarly, other qualities are generally, though not precisely, apt in framing a legislative code. Propriety, honesty, candor, confidentiality, fairness—indeed all human ideals—are essential ingredients, but their meanings must be specifically defined when they are used by a legislator acting as a delegate or trustee and operating in a political context. I say "delegate or trustee," for notwithstanding the age-old argument, the legislator is sometimes one, sometimes the other, and usually both. The facts of legislative life simply will not yield to compartmentalization, notwithstanding how convenient it would be if they did. We must go beyond Edmund Burke's exhortation:

> It is therefore our business carefully to cultivate in our minds, to rear to the most perfect vigour and maturity, every sort of generous and honest feeling that belongs to our nature. To bring the dispositions that are lovely in private life into the service and conduct of the commonwealth; so to be patriots, as not to forget we are gentlemen.

However admirable these sentiments, they are unenforceable.

How then should we structure this set of ethical requirements which we have been careful to differentiate from other codes of moral conduct? It would be redundant to restate the broad objectives of a code so well defined and circumscribed by Callahan. He has given the task its form and has provided some theory on which to base his construction. He has compared and distinguished other codes as they relate or fail to relate to the special problems of legislative ethics. He has explained what the constituent elements of a code ought to be and shown that it must be open to observation. He has spoken of legislators in their numerous roles and shown the need for code provisions relevant to these roles. I can offer no useful additions to, or enlargements on, his exposition.

I would like to suggest that in actually drafting a working code (see Table 1), it would be helpful to look at both the beginnings of proposed legislative codes and their ends, that is, their implementation. If we were to look at the beginnings, we would start with all the behavior of legislators. Now some aspects of a legislator's behavior are subject to legislative enforcement, whereas other aspects are not. Certainly we would all agree that use of one's office for private gain is proscribed behavior, rightly subject to legislative enforcement.

However, when it comes to behavior that might bring discredit to the member personally, such as a traffic offense or even adultery, but would not discredit the institution, such behavior ought not to be subject to legislative enforcement. In the case of the first example, the traffic offense, enforcement would fall upon the courts under the law of the land. In the case of the second example, adultery or any question of general moral turpitude, enforcement should be limited to press, peer, and public pressures and the adversarial nature of politics. I submit that a code of ethics should be established to address these latter forms of behavior. Containing generally admonitory or aspirational points of observance, a code of ethics would assist citizens in assessing the politically enforceable activities of their elected representatives.

It is appropriate that in exchange for (1) receiving compensation that is fair and equitable for the comparable services, responsibility, and station evidenced in other walks in life and for (2) being provided adequate resources to engage in legislative dialogue free of special interest influence the representative should be held accountable by the electorate to a code of ethics. This generally admonitory or aspirational code could include the following: (1) promote the public interest, (2) provide public accountability, (3) promote constituent interest, and (4) be informed. This code would supplement any legislator's personal moral code and would set forth standards of honesty, truth, and fairness providing a guide to the representative in performance of his or her duties and a guide to the citizenry in their assessment of that performance.

For behavior that would bring discredit upon the legislator and be enforceable by the courts under the law of the land, as exemplified by traffic offenses or even personal assaults, there are instances whereby discredit would be brought upon the institution as well as the member, for example, bribery. In instances such as bribery, the act implicates not only the law of the land but also the institution and as such brings into question what I would call the "representational fitness" of the legislator. Hence a second code is required—a code of conduct—a violation of which would bring discredit on the institution and call into question the fitness of the representative to be a member of that institution.

Table 1. All Behavior of Legislators

	Not subject to legislative enforcement	Law of the land		Subject to legislative enforcement	
	Code of ethics	Not involving representational fitness	Involving representational fitness	Code of conduct	Code of regulation
Explanations	This code should contain generally admonitory or aspirational points of observance. Discipline over this code should be limited to press, peer, and public pressures and the adversary nature of politics. A violation of this code would bring discredit on the *member*.	Violations not involving representational fitness should be left entirely to the courts.	Only those laws of the land involving representational fitness should be simultaneously prosecuted at the legislative level. [a]	This code should contain subjectively stated but enforcement-demanding principles. A violation of this code would bring discredit on the *institution*.	The remaining body of rules of conduct—the objectively stated requirements—should be included here.
Examples	1. Promote the public interest 2. Provide public accountability 3. Promote constituent interest 4. Be informed 5. Advise, consent, and confirm	1. Traffic offenses 2. Assaults	1. Treason 2. Bribery 3. Sedition	1. Obedience to the Constitution, laws, and rules 2. Use of office for private gain 3. Proper expenditure of public funds 4. Fair use of employees	1. Financial disclosure 2. Use of letterhead 3. Franking 4. Gifts 5. Honoraria 6. Earned income limitation

Violation of a code of conduct would be subject to legislative enforcement. Only those laws of the land involving representational fitness should be simultaneously prosecuted at the legislative level as well as in the courts. Crimes that should be left entirely to the courts, such as those mentioned earlier, traffic offenses or assaults, do not involve the member's representational fitness. Examples of crimes that are subject to enforcement by both the courts and the legislature—a violation of the law and a code of conduct—would include treason, bribery, and sedition.

The legislator and the citizenry would both recognize and accept that the legislator is not only to abide by all duly enacted laws of the several jurisdictions of the land, but to the extent to which the legislator fails to do so, he or she shall be held to a higher standard of accountability than ordinary citizens. If the legislator should commit an offense not involving representational fitness, he or she may be prosecuted under the law alone. If the offense involves representational fitness, the legislator would be prosecuted simultaneously, or in an otherwise timely manner, under the code of conduct by the representational body.

The code of conduct should be comprised of subjectively stated but enforcement-demanding principles peculiar to the systems and operations of the legislature itself. Examples of such subjective principles, a violation of which would discredit the institution, could include: (1) obedience to the Constitution, laws, and rules; (2) use of office for private gain; (3) proper expenditure of public funds; and (4) fair treatment of employees.

Now there are a number of legislative rules of conduct that are comprised of objectively stated requirements. These, I submit, ought to be embodied in a third code, a code of regulations. Examples that could be included in this code of objective requirements are (1) financial disclosure, (2) franking, (3) acceptance of gifts and honoraria, (4) use of letterhead, and (5) earned income limitation. This code would, in effect, encompass those rules and regulations necessary for the proper and efficient operations of the body that are directly relevant to and harmonious with both the code of conduct and the code of ethics.

It is incumbent upon the legislature to provide any accused with the maximum feasible due process when enforcing a code of conduct and code of regulations. A mechanism ought also be established to provide legislators with advisory opinions to assist in guiding contemplated conduct. The details of the mechanics of advice and due process are quite important as well. They need not be elaborated here, but recognition must be given to their consideration in any thorough exposition on legislative codes.

I conclude with the observation that, as set forth in a most skeletal and tentative fashion, the relationship between the legislator and the citizen can be best envisioned as essentially a contractual relationship. In exchange for adequate compensation and resources freely to perform their duties, legislators agree to abide by three separate codes—the aspirational but politically enforceable code of ethics, the institutionally enforceable, subjectively stated code of conduct, and the institutionally enforceable, objectively stated code of regulations.

This representational contract need not have the implications of the social contract theory of Hobbes, Locke, or, for that matter, Rousseau. Rather, I feel that it is within a tradition closer to the observation of Justice Brandeis: "The old idea of a good bargain was a transaction in which one man got the better of another. The new idea of a good contract is a transaction which is good for both parties."

The representational contract can be viewed as being good for both parties. I maintain that the concept may offer a basis for the further thinking needed to allow a just compensation for members of our legislature and an allocation of resources necessary to keep representatives free from the potential distortion of special concerns while seeking the electorate's approval. These questions must of necessity be addressed if we are going to follow upon Callahan's appropriate admonition, namely, that legislative codes "ought to be taken seriously, in their formulation, their publication, or their implementation." After all, as Plato observed in the *Republic,* "Our discussion is on no trifling matter, but on the right way to conduct our lives."

IV

LEGISLATIVE ETHICS IN THE STATES

13

Ethics in the States
The Laboratories of Reform

ROBERT M. STERN

When an attempt is made to review ethics in the state legislatures, an initial temptation is to plead helplessness. How can the California legislature, with its members representing districts of 250,000 to 500,000 constituents, be compared with New Hampshire, where 424 legislators represent districts which in some instances have fewer than 2,000 voters?

In a nation as diverse as ours, how can conclusions be drawn from states that are essentially one-party dominated as compared to states that have different parties controlling the two houses? How does one compare ethics in a state that pays salaries of only $100 a year to its legislators to a state that pays $50,000 to its elected representatives? Finally, there are more than ten times as many state legislators as there are congressmen—7,482 representatives in the fifty states as compared with the 535 federal senators and representatives.

Nevertheless, after talking to leaders in several states, one comes to the opposite conclusion: there is not that much difference in the attitudes, the problems, and the ethics in the various states. The same questions arise in the biggest and smallest states: What ethical standards should be established? What should the legislators be paid? Should a legislator represent a client before a state agency? Should campaign funds be used for personal purposes? Should lobbyists make gifts to officials whom they are lobbying? All of these questions are being addressed by the states—either by the legislators, by the press or by both.

The answers to these questions clearly demonstrate that the states

ROBERT M. STERN ● California Commission on Campaign Financing, 10951 W. Pico Boulevard, Los Angeles, California 90064.

have become the laboratories of reform. Their solutions are diverse, creative, and noteworthy; many of these solutions will be discussed below.

Alan Rosenthal, who wrote the book *Legislative Life,* says there is very little interaction between legislators and academicians. He quotes one observer as saying that political scientists regard legislators in the same way that upstanding women regard prostitutes—with a sullen envy and with a confidence that if they wished to go commercial, they could do it better.[1] Most academicians only want to examine legislative turnover, an easy task because the numbers are there and can be plugged into a computer.

There is so little research that there is no single source which lists how many legislators have been indicted, resigned under pressure, or penalized by an ethics commission or ethics committee.

Fortunately, there is a new organization which consists of the governmental agencies which are regulating ethics, campaign disclosure, economic disclosure, and lobbyist laws. The Council on Governmental Ethics Laws, founded in 1979, has over forty member agencies, federal, state, and even Canadian. It publishes annually a summary of the reform laws as well as quarterly bulletins.

Legislatures are under seige by the general population. According to the Gallup Poll published in *Parade Magazine* on January 17, 1982, only 12 percent of the population rate the ethics of state officeholders as very high or high. Only insurance agents (11 percent), advertising practitioners (9 percent), and car salesmen (6 percent) received lower ratings. Clergymen (63 percent) and pharmacists (59 percent) rated highest. Of interest is the fact that all other elected officials ranked higher in ethics than did state legislators: United States Senators, 20 percent; United States Representatives, 14 percent; and local officeholders, 14 percent, although none of the other public officials can be very proud of their ratings.[2]

This chapter will put into perspective the various ethical questions being debated on the state level. First, the state legislatures will be surveyed on the compensation paid to their elected representatives. Next there will be a discussion of the important ethical issues being addressed throughout the states. Then there will be discussion of the legislative ethics committees: how they function and what enforcement actions they have taken.

---

[1] Robert Herman, from an address January 12, 1979, at a National Conference of State Legislatures session in Dallas, as cited in Alan Rosenthal, *Legislative Life: People, Process and Performance in the States* (New York: Harper & Row, 1981), p. 2.

[2] "Occupational Perceptions," *Parade Magazine,* 17 January 1982, p. 10.

Finally, the chapter will conclude with specific recommendations as to how legislative bodies can improve their ethics as well as improve the public's perception of their ethics. This is perhaps the crux of the problem facing elected officials today. No matter how honest or moral the great majority of legislators may be, the public's attitude toward our officials has been declining dramatically. Each new revelation of scandal does not cleanse the political process—rather, it merely reinforces the public's view that all elected representatives are corrupt money grubbers. How to improve the ethics and enforce these new ethical standards without causing public confidence to sink even further is the question which calls out for an answer.

BACKGROUND

Before addressing in depth the ethical issues confronting state legislators, it is necessary to understand the structures of legislative bodies throughout the country.

The length of legislative sessions varies tremendously. Some legislatures meet for less than thirty days. Others can be in session year round. However, most state legislatures meet for less than six months in a year. Thirty-five of the fifty states call their legislators citizen-legislators as opposed to full-time professional politicians.[3]

Most of the legislatures have some type of staff assistance, but only a few have full-time professional help for each of the legislators. Many more have committee staff members who are specialists in their fields. Finally, a majority of states have legislative counsel bureaus and budget analysts. Recently, legislatures have been adding staff even as they cut back other state agencies' budgets. Many observers believe that an independent legislative staff is essential if the legislature is to be a truly coequal branch of government. A staff that can analyze bills and help the members study the issues acts as a buffer to "the third house," the lobbyists who can sometimes overwhelm an overworked member with data. Unfortunately, the more staff a member hires, the greater is the temptation to use that staff for political rather than governmental purposes.

The number of legislators in the states ranges from a maximum of 424 in New Hampshire to 49 in the unicameral state of Nebraska. In contrast

---

[3] Council of State Governments, *The Book of the States 1982–83*, Vol. 24 (Lexington, Kentucky: 1982), pp. 181–201.

to New Hampshire, California's state senators represent more constituents (over 500,000) than do California congressional representatives.

LEGISLATIVE SALARIES

> Higher salaries is the cryin' need of the day. . . . You can't be patriotic on a salary
> that just keeps the wolf from the den. . . . But when a man has a good fat salary, he
> finds himself hummin' "Hail Columbia."
>
> George Washington Plunkitt[4]

The compensation question appears to be the toughest issue (ethical or otherwise) that legislators have to face year in and year out. One state, New Hampshire, pays its elected representatives the munificent sum of $100 a year to serve in its hallowed legislative halls. Obviously, it is more of an honor than a profession in New Hampshire to serve as an elected representative. On the other hand, California pays its elected representatives $50,000 when salary, per diem expenses, pension payments, and other perquisites are totaled. However, California's basic salary of $33,732 ranks only third and is not keeping pace with inflation since legislators may increase their own pay only by a maximum of five percent a year. In some years, the political heat or fallout has been so great that these cost of living increases have not been granted.

It is clear that few states pay their legislators high salaries. Only eight states pay more than $20,000 a year in basic wages. Most of the states (twenty-seven) pay less than $10,000 a year.[5]

On the pay issue there seems to be little difference which level of government one observes: local, state, federal, or even Canadian. Pay raises for elected officials generate intense resentment from the electorate. The California legislature attempted an end run around the voters when in 1978 it put on the ballot a constitutional measure which would have established a commission with the power to set the salaries of elected officials. The voters overwhelmingly saw through this back-door attempt to legitimatize salary increases and by a margin of 62 to 38 percent turned down the proposal.[6]

Congress, year after year, struggles with attempts to raise its pay. It finally established a commission to make recommendations. But a 1977 law which also established congressional rules of conduct and disclosure of financial activities revised the procedure so that both houses have to vote affirmatively for any pay raise.

[4] William L. Riordon, *Plunkitt of Tammany Hall* (New York: E. P. Dutton, 1963), p. 56.
[5] *The Book of the States*, pp. 192–93.
[6] Secretary of State March Fong Eu, *Statement of Vote and Supplement: Primary Election, June 6, 1978* (Sacramento: 1978), p. 38.

Salaries do not provide a complete picture of compensation. Most states pay a per diem for each day the legislature is in session. Per diem payments range from $15 (Utah) to $105 (Alabama) a day. Some states will pay per diem even for the weekends.[7]

Another common fringe benefit is a lucrative retirement system which provides for generous benefits for a minimal amount of service at an early age. However, one should remember that there is no guarantee of continued tenure for legislators; at any two- to four-year period they may be involuntarily retired by their constituents. Further, it may be desirable to encourage legislative retirement so that new blood continues to stimulate the system.

Some states provide new automobiles to legislators along with gasoline credit cards for fuel and repairs. There are other nonmonetary benefits, such as sergeants-at-arms, who may act as personal valets for the members; these sergeants drive members to the airport, pick up dry cleaning, frame pictures, and perform other similar tasks.

Nearly all states provide some form of staff for their legislators (only Idaho and South Dakota do not). However, only nineteen states give personal staff to individual legislators on a year-round basis and another nine states allow their legislators personal staff during the session.[8]

Thus it is extremely difficult to place a value on overall compensation for our lawmakers. Nevertheless, most solons feel that they are underpaid and most must turn to outside sources to supplement their pay. Many have full-time professions which they can pursue when not attending legislative matters. Lawyers used to dominate the state houses, but the percentage of attorneys is on the decline.

Some legislators must rely on the people they are regulating to assist them in making ends meet. In Congress, senators in particular have turned to the lecture circuit to supplement their $72,500 salary. Some senators had been able to earn over $100,000 in honoraria, compensation coming from the special interests. But recently, both houses placed a limit on outside earned income—including honoraria. State lawmakers are not so easily able to take advantage of honoraria, but compensation for such speeches may be on the increase. In California, the Senate Minority Leader and the Speaker of the Assembly have each reported receiving over $20,000 in outside compensation for speeches, nearly equaling their legislative salaries.[9]

[7] *The Book of the States*, pp. 192–93.
[8] Ibid., p. 219.
[9] California Fair Political Practices Commission, *Report of Financial Interests, January 1–December 31, 1981* (Sacramento: May 1982), pp. 17, 45.

State legislators have never served for the salary paid to them, for in no state is the salary by itself an attractive enough reason to put up with the tribulations of being a legislator. But the prestige and power of being a legislator has been a sufficient incentive. Today the prestige has waned but the power has increased. A legislator used to be highly regarded in the community—a leading businessman or former mayor whose career was capped by serving in the state capital, or an attorney who practiced law during the off-session. In some cases an attorney's legislative office in the district served as his law office as well. As a legislator, he became known to potential clients through newspaper stories which carried news of his legislative activities. He brought prestige to his law firm, which was willing to let him go away for a few months to the state capital.

However, as the cynicism of the public toward its public officials increases and as the job becomes more and more demanding, legislators are not satisfied with their positions. Increasingly, turnover is rapid as legislators indicate that the job is not worth the sacrifices (loss of privacy, lack of public esteem, low pay, long hours).

One young legislator who was making $30,000 a year plus per diem complained that his wife could not afford to buy a new couch because his salary was so low. He wistfully remarked that he could be making five times as much in the private sector working on political campaigns as a consultant. When asked why he did not quit, since nobody was forcing him to be a legislator, he admitted that he liked being a legislator because of the power.

As the administration in Washington continues to defederalize programs and return the management of these huge programs to the states, the states in turn have more responsibility and control over billions of dollars and hundreds of programs. But with this new increasing power (and money) comes the pressures of the people who are going to be affected by these state decisions. And with the pressures come the campaign contributions.

Increasingly, at all levels of government the receipt of campaign contributions from special interests which have legislative agendas before the legislature is commonplace. Campaign contributions are called legal bribes by some political observers. In most states they are fully disclosed by the official on campaign statements filed with election officials; in no states are they illegal. Although the disclosure of campaign contributions is receiving more and more press scrutiny, no one as yet is calling for their prohibition because it takes money to run for office.

As campaigns for legislative races become more and more expensive (in 1982, the average legislative race in California cost $429,000[10]), the

[10] California Fair Political Practices Commission, "1982 Campaign Costs Shatter Records," Press Release (Sacramento: 25 February 1983), p. 2.

role of money in politics (and in governmental decisions) dominates the legislative halls to an even greater degree.

The source of the campaign money is no longer the individual who gives $10 to his or her favorite representative. Despite very favorable tax treatment for political contributions (a 50 percent tax credit for contributions totaling $100 or less[11]), it is estimated that less than 3 percent of the public makes political donations. In a detailed report the size of a small telephone book, the California Fair Political Practices Commission found that 77 percent of the contributions raised by legislative candidates in 1980 came from outside the districts of the candidates. Only 23 percent came from within the district. Just 14 percent of the money came from individuals; 66 percent was contributed by political action committees and businesses.[12] Clearly the day of the mom-and-pop contributor and the $20 spaghetti feed are over. The locus of legislative fund raising has shifted away from the districts to Sacramento, where the decisions are made which affect the contributors.

The effect of campaign contributions on governmental decisions is not easily measurable. One cannot draw conclusions that a campaign contribution to a legislator means a vote from that legislator. But there is a perception in many state capitals that the lack of a campaign contribution may mean no access to the time of the legislator and may mean as well no opportunity to rebut the opposition. The perception that it is necessary to make campaign contributions in order to ensure a proper reception in the legislative halls may only be a perception. But this belief, because it is growing, may become a self-perpetuating reality.

PERSONAL USE OF CAMPAIGN FUNDS

Campaign contributions are supposed to be used for campaign expenditures. But a new and disturbing trend is becoming more and more common as the contributions received by the candidates escalate to unparalleled proportions. Campaign funds left over after the completion of the campaigns are being converted to personal use or are being taken by the legislative official upon retirement.

Personal use of campaign funds is an example of honest graft but dishonest ethics being practiced at the state legislative level.

---

[11] Internal Revenue Code, 26 U.S.C. sec. 41.

[12] California Fair Political Practices Commission, *Sources of Contributions to California State Legislative Candidates for the November, 1980 General Election* (Sacramento: 6 August 1981), p. 1.

Two states had bitter legislative battles over proposals to ban the personal use of campaign funds, and in both instances the reformers eventually prevailed. In Nebraska the struggle to impose a ban was heated but swift; in California the debate raged for three years before finally being resolved at the last minute by a legislature tired of numerous editorials, articles, and a threatened drive to place another reform initiative on the ballot.

Nebraska's debate over personal use of campaign funds began with revelations that Senator Johnny DeCamp had spent $19,999 in campaign funds for mortgage payments, personal family medical expenses, gold coin investments (Krugerrands), office furnishings, and a fish tank.

In retaliation for the provisions of the bill limiting the personal use of campaign funds, allies of DeCamp offered amendments to the bill to gut the provisions of the entire Sunshine Act. Even the lobbyists watching the proceedings offered their own amendment which would have prohibited them from buying campaign fund raising tickets. When the senator offering the amendment was questioned by his colleagues on its meaning, he reportedly rushed to the door and said to his lobbyist friends: "You got me into this, now tell me what it means."[13] Finally, the bill passed by a vote of 32–1 and was sent to the governor.[14]

In California the debate began in 1979 when it was revealed that state legislators were spending campaign funds on, among other things, furniture for a condominium, payments to attorneys handling a legislator's divorce, a new sports car, payment of personal income taxes, and repayments of personal loans. It was common practice for retiring state legislators to take their surplus campaign funds with them. These funds ranged from $3,000 to $25,000 and were referred to by one former legislator as "severance pay for guys who leave public office."[15] One former legislator who urged a ban on such use testified: "If I had wanted to be a real crook, I could have amassed $200,000 to $300,000 over a period of time. It's very easy to do."[16]

Each year the bill prohibiting such use of contributions was introduced by a different legislator. One year the Speaker of the Assembly sponsored the measure, but after he had shepherded it through the Assembly, he was able to get only one positive vote in the first Senate committee which heard the measure.

[13] "Sunshine Bill Sparks Chaos, Theatrics, High Oratory," *Lincoln Star,* 15 May 1981.
[14] "DeCamp Rewrites Accountability Bill," *Alliance Times Herald,* 19 May 1981.
[15] "How legislators use the spoils of their warchests," *Redwood City Tribune,* 24 December 1978, p. 1.
[16] "Closing a Loophole in Campaign Funds," *Stockton Record,* 24 January 1979.

However, two years later a tough bill passed the California legislature in the waning days of the 1981 session. Three factors can be credited for the turnabout: intense press attention, a threat by the reform commission to pass an even tougher regulation, and the announcement of an initiative which not only would have banned the personal use of campaign funds but also would have prohibited transfers of funds from one candidate's campaign to that of another.

LEGISLATORS REPRESENTING CLIENTS BEFORE STATE AGENCIES

One of the major ethical questions facing several state legislatures involves legislators representing clients before state agencies.

It is not illegal in most states to practice law before state agencies over which the legislators have at least budgetary if not statutory control. However, the ethics of such practices have been questioned by political observers throughout the country.

This ethical question can be traced back to 1845 when John Quincy Adams (former president, then a member of Congress) wrote in his diary:

> It occurs to me that this double capacity of a counselor in courts of law and a member of a legislative body affords opportunity and temptation for contingent fees of a very questionable moral purity.[17]

Adams had been asked to appear before the United States Supreme Court on a constitutional question involving a private party.

For over a hundred years congressmen have been prohibited from representing paying clients before federal agencies, other than the courts.[18] In addition to the federal statute, Senate rules prevent senators from establishing an affiliation with a law firm or partnership. The senator's name may not be used in the firm's name or on its stationery. In addition, senators may not practice law during regular office hours.[19] By House rules, representatives may not receive income from partners or any others who practice before federal agencies or departments.[20]

---

[17] XII, Memoirs of J. Q. Adams 225, as quoted in California Fair Political Practices Commission, *Legislators as Advocates Before State Agencies: Avoiding Conflicts of Interest* (Sacramento: 12 January 1981), p. 12.

[18] 18 U.S.C. sec. 203.

[19] United States Senate, Code of Official Conduct, sec. 101, rule XLV, no. 6.

[20] United States Congress House Committee on Standards of Official Conduct, Advisory Opinion No. 1, 26 January 1970.

According to *The Blue Book: A Compilation of Campaign, Ethics and Lobbying Reform Laws,* published by the Council on Governmental Ethics Laws, twenty-six states plus the District of Columbia have some restrictions on public officials' representing clients before public agencies.[21] However, after analyzing the statutes, it is clear that there is a wide range of regulation. Only Florida and the District of Columbia completely prohibit legislators from appearing before all agencies under the jurisdiction of legislative officials.

The Florida State Constitution—adopted by the people, not by the legislature—has been interpreted by the Florida Ethics Commission to mean that a legislator cannot represent a paying client before any state agency even on a ministerial matter. Thus, a legislator is prohibited from filing incorporation papers for a client. Legislators are permitted to practice in Florida courts; however, they are not permitted to sue state agencies since they might enter into settlement negotiations with the agency.[22] The District of Columbia prohibition[23] is similar to Florida's in that it restricts representation before any agency other than the courts.

Five states—California,[24] Massachusetts,[25] Ohio,[26] Wisconsin,[27] and Texas[28]—prohibit legislative representatives from practicing before state agencies unless the matter is ministerial. Examples of ministerial action include: filing or amendment of tax returns, applications for permits or licenses, and incorporation papers.

Some states restrict legislators from appearing before certain agencies: Alabama, the Public Service Commission or the State Board of Adjustment;[29] Illinois, the Court of Claims or the Industrial Commission when the state is the respondent;[30] and South Carolina, the Public Service Commission, the Dairy Commission, or the Insurance Commission in rate- or price-fixing cases.[31]

Finally, there are some states which do not prohibit such activity but do require additional disclosure. Alabama requires disclosure of such representation to the Ethics Commission within five days of the appear-

[21] Council on Governmental Ethics Law, *The Blue Book: A Compilation of Campaign, Ethics, and Lobbying Reform Laws,* (Sacramento: 1981), p. 10.
[22] Florida Commission on Ethics Opinions 77–168, 78–02, 79–58, 79–64, and 79–68.
[23] District of Columbia Code 1-1181 (h).
[24] California Government Code sec. 8920.
[25] Massachusetts General Laws chap. 268A, sec. 4, par. 5.
[26] Ohio Statutes sec. 102.04.
[27] Wisconsin Statutes sec. 19.45 (7) (a).
[28] Texas Rev. Civ. Stat. Ann., Art. 6252-96, sec. 7(a).
[29] Alabama Statutes, sec. 8 of Act 130 (1975).
[30] Illinois Rev. Stat. 1979, chap. 127, sec. 2-104.
[31] South Carolina State Ethics Act, sec. 18-470.

ance;[32] Kansas, ten days after the employment has been accepted or the first appearance has been made, whichever comes first;[33] and Virginia, if the legislator is paid $1,000 or more for representation before a state agency or if the legislator is a partner of lawyers appearing before state agencies.[34]

The lawyer–legislator issue was intensively debated in the California legislature in 1981 and 1982 after it was revealed that several legislators had been appearing before state agencies for clients. California's Fair Political Practices Commission issued a report naming several legislators who had engaged in such activities, including the present Speaker of the Assembly, who represented clients before the Alcoholic Beverage Control Department, the Department of Motor Vehicles, and the San Francisco Bay Conservation and Development Commission.[35]

Following the issuance of the Fair Political Practices Commission's report, two bills were introduced in the California legislature, one sponsored by the commission and one sponsored by the chairman of the Joint Committee on Legislative Ethics, Senator Robert Presley.

There were several differences between the two bills, although both generally prohibited legislators from representing paying clients before state agencies. The commission bill amended the Political Reform Act so that enforcement of the bill's provisions would come under an independent agency, the commission. The commission had not been reluctant to bring enforcement actions against state legislators, having fined one state senator $36,000. The commission bill did not prohibit state legislators from appearing before local agencies; the Presley bill included such a prohibition.

Senator Presley was adamant about not giving the commission jurisdiction to bring enforcement actions or to administer the provisions of the bill. His stated reason was that the commission should not be interfering with the internal ethics of the legislature.

The bill sponsored by the commission was quickly defeated in the first committee to hear both bills; the Presley bill was passed with both Republicans and Democrats supporting it.

The reasons for a ban on legislators' appearing before state agencies

---

[32] Alabama Statutes sec. 8.
[33] Kansas Statutes Annotated 46-239.
[34] Code of Virginia, 2.1—358(d) (iv).
[35] California Fair Political Practices Commission, *Legislators as Advocates Before State Agencies: Avoiding Conflicts of Interest* (Sacramento: 12 January 1981).

are best documented by the following quotations from California legislators who were surveyed:

- An agency might feel "intimidated" if a legislator on its budget committee appeared as an advocate.

- The appearance of an attorney–legislator on behalf of a client before a state agency inevitably creates "an aura of a threat of political repercussions if the result is unfavorable."

- A legislator who takes a fee to represent a client before a state agency is in a "dual role," and is "serving two masters."

- An agency would "feel under pressure" if a legislator appeared on a non-routine matter for a client.

- A part of a legislator's job is to represent constituents before state agencies—as vigorously as possible. He should not receive extra pay for doing his job, nor should non-constituents have the advantage of the extra "clout" of a legislator representing them before state agencies.[36]

A few legislators disagreed, citing financial hardship in serving as a full-time legislator with a salary of less than $30,000:

> In general, the more difficult we make it for attorneys to practice while being legislators the less attractive it will be to them to become legislators. Now of course we will always be able to find *Someone* who will run for office, but to attract the kind of talent we really need in the legislature we will either have to pay them much more than they now get, or allow the talented ones to obtain outside income. Certainly, it is preferable for them to earn it through their professions than to receive it through the third house.
>
> How much of your economic life as an attorney must you write off to go into public service? The question is whether a prohibition or limitation on attorney–legislator's practice will "limit public service to the independently wealthy."[37]

ETHICS CODES IN THE LEGISLATURES

According to *The Blue Book* published by the Council on Governmental Ethics Laws, at least forty-seven states have some type of ethical codes or standards for their legislatures, and at least forty-two states

[36] Ibid., p. 25.
[37] Ibid., p. 26.

require their legislators to file some type of financial disclosure statements.[38]

There is a vast variety in the specificity and extent of the laws, but generally they tend to concentrate on financial conflicts of interests rather than on moral creeds. There is one significant exception: the Code of Ethics for the Tennessee State Senate.

The Tennessee State Senate's Code of Ethics is standard boiler plate until the end; Article V states: "Thou shalt have no other gods before me." Article VI begins: "Thou shalt not make unto thee any graven image. . . ." Following the Ten Commandments is the Golden Rule: Article XV: "Love one another; as I have loved you, that you also love one another," and Article XVI: "Therefore all things whatsoever ye would that men should do to you, do ye even so to them: for this is the law and the prophets."[39]

In 1976, the Tennessee State Senate, stung by bribery indictments brought against a fellow senator, attempted to enact a tough financial disclosure measure. However, in order to adopt this measure the Senate was forced to add to its text the Ten Commandments and the Golden Rule.

Unfortunately, no other state has a code of ethics as interesting as Tennessee's. Typically, the codes concentrate on financial matters.

These codes prohibit the following conduct:

1. Using the official's public position to obtain personal benefits.
2. Using confidential information for personal gain.
3. Entering into contracts with the public agency for private gain.
4. Receiving gifts of over a certain value from those who are attempting to influence the official.

The prohibition on receiving gifts from persons who have legislation pending can be precise or so vaguely worded that it is impossible to enforce. In California, lobbyists are prohibited from making gifts of over $10 a month to any legislator; the $10 limitation applies to all gifts, including meals.[40] This section in the California Political Reform Act is subject to criminal, civil, and administrative penalties if it is violated.

At the other end of the spectrum is the provision in the Illinois Governmental Ethics Act which prohibits gifts to legislators of over $100 per calendar year from a person who has legislative business pending "under circumstances from which it could reasonably be inferred that a

---

[38] Council on Governmental Ethics Laws, p. 11.
[39] Tennessee Senate Resolution No. 41.
[40] California Government Code sec. 86203.

major purpose of the donor is to influence him in the performance of his official duties."[41] Needless to say, the Illinois prohibition has not been enforced.

The disclosure of financial interests is fairly standard in most of the states. Normally, legislators are required to disclose interests in real property located within the state, investments of companies doing business in the state, income from persons doing business within the state, directorships of corporations, and gifts.

Few states require that an official list net worth. Generally, the disclosure of assets is by category: for example, over $1,000, over $10,000, over $100,000. Thus, it is impossible to determine how much an official is worth. News reporters are frustrated by this lack of precision since they believe that the public is primarily interested in the wealth of the officials about whom they are writing. But the rationale behind the disclosure is not to divulge wealth; rather, it is to disclose what assets might be affected by the official's actions. These "Statements of Economic Interests" are filed annually and are public records.

In most states legislators are not prevented from voting if there is a conflict of interest unless that conflict is personal. In other words, a lawyer may vote on a proposed statute which may affect his business provided it affects all similar lawyers. Similarly, insurance agents and bank executives are free to participate in legislation which may enrich them in the same manner as executives in the same professions. However, if the proposed legislation will affect only the legislator (a bill to purchase land which the legislator owns), then the legislator must abstain from voting or participating in the measure.

In some states the disqualification laws are tougher on executive officials and local officials than on the legislators. This may be due to the fact that legislators are more likely to impose such restrictions on others than on themselves. But there may be other reasons. In California, the Political Reform Act prohibits all officials from participating in decisions which affect their financial interests, but legislators cannot be penalized or restrained from such conflicts. There are absolutely no penalties for violating this provision.[42] This exemption cannot be blamed on legislators; this apparent gaping loophole is part of the initiative circulated by citizens upset that the legislature had not responded to their calls for reform.

Many other states merely require the lawmaker to announce a conflict but permit him or her to vote and participate on the matter.

[41] Illinois Rev. Stat. 1979, chap. 127, sec. 3-101.
[42] California Government Code sec. 87102.

ENFORCEMENT

> Back in 1975, the chairman of the Joint Legislative Ethics Committee, Assemblyman Harvey Johnson, called the committee "worthless" and said it should be abolished. Although most legislators probably agreed with Johnson, they didn't abolish it—perhaps they preferred a weak, worthless committee to one that would adopt and enforce a tough ethics code on the legislature.[43]

So stated the *Sacramento Bee* in an editorial on May 16, 1981, urging the legislature to put some teeth in a bill by giving the enforcement of the bill's provisions to an outside agency rather than to the Legislative Ethics Committee.

After surveying all fifty state legislatures to determine how active their ethics committees are, we can see clearly that the *Bee's* editorial could apply to most, if not all the other states. Twenty-one states reported that they had ethics committees, but of these only ten reported that they had met at least one day in either 1980 or 1981.

From the survey results, it appears that Maryland has the most active committee, which reported meeting 26 times over the two-year period. The Maryland committee also reported receiving the most complaints— 14 out of a total of 50 received by all the ethics committees.

If one merely examines the survey results, it would seem that there were no ethical problems in the state legislatures. But a look at the news stories throughout the country and the number of legislators indicted or convicted of crimes paints a different picture.

There is no one source which has tallied the number of legislators indicted, convicted, expelled, or forced to resign under pressure from their state bodies, but in the last few years the following states have reported problems: Maryland, Alaska, Louisiana, South Carolina, Oregon, Florida, Washington, North Carolina. Actions are pending in Nevada.

Reports from two Southern states perhaps sum up the reason why state legislatures are so reluctant to proceed against their own members. Both reflect the attitude of legislators when confronted by ethical problems by their colleagues.

In 1980, South Carolina State Senator Eugene Carmichael was convicted of conspiracy to buy votes, obstruction of justice, and vote buying. The Senator was sentenced to ten years in prison by the federal judge. After his conviction, the senator refused to resign pending an appeal. The Senate attempted to expel him, but he staved off the expulsion when he and twenty-one other members of the body voted to

---

[43] "A Stab at Ethics," *Sacramento Bee* Editorial, 16 May 1981, p. B6.

dismiss the charge of misconduct against him. It was only after an alarmed press and electorate demanded his resignation in a series of editorials and letters to the editor that the senator finally left the Senate voluntarily.

One letter said: "It is a sad day in the State of South Carolina when its highest legislative body condones the actions of a convicted felon." Another reader wrote: "It continually amazes me that our legislators downgrade the intelligence of the electorate—the same people who evidently were stupid enough to elect them."[44]

Several letter writers quoted South Carolina law which requires any *other* public official indicted of a crime to be automatically suspended from his position upon indictment; upon conviction, the official's position is terminated. Following the outcry and apparently because of pressure brought on him by fellow senators, Senator Carmichael resigned.

In a similar situation, Louisiana Senator Gaston Gerald was convicted of attempted extortion but refused to resign and continued to draw salary and per diem payments while serving his sentence in federal prison. Following his conviction in 1979, he was reelected and seated by the Senate, pending appeals. Finally, after exhausting all appeals, Gerald was ousted by the Senate. However, before the expulsion, the Senate had to establish rules of procedure since there had been none.

The situation in South Carolina, whereby legislators who are indicted are allowed to continue to serve whereas other state officials are suspended, is a vivid example of what is true in many other states. Legislators are eager to impose rules on state agencies but loathe to impose these same rules on themselves. In California, no state or local agency may hold secret meetings to discuss policy, but there is one exception: the legislature. In Texas, the 1983 legislature passed a law requiring disclosure of conflicts of interest for local officials. A similar proposal for state officials was defeated.

CONCLUSION AND RECOMMENDATIONS

When all is said and done, how do the ethics of our legislators stand in relationship to the rest of society? Pick one hundred citizens selected at random and ask them to serve as legislators. Subject them to the pressures of lobbyists, budgetary constraints, the intense scrutiny of a distrustful media, and a cynical public. Our legislatures are a mirror of our citizens, and their ethics are probably far superior to the ethics of the

[44] "Letters to the Editor," *The State* (Columbia, S.C.), 4 March 1982, p. 13-A.

average businessman, labor leader, or pillar of the community. How many citizens can be audited by the Internal Revenue Service and not owe any money? How many of our citizens would turn down money in exchange for a favor (a vote)?

Unfortunately, each time an enforcement action is brought against a lawmaker the reputation of the body and the others who are serving suffers. But the answer cannot and must not be fewer enforcement actions and fewer regulations. On the contrary, swifter justice brought by impartial agencies should in the long run improve the reputation of our leaders while at the same time serving as a deterrent for those lawmakers who have the perception that they can walk or cross the fine line and escape.

There are a number of recommendations which should improve the ethics of our legislatures and the public's confidence in our elected officials. But none of these suggestions by itself will stop the sliding loss of confidence on the part of the public. Today's problems facing our government officials are so complex, and perhaps so nearly unsolvable, that an absolutely clean and ethical legislature may still be poorly regarded by the electorate.

But there are some suggestions which will better the legislative process. These include the following:

1. Establish an independent agency to enforce ethical standards. This may be the most important—but also the most unrealistic—of the recommendations since few legislatures are willing to give enforcement powers to another body. In most states, the legislature is given the authority to be the judge of its members by the state constitution. However, provided that the independent agency is not permitted to expel members, the constitutional provisions should be no barrier to an outside agency's imposing fines on errant members of the legislature.

An independent agency given the enforcement tools to penalize lawbreakers will serve many purposes. First of all, if it clears a legislator who has been charged with violating the law, the public and the press are more likely to accept its verdict. Second, if it brings actions and imposes appropriate penalties, the fact that there is such an agency ready to impose enforcement remedies will serve as a deterrent. Independent enforcement agencies should not be given criminal authority. Civil or administrative remedies are just as appropriate when applying penalties to elected officials. In most cases, a monetary penalty or an order to comply with the law is almost as devastating to an official as criminal action, which is rarely brought by overworked criminal prosecutors.

2. Require extensive disclosure of economic interests. As discussed before, most states already have some form of economic disclosure.

Disclosure of wealth is not necessary, but detailed disclosure of investments, real property, income, and gifts is vital.

3. Prohibit legislators from representing clients before state or local agencies. In state after state, this issue has arisen and been resolved.

4. Abolish the personal use of campaign funds. Most smaller states have not seen the problem emerge since their campaigns are not that expensive. But if trends continue, this issue will reach each state.

5. Tie the compensation of legislation to a cost of living index, or allow some other body to set the salaries. Nothing infuriates citizens more than the salaries of legislators (and sports figures). Raising their own salaries is the most painful decision for legislators at all levels of government. But without pay raises for these officials, who handle millions and billions of dollars in appropriations, the electorate may face the choice of wealthy or corrupt officials.

6. Limit campaign contributions by individuals, businesses, labor unions, and political action committees. Contribution limitations are the law in several states and will be debated in other states. Nearly all states have adequate disclosure laws. Campaign limitations and possibly public financing of campaigns will be the next step which will be taken in those states which are being flooded with campaign money.

7. Finally, the role of the media in legislative ethics must be enhanced. The ethics of legislators (or of anyone) is stronger when someone is watching to ensure that there are no underhanded activities. If the reporters are vigilant, there is less need for an independent agency to bring enforcement actions. If stories are written about unethical conduct and the editorials condemn such behavior, public officials will fear the consequence of defeat at the next election.

REFERENCES

Benson, George C. S. *Political Corruption in America*. Lexington, Mass. Lexington Books, 1981.

Bernstein, Marver H. "Ethics in Government: The Problems in Perspective." *National Civic Review,* July 1972, pp. 341–47.

California Fair Political Practices Commission. *Legislators as Advocates Before State Agencies: Avoiding Conflicts of Interest*. Sacramento, 12 January 1981.

California Fair Political Practices Commission. "1982 Campaign Costs Shatter Records," Press release. Sacramento, 25 February 1983.

California Fair Political Practices Commission. *Report of Financial Interests, January 1–December 31, 1981*. Sacramento, May 1982.

California Fair Political Practices Commission. *Sources of Contributions to California State Legislative Candidates for the November, 1980 General Election*. Sacramento, August 6, 1981.

"Closing a Loophole in Campaign Funds." *Stockton Record*, 24 January 1979.

Cooper, Melvin C. "Administering Ethics Laws: The Alabama Experience." *National Civic Review*, February 1979, pp. 77–81, 110.

Cooper, Terry L. *The Responsible Administration: An Approach to Ethics for the Administrative Role*. Port Washington, N.Y.: National University Press, 1982,

Council of State Governments. *The Book of the States (1982–83)*. vol. 24. Lexington, Kentucky, 1982.

Council on Governmental Ethics Laws. *The Blue Book: A Compilation of Campaign, Ethics, and Lobbying Reform Laws*. Sacramento, 1981.

"DeCamp Rewrites Accountability Bill." *Alliance Times Herald*. 19 May 1981.

Eu, March Fong. *Statement of Vote and Supplement: Primary Election, June 6, 1978*. Sacramento, 1978.

Florida Commission on Ethics Opinions. 77-168, 78-02, 79-58, 79-64, and 79-68.

Homer, John. "Ethics in Government." *Editorial Research Reports*. 16 May 1973, pp. 373–96.

"How Legislators Use the Spoils of Their Warchests." *Redwood City Tribune*, 24 December 1978, p. 1.

"Letters to the Editor." *The State*, Columbia, S.C., 4 March 1982, p. 13-A.

Modie, Graeme C. "On Political Scandals and Corruption." *Government and Opposition— A Journal of Cooperative Politics*, Spring 1980, pp. 208–22.

"Occupations Perceptions." *Parade Magazine*, 17 January 1982, p. 10.

Riordon, William L. *Plunkitt of Tammany Hall*. New York: E. P. Dutton, 1963.

Rosenthal, Alan, *Legislative Life: People, Process and Performance in the States*. New York: Harper & Row, 1981.

"A Stab at Ethics." *Sacramento Bee*, 16 May 1981, p. B6.

"Sunshine Bill Sparks Chaos, Theatrics, High Oratory." *Lincoln Star*, 15 May 1981.

United States. Congress. House Committee on Standards of Official Conduct. Advisory Opinion No. 1, 26 January 1970.

United States. Congress. Senate. *Code of Official Conduct*, 1977.

"Wave of Corruption at the Grass Roots?" *U.S. News and World Report*, 11 January 1982, pp. 43–44.

14

An Insider's View of
State Legislative Ethics

JEAN FORD

Like their counterparts in Congress, state legislators often face troubling ethical dilemmas and, as responsible public servants, they must make difficult choices. Here are some examples:

- The Assembly Government Affairs Committee, on which I serve, is divided on a bill mandating compensation for private physicians who are assigned by a county medical society to shifts of duty on public wards of the county hospital. My husband is one of the doctors subject to this assignment. I cast the deciding vote in favor of the bill. Is this an ethically unacceptable conflict of interest?

- My mail is running three to one against ratification of the Equal Rights Amendment, yet I feel my constituents have been misled by propaganda and do not understand the issue. My research has convinced me that each individual's rights will be better protected through passage of ERA. Do I base my vote on the "will of the people" in my district or on what I feel is "right" and in their best interest?

- My top priority bill, expanding public library services, needs two more votes for a "do pass" from the Senate Finance Committee. The chairman, whose vote I need, will vote yes if I agree to support his land use bill in my committee. I feel his bill is bad public policy but it will not affect my district. Should I agree to support his bill?

JEAN FORD ● Las Vegas, Nevada 89109.

- I sit on the Senate Judiciary Committee where major gaming control legislation is pending affecting all hotel casinos. My guest and I have finished dinner in the gourmet room of Harrah's Lake Tahoe and I ask for the check. The waiter informs me that it has been "taken care of," compliments of the hotel manager. I accept the "comp" and later write a "thank you" to the manager. Is this the right thing to do?

- By Constitutional limitation, my legislative pay of $80 a day ended on the sixtieth day. Now I face the prospect of using my personal savings to augment my per diem to cover expenses for the estimated six weeks more until adjournment. Each Monday I can turn in a voucher for travel cost reimbursement by certifying that I drove to my district on the weekend and indicating the mileage for the trip. Several of my colleagues do this each week and receive the money whether or not they travel, saying "it's only fair" to balance out other session-related expenses that are not reimburseable. Should I do the same?

- Our campaign finance law requires disclosure by source of all contributors giving over $500 to one candidate. A prominent businessman calls to say he is giving me $1,000 but does not want it made public, so half will be sent under someone else's name. Should I accept?

I served three terms in the Nevada Legislature, with experience in both the Assembly, 1972–76, and the Senate, 1978–82. Particularly during legislative sessions but also while engaged in interim activities and pursuing my private economic interests, I was confronted with numerous situations such as those described above in which decisions had to be made. Some were easy, appearing to be primarily a matter of common sense; others I felt placed me in a moral dilemma where the choice between right and wrong was not so clear. I knew that many others were in the same boat, and yet there were only a few of my colleagues with whom I felt comfortable discussing these issues.

Theoretical discussions of legislative ethics are helpful, but if they are to provide practical guidance they must be tempered by the "real world" experiences and frustrations of legislative service. Robert Stern's chapter provides a good overview of legislative ethics issues at the state level. Here, I propose to offer an "insider's" view of the real world within the political arena of state legislatures. Drawing on my personal experience as a state legislator, I aim to apply this perspective to the ethical issues involved in legislative representation and to offer some ideas on how to create a climate that encourages ethical behavior and improves the public's perception of legislatures and legislative action.

During the four years I represented Nevada on the Ethics, Elections and Reapportionment Committee of the National Conference of State Legislatures, I got to know legislators from many states, and our discussions made it clear that we were all dealing with the same questions regarding ethical standards, compensation, conflict of interest, personal use of campaign funds, and so on. Although those issues apply to the congressional scene as well, the major difference, as Stern recognized, is that legislators in most states serve part-time and must make their living in other ways, adding another dimension to the potential for ethical conflict. It is obvious that problems relating to ethical behavior will exist in state legislatures if we look at some of the elements present: individual legislators and their election process, the task or mission at hand, the environment in which they work, interaction with each other, staff, pressure groups, media, and of course, their constituents back home.

THE INDIVIDUAL LEGISLATOR

Men and women run for state legislative seats for a variety of reasons and frequently have no idea of what they are getting into regarding the nature of the job and the environment in which they will work once they are elected.

Generally, candidates do not run for office because they have some lofty ideals and want "to do good things" for society. Admitting that there can be on occasion some degree of altruism, I suggest that the overwhelming majority of candidates have an agenda involving one or more specific issues of major concern, the desire to gain visibility to enhance private economic interests, a general desire for a political career and the prospect of exercising power, or simply a desire to unseat the incumbent. Motives can range from altruism to the desire for personal gain and all shades in between.

Once elected, freshmen legislators find little help from their political party, their peers, or legislative leadership in learning how to deal with their responsibilities or understand the struggle for power in which they are engaged. Even at presession orientations which have become popular over the last ten years, there is a minimum of attention given to genuine instruction on social norms or consideration of ethical issues. Similar to the treatment given medical interns, Marines at boot camp, or a construction worker's first day on the job, the attitude seems to be "Let them learn the hard way, just as I did."

THE MISSION

What is the role of a state legislature? Basically, in concert with the executive and judicial branches, it is to provide a system of order which is fair and equitable to all. Specifics are stated in each individual state constitution, but the overriding charge to the legislature is to perform as the heart of the state's lawmaking process. Some call it the "people's branch of government," which in fact closely represents the people in all their diversity.

The legislature's work involves many things: allocating public resources through the state budget, exercising continuing oversight over the executive branch, acting as an ombudsman for constituents, and, its chief duty, formulating public policy "in the public interest." To examine how this gets done involves a look at the legislature's environment.

THE LEGISLATIVE ENVIRONMENT

Important elements affecting legislative behavior include people, resources, the formal and informal rules that affect the process, and the salient issues of the day.

A legislator interacts with several categories of people, both individually and collectively: legislative colleagues, constituents, lobbyists, pressure groups, other public officials from the governor to city and county councils, and the media.

Colleagues will have differing philosophies about public policy, from liberal to conservative; procedure, from fair to ruthless; and representation, from free agent (trustee) to constituent agent (delegate). They can believe the "public interest" is the greatest good for the greatest number or that it results from the sum of all private interests combined.

What a new legislator begins to realize is that even if the entire legislature were handpicked to include only the finest minds and purest motives, there would still be disagreement as to the role government should play in our lives and the best public policy for a given issue with its impact on money, property, and personal rights. One learns quickly that in order to get agreement among those with competing values so that action can be taken, negotiation, compromise, and bargaining are the tools of the trade. There are few "right" answers. As Austin Ranney stated in *The Governing of Man*, "There is no scientific way of deciding matters of good and evil."[1]

---

[1] Austin Ranney, *The Governing of Men* (rev. ed.; New York: Holt, Rinehart & Winston, 1966), p. 18.

Alan Rosenthal, in *Legislative Life,* describes the scene so well when he says that "the people" (from legislators to media and all others listed earlier) "shape the process, and people and process together are mainly responsible for legislative performance."[2] A part of the process is the influence of conduct-guiding rules based on law, custom, and moral precepts.

Another important element in the process is the availability of resources, both staff and money. Recent years have seen an increase in both in many states, but it is hard to see the degree, if any, to which better public policy and higher ethical behavior are the result.

In my own state it is still a financial sacrifice to serve, greatly limiting the types of people who can run for legislative seats to the retired, the independently wealthy, or those subsidized by friends, spouses, or business interests. When the pay has ended (by constitutional mandate) and there is still much work to be done, one can begin to feel like a martyr and be tempted to respond to the pressures of special interests who show appreciation in many ways rather than base action on the merits of the issue.

In summary, there are many strains on legislators as they try to do their job: too many issues, inadequate compensation, not enough time, disrupted family life, constant visibility, pressure demands from many competing interests, and public attitudes of apathy, indifference, contempt, and distrust. At times there does not appear to be much evidence that anyone really cares whether legislators are conscientious or moral.

WHERE DO WE GO FROM HERE?

In spite of my somewhat negative description of the realities involved, I do have positive thoughts on the value of the legislature as an institution and its potential for serving society.

Robert Stern does an excellent job of outlining many of the ethical questions receiving attention and some of the types of codes and enforcement actions being tried in the various states. His recommendations for further action are sound and should be seriously considered by all parties involved.

I now offer some additional observations and suggestions which I feel merit serious consideration:

1. Although it is true that the states have been laboratories of reform

---

[2] Alan Rosenthal, *Legislative Life: People, Process and Performance in the States* (New York: Harper & Row, 1981), p. 341.

in a limited way, I believe another avenue of reform must come from the community at large. The voting public must choose its representatives with greater care. It should be much more concerned about the basic character of candidates, their track record in personal and business dealings, evidence of basic integrity, consistent use of good judgment. Why? Because legislators can be briefed on the pros and cons of key issues, can learn the skills of chairing meetings and managing staff, but the basic character they bring to the office is the one that will continue to influence behavior throughout their careers.

Felix Nigro calls that individual's own sense of responsibility "the inner check." Although in the following Nigro is referring to professional government personnel, I suggest that his observations apply to elected officials as well:

> The official's sense of responsibility is, of course, the product of his entire previous history. This is why discriminating practices in the original selection of personnel are so essential. No code of ethics will make much of an impact on someone who for long has been convinced that the smart man does not let his conscience bother him about the methods he uses in attaining his ends.[3]

Some say legislators are in fact a mirror of the electorate. An article by Janet Beardsley in *State Legislatures* quotes Majority Leader John D. Schneider of Missouri: "The legislature reflects the public with all its weaknesses. There are some legislators that just represent their own group and advance their own clout. It ought to scare the hell out of people to realize that the legislature really does represent the people."[4]

The problem with this attitude is that it underestimates the legislator's capacity to exercise moral and political leadership. I believe that the voters should expect more of their representatives and work at electing those with clear records of integrity and competence. They should question a candidate's motives carefully, get to know their past record of activity in the community, and obtain whatever financial disclosure information is available to ascertain potential conflicts regarding economic interests.

Every candidate who is elected to serve in a part-time legislature automatically has conflicts of interest; therefore the voter must judge how that person will handle the areas of conflict when they arise.

2. Voters must be willing to support financially the candidates of their choice as well as endorse more public financing of materials, public debate, candidate forums, so that candidates are not forced to obtain the majority of their funds from organized special interests.

[3] Felix A. Nigro, *Modern Public Administration* (New York: Harper & Row, 1970), p. 417.
[4] Janet Beardsley, "Leadership Today," *State Legislatures*, February 1980, p. 5.

It was always a source of wonderment to me to find how difficult it was to get even a $10 contribution from some of my strongest supporters. Somehow giving a check to a politician wasn't "nice." Unfortunately, candidates must raise money to get their message across; most prefer a broad base of "grass-roots" support but often have no choice but to appeal to large business interests or single-issue political action committees.

3. Increased attention must be given in all colleges and universities to the issue of ethics in government. In political science, government, philosophy, and public administration classes at all levels there should be more emphasis on the mission of the legislature and its health as an institution. There should be a lively dialogue about the characteristics of people who should be elected to legislative office and the ethical behavior expected of them. This should be carried on in interaction with political party leaders, officeholders, and interested community activists.

I have sat through many classes on these topics where the lectures and discussion never got beyond theory into its application to the problems of today. Professors showed absolutely no interest in the political actions within their own community and made no attempt to encourage students to get involved or give them a vision of the influence they could have if they chose.

4. The media must reexamine their roles and responsibilities in maintaining the health of the legislature as an institution and must be willing to give a more balanced account of legislative activity. I know that a fistfight between a legislator and a lobbyist sells more newspapers than a feature on a conscientious lawmaker's weekend home visits with constituents, but there has to be a way to make the public aware of the behind-the-scenes struggles of many legislators and staff to improve the system and deal with the nitty-gritty of government serving the people, day in, day out.

The media, by their emphasis on the controversial and politically "juicy" stories of the day, perpetuate an atmosphere in which the public automatically questions everyone's motives and assumes the worst regarding all candidates and officeholders.

There is much the media could do to help the public to become better educated regarding the legislative process, candidates, and issues. There should be some public financing of television and radio appearances for all candidates, a major cost of any campaign.

The media have played a major role in the current crisis of confidence. Corrupt and unethical behavior on the part of a few public officials has undermined the faith and trust of the governed; those who exhibit good deeds and hard work and refuse to succumb to unethical practice should also receive recognition.

By the way, the media have provided their share of unethical practice also, as the owners and publishers editorialize for legislative actions that will promote their private economic interests and crucify lawmakers who dare to oppose them in any way.

5. Legislative leaders must take more responsibility for setting the tone and performing as role models for ethical behavior. Presession orientations, particularly for the newly elected, are essential and should include review of the laws and rules of procedure, sources of information and counsel, and candid discussion of social and ethical norms and how potential problems can be avoided.

Strong, influential leaders of visible ethical convictions and impeccable behavior can establish an environment that will make corruption unlikely and unwelcome.

This type of leadership combined with strong ethical codes and their vigorous enforcement can help dispel common suspicions that cronyism and unethical personal gain from public service are necessary costs of the democratic system.

A fascinating article in the *Training and Development Journal* entitled "Integrity Awareness Training for Managers" is quite relevant.[5] Although its discussion of integrity "on the job" relates to a special training program within the Internal Revenue Service and is geared to its application in the business world, the principles and suggested avenues of action can easily apply to legislative "managers" in the form of majority leaders, speakers, and committee chairs.

According to author Jack Eckner, "Corruption has three components that are controllable—opportunity, incentive and risk—and one that is not—personal honesty."[6] He says that leadership can provide an environment that increases the risk that goes with corruption, decreases the incentive, and reduces the opportunity. It should provide a signal to employees (colleagues) that their concerns are in concert with management (legislative leadership) concerns and that a breakdown in integrity will not be tolerated. Techniques used in the integrity awareness training include completion and discussion of an ethical dilemmas questionnaire regarding "appearance of impropriety" situations, examining high-risk activity, surveying control weaknesses (gaps in ethical codes?), and management strategies. Most legislators would welcome this kind of

---

[5] Jack O. Eckner, "Integrity Awareness Training for Managers," *Training and Development Journal* (July 1983) p. 47.
[6] Ibid., p. 48.

leadership, and it certainly would be refreshing to most observers of the legislative scene.

CONCLUSION

When discussing legislative ethics, it is important to recognize that even in the best of times with the best of people we shall find conflict in the legislative arena because of competing values. Drawing from my experience and observations, I have discussed briefly the dilemma of the legislator regarding campaign contributions, limited time, personal financial sacrifice, the struggle for power in a system not based on merit and logic, the reality that one cannot be all things to all people, the decisions regarding serving conscience or constitutents, the need to establish rapport with legislative colleagues who represent diverse interests and philosophies, and the necessity for dealing with negotiation and compromise.

I have suggested action in several areas relating to candidate recruitment, campaign finance, the teaching of politics and government, the responsibility of the media, and the role of legislative leadership. I now join those who call for a renewed appreciation by people of the value of their political institutions, particularly state legislatures, and a commitment to create a supportive environment for legislators of competency and integrity.

Let us get on with the dialogue—and with the actions necessary to encourage public confidence in legislative integrity, to maintain high ethical conduct among legislative officials, to prevent the use of public office for private gain, and to insure the appeal of public service to those best qualified.

15

Legislative Ethics at the State and Federal Levels
A Comparison

RICHARDSON PREYER

Our federal system was unique when it was created in 1787 and still is. It has given us more governments than any nation on earth. In addition to the federal government and the fifty state governments, we have about eighty thousand local governments. Among the thousands of public officials who make these governments run—and among the citizens they serve—one finds many different ways of looking at the world and many different perspectives on politics. Daniel Elazar, for example, has identified three political subcultures within the American political universe: the *moralist*, deriving from the New England Puritans, intolerant of corruption, supportive of reform movements; the *individualist*, in which politics is viewed as just another business, run by "machines" and bosses; and the *traditionalist,* in which politics supports the values of family, community, and tradition, a subculture particularly strong in the South.[1]

Further adding to this pluralism, the United States probably has more "free enterprise" politicians than any nation on earth. They tend to be individualistic and increasingly independent of party. They "go into

---

[1] Daniel J. Elazor, *American Federalism: A View from the States*, pp. 79–140, as cited by Walter Dean Burnham *Democracy in the Making* (Englewood Cliffs, NJ: Prentice-Hall, 1983), pp. 22–23.

RICHARDSON PREYER ● School of Law, University of North Carolina, Chapel Hill, North Carolina 27514.

business for themselves, as far as the law and the voting public will permit them to do so."[2]

It is hardly surprising, then, that our fifty state legislatures vary enormously. Some are strong and independent; some are dominated by the governor. Some are unprofessional and disorganized, with minimum salaries and inadequate staffs; some—New York, California, Pennsylvania, for example—have a high level of professionalism, staffing, and salaries. Some state legislators take pride in being "professional legislators"; others take equal pride in calling themselves "citizen legislators."

What is surprising, in view of this diversity (some might say this pluralism run riot), is that there is so much agreement among the state legislatures, as Robert Stern's paper points out, on the basic problems of legislative ethics. At the federal level, there is common ground on these same broad concerns—to avoid conflicts of interest, to require financial disclosure, to have procedures for ethics enforcement (but not too much). State and federal legislative codes of ethics are also alike in that, without exception, they are in reality codes of conduct—basically a list of "Thou shalt nots"—which discourage members from pursuing their own interests but offer little encouragement to them to act in the public interest. They do not lay out the moral obligations of the legislator and of the institution in which the legislator serves. (The Tennessee Code of Ethics, which includes the Ten Commandments and the Golden Rule, might be viewed as an exception. One wonders about enforcement; for example, "Thou shalt not covet thy neighbor's wife" would seem to cast a broad net.)

Most surprising of all is the agreement of both state and federal legislators on the necessity of some kind of written code. In addition to both houses of Congress, Stern reminds us that forty-seven states have some type of ethics codes. There appears to be little support for the idea that only the law should regulate the conduct of public officials. On the contrary, there is general recognition that actions other than violations of law may cast discredit on the institution and affect a member's performance.

What then are the differences in state and federal legislative ethics concerns? There are three factors that generate, or should generate, differences in the content of codes of ethics at the state and federal level. One arises from the contrast in the concepts of citizen legislator and professional legislator. A second is the differing impact of the "special interests" at the state and at the federal level. A third factor grows out of the difference in media coverage at the state level and at the federal level.

[2] Burnham, p. 588.

THE CITIZEN LEGISLATURE

In most states the citizen legislator is a revered concept. Thirty-five state legislators meet for less than six months a session. Only seven states pay over $20,000 in salary. Only one half of the state legislatures provide office space and staff. The turnover in state legislatures averages over 25 percent—far higher than in Congress.

Although revered, the species is endangered. The growing problems of society are reflected in the legislative load, and many citizen legislatures are extending their sessions beyond six months. This is having a profound effect on the type of citizen who is willing to serve. The citizen legislature pay scale is based on Lord Bryce's adage: "The way to get efficient men is to pay them well—The way to get honorable men is to pay them nothing."

Since citizen legislatures opt for honorable men, the pay does not compensate for the months away from a legislator's normal occupation. Yet higher pay is not viewed as the answer; the time limitation is seen as more important, and citizen legislatures are moving in the direction of streamlining procedures to shorten the length of sessions rather than increasing pay. In the meantime, "fewer qualified people will seek legislative office because they cannot afford the financial and personal sacrifice."[3] Increasing numbers of retired people, instead of young lawyers, are now serving in state legislatures. Control goes to the older members with more free time.

But though endangered, the citizen legislature still predominates. We must ask, then, what kind of code of ethics is appropriate for such a body? What kind of code will encourage the more qualified to serve? What kind of code will make it most likely that the individual citizen legislator will act in accordance with public rather than private interests?

When legislators are not full time, they obviously need outside income. A code of ethics that places strict limitations on outside earned income and outside professional activities (like the practice of law) is appropriate for Congress, but it would be unworkable at the state level.

Moreover, privacy should be given more weight in the case of the citizen legislator. Full financial disclosure is more likely to deter qualified citizen legislators from running than the professional legislator. They should be compelled to disclose less of their private lives—e.g., lists of clients or customers should not be required. Yet to control conflicts of interest, adequate financial disclosure and regulation by an independent

---

[3] North Carolina Legislative Study, cited in "Virginia, North Carolina Legislating," *Greensboro Daily News*, 17 April 1983.

commission appear to be essential. To give more protection to privacy, perhaps some items could be disclosed only to the commission. Since most state legislatures are short on staffing, an independent commission rather than a legislative commission is a must.

Almost every member of a citizen legislature has conflicts of interest. Because of the number of conflicts, a more tolerant attitude is requisite. For example, disqualification or divestiture should not be required. What must be sought is not the elimination of conflicts of interest but the *abuse* of self-interest.

Although a proper code for a citizen legislator, if it is to be enforceable, should be less rigid and detailed than that for the professional legislator, it is even more necessary that such a code be broader in scope than existing codes. Citizen legislators need some broad understanding of what is expected from them. Such a code should set out the philosophical and ethical foundations of the concept of the citizen legislator, trace the tradition of the institution in which the legislator serves, and furnish guidance and understanding of the representative process to the individual legislator and to the public. One can hear the guffaws of the hard-bitten legislator or press correspondent. Yet a well-drafted code may assist in restoring pride and dignity to the office holder and may even lead the public to appreciate the idea that public office is an honorable pursuit. There are many causes of the public misconduct of public officials—greed, political gain, the desire for social approval, the secularization of society. But surely one of the causes is ignorance of our basic political and ethical ideas.

INTEREST GROUPS

Interest groups of all kinds have increased dramatically in numbers in recent years, of course, at all levels of government. These groups find a more vulnerable target at the state than at the national level. For one thing, the weakness of political parties makes interest groups stronger, and state political parties are notoriously much weaker as a political force than the national parties.

Also, state legislators are more vulnerable to the special interests because they lack not only the screen of the political party but also the screen of a large staff. *Staff* for state legislators is a dirty word, as far as most voters are concerned. It is simply easier for the special interests to "get at" the state legislator. Furthermore, because most state legislators are part-time legislators they have expertise in the field of their occupations—banking, the law, farming, for example—but are unlikely to be experts in other areas. Since they have little staff help, the vacuum in expertise is likely to be filled by interest groups, which always stand ready to assist.

No code of ethics can solve this problem, but clear guidelines and strict restrictions on gifts from lobbyists, honoraria, and travel expenses, combined with media access to this information, are essential. There appears to be no other practical or constitutional way to regulate lobbying. Unfortunately, in this area wherein state codes should be as strict or stricter than at the federal level, the reverse is the case. Stern tells us that gifts from lobbyists are not illegal in most states, and enforcement of such restrictions as do exist is woefully weak. Nor can it be argued that gifts from lobbyists are essential to get good people to run for office.

Here, too, a broader type of code could make a contribution. In addition to the "Thou Shalt Nots," the code should emphasize the positive duties of the legislator as a democratic representative of the citizenry. It is a duty of the legislator to represent all of his or her constituents, to be familiar with their views, and not to represent only those citizens who come to the office. By and large, interest groups represent the middle and upper classes. It has been left to the political parties to champion the interests of the poor, and the parties' weakness in most states puts a heavy burden on the legislator. It bears emphasizing in a code that a public office is a public trust and that the legislator must not subordinate the public interest to the particular interest of any individual or group.

MEDIA COVERAGE

United States congressmen have much greater resources to manage the news than do state legislators. The average congressional office resembles the cabin of a space ship, with Xerox machines, WATS lines, and computer technology grinding out personalized letters and targeted mailings. Most offices have a press secretary who knows how to use radio and television to deal with actualities in the district, how to produce public affairs programs in the congressional radio and television studios, and how to produce newsletters (with no more than seven first-person pronouns per page). In addition to these in-house media, congressmen benefit from expensive campaign media to a far greater degree than do state legislators.

These advantages are only partially offset by the attention given to Congress, unlike state legislatures, by the national press. The national press is regarded as hostile by most congressmen, in contrast to the "soft" local press. Yet the hostility is directed more to the institution than to the individual congressman, at least in the House of Representatives. The individual congressman is rarely mentioned in the national press unless he or she is a subject of scandal, resulting in the public attitude, "We love our congressmen but dislike Congress."

In short, the members of Congress have learned to cope with the media, primarily by using the new technological resources to manage the news concerning their activities.

State legislators cope in a different way. There is a marked difference between the state legislator's and national legislator's relationships to the press; there is more distance between the press and the legislator in Washington than there is at the state level. Partly this is because the congressman's staff acts as a buffer. More important are the personal relationships that arise between the state legislator and the press. Part-time state legislators usually stay in motels, without their spouses, for a relatively brief period of time. They may frequent the local "Democratic bar" or "Republican bar," along with the press. There are many opportunities for direct personal contact with the press and for the forming of friendships. This is rarely possible in Washington, although something akin to this same coziness of relationship may arise for a local reporter covering his or her state's delegation in Washington.

The legislator–press relationship is complex; legislators and corre-spondents help each other and exploit each other. Douglass Cater noted that the member of Congress "lives in a state of intimacy with the newspaperman baffling to outsiders who mistake this vital relationship for pure cronyism."[4] The personal friendship between correspondent and legislator is rarely cronyism; there are too many inherent conflicts. Yet the correspondent covering the state legislator, or his state's delegation in Congress, must be on his guard lest his personal relationship with the legislator, or his approval or disapproval of the legislator's goals, make his a less than zealous exposer of wrong-doing by the legislator. In some cases it may even cause the correspondent to impose a deliberate censorship on some of the legislator's activities.

Because they often face a less critical, less probing form of press coverage, the challenge of internal self-regulation to ensure high stan-dards of ethical conduct is even more of an issue for state legislators and state legislatures than it is for their counterparts at the federal level.

This leads to the final general point I wish to raise: the role of the legislator as a political educator in a democratic society. On both the

---

[4] Douglass Cater, *The Fourth Branch of Government* (Boston: Houghton Mifflin, 1959), p. 47.

federal and the state level, the American legislative process is increasingly preoccupied with the use of the media. We have a new world of a politically oriented media and media-oriented politics. But there are troubling indications that this preoccupation is not working to strengthen the democratic process.

The press presents political campaigns as a special kind of sporting event. Television, as an entertainment business rather than a news business, presents political campaigns as a series of media events.

For their part, all good politicians are entertainers. They have mastered the state of the art and effectively use the media. They have also learned to circumvent the media by the use of the new technology of direct mail to appeal to many bits of the culture. The result is a climate of political debate that depends on advertising techniques rather than on rational public opinion, as in the traditional conception of representative government. Moreover, the practice—followed by politicians and special interest groups and facilitated by direct mail, narrow band broadcasting, and other communications technologies—of saying different things to different, carefully targeted audiences actually fragments our public culture in the long run and makes it more difficult for legislators to forge the broad public consensus they need in order to govern effectively.

A distinguished political philosopher, Maurice Cranston, has seen the broad implications of this problem:

> I believe that modern man is very largely denaturized, is a product of culture much more than nature. And culture has become oppressive nowadays, even intrusive. It is not education that shapes us, because what deserves the name of education is something that we receive less and less of. . . . What we receive is a culturization imposed upon us by modern media, and modern institutions, so that modern man is no longer the political man as he was intended by God, by nature, or by Aristotle to be. Nor does modern man know what politics is. Modern ideologies—nationalism, communism and so forth—provide a kind of imitation political experience for people. . . . But I think, perhaps, that democracy will, with difficulties, survive and improve itself in places where it is well rooted, and where people understand what democracy is, provided that people's understanding of it is enlarged.[5]

Surely one of the most important ethical challenges facing legislators today is their responsibility to be leaders and educators and to enlarge the people's understanding of our system. That is a challenge which both state and federal legislators must meet in the years ahead.

---

[5] Maurice Cranston, ''A Dispute on the Future of Democracy,'' in *The Great Ideas Today, 1978* (Chicago: Encyclopedia Britannica, 1978), pp. 46–47.

V

REPRESENTATION IN
NONLEGISLATIVE SETTINGS

16

Representation without Elections
The American Bureaucracy and Its Publics

JAMES A. MORONE

> *They may be every bit as intelligent as you say,*
> *but I'd feel a whole lot better about them if just*
> *one of them had run for sheriff once.*
>
> —Sam Rayburn [On the Kennedy cabinet][1]

Officials who do not stand for election hold a peculiar place in American thought. They are viewed, alternately, as a threat to democracy and a refuge from its worst consequences. Questions of public administration have repeatedly been turned into disputes about accountability to the public. This chapter reviews the shifting standards of representation that have been pressed on bureaucratic administrators, both by past reforms and by contemporary theories.

The other essays in this volume chart the dilemmas of representation and ethics within legislatures. There are formidable issues to puzzle out; however, they ultimately rest on clear representational mechanisms, on elections. Even this weak guide is absent in bureaucratic settings. There are no elections, no formally drawn constituencies. It is difficult to know

[1] Cited by Lawrence Dodd and Richard Schott, *Congress and the Administrative State* (New York: John Wiley and Sons, 1979), p. 7.

JAMES A. MORONE ● Department of Political Science, Brown University, Providence, Rhode Island 02912.

how representation should operate. Who ought to be represented? How can constituents convey desire or express displeasure? Should officials even be concerned when they do?

THE DEVELOPMENT OF A NATIONAL ADMINISTRATION

The American bureaucracy developed slowly through, very roughly, four stages. Each was founded on charges that previous arrangements did not properly represent the public or its interests, although ideas about whom bureaucrats ought to represent and how have changed enormously. The issues have been complicated by the American suspicion of centralized political power. With notions of individualism and liberty ascendant, the ideal has been a political system in which "nobody. . .is. . .running this place."[2] Throughout, there has been a steady erosion in the capacity of elected officials to control unelected administrators—the most traditional view of democratic governance undermined in a quest to return the government to the people.

Administration by Gentlemen (1789–1828)

The original cabinet had three officers, the largest agency (the Department of State), nine members. Officials were drawn from the patrician elite. Although President Washington emphasized "good character, good management and loyalty to the Constitution,"[3] good character was reckoned by family background and education.

The governing vision was unabashedly trustee—administrators were expected to make proper rather than popular choices. However, that standard was disputed from the start. In organizing the first agencies, Congress had to vest the power to fire administrators. The issue raised the fiercest conflict of the First Congress. It was repeatedly argued that since the House of Representatives was directly elected (the Senate and the president were not) and therefore closest to the people, it should exercise the responsibility. If the president could both hire and fire, he would resemble a monarch.

The appeal to democratic principles was answered, not with a

---

[2] Brian M. Barry, "The Private Morality of Public Servants," *The Hastings Center Report*, June 1980, p. 39.

[3] Paul P. Van Riper, *History of the United States Civil Service* (Evanston, Illinois: Row Peterson and Company), 1958, p. 17.

competing value such as efficiency, but with an assault on its egalitarian premise: "Your people," Hamilton commented, "Your people, sir, is a beast."[4] From the beginning, questions about public administration were construed in terms of democratic representation.

Despite the executive's victory and an acknowledged ideal of government officials as trustees, administrators and their politics remained at issue. John Adams made dramatically partisan "midnight appointments" after he and his party lost the presidency. Jefferson sought a balance between the parties. And throughout the period the dominance of wealthy freeholders, with their trustee ideas of administration, came increasingly under attack. An antiaristocratic, antiintellectual impulse focused first on Jefferson, then spread through both political parties. John Quincy Adams repeatedly stirred it up, sticking doggedly to a nonegalitarian view of public office. He championed administrative schemes drawn from European models (more efficient postal service, for instance), seeking to blink their unpopularity by urging Congressmen not to " 'fold up' our hands and declare that we are palsied by the will of our constituents."[5]

However it was precisely that will which was ascendant. With Andrew Jackson's election in 1832, the rule of America's gentry was thrown over.

The Spoils System (1828–1883)

Andrew Jackson articulated a new philosophy for public officials, replacing the trustee vision with a profoundly egalitarian one.

> The duties of all public offices are. . .so plain and simple that men of intelligence may readily qualify themselves for their performance;. . . more is lost by long continuance in office then is gained by their experience.[6]

Any man—everyman—could do the job. Legitimacy no longer resided in wisdom or "good character" but in democratic roots. Officials should turn over constantly (Jackson favored a four-year limit on administrative appointments). They should remain close to the people who were no longer "a beast," "palsying the will of public officials." Rather, Jacksonians sought to inject "republican virtue, simplicity and decency

---

[4] Riper, *History of Civil Service*, p. 18.

[5] Richard Hofstadter, *Anti-Intellectualism in American Life* (New York: Vintage Books, 1962), p. 158.

[6] Frederick Mosher, *Democracy and the Public Service* (New York: Oxford University Press, 1968), p. 62.

into public life."[7] Elaborate myths, often turning on family life in log cabins, were devised to demonstrate that political candidates were of the people; administrative offices were ruled by the same spirit. Expertise and experience were rejected in favor of common sense and popular approval. Officials held their positions by virtue of their politics, their party loyalty.

Each time the presidency changed party hands (and it did so an extraordinary five out of six times between 1836 and 1860), there was a more sweeping turnover throughout the government service. In 1860 Lincoln turned out ninety percent of the incumbent administrators. The Senate exerted tight control over patronage, steadily extending the positions available. Although the spoils system is often viewed through the scandalized eyes of subsequent critics, it resulted in a sort of participatory people's bureaucracy. Large numbers of citizens passed through the public service.

Naturally, the system retarded the development of effective administration. However, even this could be set in democratic terms. Tocqueville, for instance, observed that "all offices are elective offices in the United States," that "it has been impossible to introduce the rules of hierarchy anywhere" (although New York came closest, even then). Although acknowledging the "tiring results" that no European would find "tolerable," he viewed the system in the same republican terms as his American contemporaries: it fostered a democratic, civic spirit, and a sense of private initiative.[8]

Reform (1883–1920)

The spoils system flourished until after the Civil War. Then the enormous extension of the American economy and society began to strain the people's bureaucracy. Its raw partisan politics—the buying and selling of public offices, the intense party affiliation of public administrators—came under attack. The same cry that had ushered in the system now went up against it: "a new aristocracy of plunder and patronage" had usurped public offices to private ends.[9] Inexpert citizens rotating through public office with every election turned from an emblem of republican virtue to one of grasping corruption.

First the Populists, then the Progressives sought to restore adminis-

---

[7] James Q. Wilson, "The Bureaucracy Problem," *Public Interest,* (Fall 1975), p. 82.

[8] Alexis de Tocqueville, *Democracy in America,* ed. by J. P. Mayer (Garden City, NY: Doubleday, 1969), pp. 87–89.

[9] Riper, *History of Civil Service,* p. 81.

tration to the public by purging it of politics. Officials were shielded from elections, their aptitude for office measured by ostensibly objective civil service exams rather than loyalty to a victorious party.

The new administrators would be guided by their expertise and professional norms. Using quantitative, objective measures, they would do what was correct, regardless of political expedience. The techniques of scientific management, then being popularized by Fredrick Taylor, would chart the public interest.[10]

To accommodate scientific decision making, administrative agencies were redesigned and buffered from political institutions such as Congress. They were given authority over narrow issue areas—regulating railroads, for instance—so that their specialized expertise could more easily be brought to bear on public problems.

Administrative constituencies had shifted from political parties to carefully defined problem areas, the public interest reconceived, from subjective preferences expressed by the electorate to solutions discerned by an expert. The participatory bureaucracy of the spoils system was replaced by one that aspired to scientific trusteeship.

Yet for all the changes, there remained an underlying similarity. The spoils system rested on an interpretation of administrative tasks that precluded a highly bureaucratic, self-conscious administrative apparatus. The state could be thought of as a reflection of societal preferences rather than a self-conscious force. For the Progressives, science would yield the public interest, correct decisions flowing from correct technique. But like a self-equilibrating free market economy, the new agencies would produce the public good without conscious choices from the center. The Progressives replaced the spoils system, promising good, even active government; but they did so without threatening to introduce self-conscious public power.

A National Administration

Contemporary bureaucratic administration has been built over the Progressive foundation of agencies with a narrowly defined scope, staffed by professional administrators (protected from the vicissitude of electoral politics by the civil service system) and often characterized by some independence from Congress and the president. One consequence of the narrowly defined jurisdiction of many agencies has been an enormous

---

[10] See Grant McConnell, *Private Power and American Democracy* (New York: Alfred Knopf, 1966), chap. 2.

fragmentation of government authority in a system that is already divided by federalism and an extensive array of checks and balances. It has proved difficult to aggregate the policies of different agencies into systematic national programs that cut across specific issue areas. Railroads, airlines, and highways, for instance, each operate under a number of different agencies whose overlapping, sometimes contradictory, programs do not cohere into a national transportation policy.[11]

Worse, the professional administrators who have staffed the growing number of government offices found the public interest elusive from the start. The techniques of scientific decision making were useless before the ultimately political questions that they were asked to solve. For instance, the Progressive demand for railroad regulation led to the creation of the first independent regulatory agency, the Interstate Commerce Commission, in 1887. Its legislative mandate was broad and vague in the Progressive fashion: the commission was to insure that railroads charged "just and reasonable rates." Unfortunately, the principles of scientific management provided no guide to the quickly bewildered commissioners who lamented in their first annual report:

> The question of reasonableness of rates is quite impossible to deal with on purely mathematical principles, or any other principles whatsoever.[12]

The perplexity of the ICC commissioners remains relevant. Most administrators operate with some political "independence," protected from elections by the civil service system. Like the ICC commissioners, they act within institutions designed to promote a sort of trusteeship—a search for the public interest, guided roughly by their expertise (if not exactly "mathematical principles"). However, trusteeship implies some knowledge, wisdom, or skill that the constituency does not possess. If administrators, despite their merit qualifications, have "no principles whatever" to guide them, how are they to make choices? One possibility is to rely on the public for direction—a delegatory stance within institutions originally designed for trusteeship.

---

[11] For instance, authority over railroads is shared by the Federal Railroad Administration in the Department of Transportation, the Interstate Commerce Commission, and the Railroad Retirement Board; airlines are divided into the Federal Aviation Administration and the Civil Aeronautics Board; an entirely independent National Transportation Safety Board should not be confused with the National Highway Traffic Safety Administration, which is distinct from the Federal Highway Administration. None of these agencies is in the Department of Commerce.

[12] Robert Heilbronner, *The Economic Transformation of America* (New York: Harcourt Brace Jovanovich, 1977), p. 118. See also Robert Wiebe, *The Search for Order* (New York: Hill and Wang, 1967).

However, given the logic of political action, it is often the most concerned, those with an economic stake, that come forward. The ICC commissioners, for instance, eventually turned to the railroads for guidance in determining "just rates," at least until the truckers arrived on the political scene.

In addition, many departments are explicitly designed to promote the interests of well-defined groups. The interests receive an institutional advocate within the government. The Department of Labor was created for—and by—labor, Education for educators, Agriculture for farmers. Each has developed extremely close relations with a small number of organized groups that speak for the same interests as the agency. The National Association of Wheat Growers, the National Milk Producers Federation, and the National Cotton Council are extremely influential in the Department of Agriculture's deliberations over programs that affect their commodities.[13]

REPRESENTATION AND THE AMERICAN BUREAUCRACY

European bureaucracies were shaped primarily by the imperatives of efficiency.[14] In contrast, American administration has evolved around fundamentally representational issues, driven by a recurring urge to link the public service more closely to the public. The dispute about "the people" that split the First Congress, the Jacksonian revolt for the common man, the Progressive reaction against the politics that resulted, and many of the interpretations of contemporary bureaucracy, discussed below, all turn on different notions of representation.

Today, over two-and-a-half million unelected federal employees operate within a far-flung, decentralized, fragmented, bureaucracy. Their proper relationship to the public remains widely disputed. The traditional view, overhead democracy, seeks to link them through elected representatives, through congressmen and the president. The best known alternative, pluralism, turns to interest groups to carry civic wishes

[13] See Grant McConnell, *Private Power*, chap. 7.
[14] See Ernest Barker, *The Development of Public Services in Western Europe* (Hamden, Conn.: Archon Books, 1966); Alexis de Tocqueville, *The Old Regime and the French Revolution*, translated by Stuart Gilbert (Garden City, NY: Doubleday & Co., 1955); and *The Formation of National States in Western Europe*, ed. by Charles Tilly (Princeton,N.J.: Princeton University Press, 1975). Naturally the European nations differed enormously in the ways their bureaucracies developed. England, which was consciously emulated by Progressive reformers, is generally contrasted to the more specialized and bureaucratic Prussian and French cases.

directly to administrators. Other theories seek to convert administrators themselves into representatives. Each prescription involves a different set of answers to the central questions of representation.

First, who is to be represented? Without a formal mechanism of representation (like an election), there is no clearly delineated constituency. Administrators might represent the entire nation, a sector, an industry, a district. Should the Department of Agriculture protect farmers? Or consumers? How does its institutional design bias the possibilities?

Once the constituency is defined, how should unelected officials relate to it? The Progressives sought to establish a trustee relationship, the Jacksonians a more responsive one. Should officials be partisan, actively promoting constituent interests? If so, how are they to choose among competing claims? What about claims that are not articulated?

Finally, what mechanisms ought to link representatives to the represented? Congress or interest groups can convey preferences; expertise or shared demographic traits (like race or sex) may help a representative understand constituent interests. At different times each has been proposed; in various corners of the American state each is presently pursued.

Overhead Democracy

The traditional solution dismisses bureaucratic representation and restores each institution to the tasks it is designed to perform. Elected representives make the political choices, administrators put them into effect. In Mill's terms, legislatures "represent the will," unelected officials "the skilled labor, special study and experience."[15] The implicit chain of accountability is clear: lower-level administrators answer to their bureaucratic superiors who respond to elected officials who are accountable to the public. If representation is fostered directly within bureaucracies, questions resolved by one set of representatives will be reopened by an entirely different set. Proper bureaucratic representation is no more than the control that elected representatives exert over bureaucrats.

Overhead democracy requires a sharp division of tasks and distinct lines of authority. Legislators must make clear choices, oversee their implementation, and intervene if administrative decisions stray from legislative intentions. The bureaucracy simply effects congressional man-

---

[15] From "The Representative as Agent," in *Representation*, ed. by Hanna F. Pritkin (New York: Atherton Press, 1969), p. 232.

dates, acting as "an Aristotelian slave," incapable of independent thinking.[16] Ultimately, Congress makes ethical or value judgments, administrators factual determinations.

Past reforms challenged both sides of this equation. The spoils system was premised on a derogation of expertise, the Progressive reforms on an effort to protect it from political oversight. The institutions that emerged have complicated the task of setting Congress firmly over the bureaucracy—a difficult arrangement even when national institutions are designed to try.

One problem is the uneasy distinction between legislative value judgments and factual administrative ones. Implementing even carefully drafted legislation requires a series of choices, many with sweeping political and ethical ramifications. Officials aspiring to technical precision commonly find important value conflicts thrust into their cost–benefit analyses, sometimes despite earnest efforts to ignore them. For instance, Medicare seemed a relatively straightforward choice to finance some medical expenses for the elderly. Benefits, beneficiaries, and revenue sources were all specified in the statute, leaving administrators only such apparantly technical decisions as how to compensate hospitals. Yet their choices ended widespread racial segregation in American hospitals, dramatically improved the wage scale for workers performing menial tasks in health care institutions, and helped turn moderately rising costs into hyperinflation.

A lingering Progressive spirit acknowledges that facts cannot be fully extracted from values but contends that administrative experts are likely to make better choices than politicians. Experts are guided by internal norms such as professional ideals; they are likely to care about the judgments of their peers and the standards of professional societies. Public administrators may even promote enlightened reform, counseled by law journals and the most respected members of their profession. In the best cases, they will cultivate a "fellowship of science."[17] This view envisions an enlightened trusteeship by carefully trained professional administrators, searching for the public interest more diligently than politicians are apt to do. Objections regarding representation are met with a vague wave toward overhead democracy, which is expected to keep administrators within very roughly demarcated boundaries of acceptable choice.

---

[16] Norton Long, "Bureaucracy and Constitutionalism," in *The Politics of the Federal Bureaucracy,* ed. by Alan Altshuler (New York: Dodd, Mead, 1968), p. 17.

[17] Carl J. Friedrich, "Responsible Government Service Under the American Constitution," in *Problems of the American Public Service* (New York: McGraw Hill, 1935), p. 38.

However, administrative decisions are more often shaped by the ethos and interests of the bureau than by the detached expertise of the bureaucrats. The organization itself profoundly affects the way in which issues are viewed. Decision-making routines blunt professional ideals; procedures and deadlines deflect philosophical questions. Administrators often become isolated from both their peers and the public.

Congressmen are often accused of "running against Congress," of promoting their own careers at the expense of their institutional chores. Administrative agencies reward precisely the opposite behavior. Advancement comes from within the agency, not from an external public. Officials tend to develop an exaggerated concern for maintaining or enhancing their organization, even to the point of neglecting its ostensible purpose. Consider the celebrated Pentagon "whiz kids"; for all their technique and good intentions they grew increasingly isolated and, deceiving themselves, drifted into a senseless war. Again, professional judgment (much less the "fellowship of science") was conspicuously forgotten as the American Medical Association stridently fought the passage of Medicare for embarrassingly selfish reasons. And welfare agencies have become notorious for placing the interests of poverty professionals before those of the poor.[18] Repeatedly, studies of organizational behavior find experts spurning outside opinion, acting in an increasingly rigid and stultifying fashion, protecting their own interests (primarily autonomy and power) in the name of professional judgment.

Furthermore, there is enormous power in the information that bureaus accumulate and wield. It is enhanced by their tendency to be secretive—thus the reflex for classifying documents. Expertise and secrecy effectively parry criticism and extend autonomy. Bureaucracies often come to view political commands—the mainspring of overhead democracy—as the "occasional ideas of a dilettante."[19]

The structural legacies of Progressive reform—semiautonomous agencies with authority over narrow issue areas—make controlling administrative agencies particularly difficult. Effective overhead democracy requires that political choices be made at the center; the authority over narrow issue areas must be removed from dispersed administrative offices and exercised by elected officials. Congress, in particular, would have to fashion more precise policy and track its implementation more carefully.

---

[18] See David Smith, "Professional Responsibility and Political Participation," *Participation in Politics: Nomos XVI,* ed. by J. Roland Pennock and John W. Chapman (New York: Lieber-Atherton, 1975), pp. 213–232.

[19] Max Weber, *Economy and Society,* Vol. 2, ed. by Guenther Roth and Claus Wittich (Berkeley: University of California Press, 1978), p. 993.

However, Congress has been reluctant to assume a vigorous role. The Constitution forbids its members to hold administrative offices (as parliamentary leaders assume ministerial portfolios). This proscription checks the most straightforward form of overhead control—direct congressional responsibility for administrative decisions.

Instead, legislators are rewarded for being individual entrepreneurs. Their most obvious electoral incentives are to distribute benefits to self-conscious beneficiaries (that is, those who know enough to be greatful when it is time to raise funds). The more difficult task of governing the federal establishment, of working with other legislators to craft systematic policies and watch over their implementation, is less apt to enhance a political career. Both individual and institutional incentives lead Congress to buy out a town ruined by toxic chemicals (a distributive benefit with no enemies) rather than restrict the chemicals and avoid the disaster in the first place.

Congressional behavior is often interpreted within this rubric of distributing obvious benefits or avoiding difficult choices. For instance, Congress appears to create bureaucracies to deflect problems or satisfy demands; individual legislators then intervene—more or less as ombudsmen—to constituent complaints about agencies that they have established. In more sweeping terms, American legislation is criticized for providing unelected officials with a "broad delegation of power" rather than a series of carefully specified commands.[20] Responsibility for solving national problems, as well as the discretion required to do so, is ceded from elected representatives at the political center to unelected administrators scattered throughout the government.

Of course, vague mandates may be a consequence of the volume and complexity of the issues that confront a relatively small number of legislators. Even the tax code, which runs a meticulous 1,100 pages, prompts 6,000 additional pages of regulation.[21] However, the key to effective overhead democracy lies less in what administrators do, as in whether they do it within parameters set by the legislature. Even complicated programs can be overseen for broad policy effects.

In the United States, administrative oversight is performed in an ad hoc, haphazard manner. It is not important to either the programmatic or the political concerns that dominate Congress. Oversight is peripheral to drafting legislation and writing budgets; it can hamper the provision of constituent services. Furthermore, the task is not centralized but scat-

[20] Theodore Lowi, *The End of Liberalism* (New York: W. W. Norton, 1969), p. 121.
[21] Kenneth Meier, *Politics and the Bureaucracy* (North Sciuate, Mass.: Duxbury Press, 1979), p. 137.

tered over a tangle of subcommittees, each jealous of its authority. It is more a tactic in the political maneuvers among committees than a means for controlling national government. Centralized oversight might be more effective, but it would threaten the authority of congressional committees, the autonomy of administrators, the power of allied interest groups, and the electoral interests of individual legislators. The same incentives that send political decisions from Congress to the bureaucracy undermine rigorous oversight of the choices that are made there.

In the end, Congress is poorly organized to assert control over the American bureaucracy. Its members have neither the incentives nor the institutional mechanisms for asserting their collective will over administrators who are equally reluctant to submit to it. The president has clearer incentives but equally blunt mechanisms. For example, he can appoint six hundred administrative officials who, in turn, appoint about five hundred more. Beneath the political appointees sit over 2.5 million civil servants—roughly 2,300 administrators for each presidential appointee. An extended civil service system bars effective political control over civil servants, precisely as its Progressive authors intended.

Both the president and Congress represent diverse constituencies which can enforce their preferences with electoral sanctions. Any theory of representational bureaucracy must operate in the context of these institutions. Numerous reform proposals—invigorating political parties, introducing a parliamentary system—seek to tie elected officials more closely to administrative offices. However, such ambitious ideas spark little enthusiasm. At the same time, a widespread sense that elected officials have abdicated their responsibility over the bureaucracy—that overhead democracy provides too weak a link between public and policy—has led to numerous schemes that would make bureaucratic officials answer more directly to the people.

Pluralism

Contemporary government seems an unlikely setting for the Jacksonian vision of inexpert administrators guided by public sentiments. Yet precisely that antitrustee notion underlies the dominant postwar theory about unelected officials. First proposed (though scarcely noticed) in the waning of the Progressive era, pluralism links extensive political participation to the decentralized administration of contemporary American government.[22]

---

[22] See Arthur Bentley, *The Process of Government* (Cambridge, Mass.: Harvard University Press, 1967). The pluralist argument is developed by David Truman, *The Governmental*

Pluralists consciously repudiate Progressive rationalism. They deny objective interests or conceptions of the public good—"ends cannot be imputed to society by philosophers."[23] Instead, interests are defined by action. When an interest is felt, a group is expected to form and enter politics to pursue it. That group interacts with other groups concerned with similar issues. Political decisions emerge from the "mutual adjustment"—the bargaining and compromise—among interested groups throughout the government. The political system measures competing political utilities, even taking into account their varying intensities. In principle, it is a far more sensitive measure of public preferences than the party competition of the last century or the careful congressional oversight prescribed by overhead democracy.

Government agencies themselves are neutral arbiters of competing interests, they are citizen forums more than self-conscious forces. The measure of good policy is purely procedural: Are all groups, all interests, heard somewhere in the decision-making process? Pluralism blurs the distinction between public institutions and private interests—a felicitous result in a polity suspicious of government power. The analogy to economic markets, to an invisible hand guiding self-interested actions so that they sum to a common good, is explicit and quite exact.

The pluralists found reform more than they promoted it, reinterpreting nonelective institutions in a sweepingly democratic fashion. They transformed a national administration into a passive reflection of expressed societal preferences. Politics again eclipsed expertise as the standard for administrative life.

In the past two decades, almost every aspect of the pluralist model has come under attack. The most relevant critique suggests that it is systematically biased. The cost of hiring representatives—of forming a group and sustaining it over the life of a political issue—is extremely high. Economic elites with a great deal at stake have more incentives to participate and can mobilize greater resources when they do. They can afford lawyers and lobbyists. Government officials (not neutral umpires, after all) often find the steady pressure irresistible, particularly when it is not balanced by other groups articulating other interests.

The Progressives designed their agencies to be independent of corrupting political forces. They envisioned administrators pursuing the public interest, beyond the reach of selfish private powers. Although the

---

Process (New York: Knopf, 1951), and Robert Dahl, *A Preface to Democratic Theory* (Chicago: University of Chicago Press, 1956).

[23] Charles E. Gilbert, "Operative Doctrines of Representation," *American Political Science Review* (September 1963), p. 613.

public interest proved elusive, pluralists came to celebrate the same institutions for exactly the contrary reason—they were open to the public through the lobbying of pressure groups. Institutions originally designed to foster trustee administration were extolled for being responsive. However, now critics have been charging that the pressure groups that come forward do not sum to broad publics but to a series of self-interested powers seeking selfish gains.

Though usually viewed as an argument about power, pluralism articulates a comprehensive theory of representation in administrative agencies: popular preferences are mediated by interest groups. Government officials are like delegates; rather than acting on their own volition, they simply legitimate the policy conclusions that emerge from interest group interactions.

The central flaw in the theory lies in its sanguine expectation that every interest will develop a group and achieve representation before a government agency. Reliance on the spontaneous generation of interests may sooth a yearning for unfettered political markets, but it results in a systematic bias toward the concentrated interests that are most likely to organize. Pluralism might have accurately portrayed some aspects of interest group politics in America. However, the narrow range of interests—the narrow constituencies—that administrators actually hear makes it an insufficient model of bureaucratic representation.

Bureaucratic Representation[24]

In the past two decades, numerous programs have sought a more direct connection between administrators and public. Sunshine laws mandate public access to agency proceedings, minorities are recruited into government service, government bureaus assign citizens to advisory committees. Though often viewed as one broad "citizens' movement," such reforms are rooted in very different conceptions of representation.

Perhaps the best known view treats administrators themselves as representatives. Although they are not elected—and, in some variants of the theory, because they are not—administrators "are more likely to be in touch with the public" than elected officials.[25] They do not need to cater

---

[24] For an extended discussion of the themes in this section, see James A. Morone, "Democratic Wishes and Sensible Reforms," in *Health Care Politics*, ed. by Theodor Littman and Leonard Robbins (New York: John Wiley, 1984); and James Morone and T. R. Marmor, "Representing Consumer Interests: The Case of American Health Planning," *Ethics* (April 1981), pp. 431–450.

[25] Norton Long, "Bureaucracy and Constitutionalism," p. 21 and *passim*.

to campaign contributors or compromise themselves to win election (again the Progressive apprehension of politics). The crux of the argument, however, is that bureaucrats look like the public. They are far more likely to be women or minorities or members of the middle class than are congressmen. The implicit argument is that if public officials are recruited from a broad mix of social and demographic backrounds, they will be better representatives.

This descriptive representation is premised on the idea that individuals with similar demographic traits will have similar interests and pursue them in roughly similar ways. Officials who look like their constituents are "more representative" than those that the constituency has elected. This is a bald form of tokenism. Bureaucrats become representatives, not because constituents approve—constituents continue to have no say in the matter—but because they are, in some dimly ascriptive sense, similar.

Although recruiting a broad descriptive mix may help legitimate policy or pacify aroused interests, it is not likely to enhance anybody's representation. Demographic characteristics do not significantly shape policy preferences; most studies find them to be a relatively weak predictor.[26] Even individuals fervently committed to an ideology often find it compromised by the imperatives of institutional maintenance and organizational process. There is no reason to expect officials who are recruited for descriptive reasons to throw off the organizational mentality and pursue the interests of an amorphous demographic constituency. Rather, recruiting administrators with the requisite social features is a facile way to conduct business as usual while claiming to be broadly representative.

Naturally, all social groups should be included in the civil service. But this is a matter of equal employment opportunities. Effectively injecting public views into the bureaucracy requires a more robust form of representation.

A second type of citizen action places citizens on boards, committees, and agencies throughout the bureaucracy. They may appear at an occasional public hearing or meet regularly to review agency decisions, making inexpert judgments like members of a jury. Using citizens in this fashion is intended to deflect administrators from reflexive ways of thinking, give them a sense of community opinion, open their agencies to fresh ideas. It forces bureaucratic decision makers to face a portion of the public.

[26] Meier, *Politics and the Bureaucracy,* pp. 169–173, and Kenneth Meier, "Representative Bureaucracy: An Empirical Analysis," *American Political Science Review,*69 (June 1975), 526–542.

Still, difficulties remain. Who is to be selected for these positions and how? Citizens who appear at public hearings rarely speak for the entire community. They are less informative than a public opinion poll, less representative than elected officials. Broad invitations to participate—open public forums, for instance—generally yield citizens with special interests or narrow complaints or nobody at all. Furthermore, citizens who participate regularly are less likely to deflect an agency than they are to be coopted by it. Once on the governing board, they often—in John Ehrlichman's derisive phrase—"go off and marry the natives." The organizational ethos that shapes the behavior of bureaucratic officials is likely to dominate the citizen volunteers as well.

Note the premise imbedded in this form of bureaucratic representation. The concern about private domination of public office is matched by concern over autonomous government bureaus which are not susceptible to external control. Citizen representation is directed both at captive agencies serving powerful private constituents and independent ones pursuing interests that they have defined for themselves.

Finally, there is a third, more powerful form of bureaucratic representation. Political officials can designate constituencies—overlooked interests that are acutely affected by a bureau's actions—and then invite organized groups which speak for them to nominate representatives. The representatives enter into agency deliberations, joining governing boards or task forces or advisory panels.

Groups are invited rather than awaited, precisely inverting the pluralist ontology. The process of representation is tended by government officials at the political center, not left to free political markets. For instance, in designing public works, the Corps of Engineers has traditionally included local developers. Congress could mandate (or the corps itself could organize) an institutional place for environmentalists or nearby residents, extending the range of interests that are heard before rivers are dammed.[27]

Again, hospitals have long dominated local health politics. In 1975, Congress established a network of health planning agencies and mandated broad citizen representation on their governing boards. Groups representing a wide array of interests which had been silent despite a stake in health issues came forward to participate. Taxpayers, minorities, business

---

[27] See Daniel Mazmanian and Jeanne Nienaber, *Can Organizations Change?*, in *Environmental Protection, Citizen Participation and the Corps of Engineers* (Washington, D.C.: The Brookings Institution, 1979). See also Frances Rourke, "Bureaucratic Autonomy and the Public Interest," in Carol Weiss and Allen Barton, *Making Bureaucracies Work* (Beverly Hills, Cal.: Sage Publications, 1980), p. 105.

coalitions, insurance companies, and the poor all sought representation. In some cases, groups were organized (with assistance from the planning agency itself) specifically to select and monitor representatives on the agency's board. The consequences for many communities were new voices and new coalitions in health politics.

Of course, using interest groups to link the public to administrators raises awkward questions. These organizations are notorious for displacing broad public goals with narrow organizational interests. They can be fractious, jealous of one another, and unreliable. Nevertheless, they solve many of the problems that perplex bureaucratic representation.

First, they can give shape to the amorphous constituencies of bureaucratic politics—environmentalists, the poor, health care consumers. These are diffuse, often unself-conscious categories, precisely the dilemma for pluralist representation. Organizations can more easily demand an accounting from the representatives they select. Whereas general elections to political office often mobilize a geographic area, specialized elections to almost invisible boards are generally ignored.

In addition, citizen representatives who must answer to groups are less likely to naively assume the values and goals of a government agency. Organizational allegiance, bolstered by credible electoral sanctions, may check the powerful drift toward cooptation.

Bureaucratic representation mediated by interest groups may be the best of various flawed alternatives. Consider how minority representatives might be seated on a health board: elections yield either apathy or busloads of hospital workers. Administrators recruiting a required black member are apt to search for one that thinks as they do. If the NAACP is invited to do the choosing, black interests are more likely to be effectively represented.

A robust form of bureaucratic representation would define broader constituencies than administrators generally hear, linking administrators more closely to their publics. Finally, it would structure many of the obligations that are predicated of government officials.

For instance, administrators are often exhorted to "explain their choices," exposing their views to public opinion; their decisions ought to be legitimated by "elaborate mechanisms of consultation."[28] Similarly, Yates suggests an obligation to educate, to clarify issues, and inform the

---

[28] Mark H. Moore, "Realms of Obligation and Virtue," in *Public Duties: The Moral Obligations of Government Officials,* ed. by Joel Fleischman, Lance Lichman, and Mark Moore (Cambridge: Harvard University Press, 1981), pp. 3–31.

public.[29] Warwick adds that bureaucrats must steadily resist reflexive bureaucratic choices.[30] Administrators are repeatedly advised to be explicit and reflective and consultative, particularly when their choices involve competing values. The difficulty, as I argued above, is that bureaucratic organization powerfully encourages the reverse—reflexive decision making, secrecy, deference to established organizational procedures.[31]

The citizen board—when it is designed to vigorously articulate citizen interests—can disrupt these bureaucratic tendencies; it can organize the bureaucrat's obligations. Citizen boards require civil servants to translate agency jargon, articulate assumptions, and submit their choices to a regular public accounting. They provide an opportunity to educate that is not easily converted into a means of cooptation. While high-ranking officials may occasionally communicate with the public through the news media, citizen boards require administrators on every level to explain themselves regularly to public representatives. They provide a mechanism for the pursuit of public obligations which even the most responsible civil servant would be hard-pressed to find in traditional bureaucratic settings.

In short, important constituencies are identified from the political center, their representatives selected by groups. The interests that merit representation will depend on the administrative task, for in a fundamentally liberal society there are few constant cleavages. River projects, environmental agencies, health boards, and airport commissions may each require a substantially different universe of interests. Organizing the bureaucratic representation that I propose requires difficult political decisions about precisely who merits representation when.

Choices about who is to be represented before bureaucrats may appear trivial next to the sweeping reforms that would stimulate effective overhead democracy. However, the efforts are similar. Both seek to press broader constituencies onto bureaucratic agents; both require conscious public decisions about the operation of political representation; and each confronts the apparently profound American aversion to such an exercise of public power. From the Jacksonian people's bureaucracy, to the

[29] Douglas Yates, "Hard Choices: Justifying Bureaucratic Decisions," in *Public Duties*, pp. 32–51.

[30] Donald Warwick, "The Ethics of Administrative Discretion," in *Public Duties*, pp. 93–127.

[31] See Philip Selznick, *TVA and the Grass Roots* (Berkeley: University of California Press, 1949) for a penetrating case in which both administrators and citizen activists are caught in a "matrix" of organizational imperatives.

Progressive reliance on technique to the pluralist political market, the representation of public interests has been sought through mechanistic arrangements that need not be consciously structured from the center. "No one" has continued to "run this place."

Bureaucratic representation—drafting amateur administrators to review the work of the experts—makes political choice more contentious, slower, less efficient. While more voices articulating more interests are heard in any single agency, together they contribute to the centrifugal forces fragmenting the American political system. Ultimately, judgments about citizen representation must turn on the prospects for reforms that draw political authority to the political center, that fortify what I have described as overhead democracy. If such reforms seem unlikely or insufficient, the direct bureaucratic representation of carefully chosen constituencies may be the best that we can do.

ACKNOWLEDGMENTS

I am grateful to Daniel Callahan, Bruce Jennings, and Roger Cobb for their sensitive and challenging reading of this chapter.

17

Legislative Ethics and Professional Responsibility

VANESSA MERTON

The subject of legislative ethics and professional responsibility must be approached with trepidation. It is easy to be skeptical about the value and validity of comparing the moral situation of the legislator with that of the practitioner of a commonly recognized profession.[1] Such skepticism seems to wax especially strong among legislators and legislative staff members and therefore commands even greater deference than it otherwise might.

This chapter addresses that skepticism directly. It suggests some significant similarities between the responsibilities of those who make law and those who function in quite different representative roles. Its premise is that although the legislator is unlike the independent professional in many respects, it still may be useful to compare the legislator's situation with that of the professional for the limited purpose of examining legislative ethics. Legislators have largely ignored various ethical problems that preoccupy other professionals; a by-product of comparing their situations might be a broader range of issues for legislators to reflect upon in devising their own standards of conduct. One may ultimately reject the implications of this comparison on their merits, but they do not lack all

---

[1] I have been further emboldened in this undertaking by discovering, during the penultimate draft of this paper, that no less distinguished an analyst than William May also sees parallels between political and professional duty. See William May, "Adversarialism in America," *The Center Magazine*, (January/February 1981), pp. 47–58.

VANESSA MERTON ● School of Law, City University of New York at Queens College, Flushing, New York 11367.

probative force simply because there are differences as well as similarities between the legislator and the doctor or lawyer.

The chapter is divided into two major parts, one essentially theoretical, the other fairly practical:

1. I argue that in the legislative realm the fundamental tenet of professional ethics applies: special moral duties, distinct from general ethical standards, devolve upon those who assume professional roles, and the content of these special duties is to be derived from what may be called the mission of the profession. This proposition has come under attack with regard to professionals[2] and clearly invites dispute with regard to legislators. Without rehearsing that debate in full, I maintain that professionals are obligated to remain faithful to the underlying values of their professions. That does not mean slavish obedience to a rigid set of rules; professional ethics is more a matter of developing the requisite sense of judgment than of compliance with a code. Similarly, the ethical responsibilities of legislators are shaped by their representative function and can never be wholly expressed in a set of proscribed financial transactions.

2. For most commentators on legislative ethics, the problem of enforcement remains a persistent concern. Individual self-regulation according to internalized standards has not proven very satisfactory. Collective self-regulation (peer review) also has significant limitations. The intrusive oversight of outside agencies and investigative journalists may be the least desirable approach of all. The problem of enforcement is further complicated by the need to foster public confidence in legislators, which requires that they avoid the appearance as well as the actuality of impropriety.

On a highly (or is it lowly?) practical plane, the chapter draws attention to a somewhat novel strategy for discouraging not only unethical but equivocal conduct. Considering the incentives that most strongly

---

[2] Alan Goldman, for example, strenuously objects to this notion. See Alan H. Goldman, *The Moral Foundations of Professional Ethics* (Totowa, N.J.: Rowman & Littlefield, 1980). Goldman alleges that professional ethics amounts to little more than prefabricated convention, devoid of moral justification and designed for professional self-aggrandizement. He fears not that professionals will fail to live up to their standards but that they will succeed. With the possible exception of the judiciary, he claims, professionals have no warrant for treating rights and calculating utilities differently from anyone else.

Goldman specifically rejects the common argument that legislators are entitled to infringe individual rights when that seems essential to the welfare of the whole community. Along with Bernard Williams, see "Politics and Moral Character" in *Moral Luck* (Cambridge, England: Cambridge University Press, 1982), pp. 54–70, Goldman maintains that political leaders faced with such tragic choices must accept that whatever they decide, they will be doing wrong.

influence practicing professionals, it seems worthwhile to explore the potential of a legislative equivalent to the malpractice suit: the action for an equitable accounting or for imposition of a constructive trust. These venerable common-law remedies, which in the past have been sparingly employed, could serve as potent deterrents to improper legislative conduct.[3] Unlike either internal ethics committee proceedings, which depend on the action of legislative colleagues, or criminal prosecutions, which require action by another arm of the state, suits for constructive trust or equitable accounting can be brought by any citizen.

The conceptual underpinnings of these remedies depend on viewing the legislator as a fiduciary, one who can be held to standards of trustworthiness higher than those of the marketplace, and thus to a substantial extent on defining the ethical dimension of the legislative role. Otherwise there is no reason to expect legislators to refrain from the profit-maximizing, winner-take-what-you-legally-can behavior deemed morally acceptable in the private sector.

THE LEGISLATOR AS PROFESSIONAL

Some Similarities

Professionals, like legislators, exercise power that has been delegated to them by people who expect that power to be used in *their* interest—people who in a strong sense depend on the competence and character of those who represent them.[4] Such dependence engenders more or less conscious ambivalence. Clients and constituents regret and resent their surrender of some degree of autonomy even when it is their clear choice and patently best for them to do so.[5]

Legislators also have the monopoly on their function characteristic of the professional. Only legislators pass statutes. They make law and set policy in a way that no judge or administrator, let alone private citizen, can. It is certainly true that for each individual legislator this monopoly is

---

[3] The deterrent effect of these remedies may have been demonstrated to some degree by the California state legislature's recent decision to abolish them. Interview with Robert Stern of the California Fair Political Practices Commission.

[4] Even Hanna Pitkin has conceded this similarity. See *The Concept of Representation* (New York: Atherton Press, 1967), p. 167.

[5] For further discussion of client ambivalence, see Vanessa Merton, Robert K. Merton, and Elinor Barber, "Client Ambivalence in Professional Relationships: The Problem of Seeking Help from Strangers," *New Directions in Helping,* ed. by Bella M. DePaulo *et al.* (New York: Academic Press, 1983), pp. 13–44.

more contingent and temporary, more subject to divestment for reasons that have little to do with competence, than is the professional's license to practice. (On the other hand, losing an election may be closer to being fired by all your clients than to being deprived of your license; it does not deprive you of the *right* to practice your craft, just the *opportunity*.)

But for both legislator and professional, the formal power with which they are invested is always in a sense more potential than actual, more apparent than real. The exercise of that power requires the continuing assent of those who have ceded it to them. In Kateb's phrase, theirs is "an eternally chastened authority,"[6] ever subject to withdrawal by the client or electorate. Moreover, the theoretical power to do whatever seems called for may not be matched by the technical capacity to achieve it. Circumstances—inadequate resources, simple bad luck—may thwart the professional's or legislator's plans. The difficulty is that admitting to such limitations can have the unintended effect of amplifying them.

Why is it so unusual, both for professionals and for politicians, to state forthrightly that they do not know what to do, or that they have made serious mistakes?[7] Because they fear rejection by clients or constituents who prefer reassurance to realism; because it can be paralyzing to contemplate one's own uncertainty; and because the patient who hears that the doctor is not sure the medicine will work, the electorate which is told that proposed legislation may not solve a social problem, may lose faith and become unwilling to give either prescription a chance. In an aggravated version of the self-fulfilling prophecy, the mere possibility—far from prediction—of an undesirable outcome triggers its own occurrence. Legislators point out that they must also contend with competitors who do not hesitate to assert that if they were in charge all would be well. Conscientious professionals, too, can be supplanted by the quack or hack who promises an easy cure or a quick verdict. Thus the temptation to simulate certitude and to provide extravagant guarantees.

Legislators share with professionals the inability to retreat into the protected comfort of academic debate. Neither can get away with endlessly analyzing the pros and cons, the risks and benefits, that inhere in all the options which they see. A time comes when they must *decide*— reach a diagnosis, select a litigation strategy, make a policy choice—and then *act*—perform the operation, examine the witness, vote on the bill. In political life as in professional work, not to decide is to decide, not to act

---

[6] George Kateb, "The Moral Distinctiveness of Representative Democracy," *Ethics* 91 (April 1981), 357–354.

[7] David Hilfiker, "Facing Our Mistakes," *New England Journal of Medicine* (January 12, 1984), pp. 118–122.

is to act by default. And decision and action inevitably expose their perpetrators to blame when they turn out to have been wrong.

The structural characteristics of the legislative and professional roles, then—their complex dynamics of dependency and power, their unavoidable association with disappointment and failure—may account in part for the phenomenon that both politicians and professionals experience: although as individuals they are often admired and trusted, *en masse* they are not very well regarded.

Some Differences

In important ways, of course, legislators do not fit the classic definition of a professional, that is, one who uses special knowledge in the service of others to make a living.[8] Most salient is the fact that few state legislators and virtually no municipal and local legislators are paid enough for their legislative work to support themselves. Compensated on a partial or *per diem* basis (is this entirely dissimilar to a fee-for-service or continuing retainer arrangement?), they almost all engage in some other calling that supplies not only their livelihood but their primary occupational identity. Even federal legislators claim that they cannot survive on the $72,200 a year that representatives and senators currently make.[9]

The increasing professionalization of legislators with respect to compensation seems undeniable, however; a clear trend toward placing legislators on a pay scale that will enable and encourage longer-term and full-time service is emerging. Most observers endorse this trend as likely to improve the quality of legislative bodies. Legislators may be in a position comparable to that of the inchoate professions of the last century, when lawyers, healers, and ministers often were also farmers,

---

[8] Sociologists have devoted much energy to developing definitions that distinguish the "professions" from other occupational classifications. Some focus on the cognitive dimension (the professional's mastery of specialized abstract knowledge and technique), some on the normative dimension (the professional's orientation to the intrinsic rewards of work and to client needs), and others on the economic-political dimension (the professional's status, prestige, authority, autonomy, and ability to control the terms and conditions of professional work). See Walter P. Metzger, "What Is a Profession?," Columbia University Program of General and Continuing Education, vol. 3, no. 1 (New York: Columbia University Press, 1975), pp. 1–12, and Michael Schudson, review article of Magali Sarfatti Larson's *The Rise of Professionalism: A Sociological Analysis, Theory and Society,* 9 (January 1980), 215–229. Not daring to enter this fray, I use an abbreviated version of one of the more conventional definitions.

[9] City of New York Official Directory 1983–84, pp. 296–297.

artisans, and merchants.[10] As the knowledge base and the social functions associated with the professions expanded, the part-time professional gradually became an inefficient anachronism; perhaps the part-time legislator has also become a luxury that the complexities of modern government can no longer afford.[11] *De facto,* many supposedly part-time legislators already appear to be as dedicated to the vocation of politics as most professionals are to their work.

Linked to the issue of full-time career is the question of training. The ad hoc education and haphazard initiation of the legislator is nothing like the standardized, prolonged socialization process of a physician or a lawyer.[12] (The apprenticeship period of junior legislators seems comparable to that of journalists and business managers, however, both of whom often claim the appellation "professional").

But in this era of declining political party ties and the electoral success of celebrities, concern about legislators' lack of preparation for their role is growing. Several legislatures, notably Congress, have already begun to augment their orientation sessions, and legislators are forming study groups to develop positions on complex questions of public policy. The need for specialization and expertise vies with the perception that those who come to the legislature most knowledgeable about a given area tend to be more susceptible to at least potential conflicts of interest—the proverbial dilemma of banker-legislators' drafting bank regulations, for example. To the extent that comprehensive, ongoing educational programs can enhance their ability to offset the influence of lobbyists, legislators may have good reason to emulate a more professionalized model.

The most telling point of disanalogy between legislators and professionals is generally thought to be the difference between providing service to a constituency and to a client. By definition constituents are a multitude; the typical client, although more and more often a couple, a

[10] Magali Sarfatti Larson, *The Rise of Professionalism: A Sociological Analysis* (Berkeley: University of California Press, 1977), p. 13. It is worth remembering that through the nineteenth century, only 10% of physicians were graduates of medical school.

[11] But see the vehemently opposed view of Senate Majority Leader Howard H. Baker, Jr., "Congress According to Baker," *The New York Times Magazine,* 1 April 1984, pp. 68–74.

[12] It does not seem too far-fetched to imagine that those graduates of public policy and public administration programs who pursue legislative careers find what they learn to be of some practical use, perhaps even in appealing to voters. (They might easily find it as useful as professionals find much of what they are taught in professional schools.) And although universities have yet to offer degrees in campaigning and legislating, who knows what we can look forward to—at least one graduate program in lobbying *has* gotten underway. According to Jay Hedlund of Common Cause, Catholic University in Washington, D.C. has instituted a master's degree program in lobbying.

family, an association, a corporation, a class, or (in the case of public health workers and public interest lawyers) a relatively undifferentiated public, is probably still an individual. Sorting out and balancing the conflicting interests and desires within a constituency is seen as different in kind from the representation of a single client.

> Representing a constituency is not like representing a client, whose wishes on a single issue at least, are presumably unitary. A constituency, on the contrary, is rarely unified, even on a single question.[13]

One quick response to this view is that it considerably exaggerates the singleness of purpose of those who seek professional help. It is hardly atypical for a patient or client to want, simultaneously or alternatively, two completely incommensurable outcomes: to lose weight without dieting, for a trivial example, or to refuse a plea-bargain but not have to wait in jail for a trial, for a more troubling one. (When professionals inevitably fail to satisfy these contradictory demands, they become agents of frustration. Such frustration accounts for some of the client ambivalence mentioned above.)

A major component of professional work is trying to help patients or clients translate their conflicting desires into a coherent and plausible hierarchy of goals toward which they can strive without sacrificing their core concerns. This organizing and prioritizing function mirrors the consensus-building leadership that the good legislative representative tries to exert, both in reconciling the factions within a constituency and in integrating the needs of that constituency with those of a larger political entity. In each instance, the representative role entails awareness of the range of competing values in a given situation and acknowledgment of the necessity to choose, not between one side and another—the "good" client (faction within a constituency) and the "bad" competing interest— but among the various shifting aspects of the person or group represented.

In another sense, professionals continually mediate conflicts among their several clients in a way that is directly analogous to the practice of politics. Although in any given moment the professional may seem preoccupied exclusively with a particular client, in reality she or he is constantly making allocative decisions about whom to provide with how much of what service, just as legislators trade off their multiple obligations. Weighing one indigent client's need for time-consuming psychological support against another client's willingness to pay handsomely for

[13] J. Roland Pennock, "Political Representation: An Overview," *Representation*, ed. by J. Roland Pennock and John W. Chapman, *Nomas* X (New York: Atherton Press, 1968), p. 15.

much less demanding work is not, after all, so very different from the legislator's choice between spending hours on an individual constituent's problem and taking a trip to a major industry's convention. The fact that both types of activity are valid, legitimate expressions of the representative function does not mean that there are no grounds for choosing between them.

In sum, the multiplicity of legislators' roles and role-partners is certainly matched by that of professionals'. One can identify nearly a dozen different constituencies that the average senator might have to answer to: the country as a whole, the population of the senator's state, the federal government, the Senate as an institution, a political party, Senate committees and caucuses, policy or issue-oriented coalitions, staff members, and, not least, family and self. Professionals feel a comparable array of conflicting pressures from their various clients, their families, and themselves.

Some Implications

Again, the point of all this is not whether labeling legislators "professionals" is conceptually accurate in terms of linguistic, analytic, or sociological categories, but rather whether what can be learned from the discipline of professional ethics is at all relevant and helpful to reflection on the ethical problems of legislators. There is no reason to defend the comparison *per se*. The question is whether it leads to some generalizable observations about the moral problems of *representatives,* of people who act for and on behalf of others. Intended only as an heuristic device, not necessarily an accurate depiction of reality, the disanalogies of this comparison may be as instructive as its parallels.

For example, the duty to maintain confidentiality and its counterpart, the duty to tell the truth to those entitled to hear it from you, is a well-recognized dimension of professional ethics that has received scant attention from legislators.[14] If a constituent or colleague entrusts a legislator with confidential information, is that legislator free to use or transmit that information at will? For professionals, information acquired in the context of the professional relationship is sacrosanct. There are

---

[14] These positive obligations to protect secrets and to tell the truth are not derived solely from the law or ethics of the professions. They are part of the fiduciary relationship of agency, see Restatement (Second) Agency § 395 (1957), and govern all those who are empowered *to act for* another. The implications of considering the legislator an agent are more fully developed in the section on constituent remedies.

exceptions to this principle, of course, but perhaps there is a comparable baseline principle by which the legislator should be guided.[15]

Conversely, is *anything* the legislator knows properly kept secret from those whom the legislator represents? Only in extraordinary circumstances are lawyers or doctors permitted by their professional ethics to withhold information from a patient or client, but no analogous duty has been posited for legislators. This may be an area in which the professional–legislator comparison breaks down entirely; the point is that the centrality accorded questions about confidentiality and truth telling in professional ethics suggests at least that legislators ought to account for their limited recognition of the ethical problem of using information acquired in the legislative role.

Similarly, the ethical problems raised by the impaired legislator are rarely discussed. What are the obligations of legislative colleagues to a representative who has lost the capacity to function responsibly? A good example of the lack of consensus among legislators about these difficult situations is the case of Alan Sisitsky, a Massachusetts state legislator whose flamboyant feistiness gradually deteriorated into serious mental distress and eventual paranoia, culminating in his removal from the floor of the State Senate to an asylum. Prior to that, Sisitsky had once been expelled from the Senate on the grounds that his behavior interfered with the ability of the body to function; on that occasion he had moved to replace the Senate Banking Committee with "a cleaning lady with a rubber stamp." One of his aides observed that if Sisitsky had been a member of Parliament, his behavior would have been considered perfectly normal.[16]

In the professions, this type of problem has led medical societies and bar associations to develop programs for impaired professionals. Professional ethical codes not only prohibit impaired professionals' continuing to practice but require colleagues who become aware of a violation to report it to appropriate authorities.[17] Some state offices of professional regulation have introduced emergency procedures to suspend from practice professionals whose conduct may endanger the welfare of clients.

This is not to suggest that precisely these measures should be

---

[15] However, this concept is not altogether foreign to the field. In New York the State Code of Ethics explicitly prohibits disclosure of confidential information acquired in the course of official duties as well as the use of such information to further the legislator's personal interests. See N.Y. Public Officers Law § 74 (3) (c) (1966).

[16] See Richard M. Asinof, "The Wages of Stress: A State Lawmaker's Fall From Power," *National Law Journal* (July 26, 1982) p. 1.

[17] See, e.g., Rules 1.13(a) and 8.3(a) of the American Bar Association's *Model Rules of Professional Conduct,* reprinted at 52 *United States Law Week* 1 (August 16, 1983).

adopted by legislators, but only that legislators may need to think through how they wish to deal with comparable problems. What if it is two years until the next election and a legislator is successfully concealing a serious drug or alcohol addiction from constituents? One question that continues to provoke controversy among professionals is: Assuming a duty to take some kind of action with respect to an impaired colleague, do the affected patients or clients have a right to know about the problem? The parallel question for legislators is no doubt even more troubling, since to reveal the situation to the affected community would inevitably render the legislator's plight public and publicized well beyond the confines of a particular electoral district.

These are only two examples of the way in which juxtaposing the professional's ethical concerns with those of the legislator may add to the agenda of legislative ethics. First, however, some fundamental questions must be addressed: Is it legitimate to impose special moral obligations on legislators? How shall the content of those obligations be defined? and Can such obligations be enforced?

PROFESSIONAL ETHICS:
POSITIVE DUTIES, SUBSTANTIVE GOALS

Commentators on issues of legislative ethics tend to be dubious about the feasibility of defining substantive and positive moral standards for legislators, standards that can and should be enforced. Their skepticism stems from two premises: (1) the imposition of affirmative obligations is unworkable; (2) resolving value conflicts about the *ends* legislators ought to serve is beyond the scope of ethics. Professionals, however, routinely evaluate their conduct in terms of positive duties and substantive goals. Is there something instructive for legislators in the professional's approach to ethical analysis?

Moral philosophers state a convincing case for the proposition that in ordinary life it is simply impractical to try to impose positive or so-called perfect obligations (i.e., duties to care and provide for others). In theory people will do more harm than good, neglecting their own affairs and getting in one another's way in their efforts to be of help.

But when considering the special moral duties associated with a particular professional role, it is not only possible but entirely natural to define them as affirmative obligations to engage in, rather than refrain from, certain conduct. The content of these positive duties varies with the nature of the profession, of course, although certain generic types can be identified—the duty to serve those in acute need without recompense, for example. The whole history of professional regulation demonstrates that failures to act can be sanctioned as effectively as wrong action. Although it may be impossible to legislate morality, one can legislate moral acts.

Far more than reservations about positive duty, ethical relativism seems to have paralyzed the development of legislative ethics beyond a limited focus on bribery and conflicts of interest. It is a doctrine difficult to refute and disruptive of any attempt to define a substantive content for legislative ethics. From a relativist perspective, value questions constantly dissolve into political questions that must be relegated either to personal conscience or constituent control.[18]

It seems useful, therefore, to consider the arguments mounted against relativism by contemporary philosophers such as Alasdair MacIntyre and Roberto Unger. In his disquisition on the fallacy of relativism in *After Virtue: A Study in Moral Theory*,[19] MacIntyre reports that somewhere along the line in Western history, after the Athenian *polis* and Aquinas's *civitas* and the invention of anthropology, we came to the conclusion as a culture that it is possible to be value-free—to operate without commitment to a set of shared values—and also to be value-neutral—to judge all values presumptively equal and matters of individual preference. The Enlightenment determined that neither God nor Reason could justify particular normative choices. MacIntyre contends that in the absence of such shared bases of justification, moral conflict inevitably collapses into an interminable clash of subjectively calculated self-interests.

Despite his seemingly quite opposite political orientation, Roberto Unger reaches much the same conclusion as MacIntyre. In *Knowledge and Politics*,[20] Unger dissects the mass of contradictions that comprises

---

[18] A prime example of this perspective was revealed in Senator Howell Heflin's remarks at the committee hearings on revising the Senate Code of Ethics. Senator Heflin said: "I wonder whether you are attempting to regulate and legislate morality when issues involved in the public interest are such that it depends on the eyes of the beholder as to what is ethical. . . . It seems to me by attempting to be so specific, to get into so many different fields, to give lofty goals that one should aspire to, that you are losing some of the whole flavor of American democracy and representation, that minority viewpoints ought to be protected. . . . You are getting into an area . . . of what is not right or wrong from a viewpoint of morals or ethics but rather is an area involving the conduct of legislative activity." U.S. Senate Select Committee on Ethics, *Hearing On Revising the Senate Code of Official Conduct Pursuant to Senate Resolution 109* (Washington, D.C.: U.S. Government Printing Office, 1981), pp. 84, 86.

[19] Alasdair MacIntyre, *After Virtue: A Study in Moral Theory* (Notre Dame, Ind.: University of Notre Dame Press, 1981).

[20] Roberto Unger, *Knowledge and Politics,* (New York: Free Press, 1975).

liberal theory. He pays special attention to what he dubs the "principle of subjective value"—a restatement of relativism, to the effect that all desires that are the product of autonomous choice must be presumed equally valid. Like MacIntyre, Unger focuses on the tension between group well-being and individual freedom, a tension aggravated by the suspicion that any seemingly natural coincidence of individual goals has been engineered through sophisticated social manipulation. The liberal view of society as a web of artificial constraint whose encroachment must constantly be resisted by the autonomous personality precludes the possibility of genuine, spontaneous, shared perceptions of the good.

Unger and MacIntyre insist that this view is historically false. The ideal of happiness, the concept of the good life—these have not diverged so radically. On the contrary, the continuity of their basic components is evident in the recurrent themes of stories about the human condition. Major social institutions also reflect a core of nonsubjective values. Religion, art, and language, for example, are neither instinctual nor imposed by dictators. They evolve over time through interaction within a community around its perceived needs. Their survival depends on their continuing utility for the bulk of a population; a myriad of individual choices sustain them.

Perhaps the best example is language. Without threat or force, people choose to use the "right" words when they speak because they want to communicate. They experience the social structure of language as fulfilling that desire—as affirming, not constricting, individual identity and freedom. It is a confluence, not a conflict, of individual wills that generates language.

Confluence of purpose in no way implies a set of fixed rules. New words are invented, old words fall into disuse, the language changes and can be changed by individuals. Nor does it suggest the complete absence of hierarchy. Some words are better than others, depending on the underlying purpose of those using them. If precision is wanted, and understanding by a broad range of people is not necessary, then a highly technical vocabulary may be the right choice. If the purpose is to evoke a feeling rather than to describe an object accurately, poetry may be called for. Neither choice is compelled by fiat; neither is static and permanent. That the right choice changes from moment to moment does not mean that there is no right choice, or that there is only one.[21]

---

[21] For an intriguing analysis of the connections among language, tradition, and political life, see Bruce Jennings, "Tradition and the Politics of Remembering," *The Georgia Review* 36 (Spring 1982), 167–182.

MacIntyre and Unger posit an unchanging image of human nature that, paradoxically, is one of constant change. The human qualities they deem fundamental—*indeterminancy,* that is, the capacity for noninstinctual behavior; *consciousness,* the ability to reflect upon and learn from experience; and *purposiveness,* the tendency to act with a vision of the future—furnish the framework of their substantive moral scheme. It is a morality of judgment, not rule adherence; of appropriate response to unfolding situations, not rote repetition; of virtue, not law. In this respect their precepts are strikingly similar to both the ethics and the technical standards of a profession. Standards of professional practice are not immune from criticism or fixed, yet they have to be accepted for the moment in order to begin work. And it is in their acceptance that the professional manages to escape the bind of radically individualistic relativism.

THE SUBSTANTIVE STANDARD OF PROFESSIONAL JUDGMENT

Professional standards of conduct are not defined in terms of achieving or failing to achieve predictable outcomes. Professionals *cannot* promise to deliver a result, cannot guarantee success; inherent in professional work is an irreducible residue of uncertainty. The unnerving thing about professional practice is that one can do everything right, technically, and have everything come out wrong—often for reasons that have nothing to do with diligence or skill. The best cross-examination may not persuade the jury; the most adept surgery can kill the patient. In most cases, the professional cannot even specify in advance what must be done, how long it may take, and how much it will cost. All professionals can undertake is to do the best they can to help the client or patient; all they can offer is unstinting effort and unswerving loyalty. That is why the nature of the relationship is rightly one of fiduciary covenant, not contractual bargain.

In the professional's lexicon, failure is not the untoward and unintended outcome of a careful and reasonable choice; failure is making a choice that is deemed indefensible by one's colleagues, by those who can fully comprehend the limitations within which one must work. Professionals are, in the end, less expert in the abstract sense of mastery of a body of knowledge and more expert in the practical art of making the best decision possible in a particular moment.

It is just this inability to apply theoretical knowledge to particular cases in straightforward fashion that distinguishes the professional from the mechanic (*pace* Michael Bayles[22]) and the salesperson. The professional must exercise the faculty which in the literature has come to be referred to as clinical judgment. Clinical judgment is a mixture of intuition, prudence, and discretion. It requires willingness to attend and adjust to the actual results of a given intervention instead of blindly following a preconceived protocol even as its unsuitability to the task at hand becames apparent. It is a faculty that may be compared to Aristotle's prime virtue of practical wisdom.

Because professional work calls for judgment, it cannot be carried out solely at the client's behest even though entirely on the client's behalf. Clients are not the professional's only constituents. When the client hands over to the professional a certain modicum of power, it is not with the understanding that the professional will assist the client in achieving whatever objective the client identifies as desirable. The commitment of the professional is always tempered by the limited and special purpose of the professional encounter. The physician will not mutilate the patient so that the patient can more efficiently beg in the street; the lawyer has no duty, indeed is not permitted, to advise the client how best to accomplish an illegal end. One of the major functions of a professional code of ethics is to enunciate what professionals *cannot* be expected to do for clients. Ethical standards provide a source of restraint, a check on the relentless pursuit of self-interest by the client, and empower the professional to say no, not only with regard to particular means but also with respect to the client's ends. Being able to appeal beyond the client's wishes to the collective judgment of the profession enables the professional to be something more than the hired gun, the hired scalpel, the hired computer—the client's tool.

Max Weber was one of the first to explore the paradigm of politician as professional in his "Politics as a Vocation."[23] He argued that for some of the same reasons as professionals, politicians cannot simply follow the dictates of their constituents. It is independence of judgment and a sense of responsibility for the consequences of one's choices that differentiates the political leader from the civil servant. To be valid, however, that

---

[22] Michael D. Bayles, "Physicians as Body Mechanics," in *Contemporary Issues in Biomedical Ethics,* ed. by John W. Davis, Barry Hoffmaster, and Sarah Shorten (Clifton, N.J.: Humana Press, 1978), pp. 167–177.

[23] Max Weber, "Politics as A Vocation," in *From Max Weber: Essays in Sociology,* ed. by H. H. Gerth and C. Wright Mills (New York: Oxford University Press, 1958), p. 95. This address, given at Munich University in 1918, is the first significant analysis of the professionalization of political leadership that I have been able to find.

judgment must reflect more than a purely idiosyncratic value system; it must be oriented to the basic purpose of the representative role. What, for the legislator, can be the equivalent of the physician's "No, that's unhealthy," the attorney's "No, that's illegal," the clergy's "No, that would be blasphemous"?

WHAT IS THE MISSION OF THE LEGISLATOR?

As Gutmann and Thompson[24] agree, in order to define the ethical responsibilities of the representative we must resort to basic political theory, in the same way that understanding the professional responsibilities of the physician or the attorney requires appreciation of the function and purpose of medicine and law. Depending on the political paradigm, our expectations of political leaders vary. If we live in the world portrayed by liberal individualism, in which the only common good is that which emerges triumphant from contending factions, then the best we can expect of the state and its leaders is that they protect us from random and arbitrary interference with our liberty. The state, through its leaders, is supposed to maximize the opportunity we each have to pursue our individual goals. The very considerable powers delegated to the state— the power to imprison and execute, the power to conscript and make war, the power to enforce property rights and civil obligations—are legitimate only when exercised systematically and predictably, in a way that enables us to plan our lives.

The relationship of citizen to leader, under this paradigm, is essentially contractual. It is almost a commercial transaction. In exchange for our taxes and our obedience to law, our representatives either do or do not provide satisfactory goods and services. In either event, we are the passive recipients, the consumers of their product. If the state fails to deliver the liberty and security that we bargained for, we are entitled to complain.

The principal obligation of legislators under such a regime is to reflect accurately the will of the community. This version of the representative role in and of itself does not seem to demand great expertise or special qualities of moral character and leadership. It may entail the technical skills of infighting alluded to by Morone and Marmor,[25] and at a minimum

---

[24] Amy Gutmann and Dennis Thompson, "The Theory of Legislative Ethics," chapter 9 of this volume.

[25] James A. Morone and Theodore R. Marmor, "Representing Consumer Interests: The Case of American Health Planning," *Ethics* 91 (April 1981), 431–450.

it means that the legislator must in good faith carry out the mandate of his or her constituency. But this concept of the legislator dose not support very extensive claims of substantive ethical obligation—certainly none that would conflict with the imperative of electoral survival.

What if we shift to a different paradigm, one in which the state takes on the positive obligation of enhancing the quality of life of its citizens? When the state is perceived as ordained to pursue a common good, defined not just precedurally as the aggregate of overlapping private interests but substantively, according to some vision of the "good society," then it seems that the role of the representative also changes radically. The politician no longer can be simply the broker, the negotiator, the bargainer, the compromiser, the instrumental gladiator who ensures that his or her particular constituents get the most they possibly can of whatever they want.

This is not to disparage the skills of brokerage, negotiation and compromise, by the way; they are a major part of a lawyer's work and I know how hard it is to master and to teach them. But their exercise generally involves no real edification, either of one's adversary or one's client. In an unabashedly teleological commonweal, the political leader would bear the responsibility of articulating the common vision that animates that society, in a way that strives to modify and moderate the desires of its citizenry. The skills of education, not of persuasion and manipulation, ought to be the hallmark of the legislative leader.

The point is not that political leaders should make decisions for the populace and then start trying to convince the populace that it likes those decisions. But what the legislator must not do is abdicate the responsibility of struggling with the client—that is, the constituency—toward redefinition of its objectives when those objectives conflict with the legislator's perception of the shared social vision. The concept of transformational, as opposed to transactional, leadership is salient here. The legislator has to engage the populace in not only rational but ethical discourse that centers on the validity of ends as well as on the efficacy of means. The legislator must refuse to oversimplify, to scapegoat, to obscure the complexity of issues. Just as a doctor or lawyer is obliged to educate a patient or client about the risks and benefits of alternative possibilities before seeking consent to proceed with a particular course, so are legislators obliged to educate their constituents. If liberal democracy is not to lapse into Marx's "petrified civil war," political life must consist of conversation about the *reasons* for choices, not merely the choices themselves.

THE FUNCTIONAL EQUIVALENT OF A MALPRACTICE SUIT

In the professional context, the much-maligned malpractice suit complements the traditional peer-review mechanisms of censure and discipline, which often seem relatively limited in impact, and the extraordinary sanction of delicensure, which is about as rare an event as legislative expulsion. As a victim-initiated process that seeks compensation for the wrong rather than punishment of the wrongdoer, the malpractice suit affords some substantial advantages over peer review and state prosecution. A claim of malpractice can be based solely on a breach of ethical duty as well as on negligent performance of a professional task.[26]

In a similar vein, suits for restitution of financial gain obtained in violation of the ethical obligation of undivided loyalty have been brought against legislators from the local level up to Congress. The legal device through which this is accomplished is called a "constructive trust." Its theoretical base is in the common law of agency. Under agency principles, an agent who acquires any interest or performs any action adverse to the interests of the principal is accountable for this betrayal of trust, regardless of the technical legality of the agent's conduct. And as the Supreme Court of Illinois held in 1976:

> The fiduciary responsibility of a public officer cannot be less than that of a private individual. In both instances it is gain to the agent from the abuse of the relationship that triggers the right to recover, rather than loss to the principal.[27]

The major advantage of the doctrine of constructive trust from the standpoint of enforcing legislative ethics is just that: one need not prove a particular act of fraud, or show a specific, identifiable, pecuniary loss to the government. It may be that the contract arranged by the official who collects a kickback is a good deal for the government and that an honest public servant would have entered into the very same terms.[28] The regulation passed at the behest of a legislator who regularly receives "gifts" of stock from an affected corporation may be a perfectly sound and reasonable law, and no individual citizen or public entity may actually suffer from it.[29] The petitioner in a constructive trust proceeding need not show that the legislator or administrator affirmatively harmed the public

---

[26] Most professional codes of ethics contain explicit disclaimers to the effect that they are not intended for use as a basis for civil liability, but courts frequently refer to such codes when determining professional standards of conduct to apply in malpractice cases.

[27] City of Chicago *ex. rel.* Cohen v. Keane, 357 N.E. 2d 452, 456 (Ill. 1976).

[28] See U.S. v. Carter, 217 U.S. 286 (1910).

[29] See Fuchs v. Bidwill, 334 N.E. 2d 117 (Ill. App. 1975), rev'd on other grounds, 359 N.E. 2d 158 (Ill. 1977).

or broke the law. There is no need to prove illicit motivation. It is enough to establish what amounts to an appearance of impropriety or disloyalty.

First recognized in 1910 with the landmark decision of *U.S.* v. *Carter*,[30] this "venerable judge-fashioned public remedy. . . has retained its vitality."[31] As recently as 1980, in the *Snepp* case, the Supreme Court not only reaffirmed the availability of this sanction for one who breaches the public trust but praised it as "the most appropriate remedy. . . natural and customary. . . swift and sure."[32] And that it is. Although the dichotomy of actions at law and suits in equity has long since been abolished, important differences remain between equitable remedies, such as the constructive trust, and their strictly legal counterparts.

For example, a proceeding brought to impose a constructive trust or to compel an equitable accounting is not subject to the labyrinthine procedural maneuvers and preliminary motions associated with most civil litigation. It does not culminate in a full-fledged jury trial, but in a simplified, streamlined inquiry, a virtual inquest by the court. Unlike criminal prosecutors, trust petitioners do not bear the heavy burden of proving guilt beyond a reasonable doubt, nor need they establish knowing or intentional wrongdoing (*scienter* and *mens rea*). Probative evidence will not be excluded from the proceeding because it has been obtained improperly. Finally, accounting and trust proceedings seem less likely to generate the same level of psychological resistance as an indictment and punitive sanction. It can't be easy to declare that a heretofore respected political figure is a common criminal, especially on the basis of complex, perhaps equivocally shady, transactions. Arthur Lenhoff best described the limitations of the criminal process in his classic article, "The Constructive Trust as a Remedy for Corruption in Public Office":

> The statute books are replete with criminal sanctions against specific viola-
> tions of official duty. Yet these always seem inadequate to deal with anything
> but blatant thievery, for corruption is a monster with not only as many heads
> as Hydra, but as many shapes as Proteus; the legislature no sooner isolates and
> prohibits one form of official pocket-lining than another is devised. In this
> never-ending race the law-maker is doomed to lose. On the other hand, we
> cannot simply make criminal the violation of broadly-stated canons of ethics.[33]

Equitable accounting and constructive trust have been upheld despite the fact that they lack statutory authority,[34] as well as against the

---

[30] 217 U.S. 286 (1910).

[31] U.S. v. Eilberg, 507 F. Supp. 267, 271 (E.D. Pa. 1980).

[32] Snepp v. U.S., 444 U.S. 507, 514–15 (1980) (per curium), rehearing denied, 445 U.S. 972 (1981).

[33] 54 *Columbia Law Review* 214 (1954).

[34] See U.S. v. Kearns, 595 F. 2d 729 (D.C. Cir. 1978) (Bazelon, J.).

converse argument that statutes defining criminal liability and other more cumbersome civil remedies for bribery and conflict of interest were intended to replace them.[35] Nor can a constructive trust be defeated by retreating behind the mantle of legislative immunity or the speech or debate clause. The speech, the vote, the conversation, the letter, issued in corrupt violation of the legislator's fiduciary duty does not fall within the sphere of legitimate and appropriate legislative activity.[36]

The practice of invoking the doctrine of constructive trust against public officials is well established in the state courts.[37] For no apparent reason it seems to be an especially prominent feature of the jurisprudence of Illinois.[38] Among its more notable subjects of late have been Bertram Podell, former congressman from New York, and ex-Vice President Spiro Agnew.[39]

---

[35] Ibid.; see also *Lane* v. *U.S.*, 639 F. 2d 758 (U.S. Ct. Cl. 1981); *U.S.* v. *Podell*, 572 F. 2d 31 (2d Cir. 1978) (Kaufman, J.).

[36] See Bradley, *The Speech or Debate Clause,* 57 *No. Car. L. Rev.* 197–230 (1979); see also Visser v. Magnarelli, 542 F. Supp. 1331 (N.D.N.Y. 1982). Legislative immunity, which is enjoyed by all legislators, and Speech or Debate immunity, applicable only to federal legislators, are distinct but overlapping legal doctrines whose finer points are irrelevant to this discussion. It is clear, however, that the protection of legislative immunity cannot be *broader* than that of the Speech or Debate Clause. See Benford v. A.B.C., 502 F. Supp. 1158 (D. Md. 1980), aff'd in unpublished opinion, 661 F. 2d 917 (4th Cir. 1981), cert. denied, 102 S. Ct. 612. In turn, Speech or Debate immunity has never been construed to insulate *all* conduct ostensibly relating to the legislative process, but only that conduct which is "an integral part of the deliberative and communicative processes by which Members participate in. . . proceedings," Gravel v. U.S., 408 U.S. 606, 625 (1972), and, moreover, part of the "*due* functioning of the [legislative] process," U.S. v. Brewster, 408 U.S. 501, 516 (1972). See also Hutchinson v. Proxmire, 443 U.S. 111 (1979); Doe v. McMillan, 412 U.S. 306 (1975); and U.S v. Johnson, 383 U.S. 169, 172 (1966). ("No argument is made nor do we think it could be successfully contended that the Speech or Debate Clause reaches conduct, such as was involved in the attempt to influence the Department of Justice, that is in no wise related to the due functioning of the legislative process.")

   Johnson held that prosecution under a criminal conspiracy statute requiring proof of intent to impair, obstruct or defeat the lawful function of government was precluded by the Speech or Debate Clause because it involved an inquiry into Johnson's motivation. As discussed in the text, the constructive trust doctrine does *not* require such proof or involve that kind of inquiry.

[37] See Williams v. State, 315 P. 2d 981 (Ariz. 1957); Bonelli v. State, 139 Cal. Rptr. 486 (Cal. App. 1977); City of Boston v. Santosuosso, 30 N.E. 2d 278 (Mass. 1940); Agnew v. State, 446 A. 2d 425 (Md. App. 1982); Jersey City v. Hague, 115 A. 2d 8 (N.J. 1955).

[38] See Chicago Pk. Dis. v. Kenroy Inc., 402 N.E. 2d 181 (1980); Cook County v. Barrett, 344 N.E. 2d 540 (Ill. App. 1975).

[39] Professor John Banzhof of George Washington University Law School has described how Agnew was privately prosecuted after the State of Maryland refused to authorize suit

Such proceedings may be instituted not just against the legislative malfeasor but also against private parties who induce or knowingly participate in the legislator's breach of duty. Constructive trusts have been successfully imposed on the offeror as well as the recipient of a bribe,[40] on an unscrupulous lobbyist,[41] and even on political associates of the office-holder.[42] A recent example of this is the case of Joseph Margiotta, a leading *ex officio* Nassau County politician who was convicted of extortion and looting the county treasury. Nassau County itself chose not to seek restitution from Margiotta, much to the dismay of the *New York Times,* which incorrectly assumed that it would be impossible for a private citizen to pursue his ill-gotten gains.[43] However, a few Nassau County taxpayers banded together, hired counsel, and have gone after Margiotta and a host of his political cronies for $4.5 million, using the doctrine of constructive trust. The Nassau County District Attorney has joined the action in his private capacity as a taxpayer.[44]

Margiotta's case illustrates the special advantage of the constructive trust and the equitable accounting: they do not require unified action by the polity as a whole. These remedies can be invoked not only by the state but also by individual taxpayers and citizens.[45] It is in this way that they are most reminiscent of the concept of professional malpractice. An aggrieved client or patient does not have to wait for license revocation or criminal proceedings before initiating a damage claim against a professional. Similarly, through a constructive trust petition, a citizen can seek direct vindication of the right to faithful representation without having to rely on a hard-to-mobilize electorate or a state bureaucracy. At the same time, these suits do not interfere directly with the representative function of a defendant and therefore do not affect the people's right to be represented by a rascal if they wish.

This special advantage is, at the same time, a definite source of risk. We do not want legislators to begin practicing "defensive politics" as some physicians practice defensive medicine. The validity of physicians' assumptions about the causes of malpractice litigation can be called into

---

against him. See letter of John F. Banzhof 3d, *New York Times,* 29 April 1983, p. A30, col. 5.

[40] See Cont. Mgmt. v. U.S., 527 F. 2d 613 (U.S. Ct. Cl. 1975); U.S. v. Cripps, 460 F. Supp. 969 (E.D. Mich. 1978).

[41] See Village of Wheeling v. Stavros, 411 N.E. 2d 1067 (Ill. App. 1980).

[42] See Jersey City v. Hague, 115 A. 2d 8 (N.J. 1955).

[43] "Joseph Margiotta's Damages," *New York Times,* 18 April 1983, p. A16, col. 1.

[44] "Nassau County Joins Suit Against Margiotta," *New York Law Journal,* 15 July 1983, p. 15, col. 6.

[45] See Chicago ex rel Cohen v. Keane, 357 N.E. 2d 452 (Ill. 1976).

question, but the reality is that their clinical judgment is compromised at times by their apprehension. There is reason, however, to be somewhat more sanguine about legislators' exposure to action by private citizens. First, equitable actions such as the constructive trust and the accounting are far less likely to be undertaken on a contingent fee basis. Ordinarily the potential recovery on these cases is just not going to be that high. No damage will be awarded for pain and suffering or psychological distress, no punitive or exemplary damages, no compensation for loss of future earnings. These are the items that so inflate judgments in malpractice and products liability cases. Moreover, whatever recovery is obtained would redound not to the private petitioner but to the state. So the motivation behind these actions would almost have to be moral outrage, not greed.

Moral outrage can lead to even greater excesses than greed, of course. But constructive trust and equitable accounting are confined in scope to financial transgressions. They offer no remedy for claims of improvident leadership or negligent political judgment. They would be perfect analogues to malpractice actions if doctors and lawyers could be sued by patients and clients only for stealing from them, or for profiting from apparent conflicts of interest. This restriction significantly limits the utility of these remedies for the enforcement of legislative ethics, but it does serve as something of a safeguard against a "malpractice explosion." And it is with respect to the business of policing financial abuse that the expertise of legislative ethics committees seems most wasted. Perhaps self-executing remedies like the equitable accounting and the constructive trust could relieve the ethics committees of some part of that burden and enable them to concentrate on more delicate and demanding issues of legislative ethics.

CONCLUSION

Legislators, like other professionals subject to the temptations of power and the constraints of untenured position, need what Henry Clark calls a rationalization for integrity.[46] In order to escape the cynical position of the jaded Machiavellian without becoming a hapless sucker, the legislator must have a principled basis for telling constituents, colleagues, and contributors, "No." Substantive standards of legislative ethics, grounded in a full conception of the political leader's mission, can provide that basis. Enforcement mechanisms available directly to the public, not requiring official intervention, can make it all the more

[46] Henry B. Clark, "Honesty, Savvy and Vision: Integrity in the Vocation of Politics," *Humanities in Society,* 3 (Summer 1980), 28–41.

pragmatic for the legislator to be principled. Both these approaches to recurrent problems of regulating legislative conduct are derived from comparing the legislative with the professional role.

Dr. Carleton Chapman argues that politics became a profession when the role of political leader shifted from that of the exploitative victor, entitled to make the most of high office, to that of the people's servant, one obligated to do not just the minimum, but the best he or she could do on their behalf.[47] This ideal may rarely be realized, either by politicians or professionals, but it nonetheless expresses a distinctive source of moral responsibility. It is important to be cognizant of its limits, however. Professionals should not bargain with their clients to make them whole or free, and political leaders should not promise their constituents Utopia. In each instance the nature of the relationship is rightly one of fiduciary undertaking, not contract, in which the professional or the politician offers unstinting effort and unswerving loyalty, but never unquestioning obedience.

---

[47] Carleton B. Chapman, "The Importance of Being Ethical," *Perspectives in Biology and Medicine* 24 (Spring 1981), 422–439, at 424.

Index

Abscam scandal, 102–103
Absenteeism, 193
Accountability
  autonomy and, 180
  bureaucracy and, 283
  reforms supporting, 189–191
  theory and, 176–177
Administration. *See* Bureaucracy
Adversary system. *See* Interest groups;
    Pluralism
Advertising
  electorate and, 81
  fair principles statement for, 83–85
  increase in unethical uses of, 71–74
  model agreement operation in, 87–88
  problems posed by, 69–71
  purposes served by, 75–78
  regulation of, 81
  unethical practices in, 67–68
  See also Media; Press
Advertising agencies. *See* Professional
    campaign firms
American Association for the Advance-
    ment of Science Code of Ethics,
    224
American Bar Association Code of
    Ethics, 224
American Dental Association, 95
American Medical Association, 95
American Medical Association Code of
    Ethics, 224
Apprenticeship system, 111–112
  decline of, 131–132
  impatience with, 119
Automobile industry, 95
Autonomy
  accountability and, 180
  conflict of interest and, 201
  duty and, 174–175
  interest groups and, 152

Autonomy (*Cont.*)
  legislation supporting, 188
  party politics and, 200–201
  socialization and, 186
  structural supports for, 184
  theory and, 176

Baker, Richard Allan, 3–27
Bank of the United States, 8
Behavioral norms. *See* Norms; Socializa-
    tion
Bribery
  autonomy and, 175
  codes of conduct and, 26
  Congress (U.S.) and, 17, 21
  exclusion from public office, 13
  history and, 10–11
  honoraria and, 99
  lobbyists and, 35–36, 97–98
  Senate (U.S.) and, 14–15
Bureaucracy
  accountability and, 191
  bureaucratic representation, 296–300
  development of, 284–289
  national administration, 287–289
  overhead democracy theory, 290–294
  pluralism and, 294–296
  reform and, 286–287
  representation and, 283–301
  socialization and, 122
  spoils system, 285–286
Bureaucratic representation, 296–300

California Fair Political Practices
    Commission (FPPC), 85
Callahan, Daniel, 221–234
Campaign financing and funds

Campaign financing and funds
  (*Cont.*)
  censure and, 35
  Congressional context and, 120–121,
    134
  Congresspeople, 3
  electoral success and, 50
  history and, 19–21
  incumbency and, 55
  individual contributions, 63
  limits on, 56, 62
  lobbyists and, 92–93, 97
  misuse of, 24–25
  Nixon and, 23
  political action committees and,
    42, 43–44, 45, 48
  public financing, 62–63, 103, 188
  reforms and, 93–94
  regulation of, 19
  state legislatures, 249–251, 269
  structural reforms and, 185
Campaigns, 67–88
  candidate characteristics in, 79
  codes of ethics and, 228
  conceptual framework for, 74–75
  Congressional context and, 131, 133–
    136
  electorate and, 80–81
  increase in unethical conduct in, 71–74
  interest groups and, 134
  model agreement operations in, 87–88
  party system and, 133
  problems posed by, 69–71
  purposes served by, 75–78
  standards and procedures for, 81–87
  unethical practices in, 67–68
  See also Elections
Censure
  electorate and, 32, 34, 35
  history and, 6–7, 10, 14
  Senate (U.S.) and, 25
Character
  advertising and, 75–76
  bureaucracy and, 284
  campaigns and, 79
Checks and balances, 159
Citizen legislatures, 275–276
  See also State legislatures
Civil service. *See* Bureaucracy
Civil War, 10, 11–12
Codes of ethics, 221–234

Codes of ethics (*Cont.*)
  commercial activity and, 175
  contents of, 161–162, 226–230
  development of, 22–23, 24, 25–27
  effectiveness and, 213–215, 232–233
  enforcement and, 231, 235–240
  expulsion and, 311
  limitations of, 229
  motivation behind, 221–222
  new efforts in, 151
  passage of, 179
  pluralism and, 233–234
  professional groups, 223–225
  purposes of, 230
  responsibility and, 192
  Senate (U.S.) and, 225–226
  socialization and, 121–122
  state/federal compared, 274
  state legislatures, 254–256, 270, 277
  theory and, 167
Commercial activities
  accountability and, 189–190
  bribery and, 17
  codes of ethics and, 175
  conflict of interest and, 201
  Congressmen, 4
  electorate and, 36
  financial disclosure and, 222
  history and, 8, 9
  House of Representatives and, 13–15,
    23–24
  legislation and, 151
  Progressivism and, 17–18
  Senate (U.S.) and, 18–19, 24
  structural reforms and, 185–186
  See also Conflict of interest
Committee system
  decentralization of, 135
  decline of, 130
  function of, 144
  norms and, 131–132
  responsibilities for, 140–142
Competence, 76, 79
Compromise, 109
Conflict of interest
  codes of ethics and, 175
  ethics definition and, 201
  legislation in, 151
  state legislatures and, 276
  theory and, 167
  See also Commercial activities

Congress (U.S.)
  bribery and, 10–11, 17
  bureaucracy and, 284, 292–294
  campaign contributions and, 56
  commercial activity and, 8
  confidence in, 16–17
  Constitution (U.S.) and, 158–159
  context of, 130–132
  criminal prosecution and, 30–32
  elections and, 133–136
  electorate and, 29–37
  ethical code development in, 22, 24,
    25–27
  historical perspective on, 3–27
  interpersonal relations in, 119–120
  office holding and, 52
  political action committees and, 94–97
  postwar norms in, 110–116
  Progressivism and, 17–18
  representation and, 136–143
  resources of, 54–55
  responsibility to, 179–180
  role in, 142–143
  salaries in, 26–27, 246
  shifts in ethics of, 129–145
  socialization context of, 110
  state legislatures compared, 273–279
  structural safeguards in, 144–145
Congressional Research Service, 121, 123
Constituency and constituents
  changes in, 133
  clientage compared, 308–309
  ethics definition and, 199–200
  legislator and, 159, 173–174
  lobbying and, 90
  norms and, 119
  public interest and, 168
  responsibility and, 152
  socialization and, 113
Constitution (U.S.)
  advertising and, 81
  Congress and, 158–159
  elections and, 19
  ethical standards and, 4–5
  political action committees and, 62
Contracts. See Commercial activities;
    War contracts
Contributions. See Campaign financing
    and funds
Credit Mobilier scandal, 13–15
Criminal activity

Criminal activity (Cont.)
  electorate and, 30–32, 36
  legislative ethics and, 198
Customs. See Norms; Socialization

Dairy lobby, 95
Davidson, Roger H., 109–128
Democratic party. See Party politics
Democratic Study Group, 113–114, 132
Democratic theory
  bureaucracy and, 284–285, 290–294
  campaigns and, 76–77
  character and, 79
  compatibilty within, 180
  conflicts within, 180–181
  electorate and, 80
  legitimacy and, 41–42
  moral minimalism and, 158
  political action committees and, 94
  representation and, 160
  See also Theory
Direct mailings
  fair practices agreements, 86
  unethical practices and, 73
Discipline
  Civil War and, 10
  codes of conduct and, 213–216, 231
  Constitution (U.S.) and, 4–5
  electorate and, 29, 32–36, 210–211
  emotion in, 209
  ethics committees and, 211–212
  malpractice suits compared, 319–323
  party politics and, 7, 16
Disclosure
  accountability and, 177–178, 189–190
  ineffectiveness of, 222
  legislation in, 151
  state legislatures, 275–276
  structural reforms and, 185
  theory and, 167–168
Douglas Committee, 22
Duty
  codes of ethics and, 227–228
  ethics definition and, 205
  structural and, 181–182, 185–193

Education
  professionalism and, 308
  See also Norms; Socialization

Effectiveness
  ethics contrasted, 109
  moral minimalism and, 153
  socialization and, 111
Elections
  bribery in, 15–16
  campaign contributions and, 19–21, 23
  Constitution (U.S.) and, 19
  democratic theory and, 41–42
  spending and, 50
  See also Campaigns
Electorate
  accountability to, 189
  advertising and, 70, 81
  autonomy and, 187
  backlash by, 71, 73
  campaigns and, 76–77, 80–81
  Congressional context and, 133–136
  criminal activity and, 30–32
  discipline and, 32–36, 210–211
  ethics and, 29–37
  identification of, 180
  political action committees and, 49
  public confidence, 150–151
  seniority and, 54
  theory and, 170–171
  watchdog role of, 78
Elites, 171
Enforcement
  codes of ethics, 235–240
  state legislatures, 257–258
  See also Discipline
Equality, 41–42
Ethical codes. See Codes of ethics
Ethics, 168–169
  See also Legislative ethics
Ethics committees, 211–212
Ethics in Government Act of 1978, 151
Ethnicity
  bureaucracy and, 299
  representation and, 202
Exclusion
  Constitution (U.S.) and, 5
  electorate and, 34
  House of Representatives, 25
Expulsion
  Constitution (U.S.) and, 5
  history and, 5–6, 10, 11–13
  impaired persons, 311
  Supreme Court (U.S.) and, 19

Fair Campaign Practices Agreement, 84,
  85, 87
Falsehoods
  advertising, 73–74, 81–82
  fair practice agreements, 86
Family, 124
Federal Corrupt Practices Act of 1925, 20
Federal Election Campaign Act Amend-
  ments of 1974, 43, 63, 104
Federal Election Campaign Act Amend-
  ments of 1976, 120
Federal Election Commission, 120
Feedback, 78
Felons, 29
Financial interests. See Commercial ac-
  tivities
Folkways. See Norms; Socialization
Ford, Jean, 263–271
Franking system, 122
Fund raising. See Campaign financing
  and funds

General Accounting Office, 123
Gutmann, Amy, 167–195

Hedlund, Jay H., 89–107
Holidays. See Junkets
Honoraria, 97–98
  party politics and, 99–100
  regulation of, 104
  salaries and, 98–99
House of Representatives
  commercial activities and, 13–15, 23–
  24
  ethical conduct codes development in,
  22, 25–27
  exclusion from, 25
  expulsion and, 7, 10, 12–13
  incumbency and, 134
  norms in, 113–114, 118
  socialization in, 111–112
  See also Congress (U.S.); Senate
  (U.S.)
Houston, Thomas Kingsley, 67–88

Impeachment, 5–6
Incumbency

Incumbency *(Cont.)*
advantages of, 134–135, 194
campaign spending and, 55, 62
codes of ethics and, 228
electorate and, 30
feedback to, 78
finances and, 50
political action committees and, 55–56
See also Office holding
Individual contributions, 96
Influence peddling. *See* Commercial activities
Interest groups
advertising and, 76
autonomy and, 152
bureaucracy and, 295, 299
ethics definition and, 199
public interest and, 168
state legislatures, 276–277
See also Lobbying and lobbyists; Political action committees
Interstate Commerce Commission, 288
Issues
accountability and, 177
autonomy and, 187
campaigns and, 76–77
moral minimalism and, 149
theory and, 171, 172

Jacobson, Gary C., 41–65
Jennings, Bruce, 149–165
Junkets
lobbyists and, 100–102
regulation of, 104

Kirby, James C., 29–37

Labor, 95–96
Law practice. *See* Private law practice
Leadership
campaigns and, 77
Congressional norms and, 119
lobbying and, 89
political action committees and, 57
socialization and, 112
state governments and, 268, 270
Learning. *See* Education; Socialization

Lecture circuit
lobbyists and, 97–98
See also Honoraria
Legislation
autonomy supported by, 188
ethics enforcement, 151
Legislative ethics
broadening scope of, 216–219
codes of conduct and, 213–216
defined, 197–201
judges in, 210–212
professionalism and, 303–324
scope of, 201–206
standards applied in, 206–210
state/federal compared, 273–279
Legislative Reorganization Act of 1946, 21
Legitimacy
bureaucracy and, 285
democratic theory and, 41–42
Lobbying and lobbyists, 89–107
bribery and, 35–36
campaign contributions and, 92–93, 94
campaigns and, 134
direct payments by, 97–98
disclosure law for, 104–105
ethics definition and, 202
function of, 91–92
honoraria and, 100
individuals and, 96
junkets and, 100–102
pluralism and, 137
political action committees and, 48
profile of, 91
reforms and, 103–105
Senate (U.S.) and, 21
socialization and, 126
See also Interest groups; Political action committees

Mailings. *See* Direct mailings
Malpractice suits, 319–323
McCarthy, Joseph R., 23
McCarthyism, 32
Media
state legislatures and, 269–270, 277–279
See also Advertising; Press
Merton, Vanessa, 303–324
Mexican War, 9

Moral minimalism, 149–165
  case for, 154–157
  critique of, 157–165
Morone, James A., 283–301

National Association of Social Workers
    Code of Ethics, 224
National Automobile Dealer Association,
    95
New Deal, 21
Norms, 130
  bureaucracy and, 122, 287
  committee system and, 131–132
  effectiveness of, 163
  ethical learning and, 116–117
  responsibility and, 192
  tradition of, 150
  See also Socialization

Office holding
  autonomy and, 174–175
  Congressional norms and, 131
  ethics definition and, 206
  See also Incumbency
Overhead democracy, 290–294

PACs. See Political action committees
Party politics
  advertising and, 72
  autonomy and, 200–201
  bureaucracy and, 285, 286
  campaign finances and, 20, 134
  codes of conduct and, 24, 27
  decline of, 119, 130, 141–142
  discipline and, 7, 16
  elections and, 133
  electorate and, 80
  ethical conduct codes and, 24, 27
  honoraria and, 99–100
  incumbency and, 30
  lobbying and, 89–90
  moral minimalism and, 155
  political action committees and, 46–47,
      61
  professionalism and, 308
  responsibility and, 59–60, 140–142
  socialization and, 112, 113
  theory and, 170

Pluralism
  bureaucracy and, 294–296
  codes of ethics and, 233–234
  ethics definition and, 199
  lobbyists and, 137
  moral minimalism and, 156–157, 162–
      163
  state legislatures, 273–274
Political action committees, 41–65, 89
  ambiguity in, 46–47
  campaign contributions and, 93, 97
  Congressional context and, 134
  Constitution (U.S.) and, 62
  democratic theory and, 94
  effectiveness of, 94–97
  ethics and, 105–106
  incumbency and, 55–56
  influence of, 48
  leadership and, 57
  limits for, 104
  party politics and, 61
  perception of, 49
  registered types of, 43
  roll-call votes and, 47
  types of, 43–44
Political campaigns. See Campaigns
Polls and polling, 77
Pork-barrel politics, 53
Press
  accountability and, 177–178
  socialization and, 125–127
  See also Advertising; Media
Preyer, Richardson, 273–279
Price, David E., 129–145
Private law practice
  Congress and, 3
  history and, 8–9, 11
  state legislatures and, 251, 254
Procedures, 112
Professional campaign firms, 72–73
Professional codes of ethics, 236
Professionalism, 303–324
  bureaucracy and, 287
  discipline and, 319–323
  ethics and, 312–315
  legislators compared, 305–312
  representation and, 317–319
  substantive standard of judgment, 315–
      317
Progressive reforms, 17–18
  bureaucracy and, 286–287, 291

Progressive reforms (*Cont.*)
  Congress and, 19
  pluralism and, 295
Protégé system, 111–112
Public. *See* Electorate
Public financing
  campaign contributions and, 93–94
  incumbency and, 194
  reform of, 103
  responsibility and, 193
Public policy, 94–97

Railroads, 17
Redistribution of wealth, 58
Reform and reform movements
  accountability, 189–191
  autonomy, 188
  bureaucracy and, 286–287, 291
  campaign contributions and, 93
  codes of ethics, 221
  lobbyists and, 103–105
  paradox in, 193–195
  political action committees and, 56
  Progressivism, 17–18
  public campaign financing, 188
  responsibility and, 191–193
  salary increases, 188–189
  state governments, 244, 268–269
  structural, 181
Relativism, 313–314
Religion, 201–202
Representation
  bureaucracy and, 283–301
  democratic theory and, 41–42, 160,
    169–174
  dilemmas in, 136–143
  ethics definition and, 199
  ethnicity and, 202
  professionalism and, 317–319
  role of representative and, 169–174
  theories of, 204
Republican party. *See* Party politics
Resignation
  history and, 10, 19
  Nixon, 26
Responsibility
  accountability and, 180
  bureaucracy, 292
  duty of, 178–179
  ethics definition and, 203

Responsibility (*Cont.*)
  paradox and, 193–194
  reforms supporting, 191–193
  structural supports for, 184
Retirement benefits, 247
Roll-call votes
  ethics definition and, 205–206
  political action committees and, 47, 95
  symbolism and, 54
  theory and, 171

Salaries
  autonomy and, 188–189
  codes of conduct and, 26–27
  honoraria and, 98–99
  professionalism and, 307
  state legislatures, 246–249, 275
Saxon, John D., 197–219
Scandals, 150–151
Scientific management, 287, 288
Self-interest, 159–160
Senate (U.S.)
  bribery and, 14–15, 21
  campaign contributions and, 19–21
  censure and, 6–7, 25, 35
  codes of ethics of, 225–226
  commercial activity and, 14–15, 18–19,
    24
  election to, 19
  ethical code development in, 25–27
  Ethical Standards Subcommittee of, 22
  expulsion and, 5–6, 11–12
  lobbyists and, 21
  McCarthy and, 23
  norms in, 114–115, 117–118
  socialization in, 110–111
  See also Congress (U.S.); House of
    Representatives (U.S.)
Seniority
  decline of, 119, 132
  electorate and, 30, 54
  Senate and, 115
  socialization and, 111
Separation of powers, 21–22
Seventeenth Amendment, 19
Single-issue interest groups, 51
Socialization, 109–128
  Congressional context and, 110
  current Congress, 118–127
  ethical learning and, 116–119

Socialization (*Cont.*)
   postwar Congressional norms, 110–116
   responsibility and, 192
   structural reforms and, 186
Special interests. *See* Interest groups;
   Lobbying and lobbyists; Political
   action committees
Speeches. *See* Honoraria; Lecture circuit
Spoils system, 285–286
Staff(s)
   socialization and, 123–124
   state legislatures, 245, 247, 276, 277
State legislatures
   campaign fund misuse in, 249–251
   citizen legislatures, 275–276
   codes of ethics, 254–256
   context of, 266–267
   diversity of, 243, 274
   enforcement and, 257–258
   ethics legislation in, 151
   federal government compared, 273–279
   insider's view of, 263–271
   interest groups and, 276–277
   legislative structure of, 245–246
   media coverage and, 277–279
   motivation of legislator in, 265
   norms in, 163
   private law practice and, 251–254
   recommendations for, 258–260, 276–271
   reforms and, 244
   role of, 266
   salaries in, 246–249
Stern, Robert M., 243–261
Structure
   state legislatures, 245–246
   theory and, 181–184
Sunshine laws
   accountability and, 191
   bureaucracy and, 296

Supreme Court (U.S.)
   campaign contributions and, 49
   expulsion and, 19
   history and, 8–9
   lobbying and, 91
   private law practice and, 251
Swanner, John M., 235–240
Symbolism
   political action committees and, 58–59
   roll-call votes and, 54

Taxation, 60
Theory, 167–195
   duties of legislators, 174–181
   legislative structure, 181–184
   paradox and, 193–195
   representation and, 169–174, 204
   structural supports for duties, 185–193
   See also Democratic theory
Thompson, Dennis, 167–195
Tillman Act of 1907, 19

Union Pacific Railroad scandal, 13–15
United Auto Workers Union, 95–96

Vacations. *See* Junkets
Voter turnout, 80
   See also Campaigns; Electorate

War contracts, 11–12
Watchdog role, 78
Watergate scandal, 93, 103
Wealth. *See* Redistribution of wealth
World War II, 21

DATE DUE

JUN 21 '89 DISCHARGED		
DEC 20 '89 DISCHARGED		
MAY 04 '90 DISCHARGED		
DISCHARGED		
DISCHARGED MAY 1 '92		